Dynamic Assessment of Students' Academic Writing

Prithvi N. Shrestha

Dynamic Assessment of Students' Academic Writing

Vygotskian and Systemic Functional Linguistic Perspectives

 Springer

Prithvi N. Shrestha
School of Lang and Applied Linguistics
The Open University
Milton Keynes, Buckinghamshire, UK

ISBN 978-3-030-55844-4   ISBN 978-3-030-55845-1   (eBook)
https://doi.org/10.1007/978-3-030-55845-1

This Springer imprint is published by the registered company Springer Nature Switzerland AG
The registered company address is: Gewerbestrasse 11, 6330 Cham, Switzerland

For Monica, Sandesh and Sankalpa

Preface

This book originates in my long-term interest in how assessment can support student learning, particularly academic writing development. As an academic writing teacher and researcher, I have encountered issues around students' academic writing when teaching and marking assignments on discipline-based academic writing courses. I wanted to address these issues through systematic research, thereby enabling myself to formally investigate my own professional practices. For this, I undertook a research project which examined the potential of a Vygotsky-inspired assessment approach called dynamic assessment (DA) that blends assessment with teaching, to assess and promote academic writing development in business studies at The Open University, UK, as part of my doctoral study (EdD). This book draws on the data primarily from that research to demonstrate how DA-based academic writing assessment procedures in higher education may promote academic writing development, including conceptual development in a discipline.

The research reported in this book was motivated by current assessment and feedback practices in higher education. The research literature on assessment and feedback in higher education indicates that there is lower student satisfaction regarding assessment and feedback than for other aspects of higher education academic support (HEFCE 2010, 2014; Office for Students 2018; Surridge 2008; Tuck 2018). In part, the lower student satisfaction appears to be associated with the quality of the assessment feedback given (Weaver 2006; Yang & Carless 2013) which is linked with the language of assessment feedback and meaningful student engagement with it. Given the 'high stakes' nature of academic writing as the principal mode of assessment in higher education (Lillis & Scott 2007), there is a need for further investigation of how assessment could be made more responsive to student needs and their learning. The research reported in this book examines the value of an alternative assessment approach (i.e., DA) and has the potential to have a positive impact on and to inform academic writing assessment practices in higher education.

This book explores the application of DA to assessing business studies students' academic writing in open and distance learning. The application is demonstrated through cases from business studies students' writing at The Open University, UK.

DA is an assessment approach that blends instruction with assessment and focusses on learners' future and potential abilities rather than the past (Grigorenko 2009).

The book provides detailed accounts of participating students' academic writing trajectories through samples of their academic writing and their interactions with the teacher during assessment. The analysis of the student academic writing is enriched with the application of a powerful genre theory informed by Halliday's Systemic Functional Linguistics (SFL). This aspect of DA research is innovative. The book is intended to be a resource for both academic writing practitioners and researchers in higher education.

There are a number of people who have contributed to the creation of this book in different ways and I would like to acknowledge their contributions. First of all, I would like to sincerely thank all six students and three business studies teachers who participated in my research voluntarily, and without them this book could not have existed. I am indebted to two of my former colleagues, Prof. Caroline Coffin and Dr. Jim Donohue, who gently persuaded me through their intellectual conversations and research to use SFL in my research. I am grateful to Prof. Jim Lantolf and Prof. Matthew Poehner (both at Penn State University) for their inspirational work within DA which is central to this book. I wish to thank Ms. Jolanda Voogd, Ms. Helen van der Stelt and Ms. Natalie Rieborn of Springer for encouragement and the guidance in preparing this book. I am grateful to two anonymous reviewers for their very helpful comments on an earlier version of the manuscript which helped me to improve the quality of the book. A number of my Open University colleagues contributed to this book by critically reading different chapters and providing invaluable comments when they had little time or space. Their comments helped to improve the book. I am most grateful to: Dr. Maria Fernandez-Toro, Dr. Kristina Hultgren, Dr. Maria Leedham, Dr. Sarah Jane Mukherjee, Dr. Nathaniel Owen, Dr. Caroline Tagg and Dr. Jackie Tuck. Finally, I am indebted to my wife, Monica, and two sons—Sandesh and Sankalpa—for their continuous care, support and patience when I was working on the research project and spending endless hours writing this book.

Milton Keynes, UK   Prithvi N. Shrestha

References

Grigorenko, E. L. (2009). Dynamic assessment and response to intervention. *Journal of Learning Disabilities, 42*(2), 111–132. doi:10.1177/0022219408326207.

HEFCE. (2010). *National student survey: Findings and trends 2006 to 2009*. London: Higher Education Funding Council for England.

HEFCE. (2014). *National student survey results and trends analysis 2005 to 2013*. London: Higher Education Funding Council for England.

Lillis, T. M., & Scott, M. (2007). Defining academic literacies research: Issues of epistemology, ideology and strategy. *Journal of Applied Linguistics, 4*(1), 5–32.

Office for Students. (2018). *National student survey results 2018*. Retrieved February 5, 2019, from https://www.officeforstudents.org.uk/advice-andguidance/student-information-and-data/national-student-survey-nss/get-the-nss-data/.

Surridge, P. (2008). *The National student survey 2005–2007: Findings and trends*. London: Higher Education Funding Council for England.

Tuck, J. (2018). *Academics engaging with student writing: Working at the higher education textface*. Milton: Taylor and Francis.

Weaver, M. R. (2006). Do students value feedback? Student perceptions of tutors' written responses. *Assessment & Evaluation in Higher Education, 31*(3), 379–394.

Yang, M., & Carless, D. (2013). The feedback triangle and the enhancement of dialogic feedback processes. *Teaching in Higher Education, 18*(3), 285–297. doi:10.1080/13562517.2012.719154.

Contents

1 **Higher Education, Academic Writing Assessment and Formative**
  Feedback... 1
  1.1 Introduction 1
  1.2 Why This Book on Academic Writing Assessment?........... 3
  1.3 Organisation of the Book 4
  1.4 Higher Education and Academic Writing 5
      1.4.1 Broad Landscape of Learning and Academic Writing in
            Higher Education.................................... 5
      1.4.2 Academic Literacy and Disciplinary Knowledge
            Construction in Higher Education 7
  1.5 Academic Writing Assessment in Higher
      Education... 9
  1.6 Types of Academic Writing Assessment 9
  1.7 Formative Academic Writing Assessment 11
      1.7.1 Formative Feedback and Academic Writing
            Assessment 11
      1.7.2 Diagnostic Academic Writing Assessment............. 21
      1.7.3 Dynamic Assessment (DA) as an Alternative 23
  1.8 Summary... 25
  References... 26

2 **Sociocultural Theory, Dynamic Assessment and Academic**
  Writing 35
  2.1 Introduction 35
  2.2 Vygotskian Sociocultural Theory........................... 35
      2.2.1 The Genetic Method 37
      2.2.2 Four Domains of the Genetic Method 38
  2.3 Academic Writing as a Semiotically Mediated Social Action
      in Context 39
  2.4 What Is Dynamic Assessment? 40

    2.5   Key Concepts of Sociocultural Theory and Dynamic
          Assessment   42
          2.5.1   Zone of Proximal Development   42
          2.5.2   Mediation   44
          2.5.3   Imitation   46
          2.5.4   Internalisation   47
    2.6   Types of Dynamic Assessment   48
          2.6.1   Interventionist Dynamic Assessment Approaches   48
          2.6.2   Interactionist Dynamic Assessment Approaches   49
    2.7   Dynamic Assessment and Other Assessment
          Approaches   51
    2.8   A Critical Review of Dynamic Assessment   53
    2.9   Summary   55
    References   55

3   **Systemic Functional Linguistics, Dynamic Assessment
    and Academic Writing**   59
    3.1   Introduction   59
    3.2   Systemic Functional Linguistics: A Theory of
          Language   60
    3.3   Rationale for Using SFL in DA   61
    3.4   Register Variables: Field, Tenor and Mode   62
          3.4.1   Ideational Metafunction   64
          3.4.2   Interpersonal Metafunction   65
          3.4.3   Textual Metafunction   65
    3.5   SFL and Academic Writing   65
    3.6   SFL-Based Genre Theory (and Pedagogy)   67
    3.7   Case Study Analysis as a Key Genre in Business
          Studies   71
    3.8   Application of SFL in This Book   72
          3.8.1   SFL as an Analytical Tool   72
          3.8.2   SFL as a Pedagogical Tool in Research   74
    3.9   Summary   74
    References   75

4   **Application of Dynamic Assessment to Distance
    Education**   79
    4.1   Introduction   79
    4.2   Context of Academic Writing Assessment: Open
          and Distance Education   80
    4.3   Nature of Business Studies Assignments   83
    4.4   Design of Research on Dynamic Assessment of Academic
          Writing   86

4.4.1   Key Concepts Underpinning the Research Design   87
4.4.2   Specific Research Context   88
4.4.3   Participants in My Research   89
4.5   Conducting Dynamic Assessment of Academic Writing
      in Distance Education   91
4.5.1   Existing Dynamic Assessment Procedures   92
4.5.2   DA Sessions and the Intervention   93
4.5.3   Non-dynamic Assessment   99
4.5.4   Transfer Assessment Tasks   100
4.5.5   Learner Interviews   102
4.5.6   Subject Specialists' Views   103
4.6   Data Analysis in Dynamic Assessment of Academic
      Writing   103
4.6.1   Thematic Analysis of Mediation Data   103
4.6.2   SFL-Based Textual Analysis of DA and Non-DA
        Texts   108
4.6.3   Thematic Analysis of the Student Interviews
        and Business Studies Teachers' Views   109
4.7   Summary   110
References   110

5   Teacher Mediation, Learner Reciprocity and Academic
    Writing Development   115
5.1   Introduction   115
5.2   Mediation and Its Purpose in Dynamic Assessment   115
5.3   The Mediation Data Used in This Book   116
5.4   Analysing Mediational Data   117
5.5   Issues in Mediation Data Analysis   118
5.6   Mediational Moves in Dynamic Assessment of Business
      Academic Writing   119
5.6.1   Descriptions of Mediational Moves in Dynamic
        Assessment of Academic Writing   120
5.6.2   Dynamicity of Mediational Moves   126
5.6.3   Academic Writing Support in the ZPD   128
5.7   Learner Reciprocity: Insights into Academic Writing
      Development of Distance Learners   134
5.7.1   Analysing Learner Reciprocity in Dynamic Assessment
        of Academic Writing   134
5.7.2   Descriptions of Learner Reciprocal Moves in Dynamic
        Assessment of Academic Writing   135
5.7.3   Reciprocal Moves and Academic Writing
        Development   141
5.8   Summary   147
References   147

**6 Tracking Learners' Academic Writing and Conceptual
Development Through Systemic Functional
Linguistics** 151
6.1 Introduction 151
6.2 Student Written Text Data Used in This Book 152
6.3 Analysing Academic Writing Assessment Texts Using
an SFL-Based Genre Approach 153
6.4 What Is Expected of Students in a *Case Study
Analysis* Genre? 154
6.5 Tracking DA and Non-DA Students' Academic Writing
Performance Through SFL 158
6.5.1 Identifying Genres in Students' Assignment Texts 159
6.5.2 Tracking *macroThemes* in Students' Academic
Writing 168
6.5.3 Tracking *hyperThemes* in Students' Academic
Writing 170
6.5.4 Case Studies: A Detailed Look at Three Students'
Academic Writing Development 173
6.5.5 Conceptual Development 189
6.6 Summary of SFL-Based Examination of Students' Ability
to Write a Case Study Analysis Genre 192
6.7 Summary 193
References 194

**7 Transfer of Aspects of Academic Writing to Similar
and New Contexts Through Dynamic Assessment** 197
7.1 Introduction 197
7.2 Dynamic Assessment and Transfer 198
7.3 Learning Transfer Data Used 200
7.4 Analysing Transfer Data 202
7.5 Tracking Learning Transfer in DA Students' Academic
Writing Through SFL 204
7.5.1 Near Transfer of Academic Writing 205
7.5.2 Far Transfer of Academic Writing 212
7.5.3 Learner Perspectives on Dynamic Assessment 226
7.6 Summary 227
References 228

**8 Dynamic Assessment of Academic Writing and Its Future
in Higher Education** 231
8.1 Introduction 231
8.2 Why Dynamic Assessment for Academic Writing
Assessment? 232
8.3 Implications for Academic Writing Practitioners 234

8.3.1 Implicit to Explicit Mediation.................... 234
8.3.2 Dialogic Feedback............................ 235
8.3.3 Interpersonal Relationship with Learners............. 236
8.4 Implications for Academic Writing Researchers............. 237
8.5 Challenges in Conducting Dynamic Assessment............. 238
8.5.1 Expertise of the DA Practitioner................... 239
8.5.2 Time Constraints............................ 239
8.5.3 Difficulty on Large-Scale....................... 240
8.5.4 Choice of Semiotic Mediation Tools................ 240
8.5.5 Labour-Intensiveness......................... 240
8.6 Future Directions for Dynamic Assessment of Academic
Writing 241
8.6.1 Group DA................................ 241
8.6.2 Computer-Based DA.......................... 242
8.6.3 Online Synchronous Communication for
Mediation 243
8.6.4 Interpersonal Aspects of Mediation and Dialogic
Feedback..................................... 244
References 244

About the Author

Dr. Prithvi N. Shrestha an award-winning author (British Council ELTons), is a Senior Lecturer in English Language at The Open University, UK. He has co-authored English for Academic and Specific Purposes books and published research articles on academic writing assessment in distance education, language assessment and English language education. His research interests include academic writing, Systemic Functional Linguistics, sociocultural theory, writing assessment, technology enhanced language assessment and teacher development in developing countries.

Abbreviations

AfL	Assessment for Learning
C-BDA	Computer-Based Dynamic Assessment
DA	Dynamic assessment
EAP	English for Academic Purposes
GDA	Group Dynamic Assessment
IELTS	International English Language Testing System
LOA	Learning Oriented Assessment
Non-DA	Non-dynamic assessment
OU	The Open University
OUBS	The Open University Business School
SFL	Systemic Functional Linguistics
TA	Transfer Assignment
TOEFL	Test of English as a Foreign Language
ZPD	Zone of proximal development

List of Figures

Fig. 1.1   Example assignment feedback in an academic writing
             for business studies course in distance education   7
Fig. 2.1   The mediated nature of human and world relationships
             (adapted from Lantolf & Thorne, 2006, p. 62). (Reproduced
             by permission of Oxford University Press from *Sociocultural
             Theory and the Genesis of Second Language Development*
             by Jim P. Lantolf & Steve L. Thorne © Oxford University
             Press 2006.)   45
Fig. 2.2   Attributes of Mediated Learning Experience (MLE)
             (Feuerstein et al., 2002, pp. 76-80)   50
Fig. 3.1   Three meta-functions of language in context (Reproduced
             from Martin & White, 2005, p. 27, with permission
             from Palgrave)   64
Fig. 3.2   Metafunctions regarding language register and genre (Martin
             2009, p. 12). Reprinted from *Linguistics and Education, 20*(1),
             Martin, J. R. Genre and language learning: A social semiotic
             perspective, pp. 10–21 (2009), with permission from
             Elsevier.   67
Fig. 4.1   A sample TMA task from a business studies course.   81
Fig. 4.2   A sample guidance note for the TMA task in Fig. 4.1   82
Fig. 4.3   An assignment task for TMA2 in business academic
             writing course.   89
Fig. 4.4   Assignment guidance notes for TMA2 in business academic
             writing course.   90
Fig. 4.5   Mediation checklist by Haywood and Lidz (2007, p. 42.,
             Reproduced with permission of the Licensor through
             PLSclear)   93
Fig. 4.6   DA1 task   95

Fig. 4.7   Aljaafreh and Lantolf's (1994, p. 471) regulatory scale
            (Reprinted from *The Modern Language Journal, 78*(4),
            Aljaafreh, A., & Lantolf, J. P. Negative feedback as regulation
            and second language learning in the Zone of Proximal
            Development, pp. 465–483 (1994), with permission
            from John Wiley & Sons through RightsLink)   98
Fig. 4.8   Enrichment material on paragraph development   99
Fig. 4.9   Text organisation of a SWOT analysis   101
Fig. 4.10   Marking guidelines for subject tutors   104
Fig. 4.11   Data collection methods   105
Fig. 5.1   Distribution of mediational moves across DA1 and DA2   130
Fig. 5.2   Distribution of all mediational moves in DA1   132
Fig. 5.3   Distribution of all mediational moves in DA2   132
Fig. 5.4   Comparison of mediational moves: DA1 and DA2   133
Fig. 5.5   Learner reciprocity moves   134
Fig. 5.6   Distribution of reciprocal moves across DA1 and DA2.
            (1, 2, 3… refer to reciprocal moves. Moves 1–8 are more
            dependent than moves 9–16.)   143
Fig. 5.7   Distribution of reciprocal moves across learners in DA1   145
Fig. 5.8   Distribution of reciprocal moves across learners in DA2   146
Fig. 6.1   Assignment task in DA1 for Michelle and Natasha   156
Fig. 6.2   The genre staging of a typical STEP analysis   157
Fig. 6.3   The genre staging of a typical SWOT analysis   158
Fig. 6.4   First draft of the first assignment written by DA
            student Lou   160
Fig. 6.5   First draft of the first assignment written by non-DA
            student Kristie   161
Fig. 6.6   Natasha's DA1 first draft STEP case study analysis
            (P1, P2 … = Paragraph 1, 2 …)   174
Fig. 6.7   Natasha's DA2 first draft STEP case study analysis   175
Fig. 6.8   Amina's DA1 first draft SWOT case study analysis   179
Fig. 6.9   Amina's DA2 first draft SWOT case study analysis   181
Fig. 6.10   Lena's non-DA1 SWOT case study analysis   185
Fig. 6.11   Lena's non-DA2 marketing case study analysis   186
Fig. 7.1   Example of TA task completed by Lou (DA participant)   201
Fig. 7.2   Example of TA task completed by Kristie (non-DA
            participant)   202
Fig. 7.3   Comparison between DA task and TA task (key differences
            highlighted in bold)   204
Fig. 7.4   Kristie's TA text   207
Fig. 7.5   Technicality in Kristie's non-DA1 (% of the total technical
            terms)   210
Fig. 7.6   Technicality in Kristie's non-DA2 (% of the total technical
            terms)   210

Fig. 7.7   Technicality in Kristie's transfer assignment (% of the total
              technical terms).   211
Fig. 7.8   Natasha's macroThemes   216
Fig. 7.9   Natasha's hyperThemes   218
Fig. 7.10   Lou's hyperThemes   219
Fig. 7.11   **a** Technicality in Amina's DA1 (count and % of total technical
              terms). **b** Technicality in Amina's DA2 (count and % of total
              technical terms). **c** Technicality in Amina's TA (count
              and % of total technical terms).   221
Fig. 7.12   **a** Technicality in Lou's DA1 and DA2 (count and % of total
              technical terms). **b** Technicality in Lou's TA (count and %
              of total technical terms)   222
Fig. 7.13   **a** Technicality in Natasha's DA1 and DA2 (count and %
              of total technical terms). **b** Technicality in Natasha's TA
              (count and % of total technical terms)   223
Fig. 7.14   **a** Comparison of technicality in three students' DA1.
              b Comparison of technicality in three students' DA2.
              c Comparison of technicality in three students' TA   224

List of Tables

Table 3.1	Elemental genres and their purposes and stages (from Coffin & Donohue, 2014, p. 50, Reproduced with permission of The Licensor through PLSclear).	68
Table 3.2	Genre families in the BAWE corpus (from Nesi & Gardner, 2012, p. 53)	70
Table 3.3	Typical generic features of a case study analysis	72
Table 4.1	Purposes and genres in a first year business course	84
Table 4.2	Purposes and genres in a second year business course	85
Table 4.3	Summary of participant details	92
Table 4.4	Summary of assessment tasks	94
Table 4.5	Marking criteria based on Bonnano and Jones (2007)	96
Table 4.6	A summary version of the 3 × 3: a framework for describing linguistic resources of student writing in the academic domain based on Humphrey et al. (2010, p. 188)	97
Table 4.7	DA procedures	98
Table 4.8	Poehner's (2005, p. 160) mediational moves compared with those in my research on academic writing	106
Table 4.9	Poehner's (2005, p. 183) learner reciprocal moves compared with those in my research on academic writing	107
Table 5.1	Teacher-student interaction data	117
Table 5.2	Mediational moves in dynamic assessment of academic writing	119
Table 5.3	Type and frequency of mediational moves in dynamic assessment of academic writing	129
Table 5.4	Quality and frequency of learner reciprocal moves	142
Table 6.1	Business studies teachers' judgment data	153
Table 6.2	Results for genres written by the DA students	162
Table 6.3	Results for genres written by non-DA students	162
Table 6.4	Generic stages in DA students' first (DA1) assignment texts	163

Table 6.5 Generic stages in non-DA students' first (non-DA1) assignment texts............................... 164

Table 6.6 Generic stages in DA students' second (DA2) assignment texts....................................... 164

Table 6.7 Generic stages in non-DA students' second (non-DA2) assignment texts............................... 165

Table 6.8 Summary of marks awarded by business studies teachers 166

Table 6.9 Summary of results for macroThemes and hyperThemes in DA students' texts............................... 168

Table 6.10 Summary of results for macroThemes in non-DA students' texts....................................... 169

Table 6.11 Summary of results for hyperThemes in DA students' texts....................................... 171

Table 6.12 Summary of results for hyperThemes in non-DA students' texts....................................... 172

Table 6.13 Categories and their frequency of Technicality in DA and non-DA texts................................ 191

Table 6.14 Technical categories with examples 192

Table 7.1 Examples of technicality under various categories 211

Table 7.2 Summary of generic stages in DA student texts............ 213

Table 7.3 Summary of results for hyperThemes................... 217

Table 8.1 Mediational moves in dynamic assessment of academic writing 235

Chapter 1
Higher Education, Academic Writing Assessment and Formative Feedback

1.1 Introduction

Teaching and learning in higher education has been undergoing substantial changes globally. These changes have been triggered by a number of factors including changing nature of the student body in universities (e.g., increasing non-traditional students), rapid internationalisation of higher education including transnational education and the drive for student retention and success by university leaders (e.g., Cots, Llurda, & Garrett, 2014; Healey, 2015). These changes mean student diversity in terms of, among other things, their linguistic, socio-economic and educational backgrounds (Coffin & Donohue, 2014; Manchón, 2017; Turner, 2011; Wingate & Tribble, 2011). Given the heterogenous characteristics of the student population, it is important to cater for their varying learning needs in their programme of studies. One fundamental aspect of their needs increasingly accepted in most of the English medium universities in many countries is support for academic writing although this need has not widely been acknowledged (Lillis & Turner, 2001; Turner, 2011; Wingate, 2018). Yet, it is the academic discourse, specifically the academic written text, whether in print or digital including multimodality, through which students mainly need to access and build their disciplinary knowledge for their educational success (Martin, Maton, & Doran, 2020). More importantly, despite many progressive changes in higher education teaching, academic writing continues to be the main mode of student assessment in higher education as highlighted by scholars previously (Lillis & Scott, 2007). Therefore, academic writing assessment, the focus of this book, is central to teaching and learning in higher education and should be of concern to university leaders, teachers and students.

This book is concerned with the relationship between academic writing instruction including disciplinary knowledge, and academic writing assessment. In particular, this book demonstrates how academic writing assessment procedures in higher education may promote academic writing development including conceptual development in a discipline (e.g., learners' ability to use conceptual frameworks in order to produce a successful case study analysis as construed in their assessment texts). By

© Springer Nature Switzerland AG 2020
P. N. Shrestha, *Dynamic Assessment of Students' Academic Writing*,
https://doi.org/10.1007/978-3-030-55845-1_1

academic writing here I mean academic texts written by students in a particular discipline (e.g., biology) in higher education, which entails having the epistemological, linguistic and sociocultural knowledge required in order to communicate and become a part of that disciplinary community. I have used the term *writing* to mean academic or disciplinary writing throughout this book. For the purpose of this book, *academic writing assessment*, drawing on Huot's work, is defined as the range of procedures used to 'describe the promise and limitations of a writer' (2002, p. 107) working in a particular rhetorical, linguistic and sociocultural context of higher education. In this sense, it also means assessing students' ability to demonstrate *disciplinary knowledge* and *its application*, and their *use of language* to communicate such knowledge and application in their academic writing.

This book explores the application of dynamic assessment (DA) to assessing business studies students' academic writing in open and distance learning. The application is demonstrated through cases from business studies students' writing at The Open University, UK. DA is an assessment approach that blends instruction with assessment. The assumptions behind DA are that (1) traditional assessment may not be suitable for all learners, (2) assessment should consider what a learner will be able to do in the *future* (i.e., their potential to develop) instead of focusing on their *past* (e.g., actual development), and (3) information from the assessment should be used to design teaching interventions adapting them as needed (Grigorenko, 2009, p. 113). DA originated in the influential *sociocultural theory* of learning developed by the Russian psychologist, Lev Semyonovich Vygotsky (e.g., see Vygotsky, 1978; Wertsch, 1985). He argued that learning is collaborative rather than individual and takes place in social interactions. He emphasised that the focus of assessment should be on the future potential of the learner which can be revealed when the learner works with a more capable peer or teacher/adult on a task. Both Vygotsky's sociocultural theory and DA are further elaborated in Chap. 2.

This book presents the application of DA to academic writing assessment and pedagogy in an innovative way by combining DA with Systemic Functional Linguistics (SFL). SFL is a well-established theory of language use in context which treats language use including any other semiotic devices such as signs and images as a system of choices for meaning making to achieve a goal in a social context (see Martin, 2016 for a critical discussion of SFL and its origin). To date, DA and SFL have not been employed together to track a learner's academic language and conceptual development or academic writing development except in only a few journal articles (e.g., Gardner, 2010; Shrestha, 2017). These few papers demonstrate the positive impact of such a combination on the learner's academic language and academic writing development. However, there has not been a detailed treatment of DA and SFL in a book-length publication (see Chap. 3 for a detailed discussion of SFL). Therefore, the central question this book aims to address is how DA combined with SFL, as powerful and systematic pedagogic and assessment tools, can be applied to academic writing assessment and subsequently promote students' academic writing and conceptual development over a period of time. By doing so, it also presents a set of adaptable pedagogic and learning-focused assessment techniques for developing students' academic writing in higher education in the context of distance education, which are transferable to traditional university contexts.

1.2 Why This Book on Academic Writing Assessment?

The research reported in this book was motivated by two factors. Firstly, the research literature on assessment and feedback in higher education indicates that there is lower student satisfaction regarding assessment and feedback than for other aspects of higher education academic support (HEFCE, 2010, 2014; Office for Students, 2018; Surridge, 2008; Tuck, 2018). In part, the lower student satisfaction appears to be associated with the quality of the assessment feedback (e.g., specificity and clarity) given (Weaver, 2006; Yang & Carless, 2013). It has been suggested that there are many reasons for student discontent such as, among other things, an inability to understand academic discourse (Lea & Street, 1998), lack of sufficient or good quality feedback (Hounsell, McCune, Hounsell, & Litjens, 2008), feedback not being 'usable' (Walker, 2009) and student feedback literacy (Carless & Boud, 2018). Additionally, it is reported that students may be predominantly interested in grades rather than formative comments (e.g., Carless, 2006). Given the 'high stakes' nature of academic writing as the principal mode of assessment in higher education (Lillis & Scott, 2007), there is a continuous need for further investigation of how assessment could be made more responsive to student needs and their learning although there is a burgeoning literature on assessment feedback in higher education. The research reported in this book examines the value of an alternative assessment approach (i.e., DA) and has the potential to have a positive impact on and to inform writing assessment practices in higher education. Specifically, the research contributes to the field of DA and academic writing assessment by using SFL to track learners' academic writing and conceptual development, and thus extends DA research.

A further motivation behind this study is my long-term personal interest in finding out how assessment can *support* learning because, as an academic writing teacher and researcher, I have encountered issues around students' academic writing when teaching and marking assignments on discipline-based academic writing courses and when working with academic colleagues from other disciplines like early childhood studies and business studies. I wanted to address these issues through systematic research, thereby enabling myself to formally investigate my own professional practices. This type of investigation would be of use to teachers of academic writing more widely.

1.3 Organisation of the Book

Before critically examining academic writing assessment in higher education, a preview of each chapter is presented below. There are eight chapters in total.

This chapter (Chapter 1) commenced by introducing the reader to the key purpose of the book. Next, key studies on academic writing and formative feedback on academic writing in higher education are reviewed in order to contextualise the research reported in this book. The chapter shows that there are still concerns about supporting students in higher education with their academic writing for their success in studies. It then briefly introduces DA as an alternative assessment approach to academic writing assessment in higher education to address these concerns.

Chapter 2 begins by explaining sociocultural theory as expounded by Vygotsky (1978) and presenting a sociocultural view of academic writing, academic writing as a communicative purpose oriented and mediated social action influenced by cultural and contextual factors (Coffin & Donohue, 2014; Martin, 2009; Prior, 2008). The chapter then explains the concept of DA in detail in the context of mainstream and emerging language assessment and academic writing assessment approaches. By doing so, it also introduces key concepts central to DA, especially *mediation* and *Zone of Proximal Development* which were pioneered by Vygotsky (Vygotsky, 1978) in his sociocultural theory (Lantolf & Poehner, 2004; Lantolf, Poehner, & Swain, 2018). It is argued that DA provides a viable alternative assessment approach that promotes individual learners' development based on their learning potential.

In Chap. 3, I introduce Hallidayan Systemic Functional Linguistics (SFL) (e.g., Halliday & Matthiessen, 2004) as will be deployed in this book to complement DA. The chapter demonstrates how SFL contributes to researching academic writing systematically in the context of DA. It provides a rationale for using SFL to track learners' academic writing and conceptual development in their academic writing. It then introduces the notion of *case study analysis* genre as used in SFL (e.g., Martin & Rose, 2007; Nesi & Gardner, 2012). It explains different aspects of the case study analysis genre employed to analyse the learners' writing in the current study. In particular, the chapter explains two of the register variables in SFL that are examined in students' writing: Field (subject matter) and Mode (medium of communication).

The focus of Chap. 4 is on the application of DA to open and distance learning. Drawing on the DA and academic writing pedagogy literature, it outlines a set of adaptable procedures for conducting DA of academic writing in distance education. It illustrates the procedure in the context of open and distance business studies students' writing at The Open University, UK. Additionally, it introduces the research data used in Chaps. 5, 6 and 7. The data consists of student-teacher text-based interactions around drafts of students' assignments, drafts of student written assignments, business studies teachers' comments on these assignments and student interviews.

Chapter 5 presents the analysis of the DA procedures followed with distance business studies students' academic writing assessment over a period of time. Drawing on Vygotsky's sociocultural theory, the chapter explores business studies students' zones of proximal development in relation to their academic writing across two DA sessions. It outlines a set of teacher mediation typologies for assessing academic writing, as revealed by the study, which academic writing teachers can use in their academic writing teaching and assessment. The chapter also presents learner reciprocity (responsiveness) as found in the teacher-student interaction around student written assignment drafts. By doing so, it demonstrates students' *microgenetic development* (i.e., development in a short span of time) as conceptualised by Vygotsky (see Lantolf, 2000; Wertsch, 1985).

Chapter 6 shows how a Hallidayan SFL perspective provides linguistic evidence for business studies students' academic writing and conceptual development in the DA context. Specifically, this chapter tracks students' grasp of the *case study analysis* genre from the text development perspective by considering *generic stages* (i.e., stages of a text from beginning to end), *macroThemes* and *hyperThemes* (traditionally called *introduction* and *topic sentence* respectively). It also documents the trajectory of business students' knowledge about the case study analysis genre and the key business concepts required by the assignments. Again, the notion of Vygotskian microgenetic development is applied to understand students' academic writing and conceptual development.

Building on Chap. 6, Chap. 7 presents students' near and far transfer of the generic features and conceptual development to another learning context (i.e., a higher level business studies course). It is concerned with pertinent issues related to the transfer of what learners learned during the DA and non-DA process to new academic writing assessment contexts. Thus, this chapter provides evidence for DA's potential contribution to students' sustainable academic writing development and sustainable assessment (e.g., Boud & Soler, 2016).

The final chapter (Chap. 8) summarises key findings from the study reported in the book and highlight the contributions of DA to academic writing pedagogy and assessment in higher education. It concludes by making remarks about a number of future directions of DA research in academic writing assessment and pedagogy.

1.4 Higher Education and Academic Writing

1.4.1 Broad Landscape of Learning and Academic Writing in Higher Education

Learning in higher education entails having an ability to adapt to new ways of understanding and accessing knowledge in a particular discipline such as business studies. These new ways of acquiring disciplinary knowledge can be challenging, particularly to undergraduate students (Lea & Street, 1998). One reason for this is that much academic knowledge is constructed and available as written texts in higher education (Bazerman, 1988; Lillis & Scott, 2007). Unless learners can understand and interpret this new knowledge from written texts, they may be considered incompetent and may be at risk of failing in their studies (e.g., see Cummins, 2014).

Most importantly, their (in)competence is generally assessed on the basis of their written assignments which are expected to draw on discipline-specific written texts and academic lectures. This can be particularly challenging to students who come from non-traditional (e.g., without A Levels in the UK) and different sociocultural and socio-economic backgrounds (see Devlin, 2013; Ivanič & Lea, 2006) because unlike traditional HE students (e.g., students from 'rich' and 'middle class' families), they may not have familiarity with the higher education academic cultures and discourses, and the pedagogy may be less visible to them (McKay & Devlin, 2014). In addition, these learners are expected to demonstrate the socio-cultural practices of the associated disciplinary community through assignments and, more importantly, each discipline has its own practices such as differing criteria for academic excellence (e.g., see Becher, 1994) and in each discipline, there are different ways of legitimising knowledge (Hood, 2009). In order to succeed in becoming a member of this community, learners need to learn and/or be aware of such practices. Supporting learners for their success is, thus, a concern in UK higher education institutions and elsewhere (Ivanič & Lea, 2006; McKay & Devlin, 2014).

Learning and teaching in UK higher education has undergone a number of changes due to factors such as globalisation, increasing transnational education, growth of international students and changing nature of the student population. In terms of teaching and learning approaches, the shift has moved towards more creative, autonomous and transformative approaches as seen in other parts of the world (e.g., Damianakis, Barrett, Archer-Kuhn, Samson, Matin, & Ahern, 2019; Serrano, O'Brien, Roberts, & Whyte, 2017). This shift indicates that learning and teaching has been made responsive to higher education students' needs and incorporates both spoken and written modes of interactions including the use of multimodal communication. Such changes have certainly supported students who prefer different methods of accessing knowledge and learning in the discipline. However, the predominance of the written text as the main source of knowledge continues. More importantly, I argue that the higher education assessment practice continues to be in the written mode and is monologic as noted by many scholars (e.g., Ajjawi & Boud, 2017; Nicol, 2010). Therefore, there is a need for a more dialogic assessment approach.

The learning environment for students in open and distance learning institutions such as The Open University (OU) in the UK, where my research took place, is substantially different from that in traditional brick universities. The main difference is the lack of face-to-face contact with teachers and fellow students which can leave students isolated. Currently, the most common methods of communication include emails, asynchronous online forums and telephone. This shows the key role played by the written mode of communication. In distance learning, as in the mainstream higher education sector, most assignment feedback is communicated to students in writing (Chetwynd & Dobbyn, 2011) and this will continue for the foreseeable future.

The writing assessment process also features differently, compared to other higher education institutions, on the OU courses (see Chetwynd & Dobbyn, 2011). For example, each course has two to six assignments. These assignments are marked by local part-time teachers called Associate Lecturers who are often provided with

TUTOR'S COMMENTS AND ADVICE TO STUDENT:

A: 22/25
Use of source material: Information from the source material is correct and appropriate for the task.
You have taken relevant information from the case study and included it in your SWOT analysis to create a clear analysis of the business. Well done. You have covered most of the salient points that are important to identify in order to analyse the company. Be sure to not misinterpret or alter information taken from the original; everything discussed must be accurate and reliable.
Although you are not expected to be able to reference accurately in this TMA, you are expected to cite your sources. The marking criteria states sources should be referenced 'appropriately'. You have provided a good reference list and have referred to the case study in your analysis. Well done.
B: 22/25
Structure and development of the text: The structure and development of the text is clear and appropriate to its purpose.
You have produced a written analysis of the case study using the SWOT framework for your writing and you introduce each section well. You have also structured your writing to include a recommendations section at the end. The structure of your paragraphs is good and you clearly follow the framework.
When making recommendations in the future, you might want to say where the ideas have come from. For structure, you might want to try beginning a sentence with, 'It is recommended that?' so that you make the recommendation first and then follow it with the source. That way you are using the high level generalisation and low level detail structure you have been taught and you are meeting the purpose of the question and the task.
C: 22/25
Academic writing style: The text is written in effective academic English
Continue to build your business vocabulary; it is good now and continues to improve all the time. You have avoided using abbreviations, such as, bike, don't, it's, i.e., etc. Well done.
D: 15/15
Grammatical correctness: The text is grammatically accurate as written academic English
E: 10/10
Qualities of presentation: The assignment looks professional
Excellent. Your assignment is a good length. Well done. You have provided a word count. Well done and thank you. You have clearly followed the guidance in the TMA booklet about presentation and have taken time to proof read your work so you demonstrate a professional approach to communication.

Fig. 1.1 Example assignment feedback in an academic writing for business studies course in distance education

marking guides by the central course teams. Each assignment is marked and in-text comments and summary feedback are provided electronically to students. For example, see Fig. 1.1 for the summary feedback on a business studies students' assignment. These assignments are used for both summative and formative purposes. The teacher feedback is intended to help students with writing their subsequent assignments. However, recent OU-based studies (e.g., Chetwynd & Dobbyn, 2011; Fernández-Toro & Furnborough, 2018; Walker, 2009) showed that teacher feedback has not always been effective enough to meet students' needs.

1.4.2 Academic Literacy and Disciplinary Knowledge Construction in Higher Education

Academic literacy, of which academic writing is an integral part, is widely considered as central to academic knowledge building and success in higher education (Coffin & Donohue, 2014; Snow, 2010; Woodward-Kron, 2002). Academic literacy as a concept is complex and is not straightforward to define because its meaning and practices depend on the view of language and literacy one adopts (e.g., see Coffin & Donohue, 2012; Wingate & Tribble, 2011). For the purpose of this book, I use Wingate's (2018) definition that academic literacy is 'the ability to communicate competently in an academic discourse community; this encompasses reading, evaluating information, as well as presenting, debating and creating knowledge through both speaking and writing' (p. 340). Thus, academic literacy is not narrowly viewed as academic writing which is sometimes the case. Taking Wingate's definition, then, academic writing including other semiotic aspects such as images can be considered pivotal in constructing disciplinary knowledge in higher education. Thus, it is essential that students in higher education are familiar with all these aspects whether within their disciplines or through specifically designed academic literacy courses. I also acknowledge that academic literacy is influenced by institutional contexts and practices (e.g., see Tuck, 2018).

As academic literacy researchers have argued for some time, today's higher education students' academic needs are not the same as they were in the UK in the 1990s when it was assumed that students would come to university equipped with the necessary academic literacy (Coffin & Donohue, 2014; Tuck, 2018; Wingate, Andon, & Cogo, 2011). Given the increasingly diverse and changing nature of the UK higher education student population, their academic literacy needs have changed. This has become even more prominent because there are many non-traditional students entering higher education and they are often not fully prepared for the academic literacy demand of university studies in which academic writing is the main mode of assessment (Lillis & Scott, 2007). Thus, one factor that seems to have influenced a higher education institution's student retention and progression is its students' academic literacy expertise. Evidence indicates that academic language may pose challenges to many students who are at risk of underachievement and providing sufficient academic literacy support to such students is often ignored by institutions (Cummins, 2014). This point is crucial to the context where the study reported in this book took place because all students are part-time distance learners and they have little or no face-to-face contact with their teacher, leaving written academic texts being the main tool for learning and communication as mentioned in the previous section. This kind of learning environment shows that students in distance education build their academic knowledge almost solely relying on written academic language (including multimodality). This also means these students should have good academic literacy expertise to access disciplinary knowledge and succeed in their studies, without which they are bound to under-achieve in their programme of studies.

From the brief discussion above, it can be argued that academic literacy makes an important contribution to disciplinary learning and knowledge building, particularly academic writing on the basis that it requires a more conscious effort. This approach is known as 'writing to learn', which is supported in academic writing research (Bazerman, 2005; Hyland, 2013a; Langer & Applebee, 1987; Woodward-Kron, 2005) although contested by some researchers (e.g., Ackerman, 1993). Since writing often requires a more conscious effort than speech to organise one's thoughts, it is argued that writing helps to shape our thinking and consequently our learning, a view supported in Vygotskian sociocultural theory as well (e.g., Wells, 1999). This notion of writing to learn is particularly relevant to the study of conceptual development investigated in my research.

1.5 Academic Writing Assessment in Higher Education

Having considered the broader landscape of teaching and learning in higher education and academic writing above, this section presents a review of the relevant literature on formative writing assessment in the higher education context, focusing on various aspects of academic writing assessment that are generally associated with promoting learning. In particular, I review previous studies which are concerned with academic writing development in one way or another. *Academic writing development* is defined, in this book, as improvement of students' writing in terms of the use of linguistic resources, text development (i.e., genre knowledge) and disciplinary knowledge, often through an intervention resulting from assessment over a period of time.

In the rest of this chapter, I will describe the *types* of academic writing assessment, with a focus on formative academic writing assessment, followed by a review of *key studies* that fall within formative academic writing assessment in higher education. Finally, I will present DA as a possible alternative to traditional forms of academic writing assessment in view of the weaknesses found in them.

1.6 Types of Academic Writing Assessment

In the context of writing assessment, broadly speaking, there appear to be two types of assessment although they are mixed in practice: *summative* and *formative*. Summative writing assessment is generally used to *measure* learners' achievement in writing at the end of a study programme rather than supporting them during the course (Shohamy, 2001). Summative assessment is product-focussed and tends to assume that human cognitive abilities are stable. Interestingly, it is often used to predict an individual's future performance (Lidz & Elliot, 2000). Such assessment is, naturally, not concerned with learners' writing development. There are several large-scale quantitative studies in the field of summative writing assessment primarily in English language (see Weigle, 2002 for a review), often featured in the journals devoted to language assessment and testing such as *Language Testing* and *Language Assessment Quarterly*,[1] and the journal dedicated to writing assessment: *Assessing Writing* (e.g., Barkaoui, 2007; Eckes, 2008; Llosa & Malone, 2018). However, these studies have tended to examine technical aspects such as task variables, inter-rater reliability and rating scales in standardised commercial English language proficiency tests rather than the link between writing assessment and learners' writing development. In fact, writing assessment research continues to concentrate on these technical aspects as argued about two decades ago (Huot, 2002). Likewise, although a substantial

---

[1] It is also important to acknowledge that there is *Assessment and Evaluation in Higher Education* journal, dedicated to improving assessment and evaluation in higher education. Many studies reviewed in this chapter come from it and focus on student learning.

body of research on large-scale academic writing tests such as TOEFL[2] and IELTS Academic[3] exists, these tests are English language proficiency tests and scores from these tests are used for administrative purposes such as international students' entry into colleges and universities in English-speaking countries, and therefore, have no direct relevance to academic writing development as defined earlier. It should be, nonetheless, noted that a number of studies have explored the *washback* effect of these large-scale tests on teaching and learning academic writing (e.g., Alderson & Hamp-Lyons, 1996; Green, 2007). Washback refers to the effect of a test on teaching and learning regarding various stakeholders of the test (see Green, 2007 for an overview). It does not necessarily focus on writing development nor disciplinary writing, however. Some recent studies have attempted to establish a link between what these commercial writing tests assess and what students taking these tests write in universities, focusing on their predictive validity (e.g., see Riazi, 2016; Smart, 2019). Therefore, any studies oriented towards summative writing assessment with no clear emphasis on academic writing development in a discipline are excluded from the review.

As a result of the dissatisfaction with the dominance of summative assessment, an alternative form of assessment that predicts the individual's future performance and assists in designing subsequent pedagogical interventions promoting learning has become an ongoing quest in educational assessment (e.g., see Shepard, 2000). Formative writing assessment has emerged as an option for this purpose because it is geared towards learning and improvement in writing, based on assessment at different times during a course of study (Huot, 2002). As such, its purpose is to help learners guide their subsequent phases of academic writing and help teachers 'modify their teaching methods and materials so as to make them more appropriate for their students' needs, interests and capabilities' (Bachman & Palmer, 1996, p. 98). In other words, formative assessment is 'specifically intended to provide feedback on performance to improve and accelerate learning' (Sadler, 1998, p. 77). Since formative assessment is linked to academic writing instruction and assessment as conceptualised in this book, the rest of the chapter reviews the key studies that relate to formative writing assessment in higher education.

---

[2]TOEFL is an acronym for Test of English as a Foreign Language developed by Educational Testing Services in the US. The current version, TOEFL iBT, is delivered over the internet and is used to assess test takers' English language proficiency in an academic context. It has a Writing section in addition to Listening, Speaking and Reading.

[3]IELTS refers to International English Language Testing System developed by University of Cambridge ESOL Examinations, British Council and IDP: IELTS Australia. IELTS Academic includes Listening, Speaking, Academic Reading and Academic Writing. It is for test-takers who want to study undergraduate and postgraduate degrees or seek professional registration (e.g., medical doctor) in an English speaking context.

1.7 Formative Academic Writing Assessment

As suggested by its definition, formative academic writing assessment aims to contribute positively to enhancing learners' academic writing. In the context of higher education, a number of studies have been conducted in this area and are relevant to what I discuss in the subsequent chapters. However, precisely how academic writing assessment can improve student learning is still under-researched (Walker, 2009; Wingate, 2010). A number of studies have been carried out in this area. I have classified these studies into: (1) formative feedback on academic writing, (2) diagnostic academic writing assessment, and (3) dynamic assessment. Although each of these categories broadly subscribes to the principle of supporting learners with their writing through assessment, their underlying assumptions and theoretical orientations are different, resulting in their differing applications and impacts on learning or academic writing. Each category is defined and key relevant studies within each are reviewed below.

1.7.1 Formative Feedback and Academic Writing Assessment

Formative feedback emerged as an important aspect of writing instruction in North America in the 1970s as learner-centred teaching approaches started gaining currency (Hyland & Hyland, 2006a) and various sociocultural aspects of higher education drew higher education scholars' attention (e.g., Northedge, 2003). The term formative feedback is particularly common in open and distance learning and higher education in general (see Weaver, 2006). It also entails feeding forward so that students can make use of the teacher feedback on the previous assignment when they write their future assignments. Indeed, teacher formative feedback is seen as a major teaching tool and a medium of interaction with students, and a means to motivate and encourage them to continue (Gibbs & Simpson, 2004–05; Higgins, Hartley, & Skelton, 2002). If formative feedback is provided appropriately, it can help learners to control their learning (i.e., self-regulation of learning) by reflecting on their progress (i.e., strengths and weaknesses) and to take actions to further improve their learning (Weaver, 2006). In the context of academic writing assessment, *formative feedback* refers to a teacher's responses to students' written drafts or final assignments which subsequently promote academic writing development in disciplinary academic writing.

The theoretical assumptions behind studies on formative feedback appear to be that (1) formative feedback is an essential part of the learning process in higher education (Evans, 2013; Gibbs & Simpson, 2004–05; Higgins et al., 2002); (2) formative feedback provides information about students regarding the gap between actual and desired levels of performance (Sadler, 1989); (3) the current practice of feedback is generally monologic, that is, from a teacher to students (Ajjawi & Boud, 2018; Nicol, 2010; Yorke, 2003); and (4) teacher feedback can often exert power over students by using academic discourse that may be unfamiliar to students (Carless, 2006; Lea

& Street, 1998). In this book, any research on peer formative feedback on academic writing assessment is excluded although its increasing importance has been reported in the literature (for example, see a recent review of studies in Huisman, Saab, van den Broek, & van Driel, 2019). The main reason for the exclusion is that peer review was not a feature that my research examined.

Formative feedback is often considered central to student learning in higher education in the UK and elsewhere (e.g., Evans, 2013; Keppell & Carless, 2006; Sadler, 1998; Yorke, 2003). It is also recognised in the literature that research in this area is relatively sparse (see, e.g., Pereira, Flores, Simão, & Barros, 2016; Walker, 2009; Weaver, 2006). Nevertheless, there are some studies that examine the impact of formative feedback on student writing in an assessment context. They use a number of different research frameworks and instruments. It should be noted that most of the studies reviewed below were conducted on feedback provided by disciplinary experts rather than academic writing experts in an academic writing programme. This means they do not necessarily focus on language use in academic writing in their formative feedback.

Among these, the ones selected for the present review can be categorised in terms of their main research method and focus: (1) student perceptions, (2) teacher perceptions, (3) textual analysis and (4) formative feedback process.

Student Perceptions

Student perception refers to how students in higher education perceive teacher formative feedback on their written assignments. Formative feedback studies on student perception have used different data collection and analysis tools of which the most common are: survey questionnaires, various types of interview and focus group discussions with students (e.g., Carless, 2006; Handley & Williams, 2011; Walker, 2009; Weaver, 2006). Some of these studies are reviewed in detail below.

Considering formative feedback as an essential part of learning process, Weaver's (2006) study investigated the perceptions of Business and Arts and Design undergraduate students about assessment feedback. In addition, this study employed the notions of 'deep' (i.e., making sense of what is to be learned) and 'surface' (i.e., memorising facts and reproducing them) approaches to learning (e.g., see Rust, 2002). It was assumed that students following a 'deep' approach may benefit most from the formative feedback given to them. Although this study focussed on the learner, it did not consider the dialogic nature of feedback (see Yorke, 2003). Additionally, despite the combination of both quantitative and qualitative methods, the former (in this case, a survey) was the main method and thus might have missed individual learner perceptions. Yet, the findings confirmed previous and most recent research that students find assignment feedback too vague, mostly negative, lacking guidance and not necessarily relevant to the assessment criteria (Chanock, 2000; Ferguson, 2011).

Mainly framed by notions of discourse, power and emotion, Carless (2006) conducted a large-scale study in Hong Kong. As in Weaver's study, the key instrument was a structured survey (1740 participants) although this was complemented by an open-ended survey question, 15 semi-structured student interviews in English and six in Cantonese. This study appears to be more robust than Weaver's, given the scale and the integration of individual interview data with the survey. In addition to confirming previous findings as in Weaver's, Carless's study explored additional aspects such as students' perceptions of teacher-student power relationships and their emotional reactions which are recognised as aspects of research in assessment but still under-researched. Student perceptions of the emotional support were also found to be an aspect of feedback in later studies such as Poulos and Mahony (2008) and Pitt and Norton (2017), thereby supporting the finding of Carless's study. Nonetheless, Carless's study did not examine student perceptions of feedback in light of the actual teacher feedback which Weaver's study did, which may be a weakness of the study. One key message of Carless's study, highly relevant to my research presented in this book, was a call for more research on potentially valuable 'assessment dialogue' between the teacher and the student. Since his call, there does not appear to be much research on dialogic feedback in academic writing assessment in higher education (e.g., see Ajjawi & Boud, 2017; Bloxham & Campbell, 2010; Handley & Williams, 2011).

How students make sense of assessment feedback continues to be a subject of discussion in higher education. Contributing to this discussion, Hyland (2013b) examined undergraduate students' meaning-making of assessment feedback through interviews in four broad disciplines in a Hong Kong university: business, science, engineering and arts. Based on this research, Hyland argued that his study shifted the focus from teacher formative feedback practices to student meaning-making of assessment feedback. The key findings are that when the formative feedback is 'timely, individualised and focused' students are encouraged to act on the feedback and when it is 'perfunctory, delayed and unrelated', they see it as negative and unhelpful (ibid. p. 186).

Effective assessment feedback and challenges of assessment feedback in higher education appear to be continuous themes in research on formative feedback. Unlike previous studies, however, some recent studies have tended to treat formative feedback as a *process*. For example, Dawson et al. (2019) examined what makes effective feedback through student and teacher surveys in a large-scale study in Australia. As in a number of previous studies, they reported that students perceive assessment feedback effective when it is usable, detailed, interactive (or dialogic), considerate of affect and personalised. In another large-scale study with students and academic staff, Henderson, Ryan, and Phillips (2019) examined challenges of assessment feedback in Australian higher education through a survey. They found that there are broadly three areas of assessment feedback facing challenges: assessment feedback practices (e.g., content, mode, impact), context (time and scalability) and individual (attitudes and capability). The key argument made by these authors is that assessment feedback needs to be seen as an interaction between these three areas. This points to the situatedness of assessment feedback, a view which is adopted in this book too though from a Vygotskian sociocultural theory perspective.

Within the context of distance education and The Open University (OU) where my research was conducted, a few studies have already been carried out in the area of assessment feedback. Of particular relevance is Walker's (2009) study carried out with undergraduate Technology students at the OU. It aimed to explore how much assignment feedback is 'usable' (i.e., useful) for students by seeking students' views in addition to the analysis of their teachers' feedback comments (see *Textual analysis* below). Walker employed open-ended interviews with 43 students which provided in-depth insight into student perceptions. In addition to confirming previous findings by Chanock (2000) and Weaver (2006), this study suggested that if the assessment feedback is 'usable', students make use of it in their future assignments although this will rely on the student recognising the feedback as such.

To sum up, one cannot disregard the value of student perceptions about formative feedback. In fact, knowing how students perceive formative feedback can help to improve feedback techniques (e.g., Dawson et al., 2019; Orsmond, Merry, & Reiling, 2005). However, through such studies, it is often difficult to establish how exactly students apply the formative feedback to their subsequent assessment texts without analysing these texts.

Teacher Perceptions

Teacher perception refers to how teachers perceive their feedback on students' assessment texts. Given the critical role teachers can play in developing learners' academic writing abilities, their views of feedback need to be considered. These studies have mainly employed surveys and interviews as instruments to explore teacher views on formative feedback.

Assessment feedback practices from the teacher perception perspective have been researched for some time albeit less extensively than those of student perceptions (Tuck, 2012). One such study advocating 'assessment dialogue' is Carless (2006), mentioned earlier, which surveyed 460 teachers from eight universities and interviewed five teachers about assessment feedback practices. The study found that teachers perceived formative feedback to be useful for students although they contradicted their students' views by stating that students were interested in marks or grades rather than in formative feedback. Despite the contradiction, this teacher perception supports some previous findings (e.g., see Mutch, 2003) although more empirical investigation is still needed. Price, Handley, Millar, and O'Donovan (2010) also investigated teacher perceptions about feedback practices. The authors maintained that there was confusion among teachers regarding the purpose of formative feedback and called for more 'dialogue' between the teacher and the student over feedback. Like Carless's study, this study did not appear to have examined the actual teacher feedback.

Some recent studies have explored challenges in assessment feedback as experienced by teachers. For instance, UK higher education teachers' lived experiences of engaging with assessment feedback on student writing was examined in a study in which assessment feedback was treated as a social practice (Tuck, 2012). The study found that the teachers had conflicting experiences in their feedback-giving practices because they saw the practices as *institutional requirement*, as *work* and as a *dialogue with students* at the same time. In the most recent study, Henderson et al. (2019) found that challenges for teachers relate to the interplay between feedback practices (especially, comment and mode of communication), time and scalability constraints, and attitude and capacity of their own and their students. This paper posits that assessment feedback is a complex process which is socially situated, as argued in this book, and therefore, it is important to investigate how the aforementioned three variables influence one another.

A few other studies also reported that teachers see assignment feedback as a tool for learning (e.g., Orsmond & Merry, 2010). However, it was found that the actual feedback did not correlate with what teachers said. This mismatch may be linked with teachers' own view of assessment practices which might be geared towards the task in hand rather than future work. Furthermore, in spite of both teachers' and students' positive perceptions about the value of formative feedback, research still shows that students are not able to act on the assignment feedback (e.g., see Burke, 2009; Hyland, 2013b) and this may be due to the lack of assessment feedback literacy. Therefore, there has recently been a call for student and teacher feedback literacy and its research (Carless & Boud, 2018; Henderson et al., 2019). It is also important to note that why students implement teacher formative feedback into their subsequent assignments can be explained only by examining the 'feedback dialogue' between the teacher and the student. Such studies are, however, extremely rare in the literature.

While teacher perceptions of their formative feedback practices are important, as with student perceptions of formative feedback, what has emerged from these studies is that it is difficult to understand how formative feedback is actually applied by students to their subsequent assessment texts. Therefore, a different methodological approach is required to study the link between formative feedback and student performance on assessment.

Textual Analysis

In addition to perception studies, a number of studies have examined either teacher feedback and/or student assessment texts. Teacher feedback includes the written feedback comments made by teachers on student assignments either as annotations or summary feedback. I will, first, review key studies analysing teacher feedback texts.

Researchers investigating teacher feedback texts have tended to consider the link between such feedback and student writing development. Earlier studies such as Lea and Street (1998) examined teacher feedback on assignments, following an 'ethnographic style', in addition to student and teacher interviews and sample student assignments, in terms of the clarity of teacher feedback and its effect on student learning. Lea and Street found that feedback was often vague and implied teachers' authoritative voice which may have done more harm than good to the student. Additionally, teacher feedback practices varied from one teacher to another and from one discipline to another.

Following a similar methodology to Lea and Street's, Walker (2009) examined teacher feedback on student assignments in distance education. Unlike Lea and Street's study which did not provide details of the analytical tool, Walker developed a coding system for the themes emerging from the teacher feedback data to conduct a content analysis. She used the notion of 'usability' to classify the teacher comments following Brown and Glover (2006, cited in Walker, 2009, p. 69). Walker reported that teacher feedback broadly fell into two categories: content (subject knowledge) and skills development. However, Walker stated that the proportion of teacher feedback related to skills development, the most 'usable' teacher feedback, was much lower than that associated with subject knowledge. Thus, this study showed that teachers possibly did not employ a range of formative feedback that might have supported student learning.

Stern and Solomon (2006), building on a previous study by Connor and Lunsford (1993), also employed a coding system for content analysis while examining 598 undergraduate student assignments with teacher comments on them. These assignments were from multiple disciplines. Stern and Solomon developed their own coding categories considering the function of the teacher comment such as 'Paper structure and organisation' and 'Support/evidence for claims' (2006, p. 30). This study found that teacher feedback focussed on micro-levels such as grammar and spelling, and there was virtually no comment on macro-level features such as text organisation. Again, this shows the limited 'usability' (to use Walker's term) of teacher feedback.

Another study worth mentioning, following a content analysis approach to assessment feedback, is Wingate (2010). Her exploratory study examined the impact of formative feedback on the development of academic writing among first year students in a module in an undergraduate applied linguistics programme over 10 weeks. The participating students were provided formative feedback on two assignments which they could use to improve their third assignment. A content analysis of tutor[4] comments written in the margin of the student written assignments was conducted to link the comments with any improvement in the students' writing in the assignment. Particularly, the feedback was scrutinised whether it (1) considerably improved students' academic writing, (2) did not improve their writing, and (3) consistently helped them to achieve high grades across the assignments. The student assignments were analysed by using the marking criteria used to mark the assignments such as *use of evidence from appropriate sources, critical evaluation of the literature* and so on. The data were also collected through semi-structured interviews with selected students on their perceptions and how they used the formative feedback they received after they received the grades on their final assignment. The findings showed that those students who paid attention to the formative feedback improved their academic writing while those that did not heed to the feedback continued to receive the same 'criticism' in the formative feedback. Similarly, the students who improved their academic writing seemed more engaged with feedback and took actions to improve their writing. However, as noted by the author, the study did not conduct a discourse analysis of the tutor comments although it was apparent that there was a discrepancy in the comments provided to the high achieving students and that to the low-achieving students. In fact, little attention has been paid to this aspect of assessment feedback to date.

In addition to using a content analysis approach, some studies have employed linguistic frameworks to examine teacher comments on assignments. For example,

---

[4]The terms *tutor* and *teacher* are used interchangeably in this book.

Hyatt (2005) conducted a study of teacher comments on 60 education student assignments, following corpus linguistics and critical discourse analysis (e.g., Fairclough, 1995). Based on the corpus data, he developed seven functional categories of teacher comments (e.g., developmental, structural, content-related, etc.), each with their own sub-categories. This study made the assumption that academic discourse such as teacher comments implies a form of power relationship between the teacher and students as found in Carless (2006). Therefore, how much students act on these comments may be affected by the nature of the discourse. Hyatt found that the most frequent comments (60%) were content-related followed by stylistics comments (i.e., use and presentation of academic language) whereas a quarter of the comments were developmental (i.e., focusing on future assignments). This study supported the previous findings that teachers exert power over students through their academic discourse such as the use of modality (e.g., 'should', 'must', etc.) and imperatives (e.g., see Lea and Street, 1998). A limitation of this study lies in its being purely textual, a corpus of teacher comments, which could have been enriched by teacher and student interview data.

Using an SFL-based linguistic framework in an exploratory study, Gardner (2004) investigated teacher feedback by comparing the same teachers' written and spoken comments on student assignments. Although the comments were by the same teacher, they were not on the same assignments. Gardner reported that shifting teacher comments from written to spoken changed the comments into being more engaging, personal and formative (focussed on both product and process). This study additionally suggested that spoken comments were more dialogic and hence more developmental than written comments.

Woodward-Kron (2004) also employed SFL to examine teacher comments on 44 Education students' assignments in the first and the third year each. Additionally, teacher and student interview data complemented the study, something that Hyatt's (2005) study lacked. She used Halliday's (e.g., 1994) three metafunctions as her framework of analysis: experiential (i.e., topic), interpersonal (i.e., reader-writer interaction) and textual (i.e., organisation of meanings). This study followed a sociocultural perspective on academic writing which assumed that students are apprentices who may be inducted into their respective disciplinary communities by their teachers. However, Woodward-Kron reported that teacher comments played little role in socialising students into disciplinary communities because the majority of the comments fell under experiential and textual categories, with very few relating to the interpersonal, which can promote dialogue between the teacher and the student.

Likewise, using an SFL framework, Hyland and Hyland (2006c) examined aspects of interpersonal meaning in two teachers' comments on six students' written assignments in a pre-sessional English for academic purposes course. The data was complemented by retrospective participant interviews. The researchers found that the teachers' comments fell into three main categories: Praise (44%), Criticism (31%) and Suggestion (25%). They argue that teacher comments carry interpersonal meanings which may make or break the relationship between teachers and their students. Thus, this can have a negative or positive effect on students' academic writing. As noted earlier, the interpersonal dimension of assessment feedback is rarely investigated and their study further demonstrates the value of such studies.

A few other studies analysed students' assessment texts in order to track students' writing development over time. For example, using SFL as the framework, Woodward-Kron (2008) reported a longitudinal study that analysed six undergraduate students' assignments in relation to formative feedback. In particular, she tracked the use of specialist language in their assignments through the concepts of *technicality* and *abstraction*. Woodward-Kron reported that students who were capable of employing more specialist language in their assignments were more successful than those who were not. She argued that the use of specialist language in student writing is integral to their learning of disciplinary knowledge. Nonetheless, it can also be contended that a higher frequency of technicality in student writing may not necessarily equate with their increased disciplinary knowledge or ability to write. It may rather indicate novice writers, often less successfully, trying to demonstrate their familiarity with the concerned discipline by repeating specialist terms from the reading sources.

In summary, the above studies showed that while some types of teacher comments are 'usable' or useful for future assignments, others may be either limited to the task at hand or focus on mechanical issues in writing (e.g., spelling). A few studies also demonstrated that given the unequal power relationship between the teacher and the student, teacher comments further endorsed this inequality in their choice of language, leading to a limited amount of dialogue between them. Studies that examined student assessment texts indicated writing development over time to some extent. However, these studies indicate that there is still a lack of dialogue between the teacher and the student in the formative feedback process as argued by a number of scholars for some time in higher education (e.g., see Ajjawi & Boud, 2018; Dawson et al., 2019; Henderson et al., 2019; Nicol, 2010; Yorke, 2003).

Formative Feedback Process

A number of studies in higher education have investigated the formative feedback process. Here, formative feedback process refers to the feedback-revision cycle in which the teacher comments on a student's written drafts and the student revises the text before the student submits the final text (i.e., product) for assessment. In fact, such studies are more closely aligned with students' writing development than those studies reviewed in the previous sections because these consider the impact of feedback on writing over time, although such studies are rare.

Duncan (2007) investigated how teacher feedback on assignments and associated teaching interventions (e.g., one-on-one tutorial and reading students' written drafts and commenting on them) might impact on student writing development vis-à-vis formative feedback. In this small-scale study, the researcher analysed teacher feedback and scores on assignments, and interviewed the participants. Despite the interventions targeting students' needs (e.g., referencing, analytical skills), as the researcher reported, there was 'a small gain' in achievement and the participants were not convinced that the teacher feedback was valuable to them (cf. Carless 2006).

Likewise, Ellery (2008) examined the formative feedback process. Ellery's study appears to have been based on the Vygotskian concept of 'capable peer's guidance' for assessment although it is not clear how the guidance process was carried out from the Vygotskian perspective. She analysed the two drafts of the same essay and examined the feedback process through student interviews. Her findings suggested that students could learn from formative feedback given on the first draft, although each student did so to a different degree.

There are some relevant studies which examined oral formative feedback process in teacher-student academic *writing conferences* in US universities. Writing conferences, which are common in US universities, were intended for one-on-one conversations to support with individual students' needs as the whole-class instruction proved challenging to meet needs of students with diverse backgrounds (Lerner, 2005). Studies which specifically adopted a sociocultural approach to academic writing pedagogy are worth mentioning here although they are related to second language student writers (Hyland & Hyland, 2006b). Drawing on the Vygotskian sociocultural theory (see Chap. 2), some studies examined the impact of oral feedback on students' writing in writing conferences (e.g., Aljaafreh & Lantolf, 1994; Yu, 2020), an area which still seems to be under-researched (Yu, 2020). For example, Aljaafreh and Lantolf (1994) showed that it is possible to provide implicit to explicit support to students and target their changing writing needs. This study has been influential in L2 writing research and carrying out dynamic assessment (see Chap. 2). The most recent study shows that teacher-student writing conference can support students' academic writing if the teacher is not too directive but collaborative and aims to focus on students' emerging needs, keeping in view of students' personal beliefs, institutional context and interpersonal relationships (Yu, 2020).

There has been a recent shift in research to analysing written formative feedback on academic writing assessment as a dialogic process rather than formative feedback just as input or product. In particular, two recently published papers are worth mentioning (i.e., Ajjawi & Boud, 2017, 2018). Both these papers advocate assessment feedback as a dialogic process. They define assessment feedback as 'a communicative act and a social process in which power, emotion and discourse impact on how messages are constructed, interpreted and acted upon' (Ajjawi & Boud, 2018, p. 1108). They draw on the model of assessment feedback dialogue developed by Yang and Carless (2013). This model has three key dimensions: cognitive (the content of feedback, related to discipline), social-affective (relational, interpersonal and emotional) and structural (institutional organisation and management of feedback) (ibid. p. 287). These three dimensions have dynamic relationships as they constantly interact with one another. Ajjawai and Boud (2017) proposed the use of an interactional analysis approach to analysing feedback dialogue which they further elaborated in their second article (i.e., Ajjawi & Boud, 2018). The interactional analysis, in many ways, resembles linguistic analyses of interpersonal dimensions because it focuses on interactional features and negotiations between the teacher and the learner in a social context. Ajjawai and Boud (2018) argued that their study showed the interplay between the three dimensions mentioned above for sustained dialogic feedback and sustainable assessment. They found that the effect of the dialogic feedback was beyond the immediate task. The paper concludes by calling for more longitudinal research into dialogic feedback and an examination of patterns of linguistic use in relation to the three dimensions to track effects on learners. In many ways, the research reported in this book addresses this call.

Formative feedback process has also been investigated from a linguistic perspective. For example, a study following an SFL framework was carried out focusing on formative feedback process by Mahboob, Dreyfus, Humphrey, and Martin (2010). They expanded the *writing assessment scheme* for assessing academic writing developed by Rose, Rose, Farrington, and Page (2008). The scheme has an explicit focus on genre as suggested by the criteria labels such as 'Genre', 'Register' and 'Discourse' (see full criteria in Chap. 4). The criteria are further sub-divided into sub-categories (e.g., Register: Field, Tenor, Mode). Mahboob et al. adapted the writing assessment schedule in the SLATE (Scaffolding Literacy in Adult and Tertiary Environments) project designed for students studying academic writing online in Hong Kong. The key contribution of this project is its greater focus on the assessment feedback process which had received little attention in the SFL research previously. The students were offered opportunities to learn when they were writing their assignments. One of the underpinning theories of the pedagogy in the SLATE project was the Vygotskian notion of scaffolding as theorised by Bruner (1966). Following this notion, a feedback cycle was designed for the assignment. The students wrote two drafts for which teachers provided annotations and comments for improving their writing. Then students incorporated the feedback into their second draft and the final version before submitting the assignment for marking. Additionally, the SLATE team developed a 3×3 matrix (see Chap. 4) extending and simplifying the *writing assessment schedule* (see Humphrey, Martin, Dreyfus, & Mahboob, 2010 for details). The teachers were trained to follow the 3×3 matrix and a particular feedback genre having three mandatory stages: Orientation (greetings and preview)^5 Feedback (explanation of problem and solution)^ Encouragement (positive note). Mahboob et al. (2010) report that the participating students achieved some writing development. However, they have not yet tracked the students' academic writing development over time. In many ways, their project is similar to my research discussed in this book. Nevertheless, the teacher-student interaction followed in my research is different not only due to the mode of communication (i.e., emails and instant messaging) but also the flexibility allowed for the individualised feedback dialogue following the dynamic assessment process.

Despite the fact that these studies investigated the impact of formative feedback on student academic writing development, there was a lack of a clear feedback framework regarding the feedback process except in Mahboob et al.'s (2010) study. Also, studies such as Ellery's (2008) still appeared to have concentrated on the products and grades rather than focusing on which type of feedback resulted in which type of positive change or otherwise in students' writing. However, the recent research such as Ajjawi and Boud (2018) shows that there has been a shift towards dialogic

---

[5]The symbol ^ refers to the sequence.

feedback in relation to discipline-based academic writing assessment although this may be a long way away from mainstream academic writing assessment practices.

To sum up, the studies discussed here suggest that formative teacher feedback on students' written assignments does not appear to have the expected extent of positive impact on academic writing development although some studies indicate some positive signs. One of the main reasons for the lack of positive impact could be the predominance of a monologic approach to teacher feedback in higher education (see Yorke, 2003). Such an approach, as a number of higher education scholars have long argued for (e.g., Ajjawi & Boud, 2018; Lillis, 2003; Nicol, 2010; Yang & Carless, 2013), needs to be replaced with a more dialogic approach that considers students' construction of meaning in a written text in context. Most importantly, most feedback studies fail to demonstrate whether writing assessment supports academic writing and conceptual development in a discipline. Thus, a study that investigates these areas seems timely.

1.7.2 Diagnostic Academic Writing Assessment

Diagnostic assessment can be defined as a process that helps to identify strengths and weaknesses in a student's writing (Bachman & Palmer, 1996, p. 98). Based on this diagnosis, learning activities are designed to address the weaknesses. For this reason, in this review, diagnostic assessment is considered a type of formative assessment and thus relevant to my research. Diagnostic assessment is also considered to have certain features of DA (e.g., see Antón, 2018). While the other studies reviewed in the previous section did not have an explicit diagnostic purpose, the studies reviewed in this section do.

Studies on diagnostic academic writing assessment have concentrated on specific diagnostic assessment instruments used for diagnostic purposes. Only a few studies have been reported in this area regarding academic writing assessment in higher education. Furthermore, these studies are related to two diagnostic instruments that integrate academic writing support: Measuring the Academic Skills of University Students (MASUS) and Diagnostic English Language Needs Assessment (DELNA).

SFL-based MASUS (Bonanno & Jones, 2007) was developed for teaching and assessing academic writing in the University of Sydney. It has been applied in various higher education contexts including the academic writing course where my research took place.

Some studies have been conducted to measure the effectiveness of MASUS. Studies that used the MASUS tool to investigate academic writing have sought to identify students' needs in academic writing and subsequently designed programmes to support students (see Bonanno, 2002; Scouller, Bonanno, Smith, & Krass, 2008). The MASUS tool as a diagnostic instrument has shown that it can help teachers to identify the areas that students need support in (Bonanno, 2002; Donohue, 2002). However, researchers have not yet investigated the developmental process of student writing or learning opportunities during the assessment process nor during the intervention after the test as they have almost always focussed on 'end products' (see Taylor & Drury, 2007). Although an analysis of the 'end product' may indicate a degree of any improvement in student academic writing, without examining the diagnostic process, it is hard to establish a clear link between their eventual academic writing and the diagnostic intervention. Furthermore, diagnostic assessment in studies using MASUS such as Scouller et al. (2008) was carried out as in a psychometric test (i.e., measurement of static human abilities represented by scores and grades) in which students responded to a writing task in a 'controlled' environment and they received grades or scores on their performance. However, the designers of MASUS suggest variations and flexibility in relation to the use of the instrument (Bonanno & Jones, 2007, pp. 4–5). These may include, inter alia, the timing and nature of the feedback and the genre type. Yet, there seems to be no learning opportunity during the assessment. As noted by Johns (2008), the focus on texts or products and the lack of attention to cognitive learning strategies in a relevant socio-cultural context make it difficult to establish a clear link between the diagnostic test and the subsequent instruction programme.

Read (2008) investigated the use of another diagnostic academic writing assessment tool, namely DELNA, for identifying academic literacy needs of undergraduate students in the University of Auckland. Read analysed the test purpose and built his argument on the validity of the instrument (i.e., test). This diagnostic instrument also incorporates a support programme for students diagnosed as needing academic language support. However, research does not appear to have focussed on whether the programme had any impact on students' academic writing development but rather on refining DELNA (e.g., Knoch, 2009).

Only recently there has been an interest in diagnostic academic writing assessment from a sociocultural theory perspective. Fox, Haggerty, and Artemeva (2016) is a case in point. They draw on Activity Theory (e.g., see Engeström, 1999) in which diagnostic academic writing assessment is seen as an activity system which involves human participation to achieve objects through sociocultural tools such as symbols and materials. They report on a longitudinal study which examined the impact of diagnostic assessment procedures that adapted DELNA and MASUS (see above) and academic writing support in a first year undergraduate engineering programme. The purpose of the diagnostic assessment was to identify at-risk students early in the programme and provide them with individualised pedagogical support which included academic literacy embedded within a mandatory engineering course. According to the authors, there were positive outcomes such as better student engagement and participation because both the diagnostic assessment procedures and the pedagogical support were discipline-based rather than generic unlike in Read (2008).

To sum up, despite diagnostic assessment being promising, studies on it, to date, have not effectively shown how it improves students' academic writing. Furthermore, these studies have treated assessment and instruction as separate entities except in the study by Fox et al. (2016). Most importantly, these diagnostic approaches appear to concentrate on assessment rather than integrating assessment with learning in the context of academic writing in a disciplinary context.

1.7.3 Dynamic Assessment (DA) as an Alternative

DA is concerned with students' learning in the assessment process as noted in 1.1 earlier. Therefore, it is broadly considered as a form of formative assessment (e.g., see Black & Wiliam, 2009; Leung, 2007).

Although DA has been employed in education and clinical psychology for several decades (e.g., see Haywood & Lidz, 2007 for a comprehensive review), it is new to language and literacy education. DA is mainly used in face-to-face contexts. However, some studies have used computers for mediation. For example, Tzuriel and Shamir's (2002) study was conducted with kindergarten children to examine the effects of computer-assisted DA on cognitive performance and reported that this method brought about significant cognitive changes to the participants. Likewise, Poehner and Lantolf (2013) reported on the computer-mediated DA of listening and reading comprehension in French and Chinese for university students. In this DA, graduated prompts were used through the computer when students responded to tasks. Each time the learner responded a prompt was given which varied according to the appropriateness of the response. They calculated un-mediated, mediated and learning potential scores for each learner. They argued that this type of DA is easy to administer to a large number of students simultaneously and the result is quantifiable and easy to interpret. Similar findings are reported in Oskoz's (2005) study which investigated DA of Spanish learners' language skills in a US university. Unlike my research presented in this book, however, it was carried out in a synchronous computer-mediated communication environment. Besides this study, there are a few other studies in higher education reported in the literature that relate to second or foreign language learning (see Lantolf & Poehner, 2011; Lantolf et al., 2018). Among them, only a few were on writing assessment from a DA perspective and these studies are discussed here due to their methodological relevance to my research.

Among the published studies, Kozulin and Garb's (2002) study is linked with a less flexible DA approach (see Chap. 2 for types of DA). This study focussed on the English language reading comprehension skills of adult migrants. These researchers devised a formula to calculate a 'learning potential score' for each learner based on their pre-test and post-test performance. Interestingly, they do not offer any examples of student-teacher interaction during the assessment process. This may be a weakness of this study.

A few other DA studies associated with a more flexible DA approach in the context of foreign language learning have been reported in the literature. To date, the most detailed DA study in this area is by Poehner (2005, 2008) who explored the speaking skills of six advanced French learners following an open and flexible DA approach pioneered by Feuerstein and his colleagues (see Feuerstein, Falik, Rand, & Feuerstein, 2002) and adapted Aljaafreh and Lantolf's (1994) regulatory scale for mediation strategies. In Poehner's study, students were asked to construct an oral narrative in French after viewing a short video clip, which included two types of sessions: one with mediation and another without mediation. These two types of sessions were designed for comparison. There was also an individualised instructional programme for each student to support them with their problem areas which were verbal tense and aspect as identified in the DA sessions. Poehner reported that DA is an effective means of understanding learners' changing abilities and helping them resolve their linguistic problems.

A further study by Antón (2009) investigated DA procedures for the speaking and writing skills of five students in a Spanish diagnostic test for an advanced level. The DA procedures for writing were conducted following Aljaafreh and Lantolf's (1994) model in which the mediator offers assistance that ranges from implicit prompts to explicit corrections. Although Antón reported that, through the DA procedures, the mediator was able to obtain a richer and deeper description of the learners' existing and potential language abilities, the DA procedures for writing were carried out only once after the timed test and the interaction between the students and the assessor seemed very limited (i.e., asking questions). In addition, Antón does not provide the details of the DA procedures followed during the mediation.

There are a few other studies which specifically focus on writing in the context of English as a foreign language. Two papers are worth mentioning here although they are in the context of English language learning rather than disciplinary learning (e.g., biology). The first one is by Alavi and Taghizadeh (2014) who conducted their research with Iranian undergraduate students in the context of an IELTS test. The authors followed an implicit-to-explicit feedback approach to mediation with the participants. Their foci were on writing content and organisation skills and strategies. The study followed a pre-test-train-post-test design and conducted statistical analyses of the learner performance in essay writing. The authors found that, as in previous studies, the participants had different zones of proximal development (i.e., learning potential) in the areas focused on and DA had positive effects on the learners. They argue that explicit teacher feedback was the most effective during the mediation process. This paper, however, lacks detailed data about the actual mediation process or interaction between the teacher and the learners. The second study of relevance is Ebadi and Rahimi (2019) which was also conducted in the IELTS academic writing test context with three undergraduate Iranian university students. The DA procedures were conducted via Google Docs synchronously and asynchronously. The authors found that DA sessions had positive effects on the participants' general academic writing development in relation to coherence and cohesion, lexicon, grammatical range and accuracy which are the marking criteria used in the IELTS test. They also tracked participants for the transfer of learning which showed the participants' maturing writing abilities. They reported positive perceptions of the participants about DA. In many ways, this study is similar to the DA research I discuss in this book. However, unlike my research (e.g., Shrestha, 2017), this study is related to a commercial test (i.e., IELTS) and does not use a particular theory of language use description for tracking learners' microgenetic academic writing development in a discipline.

In the most recently edited volume on sociocultural theory and second language acquisition (Lantolf et al., 2018), a number of authors contribute to the theorisation and expansion of DA. Yet, the chapters in the volume do not provide any detailed account of DA of academic writing. For example, six chapters are dedicated to DA each discussing and theorising different aspects of DA building on up-to-date research which is also important for developing our DA knowledge-base. The aspects covered, for instance, include object of mediation and mediated development in DA (Poehner, 2018), mediator and learner engagement (Davin, 2018) and diagnostic features of DA (Antón, 2018). As the volume title suggests, the chapters do not address questions related to academic literacy or writing assessment except Part V of the volume which has three chapters on literacy and content-based language teaching. However, these chapters do not discuss DA but use aspects of sociocultural theory such as activity theory and social network support to examine second language literacy. These and the papers reviewed in this section indicate that there is significantly limited research on DA of academic writing in a discipline (e.g., business studies), especially in distance education.

Each DA study reviewed above reported that DA enhanced students' linguistic skills (e.g., past tenses in French) by responding appropriately to the potential of learners' zone of proximal development through teacher mediation as indicated by the improvement in the students' independent performance and the decreasing amount of assistance needed by them. However, all of these studies were conducted on learning certain formal features of a foreign or second language and there have been only a few studies on academic writing from a DA perspective. Also, none of the researchers appear to have used a comprehensive theory of language use such as SFL, a need highlighted about a decade ago by Gardner (2010). Nevertheless, as a promising and empowering pedagogical and assessment tool, DA offers an alternative to traditional forms of academic writing assessment in higher education which aligns with the call made for dialogic feedback and sustainable assessment by a number of scholars (e.g., Ajjawi & Boud, 2018; Nicol, 2010; Shrestha & Coffin, 2012; Yang & Carless, 2013; Yorke, 2003) as mentioned in this chapter. The research presented in this book is a response to this call.

1.8 Summary

To summarise, as shown in my critical review of formative assessment, many formative writing assessment studies in higher education suggest that assessment practices in higher education may still have a heavy focus on 'end products' and ignore the interdependence between the pedagogical approach and assessment. These studies reported student writing development in the assessment context only to a limited extent. The studies reviewed in this chapter explored students' writing through student and teacher perceptions, and textual analyses of teacher comments and student writing assessment texts. It should be noted that academic writing and conceptual development are not examined as interrelated components of disciplinary writing in these studies except in a few studies (e.g., Woodward-Kron, 2008). The DA studies reviewed here had a strong theory of learning (i.e., Vygotskian sociocultural theory), something that other studies often lacked. However, their weakness appears to be a lack of a clear linguistic framework for the analysis of the data and tracking academic writing development. Therefore, there is a need for developing a sound theoretical framework to examine academic writing assessment and conceptual development in a discipline over time using a combination of a robust theory of learning and development (such as Vygotskian sociocultural theory of learning) and a theory of language use (e.g., SFL). Theories such as sociocultural theory and SFL are compatible with the widely accepted view of academic writing as a social practice. The next two chapters will explain these two theories respectively as relevant to my research.

References

Ackerman, J. M. (1993). The promise of writing to learn. *Written Communication, 10*(3), 334–370. https://doi.org/10.1177/0741088393010003002.

Ajjawi, R., & Boud, D. (2017). Researching feedback dialogue: An interactional analysis approach. *Assessment & Evaluation in Higher Education, 42*(2), 252–265. https://doi.org/10.1080/026 02938.2015.1102863.

Ajjawi, R., & Boud, D. (2018). Examining the nature and effects of feedback dialogue. *Assessment & Evaluation in Higher Education, 43*(7), 1106–1119. https://doi.org/10.1080/02602938.2018. 1434128.

Alavi, S. M., & Taghizadeh, M. (2014). Dynamic assessment of writing: The impact of implicit/explicit mediations on L2 learners' internalization of writing skills and strategies. *Educational Assessment, 19*(1), 1–16. https://doi.org/10.1080/10627197.2014.869446.

Alderson, J. C., & Hamp-Lyons, L. (1996). TOEFL preparation courses: a study of washback. *Language Testing, 13*(3), 280–297. https://doi.org/10.1177/026553229601300304.

Aljaafreh, A., & Lantolf, J. P. (1994). Negative feedback as regulation and second language learning in the zone of proximal development. *Modern Language Journal, 78*(4), 465–483.

Antón, M. (2009). Dynamic assessment of advanced second language learners. *Foreign Language Annals, 42*(3), 576–598.

Antón, M. (2018). Dynamic diagnosis of second language abilities. In J. P. Lantolf, M. E. Poehner, & M. Swain (Eds.), *The Routledge handbook of sociocultural theory and second language development* (pp. 310–323). New York, NY: Routledge.

Bachman, L. F., & Palmer, A. S. (1996). *Language testing in practice*. Oxford: Oxford University Press.

Barkaoui, K. (2007). Rating scale impact on EFL essay marking: A mixed-method study. *Assessing Writing, 12*(2), 86–107.

Bazerman, C. (1988). *Shaping written knowledge: The genre and activity of experimental article in science*. Madison, WI: The University of Wisconsin Press.

Bazerman, C. (2005). *Reference guide to writing across the curriculum*. West Lafayette, IND.: Parlor Press.

Becher, T. (1994). The significance of disciplinary differences. *Studies in Higher Education, 19*(2), 151–161.

Black, P., & Wiliam, D. (2009). Developing the theory of formative assessment. *Educational Assessment, Evaluation and Accountability, 21*(1), 5–31.

Bloxham, S., & Campbell, L. (2010). Generating dialogue in assessment feedback: Exploring the use of interactive cover sheets. *Assessment & Evaluation in Higher Education, 35*(3), 291–300.

Bonanno, H. (2002). Standing the test of time: Revisiting a first year diagnostic procedure. In *Paper presented at the 6th Pacific Rim Conference*.

Bonanno, H., & Jones, J. (2007). *Measuring the academic skills of university students*. Sydney: Learning Centre, the University of Sydney.

Boud, D., & Soler, R. (2016). Sustainable assessment revisited. *Assessment & Evaluation in Higher Education, 41*(3), 400–413. https://doi.org/10.1080/02602938.2015.1018133.

Bruner, J. S. (1966). *Towards a theory of instruction.* Cambridge, MA.: Harvard University Press.

Burke, D. (2009). Strategies for using feedback students bring to higher education. *Assessment & Evaluation in Higher Education, 34*(1), 41–50.

Carless, D. (2006). Differing perceptions in the feedback process. *Studies in Higher Education, 31*(2), 219–233.

Carless, D., & Boud, D. (2018). The development of student feedback literacy: Enabling uptake of feedback. *Assessment & Evaluation in Higher Education*, 1315–1325. https://doi.org/10.1080/02602938.2018.1463354.

Chanock, K. (2000). Comments on essays: Do students understand what tutors write? *Teaching in Higher Education, 5*(1), 95–105.

Chetwynd, F., & Dobbyn, C. (2011). Assessment, feedback and marking guides in distance education. *Open Learning: The Journal of Open, Distance and e-Learning, 26*(1), 67–78.

Coffin, C., & Donohue, J. (2014). *A language as social semiotic based approach to teaching and learning in higher education.* Malden, MA: John Wiley & Sons Inc.

Coffin, C., & Donohue, J. P. (2012). Academic literacies and systemic functional linguistics: How do they relate? *Journal of English for Academic Purposes, 11*(1), 64–75. https://doi.org/10.1016/j.jeap.2011.11.004.

Connors, R. J., & Lunsford, A. A. (1993). Teachers' rhetorical comments on student papers. *College Composition and Communication, 44*(2), 200–223.

Cots, J. M., Llurda, E., & Garrett, P. (2014). Language policies and practices in the internationalisation of higher education on the European margins: An introduction. *Journal of Multilingual and Multicultural Development, 35*(4), 311–317. https://doi.org/10.1080/01434632.2013.874430.

Cummins, J. (2014). Beyond language: Academic communication and student success. *Linguistics and Education, 26,* 145–154. https://doi.org/10.1016/j.linged.2014.01.006.

Damianakis, T., Barrett, B., Archer-Kuhn, B., Samson, P. L., Matin, S., & Ahern, C. (2019). Transformative learning in graduate education: Masters of social work students' experiences of personal and professional learning. *Studies in Higher Education*, 1–19. https://doi.org/10.1080/03075079.2019.1650735.

Davin, K. J. (2018). Mediator and learner engagement in co-regulated inter-psychological activity. In J. P. Lantolf, M. E. Poehner, & M. Swain (Eds.), *The Routledge handbook of sociocultural theory and second language development* (pp. 282–294). New York, NY: Routledge.

Dawson, P., Henderson, M., Mahoney, P., Phillips, M., Ryan, T., Boud, D., et al. (2019). What makes for effective feedback: Staff and student perspectives. *Assessment & Evaluation in Higher Education, 44*(1), 25–36. https://doi.org/10.1080/02602938.2018.1467877.

Devlin, M. (2013). Bridging socio-cultural incongruity: Conceptualising the success of students from low socio-economic status backgrounds in Australian higher education. *Studies in Higher Education, 38*(6), 939–949. https://doi.org/10.1080/03075079.2011.613991.

Donohue, J. P. (2002). *Genre-based literacy pedagogy: The nature and value of genre knowledge in teaching and learning writing on a university first year media studies course.* Ph.D., University of Luton.

Duncan, N. (2007). 'Feed-forward': Improving students' use of tutors' comments. *Assessment & Evaluation in Higher Education, 32*(3), 271–283.

Ebadi, S., & Rahimi, M. (2019). Mediating EFL learners' academic writing skills in online dynamic assessment using Google Docs. *Computer Assisted Language Learning, 32*(5–6), 527–555. https://doi.org/10.1080/09588221.2018.1527362.

Eckes, T. (2008). Rater types in writing performance assessments: A classification approach to rater variability. *Language Testing, 25*(2), 155–185.

Ellery, K. (2008). Assessment for learning: A case study using feedback effectively in an essay-style test. *Assessment & Evaluation in Higher Education, 33*(4), 421–429.

Engeström, Y. (1999). Activity theory and individual and social transformation In Y. Engeström, R. Miettinen, & R.-L. Punamäki (Eds.), *Perspectives on activity theory* (pp. 19–38). Cambridge: Cambridge University Press.

Evans, C. (2013). Making sense of assessment feedback in higher education. *Review of Educational Research, 83*(1), 70–120. https://doi.org/10.3102/0034654312474350.

Fairclough, N. (1995). *Critical discourse analysis: The critical study of language.* London: Longman.

Ferguson, P. (2011). Student perceptions of quality feedback in teacher education. *Assessment & Evaluation in Higher Education, 36*(1), 51–62.

Fernández-Toro, M., & Furnborough, C. (2018). Evaluating alignment of student and tutor perspectives on feedback on language learning assignments. *Distance Education, 39*(4), 548–567. https://doi.org/10.1080/01587919.2018.1520043.

Feuerstein, R., Falik, L. H., Rand, Y., & Feuerstein, R. S. (2002). *The dynamic assessment of cognitive modifiability: The learning propensity assessment device: Theory, instruments and techniques* (Revised ed.). Jerusalem: ICELP Press.

Fox, J., Haggerty, J., & Artemeva, N. (2016). Mitigating risk: The impact of a diagnostic assessment procedure on the first-year experience in engineering. In J. Read (Ed.), *Post-admission language assessment of university students* (Vol. 6, pp. 43–65). Cham: Springer.

Gardner, S. (2004). Knock-on effects of mode change on academic discourse. *Journal of English for Academic Purposes, 3*(1), 23–38.

Gardner, S. (2010). SFL: A theory of language for dynamic assessment of EAL. *NALDIC Quarterly, 8*(1), 37–41.

Gibbs, G., & Simpson, C. (2004–05). Conditions under which assessment supports students' learning. *Learning and Teaching in Higher Education, 1*, 3–31.

Green, A. (2007). *IELTS washback in context, studies in language testing series 25.* Cambridge: Cambridge University Press.

Grigorenko, E. L. (2009). Dynamic assessment and response to intervention. *Journal of Learning Disabilities, 42*(2), 111–132. https://doi.org/10.1177/0022219408326207.

Halliday, M. A. K. (1994). *An introduction to functional grammar* (2nd ed.). London: Arnold.

Halliday, M. A. K., & Matthiessen, C. M. I. M. (2004). *An introduction to functional grammar* (3rd ed.). London: Hodder Education.

Handley, K., & Williams, L. (2011). From copying to learning: Using exemplars to engage students with assessment criteria and feedback. *Assessment & Evaluation in Higher Education, 36*(1), 95–108.

Haywood, H. C., & Lidz, C. S. (2007). *Dynamic assessment in practice: Clinical and educational applications.* Cambridge: Cambridge University Press.

Healey, N. M. (2015). Towards a risk-based typology for transnational education. *Higher Education, 69*(1), 1–18. https://doi.org/10.1007/s10734-014-9757-6.

HEFCE. (2010). *National student survey: Findings and trends 2006 to 2009.* London: Higher Education Funding Council for England.

HEFCE. (2014). *National student survey results and trends analysis 2005 to 2013.* London: Higher Education Funding Council for England.

Henderson, M., Ryan, T., & Phillips, M. (2019). The challenges of feedback in higher education. *Assessment & Evaluation in Higher Education, 44*(8), 1237–1252. https://doi.org/10.1080/02602938.2019.1599815.

Higgins, R., Hartley, P., & Skelton, A. (2002). The conscientious consumer: Reconsidering the role of assessment feedback in student learning. *Studies in Higher Education, 27*(1), 53.

Hood, S. (2009). Writing discipline: Comparing inscriptions of knowledge and knowers in academic writing. In F. Christie & K. Maton (Eds.), *Disciplinarity: Functional linguistics and sociological perspectives* (pp. 106–128). London: Continuum.

Hounsell, D., McCune, V., Hounsell, J., & Litjens, J. (2008). The quality of guidance and feedback to students. *Higher Education Research & Development, 27*(1), 55–67.

Huisman, B., Saab, N., van den Broek, P., & van Driel, J. (2019). The impact of formative peer feedback on higher education students' academic writing: A meta-analysis. *Assessment & Evaluation in Higher Education, 44*(6), 863–880. https://doi.org/10.1080/02602938.2018.1545896.

Humphrey, S., Martin, J. R., Dreyfus, S., & Mahboob, A. (2010). The 3 × 3: Setting up a linguistic toolkit for teaching academic writing. In A. Mahboob & N. Knight (Eds.), *Appliable linguistics* (pp. 185–199). London: Continuum.

Huot, B. (2002). *(Re)Articulating writing assessment: Assessment for teaching and learning.* Utah: Utah State University Press.

Hyatt, D. F. (2005). 'Yes, a very good point!': A critical genre analysis of a corpus of feedback commentaries on master of education assignments. *Teaching in Higher Education, 10*(3), 339–353.

Hyland, K. (2013a). Faculty feedback: Perceptions and practices in L2 disciplinary writing. *Journal of Second Language Writing, 22*(3), 240–253. https://doi.org/10.1016/j.jslw.2013.03.003.

Hyland, K. (2013b). Student perceptions of hidden messages in teacher written feedback. *Studies In Educational Evaluation, 39*(3), 180–187. https://doi.org/10.1016/j.stueduc.2013.06.003.

Hyland, K., & Hyland, F. (2006a). Contexts and issues in feedback on L2 writing: An introduction. In K. Hyland & F. Hyland (Eds.), *Feedback in second language writing: Contexts and issues* (pp. 1–19). Cambridge: Cambridge University Press.

Hyland, K., & Hyland, F. (2006b). Feedback on second language students' writing. *Language Teaching, 39*(2), 83–101. https://doi.org/10.1017/S0261444806003399.

Hyland, K., & Hyland, F. (2006c). Interpersonal aspects of response: Constructing and interpreting teacher written feedback. In K. Hyland & F. Hyland (Eds.), *Feedback in second language writing: Contexts and issues* (pp. 206–224). Cambridge: Cambridge University Press.

Ivanič, R., & Lea, M. R. (2006). New contexts, new challenges: The teaching of writing in UK higher education. In L. Ganobcsik-Williams (Ed.), *Teaching academic writing in UK higher education* (pp. 6–15). Basingstoke: Palgrave Macmillan.

Johns, A. M. (2008). Genre awareness for the novice academic student: An ongoing quest. *Language Teaching, 41*(02), 237–252.

Keppell, M., & Carless, D. (2006). Learning-oriented assessment: a technology-based case study. *Assessment in Education: Principles, Policy & Practice, 13*(2), 179–191.

Knoch, U. (2009). Diagnostic assessment of writing: A comparison of two rating scales. *Language Testing, 26*(2), 275–304. https://doi.org/10.1177/0265532208101008.

Kozulin, A., & Garb, E. (2002). Dynamic assessment of EFL text comprehension. *School Psychology International, 23*(1), 112–127.

Langer, J. A., & Applebee, A. N. (1987). *How writing shapes thinking: A study of teaching and learning.* Urbana, Ill.: National Council of Teachers of English.

Lantolf, J. P. (2000). Introducing sociocultural theory. In J. P. Lantolf (Ed.), *Sociocultural theory and second language learning* (pp. 1–26). Oxford: Oxford University Press.

Lantolf, J. P., & Poehner, M. E. (2004). Dynamic assessment of L2 development: Bringing the past into the future. *Journal of Applied Linguistics, 1*(1), 49–72.

Lantolf, J. P., & Poehner, M. E. (2011). Dynamic assessment in the classroom: Vygotskian praxis for second language development. *Language Teaching Research, 15*(1), 11–33. https://doi.org/10.1177/1362168810383328.

Lantolf, J. P., Poehner, M. E., & Swain, M. (Eds.). (2018). *The Routledge handbook of sociocultural theory and second language development.* New York, NY: Routledge.

Lea, M., & Street, B. V. (1998). Student writing in higher education: An academic literacies approach. *Studies in Higher Education, 23*(2), 157–172.

Lerner, N. (2005). The teacher-student writing conference and the desire for intimacy. *College English, 68*(2), 186–208. https://doi.org/10.2307/30044673.

Leung, C. (2007). Dynamic assessment: Assessment for and as teaching? *Language Assessment Quarterly, 4*(3), 257–278.

Lidz, C. S., & Elliot, J. G. (2000). Introduction. In C. S. Lidz & J. G. Elliott (Eds.), *Dynamic assessment: Prevailing models and applications.* Amsterdam: JAI.

Lillis, T. M. (2003). Student writing as 'academic literacies': Drawing on Bakhtin to move from critique to design. *Language & Education: An International Journal, 17*(3), 192–207.

Lillis, T. M., & Scott, M. (2007). Defining academic literacies research: Issues of epistemology, ideology and strategy. *Journal of Applied Linguistics, 4*(1), 5–32.

Lillis, T. M., & Turner, J. (2001). Student writing in higher education: Contemporary confusion, traditional concerns. *Teaching in Higher Education, 6*(1), 57–68. https://doi.org/10.1080/135625 10020029608.

Llosa, L., & Malone, M. E. (2018). Comparability of students' writing performance on TOEFL iBT and in required university writing courses. *Language Testing, 36*(2), 235–263. https://doi.org/10. 1177/0265532218763456.

Mahboob, A., Dreyfus, S., Humphrey, S. L., & Martin, J. R. (2010). Appliable linguistics and English language teaching: The Scaffolding Literacy in Adult and Tertiary Environments (SLATE) project. In A. Mahboob & N. Knight (Eds.), *Appliable linguistics: Texts, contexts and meanings* (pp. 25– 34). London: Continuum.

Manchón, R. M. (2017). The multifaceted and situated nature of the interaction between language and writing in academic settings: Advancing research agendas. In J. Bitchener, N. Storch, & R. Wette (Eds.), *Teaching writing for academic purposes to multilingual students: Instructional approaches* (pp. 183–199). New York: Routledge.

Martin, J. R. (2009). Genre and language learning: A social semiotic perspective. *Linguistics and Education, 20*(1), 10–21.

Martin, J. R. (2016). Meaning matters: A short history of systemic functional linguistics. *WORD, 62*(1), 35–58. https://doi.org/10.1080/00437956.2016.1141939.

Martin, J. R., Maton, K., & Doran, Y. J. (Eds.). (2020). *Accessing academic discourse: Systemic functional linguistics and legitimation code theory* (1st ed.). London & New York: Routledge.

Martin, J. R., & Rose, D. (2007). *Working with discourse: Meaning beyond the clause.* London: Continuum.

McKay, J., & Devlin, M. (2014). 'Uni has a different language … to the real world': Demystifying academic culture and discourse for students from low socioeconomic backgrounds. *Higher Education Research & Development, 33*(5), 949–961. https://doi.org/10.1080/07294360.2014. 890570.

Mutch, A. (2003). Exploring the practice of feedback to students. *Active Learning in Higher Education, 4*(1), 24–38. https://doi.org/10.1177/1469787403004001003.

Nesi, H., & Gardner, S. (2012). *Genres across the disciplines: Student writing in higher education.* Cambridge: Cambridge University Press.

Nicol, D. (2010). From monologue to dialogue: Improving written feedback processes in mass higher education. *Assessment & Evaluation in Higher Education, 35*(5), 501–517.

Northedge, A. (2003). Rethinking teaching in the context of diversity. *Teaching in Higher Education, 8*(1), 17–32. https://doi.org/10.1080/1356251032000052302.

Office for Students. (2018). *National student survey results 2018.* Retrieved February 5, 2019, from Office for Students https://www.officeforstudents.org.uk/advice-and-guidance/student-inf ormation-and-data/national-student-survey-nss/get-the-nss-data/.

Orsmond, P., & Merry, S. (2010). Feedback alignment: Effective and ineffective links between tutors's and students' understanding of coursework feedback. *Assessment & Evaluation in Higher Education, 36*(2), 125–136. https://doi.org/10.1080/02602930903201651.

Orsmond, P., Merry, S., & Reiling, K. (2005). Biology students' utilization of tutors' formative feedback: A qualitative interview study. *Assessment & Evaluation in Higher Education, 30*(4), 369–386.

Oskoz, A. (2005). Students' dynamic assessment via online chat. *CALICO Journal, 22*(3), 513–536.

Pereira, D., Flores, M. A., Simão, A. M. V., & Barros, A. (2016). Effectiveness and relevance of feedback in higher education: A study of undergraduate students. *Studies In Educational Evaluation, 49*, 7–14. https://doi.org/10.1016/j.stueduc.2016.03.004.

Pitt, E., & Norton, L. (2017). 'Now that's the feedback I want!' Students' reactions to feedback on graded work and what they do with it. *Assessment & Evaluation in Higher Education, 42*(4), 499–516. https://doi.org/10.1080/02602938.2016.1142500.

Poehner, M. E. (2005). *Dynamic assessment of oral proficiency among advanced L2 learners of French.* Ph.D., Pennsylvania State University.

Poehner, M. E. (2008). *Dynamic assessment: A Vygotskian approach to understanding and promoting L2 development.* New York: Springer.

Poehner, M. E. (2018). Probing and provoking L2 development: The object of mediation in dynamic assessment and mediated development. In J. P. Lantolf, M. E. Poehner, & M. Swain (Eds.), *The Routledge handbook of sociocultural theory and second language development* (pp. 249–265). New York, NY: Routledge.

Poehner, M. E., & Lantolf, J. P. (2013). Bringing the ZPD into the equation: Capturing L2 development during Computerized Dynamic Assessment (C-DA). *Language Teaching Research, 17*(3), 323–342. https://doi.org/10.1177/1362168813482935.

Poulos, A., & Mahony, M. J. (2008). Effectiveness of feedback: The students' perspective. *Assessment & Evaluation in Higher Education, 33*(2), 143–154.

Price, M., Handley, K., Millar, J., & O'Donovan, B. (2010). Feedback: All that effort, but what is the effect? *Assessment & Evaluation in Higher Education, 35*(3), 277–289.

Prior, P. (2008). A sociocultural theory of writing. In C. A. MacArthur, S. Graham, & J. Fitzgerald (Eds.), *Handbook of writing research* (pp. 54–66). London: The Guildford Press.

Read, J. (2008). Identifying academic language needs through diagnostic assessment. *Journal of English for Academic Purposes, 7*(3), 180–190.

Riazi, A. M. (2016). Comparing writing performance in TOEFL-iBT and academic assignments: An exploration of textual features. *Assessing Writing, 28,* 15–27. https://doi.org/10.1016/j.asw.2016.02.001.

Rose, D., Rose, M., Farrington, S., & Page, S. (2008). Scaffolding academic literacy with indigenous health sciences students: An evaluative study. *Journal of English for Academic Purposes, 7*(3), 165–179.

Rust, C. (2002). The impact of assessment on student learning. *Active Learning in Higher Education, 3*(2), 145–158. https://doi.org/10.1177/1469787402003002004.

Sadler, D. R. (1989). Formative assessment and the design of instructional systems. *Instructional Science, 18,* 119–144.

Sadler, D. R. (1998). Formative assessment: Revisiting the territory. *Assessment in Education: Principles, Policy & Practice, 5*(1), 77–84.

Scouller, K., Bonanno, H., Smith, L., & Krass, I. (2008). Student experience and tertiary expectations: Factors predicting academic literacy amongst first-year pharmacy students. *Studies in Higher Education, 33*(2), 167–178.

Serrano, M. M., O'Brien, M., Roberts, K., & Whyte, D. (2017). Critical pedagogy and assessment in higher education: The ideal of 'authenticity' in learning. *Active Learning in Higher Education, 19*(1), 9–21. https://doi.org/10.1177/1469787417723244.

Shepard, L. A. (2000). The role of assessment in a learning culture. *Educational Researcher, 29*(7), 4–14.

Shohamy, E. (2001). *The power of tests: A critical perspective on the uses of language tests.* New York: Longman.

Shrestha, P. N. (2017). Investigating the learning transfer of genre features and conceptual knowledge from an academic literacy course to business studies: Exploring the potential of dynamic assessment. *Journal of English for Academic Purposes, 25,* 1–17. https://doi.org/10.1016/j.jeap.2016.10.002.

Shrestha, P. N., & Coffin, C. (2012). Dynamic assessment, tutor mediation and academic writing development. *Assessing Writing, 17*(1), 55–70. https://doi.org/10.1016/j.asw.2011.11.003.

Smart, J. (2019). Affordances of TOEFL writing tasks beyond university admissions. *Assessing Writing, 41,* 80–83. https://doi.org/10.1016/j.asw.2019.06.006.

Snow, C. E. (2010). Academic language and the challenge of reading for learning about science. *Science, 328*(5977), 450.

Stern, L. A., & Solomon, A. (2006). Effective faculty feedback: The road less traveled. *Assessing Writing, 11*(1), 22–41.

Surridge, P. (2008). *The national student survey 2005–2007: Findings and trends*. London: Higher Education Funding Council for England.

Taylor, C., & Drury, H. (2007). An integrated approach to teaching writing in the sciences. In A. Brew & J. Sachs (Eds.), *Transforming a university: The scholarship of teaching and learning in practice* (pp. 117–125). Sydney: Sydney University Press.

Tuck, J. (2012). Feedback-giving as social practice: Teachers' perspectives on feedback as institutional requirement, work and dialogue. *Teaching in Higher Education, 17*(2), 209–221. https://doi.org/10.1080/13562517.2011.611870.

Tuck, J. (2018). *Academics engaging with student writing: Working at the higher education textface*. Milton: Taylor and Francis.

Turner, J. (2011). *Language in the academy: Cultural reflexivity and intercultural dynamics*. Bristol, Buffalo: Multilingual Matters.

Tzuriel, D., & Shamir, A. (2002). The effects of mediation in computer assisted dynamic assessment. *Journal of Computer Assisted Learning, 18*(1), 21–32.

Vygotsky, L. S. (1978). *Mind in society: The development of higher psychological processes*. Cambridge, MA: Harvard University Press.

Walker, M. (2009). An investigation into written comments on assignments: Do students find them usable? *Assessment & Evaluation in Higher Education, 34*(1), 67–78.

Weaver, M. R. (2006). Do students value feedback? Student perceptions of tutors' written responses. *Assessment & Evaluation in Higher Education, 31*(3), 379–394.

Weigle, S. C. (2002). *Assessing writing*. Cambridge: Cambridge University Press.

Wells, G. (1999). *Dialogic inquiry: Towards a sociocultural practice and theory of education*. Cambridge: Cambridge University Press.

Wertsch, J. V. (1985). *Vygotsky and the social formation of mind*. Cambridge, MA: Harvard University Press.

Wingate, U. (2010). The impact of formative feedback on the development of academic writing. *Assessment & Evaluation in Higher Education, 35*(5), 519–533.

Wingate, U. (2018). Academic literacy across the curriculum: Towards a collaborative instructional approach. *Language Teaching, 51*(3), 349–364. https://doi.org/10.1017/S0261444816000264.

Wingate, U., Andon, N., & Cogo, A. (2011). Embedding academic writing instruction into subject teaching: A case study. *Active Learning in Higher Education, 12*(1), 69–81. https://doi.org/10.1177/1469787410387814.

Wingate, U., & Tribble, C. (2011). The best of both worlds? Towards an English for academic purposes/academic literacies writing pedagogy. *Studies in Higher Education, 37*(4), 481–495. https://doi.org/10.1080/03075079.2010.525630.

Woodward-Kron, R. (2002). *Disciplinary learning through writing: An investigation into the writing of undergraduate education students*. Ph.D., University of Wollongong.

Woodward-Kron, R. (2004). 'Discourse communities' and 'writing apprenticeship': An investigation of these concepts in undergraduate Education students' writing. *Journal of English for Academic Purposes, 3*(2), 139–161.

Woodward-Kron, R. (2005). The role of genre and embedded genres in tertiary students' writing. *Prospect, 20*(3), 24–41.

Woodward-Kron, R. (2008). More than just jargon—The nature and role of specialist language in learning disciplinary knowledge. *Journal of English for Academic Purposes, 7*(4), 234–249.

Yang, M., & Carless, D. (2013). The feedback triangle and the enhancement of dialogic feedback processes. *Teaching in Higher Education, 18*(3), 285–297. https://doi.org/10.1080/13562517.2012.719154.

Yorke, M. (2003). Formative assessment in higher education: Moves towards theory and the enhancement of pedagogic practice. *Higher Education, 45*(4), 477–501.

Yu, L. (2020). Investigating L2 writing through tutor-tutee interactions and revisions: A case study of a multilingual writer in EAP tutorials. *Journal of Second Language Writing*, 100709. https://doi.org/10.1016/j.jslw.2019.100709.

Chapter 2
Sociocultural Theory, Dynamic Assessment and Academic Writing

2.1 Introduction

The main purposes of this book are to investigate the application of dynamic assessment (DA) to distance learning students' academic writing assessment and its impact on their academic writing and conceptual development. The previous chapter showed that, despite a number of studies conducted on academic writing assessment, only a few combined a learning theory with a linguistic theory to examine the link between academic writing assessment and students' academic writing development. The research reported in this book aims to contribute to narrowing this gap. To this effect, my research employed two theoretical frameworks for designing research and analysing the data. The frameworks are: (1) Sociocultural theory and (2) Systemic Functional Linguistics (SFL). This chapter provides an overview of sociocultural theory as the key framework employed to design the research methodology of this study. SFL is used primarily to analyse student written assignments during my research, further explained in Chap. 3. The chapter also explains DA further by discussing various aspects relevant to the study reported. DA is subsumed within sociocultural theory as it is where DA developed as an assessment approach as introduced in Chap. 1. Therefore, the combination of sociocultural theory and DA serves as the theory of assessment and learning in my research. Chapter 3 explains SFL (i.e., theory of language use) as relevant to this book.

2.2 Vygotskian Sociocultural Theory

Dynamic assessment is based on Vygotsky's sociocultural theory of learning as popularly known in applied linguistics and second language acquisition research. It is also known as cultural-historical psychology (Lantolf, Poehner, & Swain, 2018; Lantolf & Thorne, 2006). Sociocultural theory has influenced writing instruction and research heavily in various ways over the last 30 years or so (Prior, 2008). Therefore,

© Springer Nature Switzerland AG 2020
P. N. Shrestha, *Dynamic Assessment of Students' Academic Writing*,
https://doi.org/10.1007/978-3-030-55845-1_2

it is essential to explicate the notion of Vygotskian sociocultural theory as employed in this book.

Sociocultural theory originated in the writings of Lev Vygotsky in Russia in the 1920s and 1930s. His works were unknown to the Western world until the 1960s when American scholars Michael Cole and James Wertsch visited Russia and familiarised themselves with Vygotsky's works and worked with his colleagues and followers (Lantolf et al., 2018). The first work by Vygotsky that was published in English was *Thought and Language* in 1962, the Russian original of 1932 entitled *Thinking and Speech* (van der Veer, 1987). This was followed by the publication of Vygotsky's book *Mind in Society* in 1978, the first English version and probably the most influential of his works in psychology and education in the West. It is also worth noting that Vygotsky's works have been interpreted in various ways which have led to different applications of his concepts and theory in psychology and education (for detailed discussions, see Lantolf et al., 2018). In this book, the notion of sociocultural theory and associated key concepts follows in the tradition of second language acquisition and writing research as outlined by Lantolf and Thorne (2006).

According to Vygotsky, sociocultural theory is about the study of human mind or consciousness and its higher mental functions, and it recognises the pivotal role of the social context and relationships, and the culturally constructed artefacts or tools (i.e., both physical and symbolic) in shaping human thinking uniquely (Lantolf & Thorne, 2006). This means human cognition and learning are seen as a social and cultural enterprise rather than individual. This view of learning is based on the notion that sociocultural artefacts, especially psychological tools, such as signs (including languages), symbols, and texts help individuals learn to use their own 'psychological functions of perception, memory, attention and so on' when they are internalised. Among psychological tools, literacy is considered one of the most powerful tools (Kozulin, 2003, p. 16).

Vygotsky's approach was influenced by the Marxist view of *dialectical materialism* which he applied to developmental psychology. The dialectical approach proposes that any phenomenon should be studied as processes in motion and in change. It also views human development dialectically which means although our biological changes do play an important role in the development of our higher mental functions, at the same time the artefacts or tools we have created historically and culturally enable us to control our higher mental functions and transform them qualitatively. This view is in contrast to Piaget's approach to human development which emphasises the centrality of the individual and their maturation, downplaying the role of culturally and historically created artefacts which have a central role in elaborating the account of human mind in the Vygotskian approach (Cole & Wertsch, 1996, p. 255).

Given the significance of the higher mental functions in Vygotsky-inspired research, it is important to distinguish them from elementary mental functions. Wertsch (1985, pp. 25–27) has helpfully provided four criteria that Vygotsky used to differentiate them. The first criterion is that elementary mental functions are directly influenced by the environmental circumstances whereas higher mental functions are self-regulated by the person (e.g., attention to a sudden loud noise versus attention to a conversation someone is having). The second criterion is that unlike elementary mental functions, higher mental functions are subject to "'intellectualisation' or conscious 'realisation'" (p. 26). In other words, we not only control these functions voluntarily but also realise what they are. Third, elementary mental functions have biological origins while higher mental functions have social origins and are constructed through our sociocultural activities that we participate in. Fourth, higher mental functions require the use of psychological tools, especially language or signs to mediate the self and those around them because our contact (and thus our mental functions) with the outside world is indirect and mediated by signs. It is the qualitatively transformative change that higher mental functions bring to an individual's development in which Vygotsky was interested. This fourth criterion is the main focus of the research reported in this book.

Vygotsky argued that a child's development cannot be understood by only examining the individual. It is equally necessary to understand the social environment she lives in because '[a]ny function in the child's cultural development appears twice, or on two planes. First it appears on the social plane, and then on the psychological plane' (Vygotsky, 1981, cited in Lantolf & Thorne, 2007, p. 210). As such, the social interaction, also known as a *mediated process*, provides the individual with an opportunity for the development of their higher mental functions. In particular, the development of higher mental functions is influenced by the social and cultural activity around the individual and the tools or artefacts they use in such an activity over a period of time. In educational settings, instruction and the use of any other associated cultural artefacts such as books, visuals and computers to learn represent such an activity. However, there is always a dialectical relationship between the individual's psychological process and their social interaction (Lantolf & Thorne 2006, p. 27). It is dialectical because the individual's psychological process is influenced by the social interaction they participate in and their social participation is affected by the individual's developing psychological process. Therefore, Vygotsky argued that it is necessary to study the *process* of higher mental development and not the product, which does not provide an explanation for development (Vygotsky, 1978, pp. 61–62). As his approach aims to understand the development process, he advocated a dynamic process analysis of the phenomenon.

2.2.1 The Genetic Method

In order to study such a dynamic process, Vygotsky developed a method called *genetic* or *developmental method*. Unlike other psychologists of his time, he saw research methods and theory as interdependent, arguing cogently: '*The search for method becomes one of the most important problems of the entire enterprise of understanding the uniquely human forms of psychological activity. In this case, the method is simultaneously prerequisite and product, the tool and the result of the study*' (Vygotsky, 1978, p. 65 italics in original). As Wertsch and Tulviste (1992, p. 550) noted, in the genetic method, the investigator is interested in understanding the changes higher mental functioning undergoes by tracing back through developmental changes. Therefore, Vygotsky maintained that

> '... we need to concentrate not on the product of development but on the very process by which higher forms are established... *To study something historically means to study it in the process of change*; that is the dialectical method's basic demand. To encompass in research the process of a given thing's development in all its phases and changes - from birth to deaths - fundamentally means to discover its nature, its essence, for "it is only in movement that a body shows what it is." Thus, the historical study of behaviour is not an auxiliary aspect of theoretical study, but rather forms its very base.' (Vygotsky, 1978, pp. 64–65 italics in the original)

In this method, a researcher investigates how development occurs in an individual over a span of time as a result of the goal-directed social interactions which may serve as interventions (Wertsch, 1985, pp. 17–18). The central concept in Vygotsky's genetic method is 'psychological tool' which enables humans 'to organise and gain voluntary control over our biologically specified mental functions' (Lantolf & Thorne, 2006, p. 25). The psychological tool is key to *mediation* which will be explained later.

2.2.2 Four Domains of the Genetic Method

Vygotsky suggested that in order to understand the development of human cognition fully, it is essential to study four domains of research in the genetic method (Lantolf & Thorne, 2006; Wells, 1999; Wertsch, 1985). As one of these domains is directly relevant to the research reported in this book, a brief description of each domain is crucial. The four domains are: (1) phylogenesis, (2) sociocultural history, (3) ontogenesis, and (4) microgenesis. The first domain, *phylogenesis*, refers to the development in the evolution of human species. It is, for example, about how humans differ from other species such as primates with regard to their mental functioning in the history of their evolution as outlined in Darwin's theory of evolution. *Sociocultural history* refers to development over time in a particular culture. Unlike in the phylogenetic domain, historical processes rather than biological processes play key roles in the cultural development of mind. This domain is related to higher mental functioning which is mediated by culturally created material and symbolic artefacts. Within this domain, Vygotsky identified language (and speech) as the most powerful cultural artefact which has helped humans to mediate higher mental functions (e.g., using language to discuss decontextualized objects or abstract concepts). The third domain, *ontogenesis*, is about development over the life span of an individual. Vygotsky argued that it is not possible to understand an individual's development by only looking at their biological development or maturation but also their cultural development, thus converging both phylogenesis and sociocultural history in research. He considers ontogenesis 'as a revolutionary rather than a smooth and gradual evolutionary process. It is marked by upheavals, gaps and discontinuities that can move in unexpected directions, including regression to earlier forms of thinking'

(Lantolf & Thorne, 2006, p. 52). An example of this domain could be researching an individual's trajectory of writing since they started writing. Finally, *microgenesis* is 'the development over the course of and resulting from particular interactions in specific sociocultural settings' (Wells, 1999, p. 5). Wertsch (1985, p. 55) refers to it as 'a very short-term longitudinal study' and it is the domain of research that is dominant in second language development research (Lantolf & Thorne, 2006). The study reported in this book falls within this domain of genetic method because the other three domains were not feasible within the time and resource constraints of my research. Readers interested in a more detailed treatment of the genetic method are referred to Lantolf and Thorne (2006) and Wertsch (1985).

2.3 Academic Writing as a Semiotically Mediated Social Action in Context

As noted earlier, Vygotsky emphasised the importance of language as a powerful mediating tool for developing higher mental functions (Wells, 1999). Language is a powerful human invention which, as mentioned above, relates to the domain of sociocultural history in Vygotsky's genetic theory. A large body of work in second language acquisition research has concentrated on the application of Vygotskian sociocultural theory to language teaching and research (see Lantolf et al., 2018; Lantolf & Thorne, 2006 for extended discussion). However, it should be noted that Vygotsky himself did not write much about semiotic mediation (i.e., use of language and other forms of signs to participate in a sociohistorically situated activity) despite its high place in his theory (e.g., see Hasan, 1992; Wells, 1999). If we want to understand the process of the development of higher mental functions, then, an explanation of semiotic mediation should involve a systematic analysis of language use in social contexts which is a lacuna in Vygotsky's research methodology (Hasan, 1992; Wells, 1999). This is addressed in the next chapter.

Writing is one of the complex higher mental processes using language and was developed culturally over thousands of years in the human history. Any piece of writing is situated in a particular social context and involves a form of social interaction although it may typically appear to be written by one individual in the moment. As argued by Langer and Applebee (1987) more than three decades ago, writing typically involves careful thinking and it also shapes our thinking process and how we present knowledge to others. From this perspective, writing has been seen playing a fundamental role in mediating the development of higher mental functions and helps individuals to regulate others around them. This means writing has a direct relationship with Vygotsky's sociocultural theory. Indeed, Vygotsky stresses the importance of teaching writing or written language to children as it is a complex sociohistorically created tool which is important for schooling (Vygotsky, 1978). Children need to be able to externalise their thoughts and experiences meaningfully and explicitly to others.

Vygotskyan sociocultural theory has influenced writing pedagogy and research substantially in the last 30 or more years in the West (Prior, 2008). The closest connection between Vygostky's sociocultural theory and writing or academic writing pedagogy is the focus on processes rather than products. Most writing pedagogies which focus on the process of writing have been influenced by sociocultural theory in one way or another. From this perspective, writing is not viewed just as an end product but a social activity that 'involves dialogic processes of invention. Texts, as artefacts-in-activity, and the inscription of linguistic signs in some medium are parts of streams of mediated, distributed and multimodal activity' (Prior, 2008, p. 58). In other words, writing is always collaborative and co-authored involving the other in a sociohistorical context even when only a single individual is actually writing. The individual draws on socioculturally constructed resources to externalise their thoughts and knowledge. Thus, as defined in Chap. 1, academic writing is also a semiotically mediated social activity in a disciplinary context used to communicate and participate in that disciplinary (discourse) community. Indeed, written language is the main mode of representing academic knowledge by both academics and students in higher education (Coffin & Donohue, 2014) and thus plays a significant role in developing students' higher mental functioning. In order to develop students' higher mental functioning to enable them to write in academic contexts, the role of teacher-mediator-facilitator has been considered crucial although there are variations as to how the teacher supports students to materialise their potential academic writing abilities into reality. Despite some variations, Englert, Mariage, and Dunsmore (2008, p. 209) have helpfully identified three basic tenets of sociocultural theory relevant to the teacher/facilitator which are applied to writing pedagogy and research: (1) sociocognitive apprenticeships in writing (learner as a cognitive apprentice in guided participation with an 'expert'), (2) procedural facilitators and tools (teacher provides support as needed and tools and strategies to write), and (3) participation in communities of practice (learner participates in the disciplinary community by using tools and sharing goals, standards, etc.). They also argue that there is more need to research writing from the sociocultural perspective systematically which this book addresses particularly by considering (1) and (2) above.

2.4 What Is Dynamic Assessment?

Vygotsky's theory has been widely recognised in educational psychology and education. Although the mainstream educational assessment literature still appears to focus on products, rather than the process of an individual's higher mental development as proposed by Vygotsky, there has been a growing interest from educational assessment scholars in Vygotsky's sociocultural theory. In particular, scholars looking for an alternative to traditional IQ tests have developed an assessment approach that considers the process of cognitive development because IQ tests provide only a partial picture of an individual's development (Allal & Pelgrims Ducrey, 2000). This search has led to the development of dynamic assessment (DA) in special education and clinical psychology (e.g., see Haywood & Lidz, 2007).

As explained in Chap. 1, DA is an assessment approach in which the assessor or teacher actively intervenes during the assessment procedure by targeting learners' potential ability and their response to such interventions is assessed (Haywood & Lidz, 2007, p. 1). DA seeks to assess a learner's abilities by promoting them at the same time. In DA, learner abilities are transformed through dialogic collaboration between the learner and the teacher-assessor (Poehner, 2007). Thus, teaching and assessment become a single activity in DA in contrast to the separation of these activities in other traditional forms of assessment. At this point, it should be noted that, while DA has its origins in sociocultural theory, Vygotsky himself never used the term dynamic assessment although he alluded to the 'diagnostics' of mental development in relation to the zone of proximal development (Vygotsky, 1978, p. 87).

How DA differs from conventional testing is helpfully explained by Sternberg and Grigorenko (2002, pp. 28–29). They present three major differences between what they call *static testing* for conventional assessment and DA (or *testing* to use their term). First, static testing focuses on past development while DA is concerned with the development of abilities-in-process. Second, the examiner in static testing provides no or little feedback on the performance of the learner to avoid any threat to test reliability. In contrast, mediated feedback is provided during the DA process. The feedback may be direct or indirect, depending on the learner needs or their zone of proximal development (ZPD, see 2.5.1 for details). Finally, the relationship between the examiner and the examinee is sharply different. In static testing, the examiner remains neutral and little involved in task completion because any involvement is seen to cause measurement error. In DA, the examiner intervenes and interacts with the examinee during the assessment process, thus replacing conventional 'neutrality' with teaching and helping the learner.

Although DA has been used in special needs education and clinical psychology widely, its application to applied linguistics, namely, language education and second language development is still new. There have, of course, been a number of studies conducted in second language development in this century since this approach was introduced to the field by Lantolf and Poehner (2004). Yet, its application to academic writing development is rare in the literature, with only a few notable exceptions (e.g., Alavi & Taghizadeh, 2014; Ebadi & Rahimi, 2019; Shrestha, 2017; Shrestha & Coffin, 2012).

Given that DA has its origin in and is underpinned by Vygotskian sociocultural theory, it is important to explain relevant key concepts before elaborating on DA further. These key concepts include: *zone of proximal development (ZPD), mediation, imitation* and *internalisation*. Each concept is explained below in relation to dynamic assessment.

2.5   Key Concepts of Sociocultural Theory and Dynamic Assessment

2.5.1   Zone of Proximal Development

Zone of Proximal Development (ZPD) is defined by Vygotsky (1978, p. 86) as 'the distance between the actual development level as determined by independent problem solving and the level of potential development as determined through problem solving under adult guidance or in collaboration with more capable peers'. From a Vygotskian perspective, it is more important to know what a learner may be able to do in the future rather than what they can do at present. By working in the learner's ZPD, it is, thus, possible to determine both their actual and potential abilities. DA is grounded in this notion of assessment as a process rather than a product, and is closely aligned with Vygotsky's genetic method which focuses on dynamic processes of a learner's higher mental functioning. In other words, DA is a development-oriented process which reveals learner performance problems when they are in the process of an activity and helps learners overcome them by targeting their potential ability.

However, Vygotsky did not develop a comprehensive method of assessing an individual's ZPD (Chaiklin, 2003). Nor did he carry out any substantial empirical study to validate the concept of the ZPD (Grigorenko & Sternberg, 1998, p. 78). This situation has often caused difficulty for researchers working in the Vygotskian line of research and, therefore, they have developed different but overlapping interpretations of ZPD (e.g., Chaiklin, 2003; del Río & Álvarez, 2007; Haywood & Lidz, 2007; Mercer, 2000). It is worth noting three examples to illustrate differing interpretations.

The first one is by Mercer (2000) who considered ZPD as a static concept representing an individual's mental state at any point rather than being dynamic and replaced it with his new concept *intermental development zone* (IDZ). He coined the new term to explain the changing state of both the teacher's and learners' knowledge during the educational activity in the classroom. According to him, this zone is constantly reconstituted as the teacher and their learners continue the dialogue in the shared activity. The second interpretation comes from del Río and Álvarez (2007). They argue that, as a widely used Vygotsky's concept, ZPD has been limited to individual development only. They take an ecological perspective on ZPD by considering the internal and the external, the mental and the material, and the organism and the medium. By considering both the individual's internal mental functioning and the external sociocultural environment (e.g., politics, education, family, institutions), it is possible to understand an individual's ZPD better. They propose that the notion of ZPD should be applied to the external units like family and communities if the interdependence between the internal and the external is accepted for an individual's higher mental development. Holzman (2018), a third example, has interpreted ZPD differently from many other Vygotsky scholars. According to her, 'the *ZPD is actively and socially created*, rather than it being an entity existing in psychological-cultural-social space and time. For me, the ZPD is more usefully understood as a process rather than as a spatio-temporal entity, and as an activity rather than a zone, space, or distance' (p. 45). This view of ZPD as dynamic, similar to Mercer's, seems more aligned with the purpose of DA, but scholars working in this particular field seemed to be using the concept to refer to it as a 'zone'.

Despite different but overlapping interpretations of the ZPD, it is accepted as a common feature of the ZPD that a more capable person working jointly with another individual on a given task to achieve the set goal can gain an indication of the individual's future cognitive development. Particularly, two related attributes of the ZPD have made it appealing to Vygotsky-oriented researchers including the author of this book: (1) assisted performance provided by the 'expert' to the learner and (2) the possibility of indicating both the actual and the potential cognitive ability through the process of providing varying qualities of assistance to the learner (Lantolf & Thorne 2006, p. 263). Both of these attributes of the ZPD have been instrumental in developing assessment approaches for examining the individual's higher mental functions. Depending on the interpretation(s) of the ZPD, a range of DA approaches have been developed which are explained in Sect. 2.6 (see Lidz & Elliott, 2000a, b; Poehner, 2008 for a comprehensive review of the prevalent dynamic assessment methods).

The concept of ZPD has been applied to second and foreign language education extensively and there is a large body of research within this area. However, due to space, it is not possible to delve into the review of these studies and instead readers are referred to Lantolf and Thorne (2006, Chapter 10). As previously mentioned, the ZPD is particularly relevant to academic writing as the latter is widely accepted as a socially situated activity in a discursive community (e.g., Coffin, 2006; Coffin & Donohue, 2014; Hyland, 2007; Prior, 2008). Within writing pedagogy, as reviewed in Chap. 1, the learner ZPD is targeted through tools such as drafting of texts and dialogic feedback by the teacher and peers. It is, thus, natural to consider the joint activity of the teacher and the student to produce a written assignment in addition to the student's independent performance if the goal is learning and development (also see van der Veer & Valsiner, 1991, pp. 341–343). This creates *an opportunity for assessing the student's responsiveness to the teacher's support*, a key principle of DA, because a joint activity is a better predictor of a student's future cognitive functioning than their present independent performance (Lidz & Gindis, 2003, p. 101).

The excerpt below taken from Aljaafreh and Lantolf (1994, p. 473), though not a DA study but ZPD-focused, illustrates the teacher working in the ZPD of a second language writer. In this case, the focus is on the use of the article 'the' in a sentence in the student's (N) essay.

Excerpt 2.1

[T = Teacher; N = student]

T: okay in this, okay, "Although I was preparing my travel to USA, with some time almost always we have some thing to do in the last." Do you… is there… do you see anything wrong here in this line here? "Al- though I was preparing myself"

N: I don't know!

T: Okay, "Although I was preparing my… travel to USA" okay aah

N: long travel

T: Okay, you say "preparing my…" instead of travel …what's a better word to use?

N: Trip

T: Okay

N: Is better trip?

T: Okay. Yeah "preparing my trip," okay. There is also something wrong with the article here. Do you know articles?

N: Articles, yes

T: Yeah so what's…

N: eeh on my trip to…

T: What is the correct article to use here?

N: Isn't to is … no … eeh … article?

T: What is the article that we should…

N: It

T: No. Article … you know the articles like the or a or an

N: The trip … my, is not my? no … the trip?

T: My… yeah it's okay, you say my trip

N: My trip

T: Okay

N: To United States

T: Yeah USA, what article we need to use with USA?

N: a, an, the

T: the, which one?

N: but the?

T: Okay, do we use the … ah preparing my trip to … the USA?

N: aaah ah (utters something in Spanish) ah okay when I use when I use USA use with article

T: Okay

N: The

Here the teacher (T) draws the student's (N) attention to the problem in the sentence and gradually working in the student's ZPD tells the student the use of the correct article (*the*) before the word *USA*.

2.5.2 *Mediation*

Like the ZPD, *mediation* is a central concept in sociocultural theory and is integral to DA. While the ZPD is about the individual's potential development, mediation provides an opportunity for such development. Mediation is a process that humans employ in order to regulate the material world, others' or their own social and mental activity by using 'culturally constructed artefacts, concepts and activities' (Lantolf

& Thorne, 2006, p. 79). In other words, any human activity (i.e., higher mental functions) is mediated by objects (e.g., mobile devices), psychological tools (e.g., text, language) or another human being (Kozulin, 2003; Wertsch, 2007). In the context of my research, mediation refers to the intentional and reciprocal interaction between a teacher (and/or written texts) and the learner in relation to the problems experienced by the learner and the developmental support given by the teacher, taking into account the learner's ZPD. Thus, mediation allows the teacher to collaborate on an assessment task more closely with the learner, thereby enabling the teacher to move the learner to the next level of their ZPD.

Vygotsky's notion of mediation can be graphically represented as introduced in his book *Mind in Society.* The figure below (Fig. 2.1) is an adapted version as used by Lantolf and Thorne (2006, p. 62). As indicated by Fig. 2.1, the relationship between the human and the external world can be both direct (indicated by dotted arrow) and indirect or mediated by culturally constructed artefacts and concepts (indicated by solid arrows). Although we may have involuntary reactions to objects, they have little importance in the development of higher mental functions. What is important is the mediation by cultural artefacts and concepts, especially spoken and written language, through activities which help us organise and control our mental activities to make sense of our own cognitive development and what is going on in the external world.

Vygotsky developed the concept of mediation in his theory as he tried to bring together materials or objects (physical tools), and symbols and signs (psychological tools) to understand the development of our higher mental functioning. As noted earlier, he saw a dialectical relationship between physical and psychological tools which eventually helps to develop our higher order thinking. He argued that all our higher order thinking or mental activity is mediated by culturally constructed artefacts including language in social interactions. As a result of this mediation, higher mental functions such as memory, attention, rational thinking and development develop. Despite the centrality of mediation in sociocultural theory, it appears that when it comes to analysing mediation data, most scholars working in Vygotskyan sociocultural theory do not conduct a systematic linguistic analysis of the language use in mediation (e.g., see Hasan, 2005b).

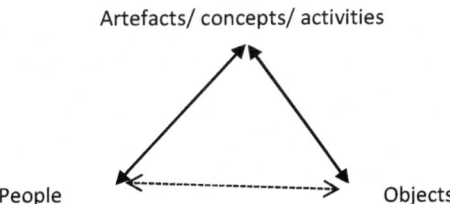

Fig. 2.1 The mediated nature of human and world relationships (adapted from Lantolf & Thorne, 2006, p. 62). (Reproduced by permission of Oxford University Press from *Sociocultural Theory and the Genesis of Second Language Development* by Jim P. Lantolf & Steve L. Thorne © Oxford University Press 2006.)

Among the cultural tools, psychological tools, also known as *semiotic tools* (see Hasan, 2005b), such as spoken and written language (including images or signs) are considered crucial for higher order mental functioning (Kozulin, 2003). As previously argued in relation to written language, individuals' cognitive development relies on their mastery of these tools. However, these semiotic tools may not work effectively without a human mediator. Therefore, in a learning context, students may not learn by just being exposed to learning materials if the material is not appropriated by a teacher (i.e., human mediator). In distance learning, it can be even more challenging given the absence of face-to-face interaction and the reliance on other communication tools such as emails and online forums (e.g., see Chetwynd & Dobbyn, 2011).

In the context of DA, and particularly the research reported in this book, semiotic mediation plays a pivotal role. Such mediation involves the meaningful use of semiotic tools such as disciplinary concepts and linguistic resources (e.g., defining concepts, explaining phenomena by using appropriate language). Semiotic mediation may be manifested in various modes of writing such as text annotations and emails during the mediating process (i.e., the interaction between the teacher and the student). The mediating process does not mean only the teacher influencing the student. As a dialectical process, both the teacher and the student are affected by each other's activity, behaviour and the semiotic tools used which move the mediating process forward although the development of the student's mental functioning may be progressing or regressing. In this process, the control of the shared activity is dynamic (i.e., shifting control gradually from the teacher to the student and vice versa). Such control is called *regulation.*

Regulation is a form of mediation (Lantolf & Thorne, 2007, p. 203). Of particular relevance to DA are the two stages of regulation: other-regulation and self-regulation. Other-regulation involves explicit or implicit mediation (i.e., varying levels of assistance) by a capable peer or teacher. In the context of academic writing assessment, other-regulation means the teacher providing hints, asking questions, etc. regarding the student text or writing the correct word/sentence/paragraph as required while working in the students' ZPD. As stated earlier, this process is *dynamic*, not linear. While other-regulation involves controlling by others, self-regulation points to the learner's ability to perform an activity without or with only minimal support from the teacher or a capable peer. Self-regulation (i.e., independent performance) is one of the goals of DA. In writing assessment, it can be observed by considering the independently written student text in response to a given assessment task. Self-regulation can only be achieved through *internalisation*, which is described after *imitation* below.

2.5.3   *Imitation*

Although imitation is an everyday term, it has acquired a special meaning in Vygotskian sociocultural theory and is relevant to DA. Imitation is *not* mindless copying of an activity. Rather, it is an intentional and selective higher mental activity which may transform the original model (Lantolf & Thorne, 2007, pp. 207–208). Imitation is linked with the ZPD and *internalisation* (see below). There is a limit as to how much an individual can imitate and thus it is connected with the ZPD (see Vygotsky, 1978, pp. 87–88). For example, someone who has never studied business studies may not be able to imitate how to write an analysis of a company's external environment as such a task will be beyond their ZPD. Imitation is the foundation step towards internalisation (Newman & Holzman, 1993, pp. 151–153). In fact, Vygotsky contended that imitation is 'the source of instruction's influence on development' (Vygotsky, 1987 cited in Lantolf & Thorne, 2007, p. 204).

Imitation plays a vital role in both DA and academic writing assessment due to its link with the ZPD and internalisation. DA targets the learner's ZPD which the teacher can observe by considering how much the learner imitates the teacher and how much they do the task themselves. What the learner imitates may be gradually internalised in the process, thus needing less assistance from the teacher to accomplish the same task. Likewise, writing in a particular discipline is often challenging for students as pointed out in Chap. 1. Therefore, they often tend to imitate[1] what experienced members of that disciplinary community write until the former become confident and internalise the new skill and knowledge. The notion of imitation as a form of academic writing development allows the teacher to see the process of student writing development. In the context of academic writing assessment, imitation may take the form of using quotations, for example, from the source text instead of paraphrasing them or using the same words as in the source material. Learners may also imitate what the teacher has written or suggested regarding their assessment text when they provide developmental feedback. However, such imitative writing needs to be done through a conscious understanding of the goal of the activity and the means by which to accomplish it (Feryok, 2009).

2.5.4 Internalisation

Internalisation is closely related to Vygotsky's argument that an individual's development occurs twice: between the individual and other people (interpsychological or social) and within the individual (intrapsychological) (Vygotsky, 1978, p. 57). Internalisation is associated with the latter. Through the process of other-regulation, the individual starts taking control of the psychological/semiotic tools such as language and concepts and appropriating them for their own use. This 'process of making what was once external assistance a resource that is internally available to the individual (though still very much social in origin, quality, and function)' is called internalisation (Lantolf & Thorne, 2007, p. 204; also see Wertsch, 1985). Internalisation enables an individual to make something (e.g., semiotic tools) their own. In other words, the individual transforms the semiotic tools (i.e., historically determined and culturally organised artefacts) and vice versa as the process is bi-directional (Lantolf

---

[1] Such imitation may result in 'plagiarism' as well, which may not be the learner's intention. For example, see Elander, Pittam, Lusher, Fox, and Payne (2009).

& Thorne, 2006; Wells, 1999). In DA, through (semiotic) mediation, learners are supported to internalise semiotic tools needed to accomplish similar future tasks to the one at hand.

In academic writing, the internalisation of discipline-related concepts and frameworks and the genre knowledge (including the linguistic resources) required to write in the discipline is an important aspect of successful learning. Unless students are able to do this, they are likely to face problems in their study.

To sum up, these sociocultural concepts have influenced the development of DA approaches in different ways. The degree of such influence is often dependent on how these constructs are interpreted. In the next section, I will review various DA approaches.

2.6 Types of Dynamic Assessment

Drawing on the key concepts explained above, various DA approaches have been developed. Given the limited space of this book, it is not possible to review all current DA approaches (for a comprehensive review, please see Haywood and Lidz (2007), Lantolf and Poehner (2004) and Lidz and Elliott (2000a, b)). According to Lantolf and Poehner (2004), there are two general approaches of DA: *interventionist* and *interactionist*. The difference between the two is indicated by how mediation occurs during the DA process. Each approach is briefly explained below.

2.6.1 Interventionist Dynamic Assessment Approaches

Interventionist dynamic assessment is based on Vygotsky's earlier writing and is oriented towards quantitative development. It employs standardised assistance. The end-point for the learner to reach is pre-specified and the support is offered and assessed on the basis of the learner's 'speed' to reach the end-point. According to Sternberg and Grigorenko (2002), there are two types of interventionist DA: 'sandwich' format and 'cake' format. The 'sandwich' format of interventionist DA was pioneered by Budoff and colleagues (e.g., Budoff, 1968; Corman & Budoff, 1973 as cited in Lantolf & Poehner, 2004, p. 55). This type of interventionist DA essentially uses a pre-test—intervention/training—post-test format (thus called 'sandwich') and is administered to an individual or a group of learners. Their pre-training and post-training scores are recorded and the examinees are placed in groups according to their scores.

The 'cake' format of interventionist DA provides mediation from a standardised menu of hints and prompts to the examinee during the assessment process (Grigorenko, 2009; Lantolf & Poehner, 2004). For example, the Leipzig Learning Test (LLT) developed by Guthke and his colleagues (e.g., Guthke & Beckmann, 2000) uses a set of five standardised prompts from implicit to explicit for all learners. The learner performance is reported in terms of scores (i.e., number of prompts and amount of time needed) and profiles (i.e., analysis of error types and responsiveness to prompts). This example shows that interventionist dynamic assessment, despite the 'cake' format being more interactive than the 'sandwich' format, still retains the psychometric properties (i.e., standardisation and scores) of traditional tests. In this respect, such assessment may not be sensitive enough to an individual's ZPD. However, the advantage of interventionist DA is its relatively easy application to a large number of learners and thus it can be cost effective. Furthermore, due to its focus on standardisation, interventionist DA has high reliability as in traditional forms of assessment.

2.6.2 Interactionist Dynamic Assessment Approaches

Vygotsky's genetic method is concerned with dynamic processes of developing mental functioning as mediated by cultural tools and human mediators. He was interested in the qualitative transformation of an individual's mental functioning as revealed by their ZPD and mediation, thus favouring an interpretative approach. Pioneered by Feuerstein and his colleagues (e.g., Feuerstein, Falik, Rand, & Feuerstein, 2002), *interactionist dynamic assessment* is interpretative and abandons the examinee-examiner relationship in favour of a teacher-student relationship in assessment. In fact, it is more aligned with Vygotsky's preference for cooperative dialoguing in assessment (Poehner, 2008, p. 18). Rather than employing a set of predetermined forms of assistance as in interventionist DA, the assistance in interactionist DA emerges from the dialogic interaction between the learner and the teacher-assessor, thus responding to the learner's ZPD. Both the teacher and the student work together to reach the ultimate goal of success. This goal may keep changing in the assessment procedure.

As interactionist DA, also known as open or flexible DA, was adopted for the research reported in this book, it deserves further explanation. In particular, Feuerstein's (Feuerstein et al., 2002) DA approach is directly relevant to the approach adopted in this book and needs to be explicated.

Feuerstein's Mediated Learning Experience (MLE)
Feuerstein is a pioneer of interactionist DA. Like Vygotsky, Feuerstein considers the key role played by mediation through symbolic and human mediators. Originally, Feuerstein's work seemed to have developed independently of Vygotsky's theory. However, Kozulin (2002) argues that there are more similarities than differences between Vygotsky's sociocultural theory and Feuerstein and his colleagues' theory of *Mediated Learning Experience* (MLE). According to Kozulin (ibid.), the main difference between the two is that Feuerstein placed higher importance on the human mediator than Vygotsky did. Feuerstein developed the MLE theory which seems to be more radical than Vygotskian sociocultural theory as MLE strongly favours cognitive modifiability of an individual through MLE. MLE refers to the intentional, reciprocal,

---

Universal attributes

- Intentionality and reciprocity
- Transcendence
- Mediation of meaning

Situation-specific attributes

- *Mediation of the feeling of competence*: making learner aware of their achievement as competence so that they are motivated to go beyond their current level of mental ability
- *Mediation of regulation and control of behaviour*: helping the learner to control their behaviour and reflect on their learning; providing feedback on learner behaviour to enable them to make appropriate decisions
- *Mediation of sharing behaviour/ Individuation and psychological differentiation*: making the learner aware of others' experiences and thoughts and encourage them to participate in thinking processes; maintaining that the learner has their own feelings, thoughts and meaning-making power as well
- *Mediation of goal seeking, goal setting and goal achieving behaviour*: helping the learner to set appropriate goals commensurate with their cognitive abilities and achieve them through problem-solving and other learning strategies
- *Mediation of challenge - the search for novelty and complexity*: mediating challenge so that the learner does not avoid novel and complex challenge; presenting the learner with a task that encourages them to go beyond current mental functioning
- *Mediation of awareness of the human being as a changing entity*: making the learner aware that all human cognition is modifiable and unique to humans
- *Mediation of search for an optimistic alternative*: making the learner aware of their potential abilities and alternatives which encourages the learner to be committed to new challenges
- *Mediation of the feeling of belonging*: enabling the learner to connect with others and develop a sense of belonging which helps with transcendence and regulation of behaviour

---

Fig. 2.2 Attributes of Mediated Learning Experience (MLE) (Feuerstein et al., 2002, pp. 76-80)

affective, and motivational learning experience provided to a learner by a human mediator. The human mediator plays a significant role by making learning highly systematic and focussed through the process of selection and transformation of the activity. Feuerstein and his colleagues (Feuerstein et al., 2002; Feuerstein, Rand, & Rynders, 1988) developed a set of criteria as MLE attributes to guide the mediation in order to modify human cognition. There are 11 of them as listed in Fig. 2.2. There are three universal attributes and eight situation-specific ones (Feuerstein et al., 2002, p. 76). The three universal attributes are: *intentionality-reciprocity, transcendence* and *mediation of meaning*. Intentionality-reciprocity means that the mediator intends to modify the learner through interaction and the learner responds to the mediator's intentionality without which learning or development is not possible. This means the mediator systematically mediates the world or an activity for the learner by engaging them in the interaction and promoting their self-regulation of mental functioning so that learning is not incidental. Transcendence refers to the learning experience gained by the learner that is applicable to new situations and contexts. This means the learner is able to apply the learning to a new and complex experience. Mediation of meaning is defined as the emotional and affective aspect of the interaction, the lack of which may mean no internalisation of learning. This mediational process involves making the learner explicitly aware of the meaning of an activity which otherwise may remain tacit. It enables the learner to search for the meaning of the activity in hand. The other eight situation-specific attributes are summarised in the figure.

Additionally, Feuerstein et al.'s (2002) instrumental enrichment (IE) programme is relevant to my research reported in this book. Its purpose is to provide a rich MLE to learners by remediating their 'deficient' cognitive functions. The IE programme seems to take a deficit approach in this sense which is not the view taken in this book. It contains 'instruments' that focus on basic cognitive functions of categorisation, analysis, comparison and so on (Kozulin, 2002). Given that these instruments are universal and domain independent (i.e., basic cognitive functions such as categorising figures) and were mainly intended to enhance children's cognitive development (Kozulin, 2002), they were not considered useful for the learners in my research. Therefore, new enrichment materials related to business studies and academic writing (i.e., domain specific, e.g., explaining business concepts) were designed instead albeit with similar principles (see Chap. 4).

2.7 Dynamic Assessment and Other Assessment Approaches

DA, as a formative assessment approach, has some similarities with other formative assessment approaches. The most relevant ones include Assessment *for* Learning (AfL) and Learning-Oriented Assessment (LOA). In particular, DA is close to AfL which is an increasingly accepted form of formative assessment, expounded by Black and Wiliam (2006) and others (e.g., Leung & Scott, 2009) regarding the school assessment system in the UK. Therefore, it is important to distinguish between DA and AfL. This will be followed by a brief review of LOA.

AfL is defined as "the process of seeking and interpreting evidence for use by learners and their teachers, to identify where the learners are in their learning, where they need to go and how best to get there" (ARG, 2002, p. 2). The two prominent advocates of AfL, Black and Wiliam (2006), have recently proposed a data-driven (i.e., based on classroom observations and interviews) theoretical framework for AfL. They used Activity Theory (e.g., Engeström, 1999) in order to theorise their praxis. Their paper made an attempt to draw on Vygotskian developmental theory. Activity Theory, originally formulated by Leontiev (see Lantolf and Thorne, 2006), views human actions as an activity system in which the activity is mediated by tools to achieve a certain goal. In this process, the responsibility is shared among participants and the 'community' of participants may create rules or codes imposed on the participants to reach the goal (Engeström, 1999). On the basis of this recent alignment with Activity Theory, it appears that AfL is committed to enhancing student learning through assessment. There are some commonalities between DA and AfL. For example, both the approaches are committed to improving student learning through assessment; they take the student's current knowledge as the starting point for assessment; and they both favour interactive feedback during assessment (Leung, 2007, p. 267). Therefore, both AfL and DA are different from traditional assessment approaches, particularly due to their explicit focus on learning.

Nonetheless, proponents of AfL such as Black and Wiliam (2009) and Leung (2007) have accepted that DA is distinct from AfL as discussed below. Most importantly, Black and Wiliam (2009, p. 6) admit that their AfL theory needs to be further systematised in the light of available theories of learning.

Given the current state of AfL, according to Poehner and Lantolf (2005, pp. 260–261), DA is different from AfL for these reasons: (1) DA is carried out systematically responding to learner needs (ZPDs) unlike AfL which is often offered in a haphazard or 'hit-or-miss fashion'; (2) DA is concerned with learners' long-term development whereas AfL may be limited to the task(s) at hand and the support may often be incidental; (3) there is no barrier between assessment and learning and thus they become a single activity in DA which does not appear to be the case in AfL; (4) DA has a strong theoretical underpinning (i.e., Vygotskian sociocultural theory of learning and development) and follows a coherent theory of mind whereas AfL seems to be based on 'good' classroom practices (e.g., see Black and Wiliam, 2009) without a clear theoretical framework guiding such practices (Poehner & Lantolf, 2005). Additionally, research on AfL to date is almost exclusively focussed on school assessment unlike DA and, therefore, a comprehensive theoretical framework of AfL for higher education is yet to emerge (Black & McCormick, 2010). However, some of these claims are contested by AfL proponents and they even propose that the two may benefit from each other (Leung, 2007).

LOA is a recent development in educational assessment which was proposed by Carless (e.g., Carless, 2007) and has been considered an alternative approach that focuses on improving students' learning (Zeng, Huang, Yu, & Chen, 2018). Carless theorised LOA in his 2007 and later papers (Carless, 2007, 2015). According to him, LOA can be 'defined as assessment where a primary focus is on the potential to develop productive student learning processes. In particular, the 'right kind' of summative assessment can be fruitful in stimulating appropriate student learning dispositions and behaviours' (Carless, 2015, p. 964). In fact, LOA is intended to create learning opportunities within summative and formative assessments. It has three components: assessment task as a learning task, students as self-/peer-evaluators and student engagement with feedback. He proposes that assessment tasks can be designed as 'ways of thinking and practising' for students. The second component, student as self- and peer-evaluator is students' evolving ability to engage with quality criteria, evaluate their own and peers' work in an informed way. For developing this expertise in students, the teacher needs to support them in doing so (Carless, 2015, p. 966). The third component, student engagement with feedback, is about students using feedback to improve their learning although how this is possible is not clearly explained. As an emergent assessment approach it appears to be promising given its integration with summative assessment. However, it has not been widely researched in terms of its applicability as mentioned by Zeng et al. (2018) in their critical review of LOA, and it still has conceptual inconsistencies and there is no systematic learning theory used or developed yet in LOA. Given the complexity of the three components in this approach, teachers may find it extremely challenging to apply it to their assessment practices.

2.8   A Critical Review of Dynamic Assessment

It has, so far, been shown that DA, inspired by Vygotsky's theory, may be a comprehensive assessment approach which not only identifies the individual's actual cognitive abilities but also targets and helps them to develop their maturing abilities. Most importantly, its major contribution to formative assessment is its emphasis on the integration of teaching and assessment into a single activity, which makes it a radically different assessment approach from others. Thus, learning and development are at its heart. However, DA has been criticised by scholars working within the mainstream assessment approaches in terms of its purpose of assessment, methodology, validity and reliability. These issues are relevant to the interactionist approach of DA rather than the interventionist since the latter closely follows the traditional form of assessment procedures such as standardisation and scoring.

The purpose of DA is sometimes questioned given its changing goal of assessment. Traditionally, the purpose of assessment is to measure an individual's existing ability at a given time whereas the goal of DA is to examine both their existing and potential abilities, and modify them. However, if abilities are modifiable and dynamic, it may be argued that it is not possible to measure them accurately (Glutting & McDermott, 1990). Furthermore, such a criticism does not appear to be valid due to DA's strong alignment with Vygotsky's notion of the ZPD and dynamic human mental abilities. In this sense, the purpose of assessment is not to *measure* per se but to *interpret* the cognitive abilities and consider how they can be further developed.

Another issue is the methodology used during the DA process. Rather than the teacher controlling the variables during the assessment process, the learner is assisted. It has been argued that this poses a threat to the procedure's reliability (Glutting & McDermott, 1990) since the assistance helps to change the ability. In DA, however, it is a success of the method because its purpose is to bring about changes in the learner through collaboration. The psychometric lens should not be used to examine DA due to its theoretical orientation (i.e., sociocultural theory) and purpose.

Changing the ability of learners is an issue for validity as well. If what is targeted in the assessment (i.e., ability) keeps moving, the validity of the assessment procedure/results is questionable from the psychometric paradigm. However, if we consider the reconceptualisation of construct validity by Messick (1989), *development* would be the construct DA researchers need to justify in their assessment procedures, not *stability* of abilities. In a recent discussion of validity of DA, Poehner (2011), drawing on argument-based approaches to validity by Kane (1992), suggests two types of validity regarding mediation: *micro validity* and *macro validity*. Micro validity is concerned with the individual mediational moves the mediator makes to assist the learner in an assessment task and the effect of these moves on the quality of mediation to the learner. Macro validity examines the whole DA procedures and its success in revealing and promoting learner abilities (Poehner, 2011, p. 256).

In addition to these criticisms, Vygotskian sociocultural theory and DA have a number of gaps and limitations. Firstly, DA is still an emerging field in applied linguistics although sociocultural theory has been used in writing research for over three decades (e.g., see Prior, 2008). Most importantly, DA's efficacy had not been investigated in the context of academic writing until recently (e.g., Shrestha & Coffin, 2012). Secondly and related to the first point, there are only a handful of DA studies that have systematically and extensively reported on the teacher-learner mediation data in the literature in the context of academic writing (e.g., see the volume Lantolf et al., 2018). Therefore, further research in this area is needed. Thirdly and *more significantly*, sociocultural theory (and, hence, DA) lacks engagement with discourse or 'concept in context' (Hasan, 2005a) despite a call for doing so (Gardner, 2010). Hasan rightly argues that sociocultural theory (and thus, DA) does not have a systematic theory of language use despite Vygotsky's preference for semiotic tools, particularly language, over physical artefacts. For this reason, DA studies investigating language learning hitherto may have focussed on micro aspects of language such as verb tenses (e.g., Poehner, 2005) rather than meaning making in context. It is surprising that even the most recent second language DA studies (e.g., Ableeva, 2010; Alavi & Taghizadeh, 2014; Ebadi & Rahimi, 2019; Part IV in Lantolf et al., 2018) have not tackled the use of a linguistic theory (cf. Shrestha, 2017) as an analytical tool to examine language development, although the use of language (spoken or written) as a mediator of social activity plays a pivotal role in learning and development (e.g., see Wells, 1999). Therefore, it is timely for DA researchers to make use of a linguistic framework for the analysis of the DA data. In order to narrow this gap, this book draws on Halliday's (e.g., Halliday & Matthiessen, 2004) Systemic Functional Linguistics (SFL) for its linguistic analysis tool as mentioned in Chap. 1. SFL offers a comprehensive theory of language. This is particularly relevant to my research which is directly concerned with students' ability to use written language to make meanings in a particular disciplinary context.

2.9 Summary

This chapter explained key concepts in Vygotskian sociocultural theory such as the *ZPD* and *mediation* to show their centrality in understanding DA. Academic writing was presented as a socially situated communicative activity in context and its link with sociocultural theory was established. The chapter demonstrated how the various interpretations of these key concepts led to different DA approaches, namely, *interventionist* and *interactionist*. In particular, interactionist DA was elaborated further as it was the approach employed in this study. The chapter also discussed two closely related assessment approaches (Assessment *for* Learning and Learning-Oriented Assessment). Despite the contributions made by DA, it was highlighted that there are still some lacunae and limitations. The research reported in this book aims to address some of these gaps.

The next chapter discusses the linguistic framework used in this book.

References

Ableeva, R. (2010). *Dynamic assessment of listening comprehension in second language learning.* Ph.D., Pennsylvania State University. Retrieved from http://etda.libraries.psu.edu/theses/app roved/WorldWideIndex/ETD-5520/index.html.

Alavi, S. M., & Taghizadeh, M. (2014). Dynamic assessment of writing: The impact of implicit/explicit mediations on L2 learners' internalization of writing skills and strategies. *Educational Assessment, 19*(1), 1–16. https://doi.org/10.1080/10627197.2014.869446.

Aljaafreh, A., & Lantolf, J. P. (1994). Negative feedback as regulation and second language learning in the Zone of Proximal Development. *Modern Language Journal, 78*(4), 465–483.

Allal, L., & Pelgrims Ducrey, G. (2000). Assessment *of* - or *in* - the zone of proximal development. *Learning and Instruction, 10*(2), 137–152.

ARG. (2002). *Assessment for learning: 10 principles.* London: Assessment Reform Group.

Black, P., & McCormick, R. (2010). Reflections and new directions. *Assessment & Evaluation in Higher Education, 35*(5), 493–499.

Black, P., & Wiliam, D. (2006). Developing a theory of formative assessment. In J. Gardner (Ed.), *Assessment and Learning* (pp. 81–100). London: Sage.

Black, P., & Wiliam, D. (2009). Developing the theory of formative assessment. *Educational Assessment, Evaluation and Accountability, 21*(1), 5–31.

Budoff, M. (1968). Learning potential as a supplementary testing procedure. In J. Hellmuth (ed.) *Learning disorders.* Vol. 3. Seattle, WA: Special Child.

Carless, D. (2007). Learning-oriented assessment: Conceptual bases and practical implications. *Innovations in Education and Teaching International, 44*(1), 57–66. https://doi.org/10.1080/147 03290601081332.

Carless, D. (2015). Exploring learning-oriented assessment processes. *Higher Education, 69*(6), 963–976. https://doi.org/10.1007/s10734-014-9816-z.

Chaiklin, S. (2003). The zone of proximal development in Vygotsky's analysis of learning and instruction. In A. Kozulin, B. Gindis, V. S. Ageyev, & S. M. Miller (Eds.), *Vygotsky' educational theory in cultural context* (pp. 39–64). Cambridge: Cambridge University Press.

Chetwynd, F., & Dobbyn, C. (2011). Assessment, feedback and marking guides in distance education. *Open Learning: The Journal of Open, Distance and e-Learning, 26*(1), 67–78.

Coffin, C. (2006). *Historical discourse:Tthe language of time, cause and evaluation.* London: Continuum.

Coffin, C., & Donohue, J. (2014). *A language as social semiotic based approach to teaching and learning in higher education.* Malden, MA: Wiley.

Cole, M., & Wertsch, J. V. (1996). Beyond the individual-social antinomy in discussions of Piaget and Vygotsky. *Human Development, 39*(5), 250–256. https://doi.org/10.1159/000278475.

Corman, L., & Budoff, M. (1973). A comparison of group and individual training procedures on the Raven learning potential measure. *RIEPrint # 56.* Cambridge, MA: Research Institute for Educational Problems.

del Río, P., & Álvarez, A. (2007). Inside and outside the zone of proximal development: An ecofunctional reading of Vygotsky. In H. Daniels, M. Cole, & J. V. Wertsch (Eds.), *The Cambridge companion to Vygotsky* (pp. 276–303). Cambridge: Cambridge University Press.

Ebadi, S., & Rahimi, M. (2019). Mediating EFL learners' academic writing skills in online dynamic assessment using Google Docs. *Computer Assisted Language Learning, 32*(5–6), 527–555. https://doi.org/10.1080/09588221.2018.1527362.

Elander, J., Pittam, G., Lusher, J., Fox, P., & Payne, N. (2009). Evaluation of an intervention to help students avoid unintentional plagiarism by improving their authorial identity. *Assessment & Evaluation in Higher Education, 35*(2), 157–171. https://doi.org/10.1080/02602930802687745.

Engeström, Y. (1999). Activity theory and individual and social transformation. In Y. Engeström, R. Miettinen, & R.-L. Punamäki (Eds.), *Perspectives on activity theory* (pp. 19–38). Cambridge: Cambridge University Press.

Englert, C. S., Mariage, T. V., & Dunsmore, K. (2008). Tenets of sociocultural theory in writing instructional research. In C. A. MacArthur, S. Graham, & J. Fitzgerald (Eds.), *Handbook of writing research* (pp. 208–221). New York: Guildford Press.

Feryok, A. (2009). Activity theory, imitation and their role in teacher development. *Language Teaching Research, 13*(3), 279–299.

Feuerstein, R., Rand, Y., & Rynders, J. E. (1988). *Don't accept me as I am. Helping retarded performers excel.* New York: Plenum.

Feuerstein, R., Falik, L. H., Rand, Y., & Feuerstein, R. S. (2002). *The dynamic assessment of cognitive modifiability: The learning propensity assessment device: Theory, instruments and techniques* (Revised ed.). Jerusalem: ICELP Press.

Gardner, S. (2010). SFL: A theory of language for dynamic assessment of EAL. *NALDIC Quarterly, 8*(1), 37–41.

Glutting, J. J., & McDermott, P. A. (1990). Principles and problems in learning potential. In C. R. Reynolds & R. W. Kamphaus (Eds.), *Handbook of psychological and educational assessment of children: Intelligence and achievement* (pp. 296–347). New York: Guilford Press.

Grigorenko, E. L. (2009). Dynamic assessment and response to intervention. *Journal of Learning Disabilities, 42*(2), 111–132. https://doi.org/10.1177/0022219408326207.

Grigorenko, E. L., & Sternberg, R. J. (1998). Dynamic testing. *Psychological Bulletin, 124*(1), 75–111.

Guthke, J., & Beckmann, J. F. (2000). The Learning test concept and its application in practice. In C. Lidz & J. G. Elliot (Eds.), *Dynamic assessment: Prevailing models and applications* (pp. 17–70). New York: Elsevier.

Halliday, M. A. K., & Matthiessen, C. M. I. M. (2004). *An introduction to functional grammar* (3rd ed.). London: Hodder Education.

Hasan, R. (1992). Speech genre, semiotic mediation and the development of higher mental functions. *Language Sciences, 14*(4), 489–528.

Hasan, R. (2005a). Semiotic mediation and three exotropic theories: Vygotsky, Halliday and Bernstein. In J. Webster (Ed.), *Language, society and consciousness: The collected works of Ruqaiya Hasan* (Vol. 1). London: Equinox.

Hasan, R. (2005a). *The collected works of Ruqaiya Hasan. vol. 1, Language, society and consciousness*. London: Equinox.

Haywood, H. C., & Lidz, C. S. (2007). *Dynamic assessment in practice: Clinical and educational applications*. Cambridge: Cambridge University Press.

Holzman, L. (2018). Zones of proximal development: Mundane and magical. In J. P. Lantolf, M. E. Poehner, & M. Swain (Eds.), *The Routledge handbook of sociocultural theory and second language development* (pp. 42–55). New York, NY: Routledge.

Hyland, K. (2007). Genre pedagogy: Language, literacy and L2 writing instruction. *Journal of Second Language Writing, 16*(3), 148–164.

Kane, M. T. (1992). An argument-based approach to validity. *Psychological Bulletin, 112*(3), 527–535. https://doi.org/10.1037/0033-2909.112.3.527.

Kozulin, A. (2002). Sociocultural theory and the mediated learning experience. *School Psychology International, 23*(1), 7–35.

Kozulin, A. (2003). Psychological tools and mediated learning. In A. Kozulin, B. Gindis, V. S. Ageyev, & S. M. Miller (Eds.), *Vygotsky's educational theory in cultural context* (pp. 15–38). Cambridge: Cambridge University Press.

Langer, J. A., & Applebee, A. N. (1987). *How writing shapes thinking: a study of teaching and learning*. Urbana, IL: National Council of Teachers of English.

Lantolf, J. P., & Poehner, M. E. (2004). Dynamic assessment of L2 development: Bringing the past into the future. *Journal of Applied Linguistics, 1*(1), 49–72.

Lantolf, J. P., & Thorne, S. L. (2006). *Sociocultural theory and the genesis of second language development*. Oxford: Oxford University Press.

Lantolf, J. P., & Thorne, S. L. (2007). Sociocultural theory and second language acquisition. In B. V. Patten & J. Williams (Eds.), *Explaining second language acquisition* (pp. 201–224). Cambridge: Cambridge University Press.

Lantolf, J. P., Poehner, M. E., & Swain, M. (Eds.). (2018). *The Routledge handbook of sociocultural theory and second language development*. New York, NY: Routledge.

Leung, C. (2007). Dynamic assessment: Assessment for and as teaching? *Language Assessment Quarterly, 4*(3), 257–278.

Leung, C., & Scott, C. (2009). Formative assessment in language education policies: Emerging lessons from Wales and Scotland. *Annual Review of Applied Linguistics, 29*, 64–79. https://doi.org/10.1017/S0267190509090060.

Lidz, C. S., & Elliot, J. G. (2000). Introduction. In C. S. Lidz & J. G. Elliott (Eds.), *Dynamic assessment: Prevailing models and applications*. Amsterdam: JAI.

Lidz, C. S., & Elliott, J. G. (2000). *Dynamic assessment: Prevailing models and applications*. Amsterdam: JAI.

Lidz, C. S., & Gindis, B. (2003). Dynamic assessment of the evolving cognitive functions in children. In C. S. Lidz, B. Gindis, A. Kozulin, V. S. Ageyev, & S. M. Miller (Eds.), *Vygotsky's educational theory in cultural context* (pp. 99–116). Cambridge: Cambridge University Press.

Martin, J. R. (2009). Genre and language learning: A social semiotic perspective. *Linguistics and Education, 20*(1), 10–21.

Mercer, N. (2000). *Words and minds: How we use language to think together*. London: Routledge.

Messick, S. (1989). Validity. In R. Linn (Ed.), *Educational measurement* (3rd ed., pp. 13–103). New York: Macmillan.

Newman, F., & Holzman, L. (1993). *Lev Vygotsky: Revolutionary scientist*. London: Routledge.

Poehner, M. E. (2005). *Dynamic assessment of oral proficiency among advanced L2 learners of French*. Ph.D., Pennsylvania State University.

Poehner, M. E. (2007). Beyond the test: L2 dynamic assessment and the transcendence of mediated learning. *Modern Language Journal, 91*(3), 323–340.

Poehner, M. E. (2008). *Dynamic assessment: A Vygotskian approach to understanding and promoting L2 development*. New York: Springer.

Poehner, M. E. (2011). Validity and interaction in the ZPD: Interpreting learner development through L2 Dynamic Assessment. *International Journal of Applied Linguistics, 21*(2), 244–263. https://doi.org/10.1111/j.1473-4192.2010.00277.x.

Poehner, M. E., & Lantolf, J. P. (2005). Dynamic assessment in the language classroom. *Language Teaching Research, 9*(3), 233–265.

Prior, P. (2008). A sociocultural theory of writing. In C. A. MacArthur, S. Graham, & J. Fitzgerald (Eds.), *Handbook of writing research* (pp. 54–66). London: The Guildford Press.

Shrestha, P. N. (2017). Investigating the learning transfer of genre features and conceptual knowledge from an academic literacy course to business studies: Exploring the potential of dynamic assessment. *Journal of English for Academic Purposes, 25,* 1–17. https://doi.org/10.1016/j.jeap.2016.10.002.

Shrestha, P. N., & Coffin, C. (2012). Dynamic assessment, tutor mediation and academic writing development. *Assessing Writing, 17*(1), 55–70. https://doi.org/10.1016/j.asw.2011.11.003.

Sternberg, R. J., & Grigorenko, E. L. (2002). *Dynamic testing: The nature and measurement of learning potential*. Cambridge: Cambridge University Press.

van der Veer, R. (1987). Book review: Lev S. Vygotsky (newly revised, translated, and edited by Alex Kozulin). Cambridge (Massachusetts): The M.I.T. Press, 1986. *The Journal of Mind and Behavior, 8*(1), 175–178.

van der Veer, R., & Valsiner, J. (1991). *Understanding Vygotsky: A quest for synthesis*. Oxford: Blackwell.

Vygotsky, L. S. (1978). *Mind in society: The development of higher psychological processes*. Cambridge, MA: Harvard University Press.

Vygotsky, L. (1981). The genesis of higher mental functions. In J. Wertsch (Ed.), *The concept of activity in Soviet psychology*. Armonk, NY: M. E. Sharpe.

Vygotsky, L. (1987). *The collected works of L. S. Vygotsky, volume 1: Problems of general psychology*. R. Reiber & A. Carton (Eds.), New York: Plenum Press.

Wells, G. (1999). *Dialogic inquiry: towards a sociocultural practice and theory of education*. Cambridge: Cambridge University Press.

Wertsch, J. V. (1985). *Vygotsky and the social formation of mind*. Cambridge, MA: Harvard University Press.

Wertsch, J. V. (2007). Mediation. In H. Daniels, M. Cole, & J. V. Wertsch (Eds.), *The Cambridge companion to Vygotsky* (pp. 178–192). Cambridge: Cambridge University Press.

Wertsch, J. V., & Tulviste, P. (1992). L. S. Vygotsky and contemporary developmental psychology. *Developmental Psychology, 28*(4), 548–557. https://doi.org/10.1037/0012-1649.28.4.548.

Zeng, W., Huang, F., Yu, L., & Chen, S. (2018). Towards a learning-oriented assessment to improve students' learning—a critical review of literature. *Educational Assessment, Evaluation and Accountability, 30*(3), 211–250. https://doi.org/10.1007/s11092-018-9281-9.

Chapter 3
Systemic Functional Linguistics, Dynamic Assessment and Academic Writing

3.1 Introduction

The previous chapter discussed Vygotskyan sociocultural theory and DA. While doing so, it was argued that despite the emphasis given to semiotic mediation and the use of language as a psychological tool in both sociocultural theory and DA, the use of a well-established theory of language use to analyse the DA data has been surprisingly ignored. In response to this gap, the research reported in this book draws on a well-known theory of language in context. This was essential because the purpose of this research was to investigate the potential contribution made by DA to learners' academic writing development which naturally requires examining language resources used by students in their meaning making. As such, a systematic theory of language compatible with DA is needed. For this purpose, in my research, I have used a linguistic theory known as Systemic Functional Linguistics (SFL), developed by Michael Halliday and colleagues (e.g., Halliday & Matthiessen, 2004; Hasan, 2014; Hasan & Webster, 2009; Martin, 2016; Martin & Rose, 2007) in Australia and elsewhere. In my research, SFL served as a key pedagogical tool and provided the main linguistic tools of textual data analysis to track students' zone of proximal development (ZPD) in academic writing. The rest of this chapter explains the SFL theory, why SFL was chosen as the underpinning theory of language and provides a description of the key SFL principles relevant to my research. Then, the SFL-based genre theory as deployed in this book is introduced which is followed by a brief discussion of the *case study analysis* genre which is the context of my research. The SFL-based genre theory offers both a pedagogical tool and an analytical tool in the application of DA to assessing distance business studies students' academic writing.

© Springer Nature Switzerland AG 2020
P. N. Shrestha, *Dynamic Assessment of Students' Academic Writing*,
https://doi.org/10.1007/978-3-030-55845-1_3

3.2   Systemic Functional Linguistics: A Theory of Language

SFL theory is concerned with the way people use language to get things done in a social context. Language in SFL is viewed as a network of systems and choices available to speakers and writers to make meaning and it is functional because people use it for their practical purposes in a particular sociocultural context (O'Grady, Bartlett, & Fontaine, 2013). The key assumptions about language in SFL are that language is (1) used for functional purposes; (2) context-specific (i.e., influenced by sociocultural context where it is used); (3) used for making meaning; and (4) a semiotic process which involves making choices of language rather than relying on rules (Eggins, 2004, p. 3). Rather than focusing on formal structures and grammar rules of a language, SFL enables us to view language as a meaning making resource in human social interactions. In particular, the focus is on how people use language in a variety of contexts and how they structure language for use in such contexts (Eggins, 2004). Language is meaningful when it is spoken or written and interpreted by a listener or reader. This meaningful instance of language is 'text' whether spoken or written. Halliday and Matthiessen (2014, p. 3) state that a 'text' is 'any instance of language, in any medium, that makes sense to someone who knows the language … [it] is a process of making meaning in context.' In this book, the term 'text' is used in this sense.

In this section, it is also important to introduce a key SFL orientation about language. This key SFL orientation is *language as social semiotic* which Halliday expounded in his 1978 publication: *Language as Social Semiotic* (Halliday, 1978). According to Halliday, language is a complex network of meanings in social context. He argued that 'language is one of the systems that constitute a culture; one that is distinctive in that it also serves as an encoding system for many (though not all) of the others' (p. 2). This SFL orientation means that language is not only always seen within a sociocultural context but also culture is mediated through language. From this perspective, all social processes and activities are semiotically mediated primarily through language which offers networks of meaning potential and choices in a culture. As in Vygotsky's sociocultural theory, Halliday saw a dialectic relationship between language and social context because 'The context plays a part in determining what we say; and what we say plays a part in determining the context' (Halliday, 1978, p. 3). The social semiotic view of language led to the development of a comprehensive theory of language that can be applied to address problems or issues in any social context.

Language as a sophisticated semiotic system offers us meaning-making choices according to what we want to communicate about, who we want to communicate with and how we want to organise our message for our purpose. In SFL, language is considered to have three broad functions or meanings, known as *metafunctions*, which work simultaneously:

- *Ideational*: to communicate about our experience of the world including our mental states

- *Interpersonal*: to interact with other people, establish relationships with them, influence their behaviours and express our attitudes
- *Textual*: to organise our message to suit the topic, purpose and social context whether spoken or written.

Let's look at an example text. Here is a business news headline text about the US-China trade war by the BBC in 2019:

US tariffs target the Chinese-made consumer goods.

All three metafunctions or meanings are at work here at the same time. One is it is about *US tariffs* on *Chinese consumer goods*. It tells us who is participating (*US tariffs*) and what is happening (*target*) to whom (*the Chinese-made consumer goods*). Another meaning is the clause structure used here. It has Participant[1] (subject) + Process (verb or action word) + Goal (object) and it is 'declarative' or informational, i.e. it gives information about the *US tariff* to the reader. The third meaning is how the text is organised. Here, the position of *US tariffs*, as the Theme (first), is the focus of the message unlike, for example, in the sentence 'The Chinese-made consumer goods are targeted by US tariffs'. These three meanings are central to SFL [see Sect. 3.4 for their details]. Due to this kind of richness in SFL, it can be argued that SFL is a 'comprehensive theory of language and social context …' (Martin, 2011, p. 101).

3.3 Rationale for Using SFL in DA

Although language plays a vital role in the mediation process, DA approaches lack a systematic theory of language use. In order to address this problem, I sought to find a language theory compatible with the DA approach. Since DA considers assessment as a social activity (both processes and products), SFL was chosen as a complementary language theory due to its focus on language as a semiotic resource and language use in social context (as discussed above). In fact, the complementarity between Vygotskian sociocultural theory (and thus DA) and SFL has been acknowledged in the literature and their combination in research and pedagogy has been proposed to address any gaps in each (e.g., see Byrnes, 2006; Gibbons, 2006; Hasan, 2005a; Wells, 1994).

Drawing on Halliday's work, SFL researchers and practitioners have developed language-based pedagogies to teach in different disciplines in higher education (e.g., see Coffin & Donohue, 2014; Dreyfus, Humphrey, Mahbob, & Martin, 2016). Halliday cogently explained the critical role of language in learning and developed a language-based theory of learning in a seminal paper published in 1993: Halliday (1993). According to this theory, a learner not only learns *language* but also learns *about* language and *through* language. In this sense, language (and other semiotic tools for that matter) is key to all meaning-making. In SFL-oriented language-based

---

[1] All SFL terms used in this book begin with an upper case.

pedagogies, Vygotskian sociocultural theory of learning has been successfully integrated. In particular, two core concepts in sociocultural theory, *semiotic mediation* and *zone of proximal development*, have been applied to genre pedagogies which will be explained later in this chapter (Coffin & Donohue, 2014; Dreyfus et al., 2016; Rose & Martin, 2012). Another reason for my choice of SFL is its emphasis on language as a social semiotic as explained above. In particular, it has connections with Vygotsky's *semiotic mediation* in which language plays a key role in an individual's conceptual development (Coffin & Donohue, 2014).

A traditional structural theory of language would not have provided the same depth of insights into the meaning-making process in a discipline that students go through in their academic writing, which SFL does. Additionally in the context of research reported in this book, the underlying language theory behind the design of the academic writing course, the context of research reported in this book, was SFL. In this book, SFL informed the academic writing pedagogy used in DA and served as a method for analysing students' academic writing assessment texts in order to track their ZPDs (see 4.5 and 4.6).

3.4   Register Variables: Field, Tenor and Mode

From an SFL perspective, language is viewed as a *resource for making meaning* in a particular social context. It considers *'texts'*, rather than sentences, as the basic unit through which meaning is made and hence the basic unit of analysis for research. It also views language as serving particular purposes or goals in a particular situation (either in speaking or writing). This means language helps to realise a social context through the choice of language used. This can be better explained with two example texts below. They are about Apple smartwatches.

Excerpt 3.1

> My husband purchased this watch for my birthday! What a great gift. I love it, it hasn't been off my wrist since. It definitely makes me want to do more exercise especially when you are competing against someone else with an Apple Watch. (A customer review of Apple watch)

Excerpt 3.2

> Apple clearly believes smartwatches are here to stay – the Watch 4 utterly proves that. The design alone is a big upgrade, with the screen offering far more visibility, and while the health benefits are only going to help a subset of users, they're welcome and show the direction Apple is heading. If it had better battery life, and thus was better able to track sleep the Watch 4 could have been the perfect smartwatch. (Review of Apple watch, Techradar: https://www.techradar.com/uk/reviews/apple-watch-4-review)

Although both the texts are a review of the same product, they have different social purposes and realise different social contexts which can be examined from three SFL dimensions of meaning. (1) *Ideational meaning*: The first one seems to be about both the review of the product by a customer and an appreciation of the 'gift' (indicated by 'purchased … for my birthday', 'great gift', 'love', 'make me want … more exercises … competing against') while the second one is purely about the product and its strengths and weaknesses (as shown by words such as 'design', 'big upgrade', 'screen offering more visibility', 'health benefits' etc.). (2) *Interpersonal meaning*: In Excerpt 3.1, the writer uses a very personal and informal tone (including emotion) which might be persuasive to customers. It also shows the writer's relationship with their husband. The wording construes less 'distance' between the reader and the writer. In Excerpt 3.2, the writer is an 'expert' as shown by the definitive statement made, which also creates a distance between the writer and the reader. They use formal and specialised language (e.g., 'upgrade', 'design', 'health benefits', etc.). (3) *Textual meaning*: The texts are organised differently. Excerpt 3.1 begins with 'My husband', thus making the person as the focus of the text while Excerpt 3.2 begins with 'Apple', the company that manufactures the smartwatch. The first text uses personal pronouns (e.g., 'I', 'you') to manage the information flow in the text whereas the second text uses the company, product or pronouns to refer to them for the same purpose. These two examples illustrate that the choice of language both varies according to social context and helps language users to construe their intended meanings in relation to a particular social context.

According to SFL, over time groups of people develop common types of spoken or written texts in similar situations to achieve the goals of their group or culture. These texts are influenced by the situations they are used for as in the two examples above. In order to describe and analyse variations of linguistic choices made by users in social context systematically and coherently, scholars in SFL have developed three fundamental linguistic register variables. A register is a functional variety of language represented by the system of lexicogrammatical features to realise a particular social context. The three register variables are: *field* (subject matter), *tenor* (reader-writer relationship) and *mode* (medium of communication). Therefore, the language structure in every text is different due to its functionality, as seen in the two example texts above—these three register variables are exemplified by the three levels of meaning (1–3) in the two examples above respectively. It is this functional view of language which helps to explain why and how students produce specifically structured texts for particular social purposes in a particular discourse or disciplinary community (see Martin, 1997). SFL also provides a means for systematically examining and assessing students' texts.

In SFL, the three register variables are realised simultaneously through the three metafunctions or meanings (mentioned in 3.2) as presented in Fig. 3.1.

Each of these metafunctions is related to one of the register variables: Ideational (Field), Interpersonal (Tenor) and Textual (Mode) (Halliday, 1994). The notion of register is also linked with the SFL genre theory as developed by Martin and colleagues (e.g., Martin & Rose, 2007) as will be explained in Sect. 3.5. Given that these metafunctions informed both the pedagogical innovation and student assessment text analysis in my research, they need further explanations. They provided a framework for understanding the social context within a distance education academic culture in which assessment texts were written by students. However, it should be noted that, in the research reported in this book, the foci were on two metafunctions

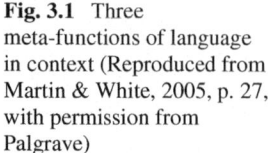

Fig. 3.1 Three
meta-functions of language
in context (Reproduced from
Martin & White, 2005, p. 27,
with permission from
Palgrave)

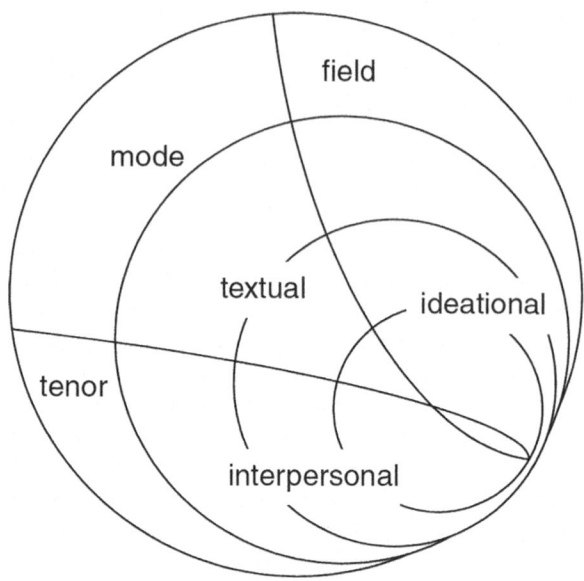

(i.e., Ideational and Textual) only because the participating students needed the most support in these two areas in the DA process (see Chap. 4). For readers' convenience and completeness, all three are explained briefly below.

3.4.1 Ideational Metafunction

The *Ideational metafunction* refers to what language is used to construe our experience of the world. It is about social processes involving people, places, things and qualities. In an academic context, Ideational meaning is represented, for example, by disciplinary knowledge such as business studies and academic cultures in a discipline. Disciplinarity, as Christie and Maton (2011a) show in their edited volume, is an important contextual variable which helps to create subject knowledge and thus shapes Ideational meaning. How the Ideational meaning is realised can be illustrated through an example:

> This report is based on a SWOT analysis of Google's new operating system called Chrome.

In this sentence, the experience of the world, the Ideational meaning, is construed as a SWOT (Strengths, Weaknesses, Opportunities, Threats) analysis report of Google's new product called Chrome. The Ideational meaning is indicated by the special and abstract terms used in the sentence (e.g., report, SWOT analysis, etc.). These terms also suggest that the activity is related to an academic discipline (decontextualized) rather than everyday commonsense (contextualised), thus realising the social context.

3.4.2 Interpersonal Metafunction

The *Interpersonal metafunction* is defined as the language used to represent social roles and relationships between participants. Language is used to interact with others or to exchange meanings. Through this interaction we establish relationships with others, influence others' actions and behaviours or explain our attitudes. The relationships may be formal/informal, equal/unequal, close/distant and so on. Academic writing is often considered formal and distant due to abstract and decontextualized language use (Coffin & Donohue, 2014). Considering the language choices in the example in 3.4.1, the writer-reader relationship seems to be formal and distant given the use of the passive voice, formal vocabulary and the absence of human Participants. It may appear that there is no interaction here, but the writer is *giving information* to the reader.

3.4.3 Textual Metafunction

The *Textual metafunction* refers to the way language is used to organise Ideational and Interpersonal meanings in a text. Textual meaning is influenced by factors such as the mode of communication (e.g., spoken versus written) and the distance between the language use and the associated social process (Martin 1984 cited in Eggins, 2004, p. 91). In the previous example in 3.4.1, the sentence organises the Ideational and the Interpersonal meanings into a meaningful coherent whole. As such, 'This report' is in the first position in the sentence which means it is the Theme of the sentence (referring to the text itself) as opposed to say, 'Google's new operating system'. This way of organising the sentence means the reader is guided as to what to expect about the report, thus, indicating information flow.

To sum up, all three dimensions of meaning are realised through the use of language in context simultaneously. The SFL perspective enables a DA researcher to not only analyse student assessment texts but also support students with overcoming any problem linked with any of these meanings as construed in their written texts. Two of the three metafunctions (i.e., Ideational and Textual) are further elaborated in 4.6.

3.5 SFL and Academic Writing

Theories, concepts and tools to teach, assess and research Academic Writing in higher education have grown exponentially over the last three decades, and there are some influential theories and approaches which have dominated the field. For example, in the US, *Rhetoric and Composition Studies* has been dominant in teaching and researching writing for a long time (e.g., see Bawarshi & Reiff, 2010 for a review).

In the UK, two dominant approaches to academic writing or literacy have been found to be widely used: *Academic Literacies* and *SFL* (Wingate & Tribble, 2011). Broadly speaking, Academic Literacies is concerned with practices in context while an SFL approach focuses on texts in context (Coffin & Donohue, 2012; Wingate & Tribble, 2011). As argued by Wingate and Tribble (2011), often, they are seen incompatible with each other although it is beneficial to draw on both for teaching and researching academic writing given their emphasis on social context or situatedness of writing. As the focus of this section is on SFL and academic writing, readers are directed to the cited publications above for a discussion of different approaches mentioned.

As noted throughout this chapter, SFL emphasises the relationship between language, text and social context. It has been widely used by both practitioners and researchers to inform teaching and researching academic writing in higher education and schools. Given the SFL view of language and other semiotic resources as a meaning-making tool, SFL has been influential in writing instruction in different ways. Especially, the notions of register and genre developed within SFL have helped to advance the field of English for Academic and Specific Purposes as an intellectual endeavour (Wingate & Tribble, 2011).These two concepts have been deployed to understand student needs and design academic writing courses by analysing disciplinary texts and associated academic cultures. As a result, different traditions of academic writing pedagogy have been developed such as Swales' genre approach within English for Specific Purposes (e.g., Swales, 1990 though not necessarily SFL-based) and the genre theory in Australia (e.g., Martin & Rose, 2007). Both of these genre theories have influenced academic writing instruction and research in the UK as noted by Wingate and Tribble (2011). In fact, the seminal corpus-based research on student academic writing in UK higher education by Nesi and Gardner (2012) adopted both Swalesian genre theory and the Australian genre theory widely known as Sydney School to analyse academic writing which led to identifying 13 genre families across four disciplines which included arts and humanities, life sciences, physical sciences and social sciences (including business studies). Due to space, it is not possible to elaborate on differences between Swalesian genre theory and the Sydney school, and therefore, interested readers are directed to Bawarshi and Reiff (2010) and Chap. 1 in Hood (2010).

In this book, the genre theory developed within SFL (i.e., the Sydney School genre theory) is adopted. In the SFL-based genre theory (hereafter), *genre* is defined as 'a staged, goal-oriented social process. Social because we participate in genres with other people; goal-oriented because we use genres to reach our goals' (Martin & Rose, 2007, p. 8). Genres in cultures are used to enact various types of social contexts. This means there are recognizable patterns used in meaning-making which can be used to predict or identify a social situation. This applies to both written and spoken communication. As Coffin and Donohue (2012, p. 66) explain, SFL-based genre theory draws on the concepts of register and genre in analysing academic texts, especially to describe and account for how language operates in academic contexts. While the notion of *genre* is used to map academic texts according to their key purposes (e.g., arguing, describing, recounting etc.), *register* variables (explained above in this chapter) are deployed to understand the relationship between the socio-cultural context of academic writing and the lexicogrammatical choices in a text. Therefore, SFL is considered a powerful tool for both academic writing pedagogy and research. The SFL-genre theory is elaborated further below.

3.6 SFL-Based Genre Theory (and Pedagogy)

SFL theory has evolved significantly over the last four decades. It has been influential in language and literacy education (Martin, 2009). As such, a particular theory of **genre**, also known as 'Sydney School' mentioned earlier, was developed by Martin and his colleagues (e.g., Martin, 2016; Martin & Rose, 2007) in Australia by extending Halliday's notion of register mentioned above (see Fig. 3.2). This expanded model included *culture* through genre which provided a means to consider the social purpose of a text more holistically.

The SFL-based concept of genre was further developed by mapping genres in primary and secondary school curricula in Australia in the 1980 and 90s (for a detailed history, see Martin, 2009; Rose & Martin, 2012). The motivation was to understand what genre types primary and secondary school students were expected to read and write in their classrooms and whether school children learned how to write those genres. It was found that school children were primarily taught how to write narratives but not other types of genres such as arguing. A typology of school genres in specific subjects such as history (Coffin, 2006) and geography (Humphrey, 1996) was developed through genre analysis of texts in those subject areas. What Coffin and Donohue (2014, p. 49) call *elemental genres* were identified which have relatively clear boundaries as prototypes and thus served as building blocks that could be explicitly taught to novice writers. The identified elemental school genres were

Fig. 3.2 Metafunctions regarding language register and genre (Martin 2009, p. 12). Reprinted from *Linguistics and Education,* 20(1), Martin, J. R. Genre and language learning: A social semiotic perspective, pp. 10–21 (2009), with permission from Elsevier

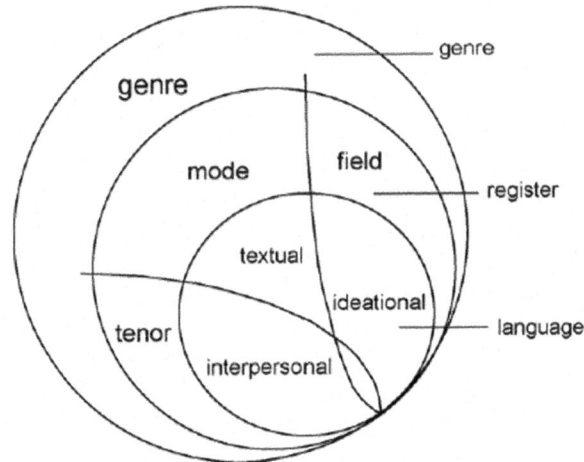

Table 3.1 Elemental genres and their purposes and stages (from Coffin & Donohue, 2014, p. 50, Reproduced with permission of The Licensor through PLSclear)

Genre	Social purpose	Generic stages
Personal recount	To retell a sequence of events in the writer/speaker's life	• Orientation • Record of events • (Reorientation)
Narrative	To tell a story	• Orientation • Complication[a] • Evaluation[a] • Resolution
Descriptive report	To describe specific things	• Orientation • Description
Taxonomic report	To classify and describe phenomenon	• Identification of phenomenon and classification • Description of types or parts[a]
Procedure	To give instructions	• Goal • Material • Steps[a]
Explanation	To explain how something works	• Identification of phenomenon • Explanation sequence
Exposition	Tto argue for a point	• Position of view • Arguments[a] • Reinforcement of position
Discussion	To consider different perspectives on an issue	• Issue • Arguments for[a] • Arguments against[a] • (Position)

[a]Recurring stage

broadly as summarised by Coffin and Donohue (2014) and given here in Table 3.1 (for a detailed map, see Rose & Martin, 2012, p. 128). These elemental genres can be categorised under three broad genre families or *macrogenres* based on their social purposes according to Rose and Martin (2012): Engaging (e.g., personal recount), Informing (e.g., reports, explanations) and Evaluating (e.g., exposition, discussion).

The SFL-based genre classification within SFL goes beyond identifying different stages of a genre to the system of grammar and lexis, called *lexicogrammar* in SFL. It is so because any choice of lexicogrammar is influenced by the purpose and context of the text. For example, in a personal recount, the key lexicogrammatical resources include personal pronoun *I*, past tense, time lexis and declarative mood.

However, soon after SFL researchers identified the elemental genres in the school curriculum it was realised in the 1990s that advanced learners need to write genres beyond the elemental ones or they have to mix genres for a particular purpose (Coffin & Donohue, 2014, p. 51). This means, within a text, it is necessary to combine two or more elemental genres, thus leading to a *macrogenre*. This type of genre is common in the context of student writing in higher education and thus learning to write in disciplines requires both teachers and students to understand what these macrogenres are. In this regard, the extensive SFL-based genre analysis conducted by the scholars who compiled a 6.5 million word corpus of university students' assessed successful academic writing in four disciplines (called British Academic Written English (BAWE)) and carried out genre analyses (Nesi & Gardner, 2012) is worth mentioning due to its large scale and influence on academic writing research and teaching in the UK and elsewhere (e.g., see Gardner, Nesi, & Biber, 2019; Nesi & Gardner, 2018). As this work, to date, is the most detailed genre analysis of large samples of assessed student academic writing in higher education, it has relevance to my research and thus for reference, the 13 'genre families' identified in the BAWE corpus are presented in Table 3.2 taken from Nesi and Gardner (2018, p. 53). It includes broad social purposes for each genre family and associated examples from the corpus. The authors mention that each genre family contained diverse genres in different disciplines but these genres had similar broad social purposes and some similarities with regard to language functions and structure (see Table 3.2). Please note the BAWE genre families and genres each have their own separate purposes, as described in Gardner and Nesi (2013), and in greater detail in Nesi and Gardner (2012).

The genre families were identified by deploying an SFL-based genre analysis and the Swalesian genre analysis approach as mentioned by Nesi and Gardner (2012, p. 11). The genre labelling has some overlap with the elemental genres mentioned earlier (e.g., recount and report). For the research reported in this book, the genre family called *case study* is relevant although the labelling is slightly different (see 3.7).

As a result of the extensive research on genre analysis both in schools and higher education in Australia, an SFL-based genre pedagogy was inevitable. A number of SFL researchers in Australia developed the genre pedagogy and was originally called the *Teaching and Learning Cycle* (TLC) in the 1980s (for details on its development, see Rose & Martin, 2012). Basically, this pedagogy was developed to explicitly teach school children how to write the identified genres in a particular school year. The pedagogical approach was mainly based on Michael Halliday's and Claire Painter's SFL-based language development studies (ibid. p. 61). Only later (i.e., turn of the century and early 2000) was Vygotsky's notion of ZPD brought into the development of SFL-based pedagogy which emphasises *dialogue* in teaching and learning (e.g., Gibbons, 2002, 2006; Hasan, 2005a, b; Martin, 1999). Viewing it as a genre, this pedagogical approach (i.e., TLC) has three distinct stages: *Deconstruction, Joint Construction* and *Independent Construction.* At the Deconstruction stage, the teacher introduces a model text of the target genre and discusses its sociocultural context, generic stages and lexicogrammatical features. The Joint Construction stage involves the teacher and their students jointly constructing (writing) another text in the same genre in the classroom (or online). The final stage, Independent Construction requires students writing a text in the same genre on their own (e.g., at home). In all these three stages, building the *field* and setting the *context* are central. The key purpose of the approach is to enable students to take control of the target genre so that they can write it and critically reflect on its role. In my research, although this approach

Table 3.2 Genre families in the BAWE corpus (from Nesi & Gardner, 2012, p. 53)

Genre families	Social purposes	Examples of genres
Exercise	Demonstrating knowledge and understanding	Calculations; data analysis; calculations + short answers; short answers; statistics exercise
Explanation	Demonstrating knowledge and understanding	Legislation overview; instrument description; methodology explanation; site/environment report; species/breed description; account of a natural phenomenon
Critique	Developing powers of independent reasoning	Academic paper review; interpretation of results; legislation evaluation; policy evaluation; programme evaluation; project evaluation; review of a book/film/play/website
Essay	Developing powers of independent reasoning	Challenge; commentary; consequential; discussion; exposition; factorial
Literature survey	Building research skills	Annotated bibliography; anthology; literature review; review article
Methodology recount	Building research skills	Data analysis report; experimental report; field report; forensic report; lab report; materials selection report
Research report	Building research skills	Research article; research project; topic-based dissertation
Case study	Preparing for professional practice	Business start-up; company report; organisation analysis; patient report
Design specification	Preparing for professional practice	Building design; game design; product design; website design
Problem question	Preparing for professional practice	Law problem question; logistics simulation; business scenario
Proposal	Preparing for professional practice	Book proposal; building proposal; business plan; catering plan; marketing plan; policy proposal; research proposal
Empathy writing	Writing for oneself and others	Expert advice to industry; expert advice to lay person; information leaflet; job application; letter; newspaper article
Narrative recount	Writing for oneself and others	Accident report; account of literature or website search; biography; creative writing: short story; plot synopsis; reflective recount

Reprinted from *Assessing Writing, 38*, Nesi, H., & Gardner, S. The BAWE corpus and genre families classification of assessed student writing, pp. 51–55 (2018). doi: https://doi.org/10.1016/j.asw.2018.06.005, with permission from Elsevier

informed the design of the study, it was not the focus of research and therefore, it is not further elaborated here. Interested readers are referred to Rose and Martin (2012).

3.7 Case Study Analysis as a Key Genre in Business Studies

The extensive research on UK university students' assessed academic writing mentioned earlier identifies *Case Study* genre as a common genre in business studies and health (Nesi & Gardner, 2012, p. 40). An earlier study by Zhu (2004) also found case studies to be the most common type of genre elsewhere in business studies. Indeed, it is a popular pedagogical method in business studies programmes, also known as Harvard case method (see Forman & Rymer, 1999b), and it is a common genre that undergraduate business studies students are required to write for their assignments at The Open University (Coffin & Donohue, 2014), the institutional context of my research. There are, however, a number of terms in the literature used to refer to broadly this type of text that students in business studies are expected to write. For example, an early study called it *case write-up* (Forman & Rymer, 1999a). Other researchers have called it *business case report* (Nathan, 2013), *case analysis* (Miller & Pessoa, 2016) and *case study* (Gardner, 2012; Nesi & Gardner, 2012). In fact, Nesi and Gardner (2012, pp. 191–194) identify *case study* as a genre family which includes three distinct business genres: Company Report (case studies pretending to address a business or shareholders, workplace document), Organisation Analysis (case studies concerned with business and management issues incorporating theoretical discussion) and Single-issue Report (case studies written in an academic style and concerned with a theme that impacts an industry rather than an organisation).

For the purpose of this book, I am using the label *Case Study Analysis* which combines a number of elemental genres and thus it is treated as a macrogenre. It was the term used in the business communication course which provided the context of my research (see next Chapter). This genre label is also used by Coffin and Donohue (2014, Chap. 7) when they discuss genres in the same business communication course. The other reason for adding *analysis* to the label is to differentiate it from the one often used in health and social care or medical education in which students are not generally required to read a case study about a patient or a practice setting but they are asked to find information about them (Coffin & Donohue, 2014). In the context of my research (at least in first year business degree programme), students are provided with information about an organisation (e.g., a business news report) and they are asked to apply business concepts and models or frameworks taught in the course to analyse the information in order to address business issues or problems and make recommendations. In a case study analysis genre, students are expected to analyse the contextualised information (case study) to produce abstract and decontextualized analysis drawing on course concepts and make business context-relevant recommendations. In this sense, as Nesi and Gardner (2012) mentioned, it is a genre preparing for professional practice and it appears to be a combination of two of the

Table 3.3 Typical generic features of a case study analysis

Social purpose	Generic stages	Lexicogrammar
Demonstrate understanding of business concepts, models, theories to teacher Prepare for professional practice	• Orientation • Application of business framework/concepts[a] (Description + Explanation + Analysis) • Evaluation/Conclusion • Recommendation	Present tense Past tense (to refer to given information about organisation) Specialist lexis related to business concepts and theories (abstract) Nominalisation Relational verbs Declarative mood Modality (especially in Recommendation)

[a]Recurring stage

genres, Company Report and Organisation Analysis, found in Nesi and Gardner's *Case Study* genre family.

In this book, a business case study analysis is considered a pedagogical genre defined as the study of an organisation at a particular time and in a specific business context through the application of a business framework or model (e.g., SWOT (strengths, weaknesses, opportunities and threats)) or a set of business concepts (e.g., business ethics) to the provided information about a real organisation to propose practical actions or recommendations. It is a pedagogical genre because business academics use it to teach business concepts and theories and assess students requiring them to demonstrate their understanding of business studies knowledge as well as its application.

A case study analysis as a macrogenre may typically have the generic features as shown in Table 3.3 below although there may be some variations in terms of generic stages (see Chap. 4).

3.8   Application of SFL in This Book

3.8.1   SFL as an Analytical Tool

SFL was employed for the analysis of the case study analysis genre texts written by the participating students in my research. The analysis helped to track the students' ZPDs in their academic writing assessment texts. Two metafunctions provided the framework for analysis: Ideational and Textual. These two metafunctions in student assessment texts were analysed because they appeared to be the difficult areas for the participants while writing a case study analysis during the initial (baseline) academic writing assessment (see Chap. 4 for details of the assessment process). For this reason, they were targeted during teacher mediation (i.e., dialogic feedback on student written drafts) in each DA session. An analysis of these two metafunctions enabled me to track any changes that occurred in the students' assessment texts during this study. The SFL analysis revealed their actual academic writing abilities and dynamic ZPDs regarding the realisation of Ideational and Textual meanings in their assessment texts. The way these metafunctions were operationalised in the study is explained below at a more general level because they are further elaborated in Chap. 6.

Ideational Metafunction

As described in 3.4, the Ideational metafunction is concerned with the representation of our experience of the world. In order to analyse Ideational meanings in the students' assessment texts, the notion of Technicality (i.e., the specialised use of a term in a particular discipline and the use of specialised terms) was applied.

Regarding the current study, teacher mediation targeted Technicality which was mainly related to business studies concepts and frameworks (e.g., SWOT), as the participants found them challenging. Also included in teacher mediation were conceptual knowledge of the case study analysis genre and the application of business studies frameworks and concepts to analysing business situations.

Textual Metafunction

Another main challenge faced by the participants as revealed by the initial academic writing assessment was how to organise the information into a coherent text, that is, Textual meaning. Textual meaning is related to managing information flow in a text, also known as Periodicity (see Martin & Rose, 2007, p. 187). As the writer is normally absent when the text is read, it is essential that the intended meaning of the text is understood. For this to happen, the writer has to scaffold the reader by using textual devices such as introductions, reference and conjunctions in a text. An effective organisation of the message through such devices enables the writer to make the social purpose and the social context clear. Such messages tend to have recognised textual features (e.g., Orientation in a story) accepted in the associated discourse community. As such, a case study analysis is organised in a certain way in business studies. Students capable of using those features in their analysis are likely to produce better texts than those who are not.

As Textual meaning was targeted during the teacher mediation, it was necessary to track any changes that occurred in the participating students' academic writing texts during this study. The focus of the tutor mediation was on (1) generic structure of the text, (2) macroThemes (i.e., introduction), and (3) hyperThemes (i.e., paragraph Theme) and hence, these needed tracking in the students' assessment texts. The analysis of these aspects of Textual meaning was informed by Martin (1993a) and Martin and Rose (2007).

More specific details about how these SFL analytical tools were employed are provided in Chap. 4. Chapter 6 discusses the key findings for Ideational and Textual meanings in student assessment texts, thereby exploring students' ZPDs.

3.8.2 SFL as a Pedagogical Tool in Research

It has already been mentioned that SFL has been widely recognised as a useful tool for teaching academic writing (also see Bawarshi & Reiff, 2010, Chap. 3). In this section, I will briefly focus on the use of SFL as a pedagogical tool as deployed to carry out DA of academic writing in my research.

The research reported in this book draws on data (including student written assignments and mediation data) from business studies students who were studying an academic writing course designed for such students at The Open University (see Chap. 4 for further details about the course and its students). Coffin and Donohue (2014) noted that this course followed the SFL genre pedagogy discussed earlier. For this reason, SFL as a pedagogical tool was *a given*. In particular, Bonnano and Jones' (2007) set of assessment criteria (known as Measuring the Academic Skills of University Students (MASUS)) adapted for the course were broadly used for any pedagogical intervention during the two DA sessions (see Chap. 4). MASUS was developed drawing on the SFL-based genre theory. The assessment criteria included (1) use of source materials—*is information retrieval and processing of visual, verbal and numerical data correct and appropriate for the task?* (2) text structure and development—*is the structure and development of the text clear and generically appropriate to the question and its context?* (3) academic style—*does the grammar conform to the patterns of written academic English appropriate for the task?* (4) grammatical correctness—*do grammatical errors interfere with communicating the message?* and (5) quality of presentation (see Chap. 4 for the full details). Additionally, the pedagogical intervention was informed by Humphrey et al.'s (2010) SFL-based 3 × 3 framework developed to assess and analyse student written texts (see Chap. 4). This framework was much more developed and detailed than the MASUS framework. For example, this framework included all three metafunctions (i.e., Ideational, Interpersonal and Textual) and specified how they can be realised at the genre and register level (social activity), the paragraph level (discourse semantic) and the clause and sentence level (grammar and expression) in the context of academic writing. Given DA's lack of a theory of language use, these frameworks became instrumental for targeting the students' dynamic ZPDs regarding their academic writing.

Although these SFL frameworks for language use in academic writing were used, as a mediator in my research, I did not use SFL and genre-related technical terms during the interactions or mediation in any DA sessions in order to avoid any cognitive overload to the participants. Instead, I used the terms that were familiar to them (e.g., *introduction* instead of *macroTheme*).

3.9 Summary

This chapter presented SFL as a theoretical framework used in my research. The main reasons for adopting this framework were its compatibility with sociocultural theory and DA, and its capability to track students' changing academic writing abilities systematically. The tracking offers insights into a learner's changing ZPDs. Despite DA being an attractive alternative to the traditional assessment approach to academic writing assessment, DA research hitherto has not included any systematic framework of language use in context. The use of SFL as a theory of language, thus, fills this gap.

In spite of the invaluable contributions each theory has made to educational research separately (sociocultural theory and DA to learning and development and SFL to language-based learning) and their compatibility as argued by both socio-cultural theory and SFL scholars (e.g., Hasan, 2005a; Wells, 1994), to date, there appears to have been a limited application of both theories to academic writing assessment research in higher education. In particular, the combination of DA with SFL to research academic writing assessment is innovative.

The next chapter explains the design of my research and the research method-ologies employed by combining the two theoretical frameworks, expounded in this chapter and the previous one, for the application of DA to open and distance learning education in higher education.

References

Bawarshi, A. S., & Reiff, M. J. (2010). *Genre: An introduction to history, theory, research, and pedagogy*. Fort Collins, COL.: WAC Clearinghouse.

Bonanno, H., & Jones, J. (2007). *Measuring the academic skills of university students*. Sydney: Learning Centre, the University of Sydney.

Byrnes, H. (Ed.) (2006). *Advanced language learning: The contribution of Halliday and Vygotsky*. London, New York: Continuum.

Christie, F., & Maton, K. (2011a). *Disciplinarity: Functional linguistics and sociological perspectives*. London: Continuum.

Coffin, C. (2006). *Historical discourse: The language of time, cause and evaluation*. London: Continuum.

Coffin, C., & Donohue, J. P. (2012). Academic Literacies and systemic functional linguistics: How do they relate? *Journal of English for Academic Purposes, 11*(1), 64–75. https://doi.org/10.1016/j.jeap.2011.11.004.

Coffin, C., & Donohue, J. (2014). *A language as social semiotic based approach to teaching and learning in higher education*. Malden, MA: Wiley.

Dreyfus, S. J., Humphrey, S., Mahbob, A., & Martin, J. R. (2016). *Genre pedagogy in higher education: (SLATE) project*. Basingstoke, UK: Palgrave.

Eggins, S. (2004). *An introduction to systemic functional linguistics* (2nd ed.). London: Continuum.

Forman, J., & Rymer, J. (1999a). The genre system of the harvard case method. *Journal of Business and Technical Communication, 13*(4), 373–400. https://doi.org/10.1177/105065199901300401.

Forman, J., & Rymer, J. (1999a). Defining the Genre of the "Case Write-Up". *The Journal of Business Communication (1973), 36*(2), 103–133. https://doi.org/10.1177/002194369903600201.

Gardner, S. (2012). A pedagogic and professional case study genre and register continuum in business and in medicine. *Journal of Applied Linguistics and Professional Practice, 9*(1), 13–35.

Gardner, S., & Nesi, H. (2013). A classification of genre families in university student writing. *Applied Linguistics, 34*(1), 25–52. https://doi.org/10.1093/applin/ams024.

Gardner, S., Nesi, H., & Biber, D. (2019). Discipline, level, genre: Integrating situational perspectives in a new MD analysis of university student writing. *Applied Linguistics, 40*(4), 646–674. https://doi.org/10.1093/applin/amy005.

Gibbons, P. (2002). *Scaffolding language, scaffolding learning: Teaching second language learners in the mainstream classroom.* Portsmouth, NH: Heinemann.

Gibbons, P. (2006). *Bridging discourses in the ESL classroom: Students, teachers and researchers.* London: Continuum.

Halliday, M. A. K. (1978). *Language as social semiotic: The social interpretation of language and meaning.* Baltimore: University Park Press.

Halliday, M. A. K. (1993). Towards a language-based theory of learning. *Linguistics and Education, 5*(2), 93–116. https://doi.org/10.1016/0898-5898(93)90026-7.

Halliday, M. A. K. (1994). *An introduction to functional grammar* (2nd ed.). London: Arnold.

Halliday, M. A. K., & Matthiessen, C. M. I. M. (2004). *An introduction to functional grammar* (3rd ed.). London: Hodder Education.

Halliday, M. A. K., & Matthiessen, C. M. I. M. (2014). *Halliday's introduction to functional grammar (Fourth* (Edition ed.). Milton Park, Abingdon, Oxon: Routledge.

Hasan, R. (2005b). Semiotic mediation and three exotropic theories: Vygotsky, Halliday and Bernstein. In J. Webster (Ed.), *Language, society and consciousness: The collected works of Ruqaiya Hasan* (Vol. 1). London: Equinox.

Hasan, R. (2005a). *The collected works of Ruqaiya Hasan. Vol. 1, Language, society and consciousness.* London: Equinox.

Hasan, R. (2014). Towards a paradigmatic description of context: Systems, metafunctions, and semantics. *Functional Linguistics, 1*(1), 9. https://doi.org/10.1186/s40554-014-0009-y.

Hasan, R., & Webster, J. (2009). *Semantic variation: Meaning in society and in sociolinguistics.* London: Equinox.

Hood, S. (2010). *Appraising research: Evaluation in academic writing.* Basingstoke, New York: Palgrave Macmillan.

Humphrey, S. (1996). *Exploring literacy in school geography.* Sydney: Metropolitan East DSP.

Humphrey, S., Martin, J. R., Dreyfus, S., & Mahboob, A. (2010). The 3 × 3: setting up a linguistic toolkit for teaching academic writing. In A. Mahboob & N. Knight (Eds.), *Appliable linguistics* (pp. 185–199). London: Continuum.

Martin, J. R. (1993). Life as a noun: Arresting the Universe in Science and Humanities. In J. R. Martin & M. A. K. Halliday (Eds.), *Writing science: Literacy and discursive power* (pp. 221–267). London: The Falmer Press.

Martin, J. R. (1997). Analysing genre: functional parameters. In J. R. Martin & F. Christie (Eds.), *Genre and institutions: Social processes in the workplace and school* (pp. 3–39). London: Cassell.

Martin, J. R. (1999). Mentoring semogenesis: a genre-based pedagogy. In F. Christie (Ed.), *Pedagogy and the shaping of consciousness: Linguistic and social processes.* London and New York: Continuum.

Martin, J. R. (2009). Genre and language learning: A social semiotic perspective. *Linguistics and Education, 20*(1), 10–21.

Martin, J. R. (2011). Systemic Functional Linguistics. In K. Hyland & B. Paltridge (Eds.), *Continuum companion to discourse analysis* (pp. 101–119). London: Continuum.

Martin, J. R. (2016). Meaning matters: A short history of systemic functional linguistics. *WORD, 62*(1), 35–58. https://doi.org/10.1080/00437956.2016.1141939.

Martin, J. R., & Rose, D. (2007). *Working with discourse: Meaning beyond the clause.* London: Continuum.

Martin, J. R., & White, P. R. R. (2005). *The language of evaluation: Appraisal in English.* Basingstoke, New York: Palgrave Macmillan.

Miller, R. T., & Pessoa, S. (2016). Role and genre expectations in undergraduate case analysis in information systems. *English for Specific Purposes, 44,* 43–56. https://doi.org/10.1016/j.esp.2016.06.003.

Nathan, P. (2013). Academic writing in the business school: The genre of the business case report. *Journal of English for Academic Purposes, 12*(1), 57–68. https://doi.org/10.1016/j.jeap.2012. 11.003.

Nesi, H., & Gardner, S. (2012). *Genres across the disciplines: Student writing in higher education.* Cambridge: Cambridge University Press.

Nesi, H., & Gardner, S. (2018). The BAWE corpus and genre families classification of assessed student writing. *Assessing Writing, 38,* 51–55. https://doi.org/10.1016/j.asw.2018.06.005.

O'Grady, G., Bartlett, T., & Fontaine, L. (Eds.). (2013). *Choice in language: Applications in text analysis.* London: Equinox.

Rose, D., & Martin, J. R. (2012). *Learning to write, reading to learn: genre, knowledge and pedagogy in the Sydney school.* Sheffield; Bristol, CT: Equinox Publishing Ltd.

Shrestha, P. N. (2017). Investigating the learning transfer of genre features and conceptual knowledge from an academic literacy course to business studies: Exploring the potential of dynamic assessment. *Journal of English for Academic Purposes, 25,* 1–17. https://doi.org/10.1016/j.jeap. 2016.10.002.

Swales, J. M. (1990). *Genre analysis: English in academic and research settings.* Cambridge: Cambridge University Press.

Wells, G. (1994). The complementary contributions of Halliday and Vygotsky to a 'language-based theory of learning'. *Linguistics and Education, 6*(1), 41–90.

Wingate, U., & Tribble, C. (2011). The best of both worlds? Towards an English for Academic Purposes/Academic Literacies writing pedagogy. *Studies in Higher Education, 37*(4), 481–495. https://doi.org/10.1080/03075079.2010.525630.

Zhu, W. (2004). Writing in business courses: An analysis of assignment types, their characteristics, and required skills. *English for Specific Purposes, 23*(2), 111–135.

Chapter 4
Application of Dynamic Assessment to Distance Education

4.1 Introduction

The study reported in this book set out to explore the extent to which dynamic assessment (DA) procedures enhance students' academic writing and conceptual development in an open and distance learning context. Specifically, it examined these four questions: (1) What insight into learners' writing development does the analysis of tutor-learner interaction provide? (2) What do the analyses of student assessment texts (including drafts) demonstrate regarding students' academic writing and conceptual development? (3) Do learners following less dynamic assessment procedures perform differently? And (4) to what extent can learners transfer the academic writing skills and conceptual knowledge learned in one writing assessment task to another?

In order to investigate these questions, the study was informed by the two theoretical frameworks described in Chaps. 2 and 3. In particular, the research design was shaped by previous studies, as reviewed in Chap. 1, and the gaps highlighted in Chaps. 2 and 3. This chapter focuses on describing the research design and methodology employed to investigate the application of DA to assessing academic writing development in open and distance education. It begins with a brief introduction to the context of academic writing assessment in open and distance education and presents a synopsis of the types of business studies assignments at The Open University Business School (OUBS) to provide the institutional context for my research. It then presents the research methodology adopted for the research and a brief profile of each participant in the study. Next, a summary of existing DA procedures in the literature is given, followed by the actual DA procedures adopted in my research. Finally, an overview of the data collection and the analytical methods deployed in my research is provided.

© Springer Nature Switzerland AG 2020
P. N. Shrestha, *Dynamic Assessment of Students' Academic Writing*,
https://doi.org/10.1007/978-3-030-55845-1_4

4.2 Context of Academic Writing Assessment: Open and Distance Education

As indicated in Chap. 1, learning and teaching in open and distance education is significantly different from traditional universities. Therefore, it is essential to understand how teaching and learning takes place in such a context. However, as in all other higher education institutions, written text is the main source of knowledge construction in open and distance education. Of course, written texts are supplemented by other relevant multimodal resources such as audios, videos and images. Unlike in other universities, students in The Open University (OU) have limited or no face-to-face contact with their teacher or their fellow students during the course of their studies because face-to-face tutorials are provided in a limited number. The attendance at these tutorials are reported to be low for various reasons such as students' time commitments and geographical distance (e.g., in Scotland, students may have to travel from home for 2–3 h to attend a tutorial). Therefore, online tutorials are increasingly becoming the norm in most of the OU courses. In terms of the study materials, all undergraduate courses provide all materials online even when there is also a printed book. While some courses continue to provide students with printed books, many courses now offer some materials in print and most of the materials online on a dedicated course website. Depending on the credit of the course, the OU courses run for six to nine months each year. Each course has its own course team that consists of academic (a course chair and two or more other academics), administrative and production (i.e., editor, online support) staff. Designing and running a course always involves collaborative teamwork across different units in the OU. Each course has a number of tutors depending on the number of students it has. An OU tutor, officially called Associate Lecturer, has 16–20 students in their group for tutorials and assessment marking. The tutor has contact with students via a private online forum called Tutor Group Forum within the course website, custom-built on the Moodle platform (it is private because it cannot be accessed by students from other tutors' groups). This online forum is used to build a community and for students to carry out learning activities in small groups. The tutor also uses email and telephone to contact their students. For tutorials, each tutor uses an online room (currently Adobe Connect®) at different points in the course; this offers students and their tutor opportunities to discuss anything related to the course in real time.

The OU students are considerably different from those in other universities for a number of reasons: they are almost all part-time students and most of them may be in fulltime employment; students are isolated and dispersed across the UK and globally rather than being in a campus. In addition, unlike those in traditional universities, most students are mature and over 30 years old (some students being over 70) although increasingly younger students (e.g., under 18 s) are studying with the OU. The other distinguishing factor is the OU's *no entry requirement* for first year (Level 1) undergraduate courses, as part of its social justice agenda and mission (i.e., open to people, places, methods and ideas).

Assessment in the OU is primarily conducted through the written mode except in Languages courses. Each course contains two to six Tutor Marked Assignments (TMAs). TMAs spread across the course and each TMA assesses a certain topic area. The TMA is designed not only to assess what students have learned in the course but also provide formative feedback that students can use in their subsequent assignments (TMAs). A typical TMA in a course in the OU has two parts to each question: *the assignment task or question* and detailed *guidance notes*. Figures 4.1

About TMA 01

TMA 01 is a simple case study based on a small- to medium-sized business. It is marked out of 100 and is worth 10% of the overall continuous assessment component.

Part I (90 marks) is intended to:

- assess students' understanding of the key learning points contained within B111 Book 1, concentrating on one study session in particular for this assignment
- develop skills such as comprehension, presenting information and communicating in writing
- introduce students to the use of short case studies in business studies and begin to develop basic skills of case study analysis.

Part I of TMA 01 is based on the following case study.

[case study – not included here]

TMA 01 question

You have been asked by [name of director], the Company Director of [company name], to help him understand his company's current situation. Using the information you have been given in the case study above and specific concepts from Session 2 of B111 Book 1, write him a short, informal report to help him understand key areas of the company's external environment.

Prepare a short report based on the following:

Part (a)

Identify the different types of stakeholders at [name of company], based on the case study, and explore their contributions and concerns.

(40 marks)

Part (b)

Briefly explain why you think a SWOT* analysis may be useful for [name of director] in understanding the strengths, weaknesses, opportunities and threats in the external environment. Perform a simple SWOT analysis for [company name] based on the case study.

(50 marks)

*SWOT = Strengths, Weaknesses, Opportunities & Threats.

Fig. 4.1 A sample TMA task from a business studies course

Guidance notes for TMA 01 Part I

You are asked to use specific concepts from one session of Book 1 only. This is to help you focus your ideas and to stay within the (short) word limit for this TMA. It is part of the purpose of this TMA to develop your skills in expressing yourself concisely and to the point. Therefore, reproducing long quotes from the case study or from B111 Book 1 is likely to be an unproductive use of your word limit.

You will find the word 'concept' used frequently in your studies. Most simply it refers to academic ideas that help improve our understanding of the world. So here you are required to select the 'concepts' or 'ideas' that help you better understand in Part (a) stakeholders and in Part (b) SWOT analysis.

When marking your TMA, your tutor will check that you are:

- making it clear which concepts from Book 1 you are using
- giving a brief explanation/definition of these concepts
- showing how the concepts you have chosen are relevant to this case study
- explaining how these concepts may be useful in helping the manager understand the situation he finds himself (and the business) in
- explaining how they would be most productive in helping [name of director] make a plan for the future.

You should write your answer/advice to the company director in the form of an informal report. It is informal in the sense that you do not have to include all the required sections of a formal report, such as an executive summary and contents page. Refer to Section 1.5 for information on what is included in the word limit. Remember to reference the theories you use at the end of your informal report. Use the detailed guidance notes on referencing in Section 1.6 of this Assignment Booklet to help you to reference correctly. If you quote from the case itself, you can make this clear by writing 'The case study says, "...."', or similar. You do not have to give a formal reference for this.

Fig. 4.2 A sample guidance note for the TMA task in Fig. 4.1

and 4.2 give an illustrative example from a first year compulsory business course called B111.[1]

As can be seen from these two figures, students are not just asked to respond to the assignment question but they are also given guidance on how to write their assignment (SWOT case study analysis here). Thus, assessment has a teaching purpose as well. Student written assignments are marked by their own tutors who are provided with a marking guide or scheme which is prepared by the central course team. The marking criteria cover these aspects: knowledge and understanding of the subject, cognitive skills, key skills, and practical and professional skills. Each course team, may, however, interpret and adapt these four areas according to the nature of their subject. As part of marking student written assignments, the tutor is required to provide both on-script comments and a feedback summary to each student, both

---

[1] Course names/codes are fictitious for anonymity.

of which are intended to provide formative feedback to students. This shows that the intention is for the tutor to 'teach' through assessment and feedback (Coffin & Donohue, 2014). The formative value of this kind of feedback or comment has, however, been questioned in previous studies (Chetwynd & Dobbyn, 2011; Walker, 2009) as noted in Chap. 1.

4.3   Nature of Business Studies Assignments

It is important to understand the type of assessment used by academics in OUBS courses to fully appreciate the application of DA reported in this book. In Chap. 3, readers may recall that I had noted *case studies* genre family being widely used in business studies assignments as shown by previous research (Gardner, 2012; Zhu, 2004). In addition to case studies, business studies students are asked to write in two other genre families, *essays* and *recounts*, in the UK business schools according to Nesi and Gardner (2012). In order to check if this is the case in OUBS, a survey of first and second year course assignments in OUBS was conducted by analysing assignment tasks and prompted genres in two compulsory courses (one in the first year and another in the second year).

Table 4.1 presents academic writing purposes and prompted genres in the first year compulsory introductory business studies course B111. There were four assignments and each assignment had differing purposes as shown in the table. However, the first two assignments were in the same macrogenre (see Chap. 3): *Case study analysis.* As can be seen in the table, they were slightly different because the second assignment included an additional elemental genre (*Evaluation*). It is also worth noting that the *case study analysis* genre here has the additional purpose of *demonstrating knowledge and understanding* of course concepts. The third assignment is distinct as it requires students to conduct a financial review of a company by drawing on course concepts. It includes genres which resemble what Nesi and Gardner call *Explanation, Critique* and *Exercise* and other elemental genres as shown in the table, as students are asked, for example, to explain the purpose of an *income statement* (profit and loss account). Finally, the fourth assignment is called an essay but it is not purely an essay genre family as described in Nesi and Gardner (2012) but a combination of *argument* and other genres such as *description, analysis* and *evaluation.* All this shows the complexity of assignment genres used in assessment in business studies.

In the second year compulsory course, the assignments are more complex than those in the first year, as shown in Table 4.2. It is also worth noting that, except for Assignment 4, all assignments are based on the same organisation the student chooses in Assignment 1. The most common genres are Case study analysis and Reflective recount which are found in almost all assignments. The first assignment is less challenging than others in that it requires students to describe—rather than analyse—an organisation of their choice. Assignment 6 has three genres, unlike the other five. In addition to a Case study analysis and a Reflective recount, it includes what Nesi and Gardner (2012) term an *Exercise.* In this Exercise, students are asked

Table 4.1 Purposes and genres in a first year business course

Assignment	Purpose	Prompted genre
1 Report to a manager	To describe/classify/explain/analyse/recommend To demonstrate knowledge and understanding To prepare for professional practice	Macrogenre: Case study analysis Description + Explanation + Analysis + Recommendation
2 Problem-solution report on own workplace	To describe (problems)/explain/analyse (problems)/evaluate/recommend To demonstrate knowledge and understanding To prepare for professional practice	Macrogenre: Case study analysis Description + Explanation + Analysis + Evaluation + Recommendation
3 Financial review of a company	To describe/explain/evaluate/discuss/recommend/argue To demonstrate knowledge and understanding To prepare for professional practice	Macrogenre: Company finance review Description + Explanation + Evaluation + Discussion + Recommendation + Argument
4 Essay (business ethics)	To describe/analyse (business situation)/discuss/evaluate To demonstrate knowledge and understanding To develop powers of independent reasoning	Macrogenre: Essay Description + Analysis (of business situation) + Discussion + Evaluation

to draw a diagram to show the information system of the organisation and classify them as core and outsourced.

The brief survey of assessment genres in first and second year two compulsory courses in OUBS above confirmed Nesi and Gardner's (2012) claim that indeed Case study analysis, Recount and Essay are the dominant genres in business studies. Given the dominance of the case study analysis genre, it was also the focus genre in the research described here. It is worth noting here that not all case study analysis assignment tasks made obvious that Recommendation was essential but implied, especially in the second year course. Similarly, Evaluation (or Conclusion) was not always expected in a case study analysis.

Having provided the context of my research, in the rest of this chapter, I explain how the research study was designed to apply DA to academic writing assessment in distance education.

Table 4.2 Purposes and genres in a second year business course

Assignment	Purpose	Prompted genre
1 Description of an organisation and reflection	To describe (an organisation) To reflect (on learning)	Description Reflective recount
2 report on operation management of organisation described in assignment 1	To describe/explain/analyse/evaluate To demonstrate knowledge and understanding To prepare for professional practice To reflect (on learning)	Macrogenre: Case study analysis Description + Explanation + Analysis + Evaluation + Recommendation Reflective recount
3 report on marketing strategy of organisation described in assignment 1	To describe/explain/analyse/evaluate To demonstrate knowledge and understanding To prepare for professional practice To reflect (on learning)	Macrogenre: Case study analysis Description + Explanation + Analysis + Evaluation (+ Recommendation – implied but not clear) Reflective recount
4 Accounting and finance analysis of a company (Dixon Retail plc)	To explain/analyse (financial information and company performance) To evaluate (impact on stakeholders) To demonstrate knowledge and understanding To prepare for professional practice To reflect (on learning)	Macrogenre: Case study analysis Explanation + Analysis + Evaluation (+Recommendation – implied but not clear) Reflective recount
5 Human resource management report on organisation described in assignment 1	To describe (chosen human resource management (HRM) functional area)/evaluate (activities in that area by applying course concepts) To discuss (organisation's HRM approaches) To recommend (ways for improvements)/apply course concepts To demonstrate knowledge and understanding To prepare for professional practice To reflect (on learning)	Macrogenre: Case study analysis Explanation + Evaluation + Discussion/Evaluation + Recommendation Reflective recount

(continued)

Table 4.2 (continued)

Assignment	Purpose	Prompted genre
6 Information management report on organisation described in assignment 1	To demonstrate knowledge and understanding To describe/analyse (information systems)/recommend To prepare for professional practice To reflect (on learning)	Exercise Macrogenre: Case study analysis Description + Analysis + Evaluation + Recommendation Reflective recount

4.4   Design of Research on Dynamic Assessment of Academic Writing

In Chap. 2, I explained Vygotsky's developmental or *genetic* method (Vogotsky, 1978) which is central to my research. In order to understand and document the development of higher mental functions such as academic writing, it is important to examine its historical development process in which changes (progressive or regressive) are dynamic and result from interactions between human mind, nature and sociocultural tools (Mahn, 1999). In this sense, the study is substantially qualitative in nature due to the inherent alignment of DA with a 'genetic' or developmental method which examines the qualitative development of individuals' higher mental functions over time (Lantolf & Thorne, 2006). As explained in Chap. 2, the high importance of *semiotic mediation* in facilitating higher mental functioning is indispensable in Vygotsky's genetic method. Specifically, the role of language and other symbolic tools including concepts is paramount in mediating activities and internalising culture. Therefore, it was essential to capture students' higher mental development process in the context of academic writing (see Sect. 4.4.1).

Complementing the developmental method, my research also followed a variant of an action research method which allows a practitioner-researcher to study the impact of a small-scale intervention to improve practice in the real world (Cohen, Manion, & Morrison, 2018). Action research is often used in applied linguistics and professional practices, allowing a practitioner-researcher to investigate a social situation in which they bring about positive changes to the participants' situation through collaboration with them. Often, the practitioner-researcher reflects on the research situation and adjusts their research process in response to participants' emerging needs (Burns, 2010). Throughout this study, the students' academic writing problems had been explored in collaboration with them in the assessment process and appropriate solutions to those problems had been found. During the process, the research activities had been adjusted to suit individual participants' dynamic needs and circumstances, which enabled the researcher (me) to gather richer data to understand the nature of the participants' academic writing development.

Action research has been criticised for its lack of rigour, reliability and validity (Mackey & Gass, 2005, p. 219). However, this criticism stems from a quantitative paradigm of research that focuses on measurement which is *not* the goal of qualitative research including action research (Feldman, 2007). Validity in this approach is dynamic and varies in response to the emerging needs of participants (Burns, 2010, p. 85). Additionally, the concept of validity in action research is related to the quality of research (i.e., how well the research describes, explains and theorises the phenomena in question) instead of any 'absolute truth' (e.g., Feldman, 2007). Therefore, the question of validity needs to concentrate on the evidence for such changes and the evidence may be drawn from multiple methods and sources for triangulation (see Sect. 4.5).

Furthermore, action research is compatible with sociocultural theory (and thus DA) as both advocate co-construction of knowledge and intervention for positive change in participants (Chaiklin, 2011; Somekh, 2010). Thus, action research is suitable and valid for DA research to study changing academic writing needs (ZPDs) of the participants in my research.

4.4.1 Key Concepts Underpinning the Research Design

This study was mainly driven by the Vygotskian concept of the *genetic* method explained in Chap. 2. Vygotsky argued that human mental development can be understood better by examining how and where it occurs in growth (i.e., process) as the product of development alone is not sufficient for this purpose (Wertsch, 1985). As described in Chap. 2, Wertsch (Chap. 2, 1985) divides Vygotsky's genetic research method into four domains: *phylogenetic* (i.e., evolution of humans), *socio-cultural history* (i.e., history of general human culture and particular human cultures), *ontogenetic* (i.e., development of an individual) and *microgenetic* (i.e., development of a specific process during ontogenesis). Among these, the fourth domain, microgenesis, is central to the research reported in the book. It allows the researcher to observe learner development (changing ZPDs) in a specific domain over a short span of time (Lantolf, 2000; Wertsch, 1985). Wertsch calls this type of study 'a very short-term longitudinal study' (1985, p. 55).

In Vygotskian sociocultural theory, an individual's microgenesis or development is generally evidenced through the analysis of semiotic mediation. The analysis is conducted to identify instances of the individual's changing ZPDs. For demonstrating changing ZPDs, as argued by Hasan (2005b), Vygotsky-inspired studies have, however, tended to focus on concepts and logic (ideational meaning) without giving much importance to the discourse in context and this applies to DA research as well. Hasan (2005a) further argues that Vygotskian sociocultural theory lacks a theory of language use and proposes SFL as a complementary theory. Following Hasan's view, in order to address the problem, this study employed the SFL notion of *logogenesis* for identifying students' changing ZPDs and the impact of tutor mediation. Logogenesis is one of the three levels of semiotic development (i.e., semogenesis) in a time frame. It refers to 'the instantial construction of meaning in the form of a text' (Halliday & Matthiessen, 1999, p. 18). Logogenesis is the manifestation of text development over a short time. It is, thus, compatible with microgenesis because both relate to development in a short span of time. The microgenesis of individual students' academic writing (ZPDs), potentially resulting from teacher mediation, can be evidenced through an SFL analysis of their assessment texts (logogenesis).

4.4.2 Specific Research Context

The participants for my research were recruited from a first year academic writing course for business studies students in OUBS. It was designed for those students who were studying or planning to study business studies at the OU. The course was designed to enhance academic reading and writing skills that students would need for undergraduate business studies.

This course was designed following an approach which sees academic reading and writing as situated social practices in particular contexts and communities (e.g., Hyland, 2003) and this design was informed by an SFL-based genre theory (Coffin & Donohue, 2014). As such, this course aimed to enable students to participate more effectively in business studies contexts. In particular, students on this module were familiarised with a number of common text types encountered in business studies. Broadly speaking, these text types included case studies, essays and reports which students are required to produce in response to business studies assessment tasks. Students were taught how to analyse texts in these genres as well as create them by using appropriate content knowledge and language resources in the context of business studies.

Generally, students on this course came from both traditional and non-traditional educational backgrounds. At the time of this research, almost all students on this particular course were in employment and the majority of them used English as their mother tongue.

As in other OU courses, a tutor was allocated to a group of around 20 students and was responsible for supporting these students, marking their assignments and providing feedback on them. Tutor support was mainly provided via an online tutor group forum and emails although students could also contact their tutor by phone if they preferred. As a practitioner-researcher, I worked as a tutor on this course to enable myself to conduct my research.

Assignment Tasks in Business Academic Writing Course

Given that the business academic writing course was designed to support students' writing in business studies, the assignment tasks aimed to reflect the genres that appeared in business studies assignments presented in Tables 4.1 and 4.2. There were four Tutor Marked Assignments (TMAs), targeting different text types: case study analysis (TMA1 and 2), business essay (TMA3) and report (workplace proposal) (TMA4). For these assignments, students were provided with real case studies of an organisation (e.g., Nike) or they were asked to consider their own workplace. A common feature of all these texts is the application of business (studies) concepts

> **Task**
>
> This part of the TMA is intended to assess your ability to analyse a business case study by applying a SWOT framework of analysis. You are also required to demonstrate the application of your tutor's feedback on TMA1 to this second assignment.
>
> Use the SWOT framework of analysis to critically examine the internal and external environment of Brompton Bicycle as described in the case study. Provide recommendations to Brompton Bicycle about future actions they should take for business success.
>
> Complete the task by reading and analysing the case study that follows and the three expert opinions at the end. Take into account your tutor's feedback on TMA1 in writing this analysis.
>
> You should submit your assignment by the given deadline. Your assignment should not exceed 800 words. Any figures or diagrams should be included in the body of the main text and will form part of the total word count.
>
> [case study – not included here]

Fig. 4.3 An assignment task for TMA2 in business academic writing course

and/or frameworks (e.g., business environment, SWOT) to an organisation's business situation. Each assignment task was accompanied by guidance notes. Here is an example of an assignment task and guidance notes from the course (Figs. 4.3 and 4.4).

The guidance notes for the TMA ask students to apply the SWOT business framework, explained earlier, to Brompton Bicycle (a UK-based folding bicycle company), by focusing on the concepts of *strengths, weaknesses, opportunities* and *threats* in an organisation's *internal* and *external business environment*. Such an application needs an understanding of the SWOT framework and its associated concepts as well as the linguistic resources and the target genre knowledge needed to produce an effective case study analysis, explained in Chap. 3 and Sect. 4.3 above.

Additionally, students are provided with detailed assessment criteria, adapted from Bonanno and Jones (2007), focusing on five areas: use of source materials, text structure and development, academic style, grammatical correctness, and presentation.

4.4.3 Participants in My Research

The research described in this book had participants from the business academic writing course described above. Following the institutional ethics approval of my research, the potential participants were sent an initial invitation via their online tutor group forum and anyone who expressed an interest in the study was sent an introductory letter with the details of the study and a consent form by email. Initially, ten students expressed interest in the project. Ultimately, only six of them were able to participate from the start to finish of the study. Of the six students, two participated

Guidance notes

Use the SWOT analysis framework introduced and discussed in Session 4 of Book 1 and draw on the other case study analysis skills you have practised in Book 1. These include the active reading process, framing the case, identifying influences and impacts, proposing solutions and writing persuasively.

Note that the complete case study presented here includes the extract on Brompton Bicycle you read for TMA1, with some additional information, and three expert views.

Using the feedback you received from your tutor for TMA1 and reading carefully the full case study given below, identify the strengths and weaknesses of Brompton Bicycle, and the opportunities and threats that face it.

This task requires you to frame the case study analysis using a SWOT framework. First, you should complete the mapping of the case which you began in TMA1. Then you should create a SWOT analysis table using brief noun groups. You should then write up the analysis in paragraph form, using the SWOT analysis table to help you, and include the SWOT table in your text. You may use the paragraphing structure of Text 4.3 in Resource Book 1 as a guide. End your analysis with recommendations to Brompton Bicycles about their best way forward to business success. There are three expert views at the end of the case study. In your recommendations, you can combine what is written by these experts; or you can decide to use some of their recommendations but not others; or you can make up your own recommendations.

You should try to get accustomed to referencing in this TMA. When you use information from the case study you should include both an in-text reference to it and give the full reference in a References list at the end.

Fig. 4.4 Assignment guidance notes for TMA2 in business academic writing course

in non-DA sessions and four were in DA sessions by self-selecting the sessions. The main reason for choosing non-DA sessions over DA sessions was the demand on the participants' time. Whilst the DA sessions required more interaction with the tutor (i.e., more time), the non-DA sessions needed limited interaction (i.e., considerably less time). This was explained to the participants at the beginning. Those students with less free time due to other commitments opted for the non-DA sessions and those with more time went for the DA sessions. However, it is important to remember that the DA sessions were distinct from non-DA because of the dialogic process followed rather than the amount of time spent/required. These students were studying towards a qualification in business studies. The profile for each participant is given below.

The first of the six participants, Michelle, was a native speaker of English and originally came from Trinidad. She had achieved nine GCSEs. She worked as an administrator at a children's centre in a metropolitan city where she had to communicate with clients very frequently via emails (e.g., to update services). Michelle chose to participate in DA sessions.

The second participant, Natasha, used Hungarian as her mother tongue and English and German as additional languages. She had obtained a first degree in horticultural engineering. She worked as a garden designer in a garden centre in a cosmopolitan city. Like Michelle, Natasha took part in the DA sessions.

Amina, the third DA participant, spoke Urdu as her first language and English, Hindi, and Punjabi as additional languages. She had studied English and Urdu formally. Regarding her academic qualifications, she had obtained qualifications equivalent to A levels in Pakistan, and a Diploma in IT. At the beginning of the study, she was working full-time and studying. Later she had a baby and had quite limited time for this research.

The fourth participant was Lou who participated in the DA sessions. She was a native speaker of English and had learned French and German at school. Lou had begun her career as a fashion designer but had left it in order to work as an administrator in prison services. Her job required writing workplace documents.

Kristie, a non-DA participant, spoke French as her first language and English as a second language. Although she was originally from France, she had been living in the UK for over 30 years. Kristie had BEPC (a French qualification equivalent to GCSE) and Baccalaureate G1 as academic qualifications. She worked as a strategy and planning manager for one of the UK National Health Services trusts in a cosmopolitan city. At work, she had to write work-related documents.

The sixth participant (non-DA), Lena, was originally from former Czechoslovakia. She was a bilingual Czech and Slovak speaker and spoke English as an additional language. She also spoke basic German. At the time of this research, she was working full-time in an IT company.

Both Kristie and Lena stated that they had very little time and therefore would participate in non-DA which required less time than DA. In fact, their decision helped me with the allocation of the participants to DA and non-DA.

The information about the participants is summarised in Table 4.3.

4.5 Conducting Dynamic Assessment of Academic Writing in Distance Education

In order to investigate the application of DA to academic writing assessment, as explained in Chaps. 2 and 3, DA was integrated with SFL, the former providing a comprehensive theory of assessment and learning and the latter a comprehensive theory of language use. The data collection methods were shaped by these two theories in order to explore the application of DA to assessing academic writing in distance education and its impact on academic writing development. As such, the data was collected from two DA sessions, and two non-DA sessions. In this study, a DA session refers to the assessment period from the first written draft to the final draft produced by the student and the formative feedback on these drafts over several weeks/months. Additionally, the data was collected from one transfer session. The transfer session involved writing an assignment without tutor support. Learner interviews and subject teachers' views on student written assignments were

Table 4.3 Summary of participant details

Participants (pseudonyms)	Age	Nationality	Language(s) spoken	Qualifications	Employment	DA/non-DA
Michelle	31	Trinidad	English	GCSEs	Full-time	DA
Natasha	30	Hungary	Hungarian, German, English	First degree in horticulture engineering	Full-time	DA
Amina	26	UK	Urdu, Punjabi, English	A levels, diploma in IT	Full-time	DA
Lou	42	UK	English	Higher national diploma	Full-time	DA
Kristie	50	France	French, English	BPEC, Baccalaureate G1	Full-time	Non-DA
Lena	28	Former Czechoslovakia	Czech, Slovak, English	Secondary school certificate, Certificate in business studies	Full-time	Non-DA

additional complementary data sets. Before describing the data collection methods deployed in my research, it is essential to present existing DA procedures which are used in face-to-face contexts.

4.5.1 Existing Dynamic Assessment Procedures

As highlighted throughout this book, DA has been used in special needs education and clinical psychology widely (see Haywood & Lidz, 2007 for a review) and more recently it has been applied to second language learning (Lantolf, Poehner, & Swain, 2018). However, it has not been applied to distance education and academic writing assessment except my own work (e.g., Shrestha & Coffin, 2012; Shrestha, 2017). Therefore, it was necessary for me to draw on the existing DA procedures that I could apply to my research. It appears that, for interactionist DA, what Haywood and Lidz (2007) have presented as a *mediation checklist* has been widely used as reference for designing DA programmes or sessions in face-to-face contexts. Hence, I drew on this checklist for my research too. Their mediation checklist is presented in Fig. 4.5.

As can be seen in the checklist, the pre-mediation preparation and the process of the actual mediation in DA is quite broad which need to be recontextualised

Mediation checklist

To Do

❐ Determine whether the learner has the basic knowledge and skill base to proceed with this task. (If not, go back and either teach what is necessary or modify the level of the task to reflect the learner's zone of actual development.)

❐ Decide how you will present the task. How will you give directions, provide supports (e.g., visual aids), modify the task (e.g., simplify, break down)?

❐ Select the interventions that are the most promising for this type of task.

❐ Identify the basic principles and strategies of task mastery or solution.

During the interaction, remember to

❐ Provide feedback that informs the learner about what did and did not work.

❐ Elicit active conversation and input from the learner related to the work.

❐ Collect data and work samples to demonstrate and document changes in competence (show these to the learner).

❐ Be explicit about what you are thinking and decisions you are making during the assessment; model reflective thinking through self-talk related to the task.

❐ Look for opportunities to relate new work to what the learner already knows, and encourage the learner to do this as well.

❐ Gear yourself to match the learner's pace and style and be ready to adjust what you are doing and saying to make it accessible to the learner.

❐ Keep the work within the learner's reach, but also require the learner to reach just beyond what he or she already knows or can do.

❐ End on a positive note of successful accomplishment.

Fig. 4.5 Mediation checklist by Haywood and Lidz (2007, p. 42., Reproduced with permission of the Licensor through PLSclear)

for the educational context one is working in. Therefore, I had to consider how these procedures could be adapted for distance education where there is a lack of immediacy and physical presence of both the assessor/teacher and learners.

4.5.2 DA Sessions and the Intervention

Two DA sessions (DA1 and DA2) were conducted as the main data collection instrument. For these sessions, assignment tasks were designed independently of the academic writing course the participants were studying at the time. The task design and the assessment procedures are described below.

Table 4.4 Summary of assessment tasks

DA sessions	Business frameworks	Companies/products analysed	Number of texts	Length of assignment
DA1	STEP	Heineken's non-alcoholic beer	1	500 words
DA2	STEP	Safer Syringe market	1	500 words
DA1	SWOT	Google's Chrome operating system for computers	2	500 words
DA2	SWOT	Vodafone's broadband	3	500 words

Assessment Task Design

In order to reflect the common assessment task type both in business studies and the business academic writing course, as explained in Chap. 3 and this chapter, case study-based assignment tasks were designed for both the DA sessions. The case studies were selected on the basis of their topicality and potential to be interesting to read so as to motivate the participants to complete the tasks. Additionally, they were about familiar companies to the participants. For example, one case study was about Google's launch of a new operating system for computers (see Table 4.4), with which all participants were familiar.

Likewise, a common business framework was selected for its application to the case studies, which is widely practised in business studies assessments (e.g., see Zhu, 2004). For instance, SWOT (Strengths, Weaknesses, Opportunities and Threats) is a common framework applied to assess the competitive position of a product or service in its external environment (Preston, Fryer, & Watson, 2007, p. 28). The assessment tasks in this study required the participants to apply this framework to their analysis of the product (e.g., Vodafone broadband). Figure 4.6 exemplifies the assignment tasks used in this study. In addition to the SWOT framework, participants had a choice of using the STEP (Social or Sociological, Technological, Economic and Political factors) framework to their case study analyses. The STEP framework allows businesses to examine the external factors affecting them in future.

A summary of all the assessment tasks designed for my research reported in this book is given in Table 4.4.

Assessment Procedures

As explained in Chap. 2, the research reported here followed the interactionist model of DA as described by Lantolf and Poehner (2004, pp. 58–60). However, the standard DA procedures had to be adjusted for conducting DA in this research due to a significantly different context as explained earlier. Additionally, an adapted version of Bonnano and Jones' (2007) academic writing assessment criteria called Measuring the Academic Skills of University Students (MASUS) and Humphrey, Martin, Dreyfus and Mahboob (2010) framework were used to assess and comment on student assessment texts (see Tables 4.5 and 4.6). Table 4.6 is a summary version

---

Instructions

You are going to read two articles: *Google parks its tanks right outside Microsoft's gates* by John Naughton and *Google plans Chrome operating system* by Jefferson Graham. These two articles form a case study of the new operating system for computers being developed by Google. The new operating system is going to compete with Microsoft's Windows operating system. Both the articles examine the business environment of Google's Chrome operating system.

Task

Read the two articles about Google's Chrome operating system for computers mentioned above and write a SWOT analysis of this product based on the articles. Your SWOT analysis should be of about 500 words.

Guidance notes

Using the SWOT framework, analyse the internal and external environment of this new operating system by drawing on the two articles. If you wish, you can also refer to Google's blog posting by clicking here. As you are using the SWOT framework to analyse Google's business environment based on this case study, look for examples that illustrate the four categories (Strengths, Weaknesses, Opportunities and Threats) in the SWOT framework in order to produce an effective SWOT analysis while you are making notes. If you are not sure about what SWOT means, please read the documents attached to the wiki home page for this task. You can also ask me for clarification or more information.

Please note that you can ask me (the researcher) any questions related to the assessment task during any time of the writing process by email or chat or any appropriate method that allows me to record your queries and my response. For this we are very likely to use a wiki to produce the text and MSN, Yahoo or Skype chat for our interaction according to your convenience. Nearer the time, I will let you know which tool we will be using. Before I make a decision on this, I would like to know your preference.

For writing your text, I would prefer a wiki because it allows me to see all the process you follow and the changes you make to your text which are crucial to my study. You will receive information regarding the wiki shortly.

[two articles not included here]

Fig. 4.6 DA1 task

of Humphrey et al.'s framework due to space. Readers are referred to the original detailed table on p. 188 of their paper.

My research, following Feuerstein, Falik, Rand, and Feuerstein (2002) and Haywood and Lidz (2007), incorporated flexible mediation into the DA procedures. As such, my role as a tutor was to jointly engage with the learner in the task at hand and reformulate the task as needed until the learner 'mastered' it. Of particular relevance was the notion of mediation ranging from implicit (e.g., hints and prompts) to explicit (e.g., correct solutions) as proposed by Aljaafreh and Lantolf

Table 4.5 Marking criteria based on Bonnano and Jones (2007)

Marking criteria
A. Use of source material—is information from case study and other sources correct and appropriate for the task?
Uses data from the case study as evidence Information from case study and business studies texts is interpreted and transferred correctly
B. Structure and development of the text—is the structure and development of the case study analysis clear and appropriate to the title and its context?
Text structure is appropriate to the task (stakeholder categories frame the analysis, there are levels in the text, cause-effect analysis is used) Evidence is used that supports the analysis Explanations link the evidence to the analysis The information in the text is well linked
C. Control of academic writing style—does the writing style conform to appropriate patterns of written academic English?
Appropriate choice of vocabulary and sentence structure for a stakeholder analysis Appropriate use of business concept words Appropriate combinations of words Appropriate relationship with reader Appropriate evaluation language
D. Grammatical correctness
Sentence structure follows recognisable and appropriate patterns of English Noun groups formed correctly Verbs formed correctly
E. Qualities of presentation
Spelling generally correct Word processing appropriate Paragraphing reflects analysis structure Capitals, italics etc. are appropriate

(1994) for targeting learner ZPDs (see Fig. 4.7). In this research, mediation was by email, instant messaging (chat) or wiki comments, a novel form of mediation in DA. No assessment mark was given to any student.

A summary of the procedures followed in each DA session is shown in Table 4.7.

Michelle, Natasha, Amina and Lou completed two DA sessions. Each DA session consisted of the procedures listed in Table 4.7 and was spread over several months, depending on the participants' availability. For example, DA1 ran for four months as each participant's personal circumstances had to be considered, given that they were all in full-time employment and were studying part-time as well.

Based on their performance in DA1, I devised an enrichment programme for each learner and worked with them individually in order to support their writing development. This intervention was inspired by Feuerstein's Instrumental Enrichment (see Feuerstein, 1980; Poehner, 2005). The enrichment programme was designed to address each of the participants' needs identified through DA1. DA1 showed that all four DA participants had difficulties with designing the structure of the target text

Table 4.6 A summary version of the 3 × 3: a framework for describing linguistic resources of student writing in the academic domain based on Humphrey et al. (2010, p. 188)

Metafunctions	1. Social activity: Genre and register (whole text)	2. Discourse semantic (phases)	3. Grammar and expression (clauses and sentences)
A. Ideational meanings *(parts)*	Knowledge building from beginning to end Use of specialised language of the discipline (Field)	Use of definitions, classifications, logical relationships, visuals etc. as appropriate in discipline Information extended—general to particular	Use of noun groups, nominalisations, verb groups, tenses and specialised terms relevant to topic/discipline
B. Interpersonal meanings *(prosodies)*	Convincing to reader through stages of text Language use showing points and argument objectively (Tenor)	Us of informational, evaluative language, stance, citations of sources	Us of subject-verb agreement, mood choices, language of attitude and intensity, source citations, conjunctions and continuatives to manage reader expectations
C. Textual meanings *(waves)*	Use of introduction, middle and conclusion Clear signposting (including sub-headings) and coherent	Topic development through paragraphs/sentences Logical Information flow—abstract to concrete Use of cohesive resources	Thematic development, use of grammatical metaphor/pronouns/active or passive voices/abstract nouns, spelling, punctuation, paragraphing to suit purpose of text

(i.e., a STEP or a SWOT analysis of an organisation), information management, and the conceptual understanding of STEP or SWOT analysis. Samples of the enrichment materials for academic writing are given in Figs. 4.8 and 4.9.

As shown in the sample, the enrichment material included study activities targeting these areas, including explicit theoretical explanations and visuals where necessary, which were emailed to each participant. The participants were asked to go through the materials over three weeks and contact me for any further support. Then, the second DA session (DA2) was conducted following the same procedures as shown in Table 4.7.

From these DA sessions, the participants' assessment texts and tutor mediation texts were collected to examine the application of DA to academic writing. Each participant's journey of academic writing and conceptual development with regard to their ZPDs was tracked in depth (see Chaps. 5, 6 and 7).

0. Tutor asks the learner to read, find the errors, and correct them independently, prior to the tutorial.
1. Construction of a "collaborative frame" prompted by the presence of the tutor as a potential dialogic partner.
2. Prompted or focused reading of the sentence that contains the error by the learner or the tutor.
3. Tutor indicates that something may be wrong in a segment (e.g., sentence, clause, line)-"Is there anything wrong in this sentence?"
4. Tutor rejects unsuccessful attempts at recognizing the error.
5. Tutor narrows down the location of the error (e.g., tutor repeats or points to the specific segment which contains the error).
6. Tutor indicates the nature of the error, but does not identify the error (e.g., "There is something wrong with the tense marking here").
7. Tutor identifies the error ("You can't use an auxiliary here").
8. Tutor rejects learner's unsuccessful attempts at correcting error.
9. Tutor provides clues to help the learner arrive at the correct form (e.g., "It is not really past but some thing that is still going on").
10. Tutor provides the correct form.
11. Tutor provides some explanation for use of the correct form.
12. Tutor provides examples of the correct pattern when other forms of help fail to produce an appropriate responsive action.

Fig. 4.7 Aljaafreh and Lantolf's (1994, p. 471) regulatory scale (Reprinted from *The Modern Language Journal, 78*(4), Aljaafreh, A., & Lantolf, J. P. Negative feedback as regulation and second language learning in the Zone of Proximal Development, pp. 465–483 (1994), with permission from John Wiley & Sons through RightsLink)

Table 4.7 DA procedures

Participants in the research	Steps in DA interventions
Tutor (myself)	1. Design DA assessment tasks and send them to the participants by email or post them on a password-protected wiki. The initial plan was to use a wiki. But the participants preferred emails to the wiki. *Only DA1 task was posted on the wiki. Other assessment tasks were sent by email* 2. Provide formative feedback on the text by using the SFL-based criteria (Tables 4.5 and 4.6) and targeting the participants' ZPD by following flexible mediation 3. Offer further mediation based on the participants' subsequent response to previous formative feedback 4. Negotiate with the participants on the final text
Learners	1. Write the response to the DA assessment task 2. Send the text to the tutor by email. Participate in the instant messaging 'conversation' for the formative feedback if preferred 3. Ask questions when necessary 4. Revise subsequent drafts in response to the tutor's formative feedback 5. Negotiate with the tutor on the final text

4.5.3   Non-dynamic Assessment

The participants in the non-DA followed the normal assessment procedure as in the business academic writing course. In other words, there was no intervention from the tutor when they were writing their assignments. Additionally, they produced only

---

Developing a paragraph/ argument

A good text has a structure which is easy to follow. Likewise, a paragraph should have the same feature. An 'easy-to-follow' paragraph contains a good flow of information. In order to manage the flow of the information effectively, you need to pay attention to some crucial elements of a paragraph. They are theme and point, link between ideas and the movement from general to particular. Each of them is explained briefly below.

Levels in a paragraph

Each paragraph moves from a general level of meaning to a particular one. The first sentence makes a general point of the paragraph which is developed further later through explanations and examples. This is one of the ways of maintaining the information flow in the text. Let us look at a paragraph from Bonnie's essay.

Activity 1

　　Spend about 20 minutes on this activity.

　　Purpose: To notice levels of meaning in a paragraph.

　　Task: Read Extract A carefully first to find out what this paragraph is about (sentences numbered). Then complete the step diagram below to show the movement of high and low level meanings in this extract.

　　Extract A (from Bonnie's essay)

　　An important factor in economic well–being is investment. (2) '…most economists agree…that high levels of investment are associated with a healthy economy' (Lucas, 2000, p.24). (3) Nike does not invest directly in the developing countries where it operates, but it encourages others to invest by sub-contracting the production of its shoes. (4) Factories will be built and people will be employed, injecting money into the economy which will pass around and create more economic possibilities because of the 'multiplier effect'. (5) An initial income will pass from hand to hand, consuming goods and creating new income with each transaction. (6) This creates new demand for goods, which creates more demand for labour, and employs more people (Coates, 2000, p.60). (7) From the point of view of investment, a large corporation such as Nike has a very beneficial influence on the economic health of the developing countries in which it operates.

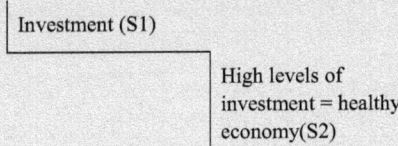

Fig. 4.8   Enrichment material on paragraph development

Compare your answer with those suggested in the Answer section.

Comment:

This paragraph has both high and low level meanings operating in it. The beginning sentence, also known as *topic sentence,* has the highest level of meaning, which is generally true to all paragraphs in a text. In this extract, the first sentence is about *investment,* which is the subject of this paragraph. The other sentences develop this concept in a specific or detailed way by applying it to Nike's investment in developing countries and its impact on their economy. Allocating a certain part of the text to a level may not always be so easy, but it is possible to notice which is more specific and which is not. For example, sentence 2 has more general information than sentence 3 because sentence 3 is not just about levels of investment but about Nike's investment in developing countries.

[five further activities on Theme and point, Information flow, Linking ideas, and explanation of SWOT and STEP]

Fig. 4.8 (continued)

one assessment text for each assessment task. The non-DA participants were asked to complete two assessment tasks (non-DA1 and non-DA2) to coincide with the DA sessions. These tasks were the same as those used in DA sessions to allow comparability between DA and non-DA. The students received standard tutor feedback from me on their assignments but were offered no assessment scores. However, one of the two non-DA participants, Kristie, asked me for a telephone 'dialogue' after non-DA2. This was allowed because of the ethical issue of fairness. This adjustment in the non-DA procedures made these procedures more dynamic for this particular learner. Nevertheless, it should be noted that the telephone 'dialogue' took place after non-DA2 and therefore this could not have benefited her non-DA2 although her transfer assessment might have been affected. Both Lena and Kristie's texts and tutor feedback were collected and analysed to compare with those who went through DA.

For ethical and equity reasons, the non-DA students also had access to the enrichment materials described above. It appeared that Kristie did use them as she confirmed during the interview. It was not known if Lena used them as she was not available for the interview.

4.5.4 *Transfer Assessment Tasks*

The success of DA lies in the learner's ability to transfer the skills and knowledge learned in one assessment task or context to another. In interactionist DA, such transfer is called *transcendence* (e.g., see Feuerstein et al., 2002), one of the universal

Text structure/ organisation of a SWOT analysis

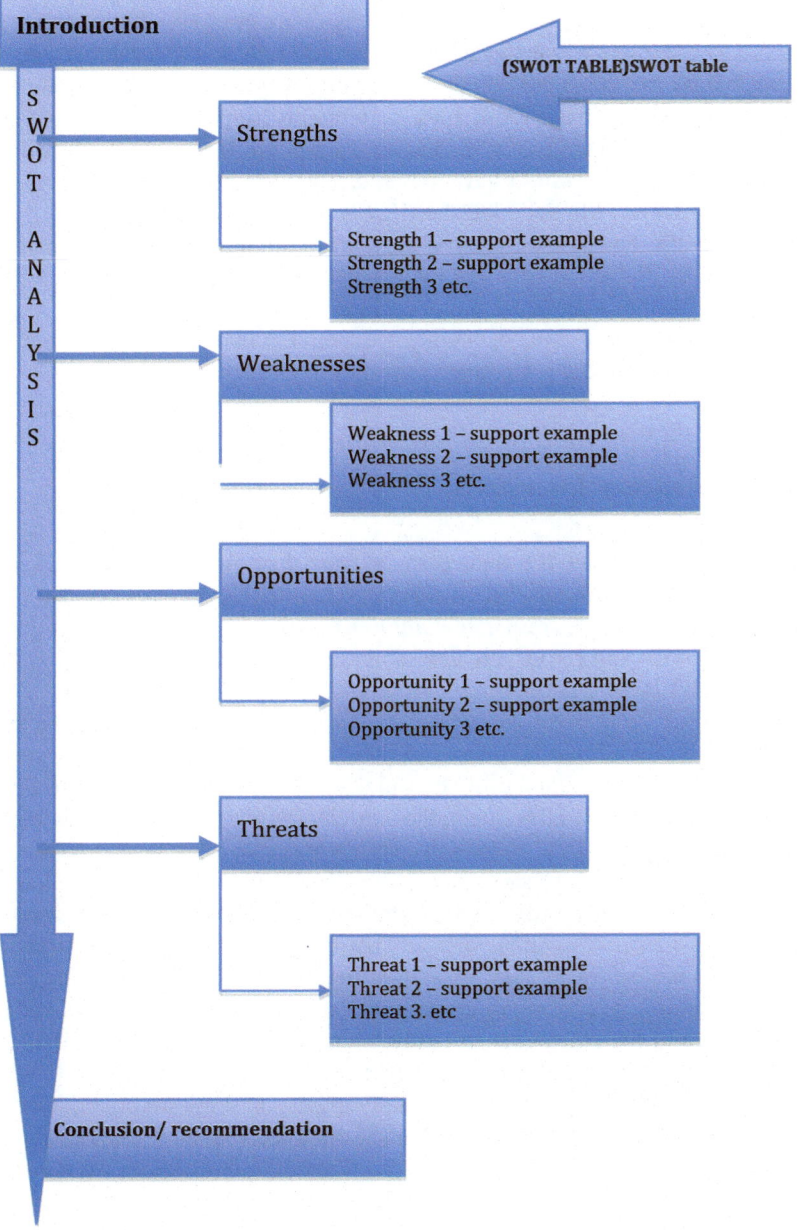

Introduction

(SWOT TABLE)SWOT table

S
W
O
T

A
N
A
L
Y
S
I
S

Strengths

Strength 1 – support example
Strength 2 – support example
Strength 3 etc.

Weaknesses

Weakness 1 – support example
Weakness 2 – support example
Weakness 3 etc.

Opportunities

Opportunity 1 – support example
Opportunity 2 – support example
Opportunity 3 etc.

Threats

Threat 1 – support example
Threat 2 – support example
Threat 3. etc

Conclusion/ recommendation

DA of academic writing Shrestha June 2020 FINAL

Fig. 4.9   Text organisation of a SWOT analysis

parameters of Feuerstein's Mediated Learning Experience stated in Chap. 2. In order to see if the learners were able to transfer their academic writing skills (e.g., writing a case study analysis) from the first two assessment tasks, all the participants were asked to complete a transfer task. While only one non-DA learner completed the transfer task that I designed, all the DA learners were asked to submit their assignment including their business studies tutor's comments from a business studies course they went on to study. These assignments were similar to DA tasks but more challenging. Ideally, all learners would have submitted an assignment from a business studies course. However, Michelle left the UK before she could complete the transfer task. Likewise, the non-DA learners were not continuing their study when they were supposed to do the transfer task and therefore, they were asked to respond to the transfer task that I designed. Lena decided to leave the project after non-DA2, but still allowed me to use the data collected from her two non-DA sessions. Therefore, only Kristie wrote the assignment in response to the transfer task.

4.5.5 Learner Interviews

In order to triangulate the data collected from the DA sessions, the DA participants were interviewed to explore their experience of writing the assignments. The purpose of triangulation in this research is *not* to capture the 'objective reality' of academic writing but to 'add rigour, breadth, complexity, richness and depth' to the inquiry (Denzin & Lincoln, 2005, p. 5).

Given the focus of my research on the process of assessment, learner perceptions can provide additional insights into their academic writing development because performance alone cannot provide explanations for what they do (van Compernolle & Williams, 2011). To this effect, the participants were interviewed twice: once after DA1 and next after DA2 to gain deeper insights into what they experienced as they went through the DA procedures. Their perceptions of the DA procedures, conceptual development and enrichment programme were explored through semi-structured telephone interviews which were recorded and transcribed. Semi-structured interviews are more flexible than structured interviews as the researcher can ask additional questions according to the response without being limited to fixed questions. It also allows the researcher to easily manage the data, unlike the data from open interviews (e.g., see Cohen et al., 2018).

Additionally, as with the DA participants, a semi-structured interview was conducted with Kristie (non-DA) after she completed all three assignments to explore her experience. The interview questions were slightly different from those asked to the DA participants to reflect the different assessment procedures they went through.

4.5.6 Subject Specialists' Views

Further triangulation of the data was conducted by seeking views of business studies tutors on the DA students' first drafts of DA1 and DA2 texts and the non-DA students' first and second assignments. For this, three business studies tutors (volunteers), with at least three years' experience of teaching business studies, were asked to assess the quality of these texts from a business studies perspective and produce a brief report. A guideline was prepared for them as reference while marking the assignments (see Fig. 4.10). The tutors used two broad criteria for marking, following the guidelines of The Quality Assurance Agency for Higher Education (QAA, 2007) for *General business and management*: cognitive skills and key skills.

The business studies tutors' judgment of the student assessment texts was expected to show the students' conceptual and academic writing development or otherwise as perceived in business studies. The use of subject specialists was successfully employed in my previous research investigating the validity of two parallel reading tests of English language (Shrestha, 2003). This method complemented the other methods used in this research (e.g., textual analysis). Most importantly, in this study, this method has been used to enhance their credibility.

To summarise, I present Fig. 4.11 which shows the sequence of DA, non-DA procedures and the data sets I have used in the subsequent chapters.

4.6 Data Analysis in Dynamic Assessment of Academic Writing

Given the nature of the context of my research being distance education and academic writing, the data analysis process is distinct from previous research on DA. Therefore, a set of specific analytical tools had to be adapted and adopted for this research which can be used for analysing data in cases where dialogic feedback and academic writing assessment from a sociocultural perspective are examined. They are also applicable to examining those aspects in action research. Each of the analytical methods is described below.

4.6.1 Thematic Analysis of Mediation Data

The mediation data (i.e., teacher-student interaction during the DA process) was thematically analysed to explore features of teacher mediation targeting learner ZPDs in the DA of academic writing in distance education. This qualitative analysis considered the amount and type of teacher mediation provided during the DA sessions which were coded by using the qualitative data analysis software NVivo 9 (QSR, 2010). Given the 'open and flexible' nature of the mediation in interactionist DA, unlike the

---

Marking guidelines for the subject tutors

Assessment guidelines (to be seen as general guidance only)

(based on the *benchmark standards* for the undergraduate level, *General Business and Management Studies 2007*, QAA)

This guidance is not intended to be comprehensive, as your view as a subject tutor on the students' assignment text is more important than whether you are able to interpret these notes accurately or not. Therefore, please use your own judgment/ discretion to comment on the areas that you would normally do when you mark your students' assignments in business studies.

When assessing/ commenting on the students' assignment texts, please, consider the following skills:

- Cognitive skills
  o Describe business concepts (e.g., SWOT, STEP) clearly (i.e., to what extent the business studies concepts are described/ defined clearly?)
  o Analyse the business case studies effectively by applying the business concepts to them (i.e., to what extent the student uses the business studies concepts to frame the analysis and how successfully?)
  o Demonstrate the relevant knowledge and understanding of the external environment in which organisations operate (i.e., to what extent the student shows that they are aware of the external environment of the company they are analysing?)
  o Identify business problems and find solutions to them (i.e., to what extent the student identifies the problem of the company and finds solutions to that problem?)
- Key skills
  o Select data, information and ideas from different sources and present in an appropriate fashion to support an argument

When you write your comments as a business studies tutor, I would like you to compare the two drafts of each student using the criteria above as far as it is possible. Your comparison of the two drafts will form a crucial aspect of my study. If you like, a table like the below can be used for marks and comments. Additionally, if you would like to make some in-text comments on the student assignment electronically, please feel free to do so.

Fig. 4.10 Marking guidelines for subject tutors

'fixed' mediation in interventionist DAs (e.g., the Leipzig Learning Test developed by Guthke and his colleagues (see Guthke & Beckmann, 2000)), it was necessary to examine the type and the amount of such mediation in detail as reported in a previous paper (Shrestha & Coffin, 2012). In order to analyse the teacher-student interaction, it was essential to develop a lens that allowed the researcher to examine it systematically. As such, the teacher-student moves during the mediation were examined by adapting Poehner's (2005) typologies of mediator and learner moves, based on Aljaafreh and Lantolf's (1994, p. 471) 13-point 'regulatory scale', which

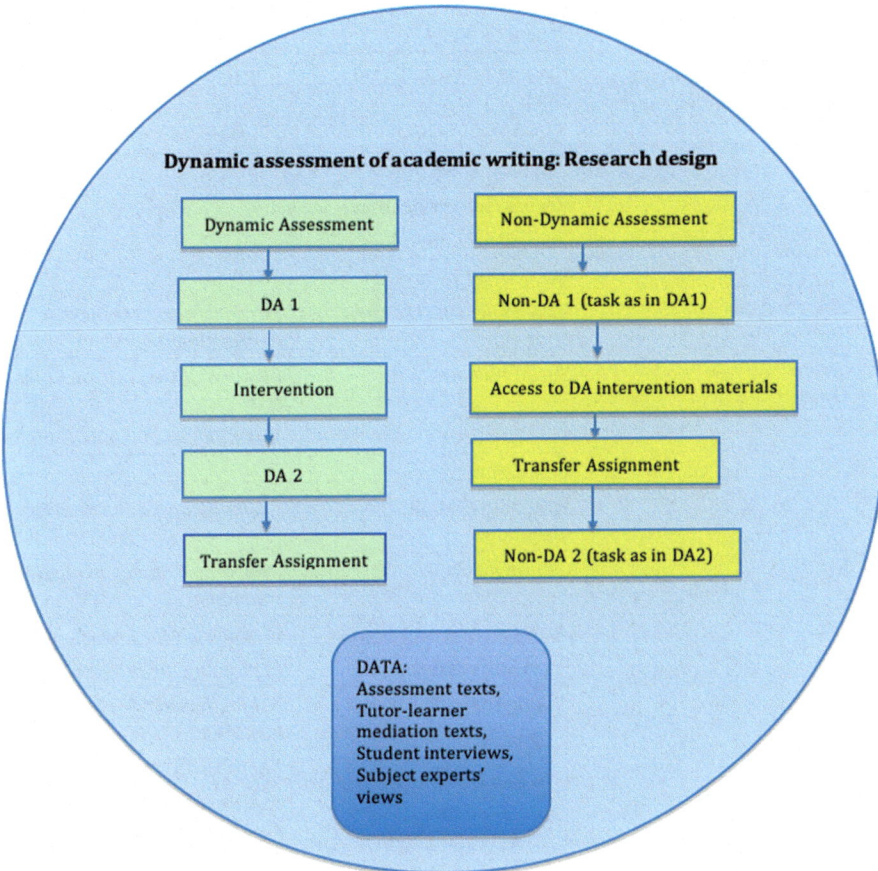

Fig. 4.11 Data collection methods

he developed in his study of advanced French learners' speaking skills. These same typologies were tested on the mediation data in my research (see Shrestha & Coffin, 2012). Inevitably, however, since Poehner's study was developed in a face-to-face context and therefore was different to my research (where the mediation took place via emails, written comments on electronic assignment texts, instant messaging and Wiki comments), these typologies had to be reworked and expanded in order to reflect the different modes of communication as well as the different subject (i.e., academic writing in business studies). A comparison between Poehner's typologies of mediational moves and those in my research are shown in Table 4.8. Any renamed and new moves are shown in bold. It is worth noting that these mediational moves, based on Shrestha and Coffin (2012), have been found effective in providing dialogic feedback in academic writing assessment in pre-sessional programmes at the English Language Centre of the University of Sheffield (Chris Smith, personal communication).

Table 4.8 Poehner's (2005, p. 160) mediational moves compared with those in my research on academic writing

Poehner's study	Current study
Helping move narration along	***Clarifying the task***
Accepting response	*Accepting a response*
Request for repetition	
Request for verification	
Reminder of directions	
Request for renarration	
Identifying specific site of error	*Locating part of the text needing improvement*
Specifying error	*Identifying the problem in the text*
Metalinguistic clues	*Providing metalinguistic clues*
Translation	
Providing example or illustration	*Exemplifying or illustrating*
Offering a choice	*Providing a choice of possible solution(s)*
Providing correct response	*Providing the correct solution*
Providing explanation	*Explaining the problem*
Asking for explanation	***Asking learner to clarify meaning***
	Showing affect
	Asking learner to identify the problem
	Providing content clues
	Rejecting the response with explanation(s)
	Asking to consider a possible solution
	Checking conceptual understanding

Among these moves, while eight moves (in italics) were retained from Poehner's mediation categories with slight adaptations, the rest of the categories (in bold) are new. These eight new categories emerged from the teacher-learner interactions in my research which did not appear in Poehner's list of categories. His list included categories such as *translation* and *request for renarration* that were irrelevant to this study. As in Poehner's study, the moves were identified as they emerged from the mediation data.

In addition to teacher moves, learner moves were analysed to consider the learner's responsiveness to teacher mediation. The student moves are called *learner reciprocity*, following Lidz (1991). Learner reciprocity is rarely investigated in the context of DA and ZPD (Ableeva, 2018; Shrestha & Coffin, 2012). Since the interaction between the mediator and the learner is dialogic, it is essential to study the learner response to the mediation which indicates learners' control (or otherwise) over their academic writing. In order to analyse the reciprocal moves, again, Poehner's typologies were adapted and expanded because the assessment context and the medium of interaction in my research were different as explained earlier. A comparison is made between Poehner's list of moves and those found in my research in Table 4.9. Any renamed and new moves are shown in bold.

As can be seen in the table, while six reciprocal moves (in italics) were retained from Poehner's typologies, **Imitating** *the mediator* was renamed as 'imitating' rather than 'repeating' as the former is commonly employed in Vygotskian sociocultural theory of learning as mentioned in Chap. 2 (see van der Veer & Valsiner, 1991, pp. 343–345; Vygotsky, 1978, pp. 87–88). The rest of the moves (in bold) were

	Poehner's study	Current study
Table 4.9 Poehner's (2005, p. 183) learner reciprocal moves compared with those in my research on academic writing	Unresponsive	*Unresponsive*
	Repeats mediator	**Imitating** *the mediator*
	Responds incorrectly	*Responding incorrectly*
	Requests additional assistance	
	Incorporates feedback	*Incorporating feedback*
	Overcomes problem	*Overcoming problems*
	Offers explanation	
	Uses mediator as a resource	*Using the mediator as a resource*
	Rejects mediator's assistance	*Rejecting the mediator's feedback*
		Asking for task clarification
		Checking conceptual understanding with mediator
		Asking for content clues
		Identifying the problem
		Explaining the problem
		Evaluating mediator feedback
		Self-assessing
		Suggesting a possible solution
		Verbalising conceptual understanding

specific to the research reported in this book. Like the mediational moves, these reciprocal moves were identified in the interaction data. I discuss the mediational data in detail in Chap. 5.

4.6.2   SFL-Based Textual Analysis of DA and Non-DA Texts

While the analysis of the mediation data provided information about the level of support given to the learners and their subsequent response, it did not give sufficient insight into learners' changing ZPDs potentially resulting from mediation while they were writing drafts of business academic writing assignments. Therefore, DA and non-DA students' assessment texts were analysed in order to complement the mediation data analysis and to examine their academic writing and conceptual development over time. For this analysis, SFL was used as the main analytical tool as explained in Chap. 3. In particular, two areas appeared to be challenging to the participants as revealed by DA1: information flow in the text (Textual meaning) and application and understanding of business concepts/frameworks (Ideational meaning). These areas were, therefore, targeted during the DA sessions and hence were examined for any academic writing development in relation to the students' ZPDs in their texts.

Textual Meanings

For Textual meanings (i.e., organisation of the message in a text), the SFL-based genre theory was used to examine both macro (e.g., macroThemes) and micro levels (e.g., hyperThemes and their development) of the texts. The analysis focussed on these aspects of the text because they featured as problematic areas during DA1 and thus were targeted in the DA process. A functional view of genre allowed the researcher to examine how well a student text was written to achieve its purpose. The specific aspects of Textual meaning examined in my research are further elaborated on in Chap. 6.

Ideational Meanings

The development of Ideational meanings in student assessment texts was related to writing a case study analysis as a genre in business studies. Producing such a text necessarily involves knowing certain business frameworks and concepts and applying them to business situations, which is a form of conceptual development. Conceptual development which formed a part of students' ZPDs in this study refers to changes in the learner's ability to use concepts in a domain such as business studies to frame phenomena in a specific context over a period of time. From a sociocultural perspective, conceptual development occurs in a situation where the learner interacts with others in a cultural group or community (e.g., see Mason, 2007; Mercer, 2008). Writing is the predominant mode in academic disciplines/communities through which students demonstrate to their teachers their conceptual development and learn disciplinary knowledge by applying such knowledge (Nesi & Gardner, 2012; Woodward-Kron, 2009). Additionally, it is widely accepted in academic writing pedagogy and research that genre awareness or genre knowledge shapes learners' thinking processes and academic writing development over time and thus it is important in academic writing development (Bazerman, 2013; Driscoll, Paszek, Gorzelsky, Hayes, & Jones, 2019; Shrestha, 2017; Tardy, 2009). Therefore, it is essential to investigate learners' developing genre knowledge. In the research reported in this book, the participants had to apply one of the two business frameworks (STEP or SWOT) and associated business concepts to their case study analysis genre. However, DA1 showed that the application of these frameworks and concepts, and the genre awareness about the case study analysis genre proved to be challenging to all the participants at varying levels, depending on their ZPDs. Therefore, the DA sessions focussed on them.

In order to measure the impact of those sessions on the participants' conceptual development, the SFL notion of *Technicality* was employed to track conceptual development (i.e., Ideational meaning) in the student assessment texts, which has been used to analyse the development of disciplinary knowledge in writing assessment research (e.g., Woodward-Kron, 2008). Technicality refers to the specialised use of a term in a particular discipline such as business studies (e.g., *marketing strategy*, *product image*). Generally Technicality is represented by definitions and taxonomies (Martin, 1993). In addition to Technicality, Abstraction is considered a characteristic of academic writing (e.g., Halliday & Martin, 1993; Hyland & Tse, 2007). It refers to abstract entities such as concepts and it is often a result of Nominalisation (e.g., turning Processes (verbs) into Things (nouns)). Nominalisations are one type of *Grammatical Metaphors* (Halliday, 1994). Abstractions are employed in academic writing to distil meanings. In this book, however, Abstractions are not treated separately from Technicality because (1) Abstractions were not an explicit focus of the DA sessions and (2) some of the Abstractions were examined under the heading of Technicality, particularly those that belonged to technical abstractions, following Woodward-Kron (2002).

The participants' genre knowledge about the case study analysis genre was also examined to gain insights into their developing academic writing repertoire. For this analysis, I drew on the notion of *Generic stages* or genre schema (potential) as it has been developed within SFL and generic staging is considered important for making meaning in academic writing (Hood, 2010; Ravelli, 2004). The specific details on Technicality and Generic stages analysed in this book are discussed in Chap. 6.

4.6.3 Thematic Analysis of the Student Interviews and Business Studies Teachers' Views

The learner interview data was scrutinised to triangulate the rest of the data and to gain an insight into the participants' experience of undergoing the DA procedures. The interviews also assisted in exploring the value of the intervention and participant perceptions of conceptual development. This data was thematically examined by looking at the features of the students' response in relation to DA procedures, conceptual development and their genre knowledge.

A thematic analysis of the business studies teachers' views on students' DA and non-DA texts was conducted to investigate the latter's conceptual and writing development as perceived in the discipline. Given the experience of these subject tutors in the field, I expected them to have a reasonably good understanding of what is valued in business studies. The purpose of this analysis was to compare subject tutors' judgment against the results from other data sets. Most importantly, the subject tutors' comments on the student assessment texts were used in order to minimise any potential researcher bias in action research (see Onwuegbuzie & Leech, 2007; van Heugten, 2004). This enhanced the validity of the results.

4.7 Summary

This chapter began with a description of the academic writing context in distance education to which DA was applied. It then described the genres of academic writing assessment in the business school, primarily focusing on the case study analysis genre which was dominant. This was followed by a description of the DA procedures used in face-to-face contexts and how these procedures were adapted and additional tools deployed for the purpose of my research. This included combining the adapted version of the existing DA procedures with the semiotic tools such as SFL-based genre theory and metafunctions (i.e., Ideational and Textual). A set of DA procedures for academic writing was provided which were unique to academic writing assessment but applicable to other academic writing pedagogy and assessment contexts in higher education. Thus, I presented an innovative approach to teaching, assessing and researching academic writing by combining a theory of assessment for learning (DA) and a comprehensive theory of language use (SFL) for evidencing learning. Furthermore, the typologies developed by Poehner were extended in this study given the nature of the subject (i.e., business studies writing) assessed and the mode of interaction (i.e., instant messaging, wiki comments and emails) employed. Since no systematic framework for examining tutor-student interactions around DA-based academic writing assessment has been reported in the literature, the typologies developed in this study provide an analytical framework for future research of this kind.

References

Ableeva, R. (2018). Understanding learner L2 development through reciprocity. In J. P. Lantolf, M. E. Poehner, & M. Swain (Eds.), *The Routledge handbook of sociocultural theory and second language development* (pp. 266–281). New York, NY: Routledge.
Aljaafreh, A., & Lantolf, J. P. (1994). Negative feedback as regulation and second language learning in the zone of proximal development. *Modern Language Journal, 78*(4), 465–483.

Bazerman, C. (2013). *A theory of literate action: Literate action* (Vol. 2). Fort Collins, Colorado: The WAC Clearinghouse and Parlor Press.

Bonanno, H., & Jones, J. (2007). *Measuring the academic skills of university students*. Sydney: Learning Centre, the University of Sydney.

Burns, A. (2010). Action research. In B. Paltridge & A. Phakiti (Eds.), *Continuum companion to research methods in applied linguistics* (pp. 80–97). London: Continuum.

Chaiklin, S. (2011). Social scientific research and societal practice: Action research and cultural-historical research in methodological light from Kurt Lewin and Lev S. Vygotsky. *Mind, Culture, and Activity, 18*(2), 129–147.

Chetwynd, F., & Dobbyn, C. (2011). Assessment, feedback and marking guides in distance education. *Open Learning: The Journal of Open, Distance and e-Learning, 26*(1), 67–78.

Coffin, C., & Donohue, J. (2014). *A language as social semiotic based approach to teaching and learning in higher education*. Malden, MA: Wiley.

Cohen, L., Manion, L., & Morrison, K. (2018). *Research methods in education* (8th ed.). Abingdon, Oxon: Routledge.

Denzin, N. K., & Lincoln, Y. S. (2005). Introduction: The discipline and practice of qualitative research. In N. K. Denzin & Y. S. Lincoln (Eds.), *The Sage handbook of qualitative research* (3rd ed., pp. 1–32). London: Sage.

Driscoll, D. L., Paszek, J., Gorzelsky, G., Hayes, C. L., & Jones, E. (2019). Genre knowledge and writing development: Results from the writing transfer project. *Written Communication*, 0741088319882313. https://doi.org/10.1177/0741088319882313.

Feldman, A. (2007). Validity and quality in action research. *Educational Action Research, 15*(1), 21–32. https://doi.org/10.1080/09650790601150766.

Feuerstein, R. (1980). *Instrumental enrichment: An intervention program for cognitive modifiability*. Baltimore: University Park Press.

Feuerstein, R., Falik, L. H., Rand, Y., & Feuerstein, R. S. (2002). *The dynamic assessment of cognitive modifiability: The learning propensity assessment device: Theory, instruments and techniques* (Revised Ed.). Jerusalem: ICELP Press.

Gardner, S. (2012). A pedagogic and professional case study genre and register continuum in business and in medicine. *Journal of Applied Linguistics and Professional Practice, 9*(1), 13–35.

Guthke, J., & Beckmann, J. F. (2000). The learning test concept and its application in practice. In C. Lidz & J. G. Elliot (Eds.), *Dynamic assessment: Prevailing models and applications* (pp. 17–70). New York: Elsevier.

Halliday, M. A. K. (1994). *An introduction to functional grammar* (2nd ed.). London: Arnold.

Halliday, M. A. K., & Martin, J. R. (Eds.). (1993). *Writing science: Literacy and discursive power*. London: The Falmer Press.

Halliday, M. A. K., & Matthiessen, C. M. I. M. (1999). *Construing experience through meaning: A language-based approach to cognition*. London: Continuum.

Hasan, R. (2005a). *The collected works of Ruqaiya Hasan. Vol. 1, Language, society and consciousness*. London: Equinox.

Hasan, R. (2005b). Semiotic mediation and three exotropic theories: Vygotsky, Halliday and Bernstein. In J. Webster (Ed.), *Language, society and consciousness: The collected works of Ruqaiya Hasan* (Vol. 1). London: Equinox.

Haywood, H. C., & Lidz, C. S. (2007). *Dynamic assessment in practice: Clinical and educational applications*. Cambridge: Cambridge University Press.

Hood, S. (2010). *Appraising research: Evaluation in academic writing*. Basingstoke; New York: Palgrave Macmillan.

Humphrey, S., Martin, J. R., Dreyfus, S., & Mahboob, A. (2010). The 3x3: setting up a linguistic toolkit for teaching academic writing. In A. Mahboob & N. Knight (Eds.), *Appliable linguistics* (pp. 185–199). London: Continuum.

Hyland, K. (2003). Genre-based pedagogies: A social response to process. *Journal of Second Language Writing, 12*(1), 17–29.

Hyland, K., & Tse, P. (2007). Is there an "academic vocabulary"? *TESOL Quarterly, 41*(2), 235–253. https://doi.org/10.2307/40264352.

Lantolf, J. P. (2000). Introducing sociocultural theory. In J. P. Lantolf (Ed.), *Sociocultural theory and second language learning* (pp. 1–26). Oxford: Oxford University Press.

Lantolf, J. P., & Poehner, M. E. (2004). Dynamic assessment of L2 development: Bringing the past into the future. *Journal of Applied Linguistics, 1*(1), 49–72.

Lantolf, J. P., & Thorne, S. L. (2006). *Sociocultural theory and the genesis of second language development*. Oxford: Oxford University Press.

Lantolf, J. P., Poehner, M. E., & Swain, M. (Eds.). (2018). *The Routledge handbook of sociocultural theory and second language development*. New York, NY: Routledge.

Lidz, C. S. (1991). *Practitioner's guide to dynamic assessment*. New York: Guilford.

Mackey, A., & Gass, S. M. (2005). *Second language research: Methodology and design*. Mahwah, NJ: Lawrence Erlbaum.

Mahn, H. (1999). Vygotsky's methodological contribution to sociocultural theory. *Remedial and Special Education, 20*(6), 341–350. https://doi.org/10.1177/074193259902000607.

Martin, J. R. (1993). Technicality and abstraction: Language for the creation of specialised texts. In M. A. K. Halliday & J. R. Martin (Eds.), *Writing science: Literacy and discursive Power* (pp. 203–220). London: The Falmer Press.

Mason, L. (2007). Introduction: Bridging the cognitive and sociocultural approaches in research on conceptual change: Is it feasible? *Educational Psychologist, 42*(1), 1–7.

Mercer, N. (2008). Changing our minds: A commentary on 'conceptual change: A discussion of theoretical, methodological and practical challenges for science education'. *Cultural Studies of Science Education, 3*(2), 351–362.

Nesi, H., & Gardner, S. (2012). *Genres across the disciplines: Student writing in higher education*. Cambridge: Cambridge University Press.

Onwuegbuzie, A., & Leech, N. (2007). Validity and qualitative research: An oxymoron? *Quality & Quantity, 41*(2), 233–249. https://doi.org/10.1007/s11135-006-9000-3.

Poehner, M. E. (2005). *Dynamic assessment of oral proficiency among advanced L2 learners of French*. Ph.D., Pennsylvania State University.

Preston, D., Fryer, M., & Watson, G. (2007). *What is a business?*. Milton Keynes: The Open University.

QAA. (2007). *General business and management*. Gloucester: The Quality Assurance Agency for Higher Education.

QSR. (2010). *NVivo qualitative data analysis software (Version 9)*. Victoria: QSR International.

Ravelli, L. J. (2004). Signalling the organisation of written texts: hyper-themes in management and history essays. In L. J. Ravelli & R. A. Ellis (Eds.), *Analysing academic writing: Contextualised frameworks* (pp. 104–130). London: Continuum.

Shrestha, P. N. (2003). *How parallel are parallel tests? A study of the two versions of the school leaving certificate (SLC) English examination (2002) in Nepal*. M.A. (TESOL), M.A. dissertation, Lancaster University.

Shrestha, P. N. (2017). Investigating the learning transfer of genre features and conceptual knowledge from an academic literacy course to business studies: Exploring the potential of dynamic assessment. *Journal of English for Academic Purposes, 25*, 1–17. https://doi.org/10.1016/j.jeap.2016.10.002.

Shrestha, P. N., & Coffin, C. (2012). Dynamic assessment, tutor mediation and academic writing development. *Assessing Writing, 17*(1), 55–70. https://doi.org/10.1016/j.asw.2011.11.003.

Somekh, B. (2010). The collaborative action research network: 30 years of agency in developing educational action research. *Educational Action Research, 18*(1), 103–121.

Tardy, C. M. (2009). *Building genre knowledge*. West Lafayette, Ind.: Parlor Press.

van Compernolle, R. A., & Williams, L. (2011). Metalinguistic explanations and self-reports as triangulation data for interpreting second language sociolinguistic performance. *International Journal of Applied Linguistics, 21*(1), 26–50. https://doi.org/10.1111/j.1473-4192.2010.00256.x.

van der Veer, R., & Valsiner, J. (1991). *Understanding Vygotsky: A quest for synthesis.* Oxford: Blackwell.

van Heugten, K. (2004). Managing insider research. *Qualitative Social Work, 3*(2), 203–219. https://doi.org/10.1177/1473325004043386.

Vygotsky, L. S. (1978). *Mind in society: The development of higher psychological processes.* Cambridge, MA: Harvard University Press.

Walker, M. (2009). An investigation into written comments on assignments: Do students find them usable? *Assessment & Evaluation in Higher Education, 34*(1), 67–78.

Wertsch, J. V. (1985). *Vygotsky and the social formation of mind.* Cambridge, MA: Harvard University Press.

Woodward-Kron, R. (2002). *Disciplinary learning through writing: An investigation into the writing of undergraduate education students.* Ph.D., University of Wollongong.

Woodward-Kron, R. (2008). More than just jargon—The nature and role of specialist language in learning disciplinary knowledge. *Journal of English for Academic Purposes, 7*(4), 234–249.

Woodward-Kron, R. (2009). "This means that…": A linguistic perspective of writing and learning in a discipline. *Journal of English for Academic Purposes, 8*(3), 165–179.

Zhu, W. (2004). Writing in business courses: An analysis of assignment types, their characteristics, and required skills. *English for Specific Purposes, 23*(2), 111–135.

Chapter 5
Teacher Mediation, Learner Reciprocity and Academic Writing Development

5.1 Introduction

In Chap. 2, I argued that research on academic writing assessment has tended to focus on 'end products' rather than the process of assessment. The research reported in this book aimed to examine both. This chapter presents the analyses of the assessment process realised through the student-teacher interaction (mediation) during the application of dynamic assessment (DA) to academic writing in business studies in a distance education context (see Chap. 4). The purpose of this chapter is to contribute to the body of research in DA regarding the value of mediation, particularly, in academic writing assessment in higher education which is under-researched. Specifically, this chapter explores what insights the learner-teacher interaction data offers into learners' academic writing development over a period of time, thus examining the *microgenetic development* (i.e., an individual's development over a short span of time) of their academic writing (see Chaps. 2 and 4).

First, I will briefly recap the purpose of mediation in the research reported, followed by a description of the data sample chosen for discussion in this chapter. Next, I will describe the process of analysing mediational data in DA of academic writing. After this, I will present and discuss the key findings based on the mediation data.

5.2 Mediation and Its Purpose in Dynamic Assessment

Vygotskian sociocultural theory contends that ontogenetic (i.e., individual) and microgenetic development cannot be fully understood through an individual's independent task performance (actual ability) alone. One needs to assess their potential ability (zone of proximal development (ZPD)) when assisted by a capable peer in order to design a learning intervention (Vygotsky, 1978). If assessment is to serve a developmental purpose, it is essential to consider the learner response during the

© Springer Nature Switzerland AG 2020
P. N. Shrestha, *Dynamic Assessment of Students' Academic Writing*,
https://doi.org/10.1007/978-3-030-55845-1_5

process of the assessment activity to which mediation is central. Mediation, as described in Chap. 2, served this purpose in my research. Such mediation created the teacher-learner interaction which helped to identify the learners' maturing academic writing abilities (i.e., ZPDs) alongside their draft assignments.

According to Vygotskian sociocultural theory (Wertsch, 2007), all human activities are mediated through physical tools (e.g., computers) or signs (e.g., language). In the context of assessing academic writing in a particular discipline, the topic of the current study, symbolic tools, particularly language and concepts, play a central role although the physical tools such as computers and other forms of information communication technology (ICT) cannot be ignored. In fact, the interaction between the teacher and the learner was enabled predominantly by emails followed by instant messaging and wiki comments. Although it is likely that the affordances of different ICT tools (e.g., synchronous versus asynchronous) influenced the nature of the interaction between the teacher and the student, my research does not specifically focus on the technological aspect. It would, however, be important to follow this up in future research. I should point out, nevertheless, that in particular the use of instant messaging had an impact on the amount and frequency of teacher moves. For a comprehensive review of research on the impact of ICT tools on student learning (and writing), readers are referred to Coffin and Hewings (2005), Crossourd and Pryor (2009), Warschauer and Ware (2008), Wertsch (2003) and Williams and Beam (2019).

The learning-assessment activities in my research were mediated by myself. The participating students and I used written English language (a symbolic tool) for all the interactions around the student assessment texts. As stated by Lund (2008), these interactions, called *semiotic mediation* in this book, were goal-directed and intentional. The semiotic mediation followed a flexible approach (Haywood & Lidz, 2007) as described in Chap. 4, in which the focus was mainly on Textual (i.e., how text is organised) and Ideational (i.e., subject matter) meanings as construed in student assignments. The nature of the technological tools used was decided through the dialogue between the teacher and the student during the assessment. The mediation ranged from implicit hints to explicit corrections depending on the response from the student.

It is worth noting that working in the learner's ZPD through flexible mediation is a challenging task. In particular, such mediation heavily relies on the mediation skill of the teacher/mediator (Haywood & Lidz, 2007). Any inappropriate mediation may lead to negative effects on learner development.

5.3   The Mediation Data Used in This Book

The *text-based interaction* between four students and me over their assignments was analysed. The text-based interaction, a form of semiotic mediation, refers to the teacher's formative feedback or comments made through computer-mediated communication (e.g., emails, wikis) on the student assignment text, which were

Table 5.1 Teacher-student interaction data

Students	Mediating tools (all written text)	DA1	DA2	Total assessment texts
Michelle	Wiki comments (DA1), emails, instant messaging (DA2), comments using Microsoft® word	4 drafts	3 drafts	7
Natasha	Emails and comments using Microsoft® word	4 drafts	3 drafts	7
Amina	Instant messaging (DA1), Emails and comments Microsoft® word	3 drafts	2 drafts	5
Lou	Emails and comments using Microsoft® word	4 drafts	3 drafts	7
Total no. of texts		15	11	26

offered to these students by following the interactionist form of DA, as described by Lantolf and Poehner (2004, pp. 54–60) and defined in Chap. 2.

This chapter discusses the teacher-student text-based interactions around 26 student assignment texts as shown in Table 5.1.

5.4   Analysing Mediational Data

The research described in this book is concerned with academic writing development of undergraduate business studies learners. In Chap. 4, I stated that this study follows Vygotsky's *genetic* method to study higher mental functioning by considering the learners' history of academic writing over a period of time, also in response to a call made by academic writing researchers (e.g., Lillis & Scott, 2007). Given the context of my research, the focus is on the learners' *microgenetic* development of writing, the fourth domain of the four in Vygotsky's genetic development research (see Chap. 2). In microgenetic research, the researcher is interested in 'the reorganisation and development of mediation over a relatively short span of time …' (Lantolf, 2000, p. 3). Following this method, the mediation data was examined to track the learners' control of academic writing development in a relatively short period of time (see Chap. 4). In particular, the mediational strategies employed by the teacher and the learners' responsiveness to such mediation in relation to the academic writing assessment tasks described in Chap. 4 (Sect. 4.5.2) were examined.

The mediation data was analysed to consider the recurring patterns of the moves made by both the teacher and the students during the mediation over a period of time. The focus of the analysis was on considering the amount and the type of the mediation provided during the DA sessions which followed 'open and flexible' interactionist DA procedures. Due to the nature of the mediation in interactionist DA, it was necessary to examine the amount and the type of such mediation in detail. Such examination helped to develop a systematic approach to analysing the mediational data. Despite mediation in DA being central, it is often challenging to carry out

(Davin, Herazo, & Sagre, 2016) and thus it is important to expand our knowledge-base through more research evidence. As explained in Chap. 4 (Sect. 4.6.1), my study adapted and expanded the list of teacher mediational moves developed by Poehner (2005) in order to suit this study and reflect the context and the subject (i.e., academic writing in business studies in distance education).

Like teacher mediational moves, learner reciprocity is rarely investigated in the context of DA and ZPD (Ableeva, 2010, 2018; Poehner, 2005, 2008; Shrestha & Coffin, 2012), let alone academic writing assessment. Since the interaction between the teacher and the learner is dialogic, it is essential to study the learner response to the mediation which indicates learners' control or self-regulation (or otherwise) over their academic writing. In order to analyse the reciprocal moves, again, Poehner's typologies were adapted and expanded as explained in Chap. 4.

5.5   Issues in Mediation Data Analysis

The teacher-student interactions were analysed by concentrating on two areas as described above: (1) mediational moves, and (2) learner reciprocity. Although it was generally clear that a teacher or learner move belonged in a particular move such as *clarifying the task*, there were occasions when the same move functioned additionally as one of the other moves, resulting in the need for 'double coding'. For example, the teacher move *locating part of the text needing improvement* appeared to function as *asking to identify the problem* as well. When this happened, the same interaction was coded more than once (i.e., belonging to more than one move), which was rare.

The difficulty in identifying the nature of a particular mediational move, as illustrated above, has been recognised in Vygotskian research on mediation (e.g., see Kozulin, 2003). One way of overcoming this difficulty is, as Kozulin (2003, pp. 21–22) proposes, to analyse the quality of mediation by considering its *type* or *purpose* and the *techniques* used to achieve the purpose. He proposed that, while analysing mediation data, it is not enough to consider what specific techniques (i.e., moves) a teacher used but also what purpose(s) they were for. When the mediational moves in my research (Table 5.2) are examined in this light, they fall into five broad pedagogical purposes, supporting Poehner's (2005) findings: managing the interaction (moves 1–3), reconsidering performance (moves 5, 6 & 8), identifying a problem (moves 4, 7, 12 & 13), probing for understanding (moves 9–11) and overcoming the problem (moves 14–16).

Likewise, it was possible that the purpose of a specific teacher move might have been misinterpreted by the learner as something else. In such a case which was rare, the mediational move was coded as intended by the teacher (i.e., myself).

5.6 Mediational Moves in Dynamic Assessment of Business Academic Writing

In this section, I present the key features of the mediational moves made by the teacher while working in the ZPD activity with the learners during their academic writing process. In my research, the mediational moves were offered for two pedagogical purposes. First, they helped to diagnose the problem areas in academic writing faced by the learner in distance education and helped identify their emerging academic writing abilities. Second, mediation, as part of a dynamic process of assessment for learning, gave the learner an opportunity to improve their academic writing skills and conceptual knowledge in business studies, thereby contributing to their academic writing development. Table 5.2 represents the mediational moves that I, as teacher/mediator, made in this study and which were first introduced in Chap. 4. Following the principle of implicit-to-explicit mediation, those moves that are more implicit are presented before those that are more explicit in the analysis of these mediational moves. A mediational move is considered *implicit* when the teacher simply offers hints or asks a question. In other words, the learner is more independent and self-regulates their learning. An *explicit* move, on the other hand, occurs when the teacher provides concrete solutions to problems or gives examples. In this case the learner is less independent (i.e., other-regulated) for their learning.

Table 5.2 Mediational moves in dynamic assessment of academic writing

Implicit (i.e., hints, prompts, etc.)	Explicit (e.g., examples, corrections, etc.)
1. Clarifying the task	9. Checking conceptual understanding
2. Accepting a response	10. Providing metalinguistic clues
3. Showing affect	11. Providing content clues
4. Asking learner to identify the problem	12. Rejecting the response with explanation(s)
5. Locating part of the text needing improvement	13. Explaining the problem
6. Asking to clarify meaning	14. Exemplifying or illustrating
7. Identifying the problem in the text	15. Providing a choice of possible solution(s)
8. Asking to consider a possible solution	16. Providing the correct solution

5.6.1 Descriptions of Mediational Moves in Dynamic Assessment of Academic Writing

1 Clarifying the Task

This move generally took place at the beginning of the session. It focused on finding out what was expected in the assessment task. The guidance notes given to the students regarding each assessment task are considered as 'clarifying the task':

Excerpt 5.1

> … As you are using the SWOT framework to analyse Google's business environment based on this case study, look for examples that illustrate the four categories (Strengths, Weaknesses, Opportunities and Threats) in the SWOT framework in order to produce an effective SWOT analysis while you are making notes… [Guidance notes, Assessment 1]

In addition, the mediator clarified what the student had to do regarding the subsequent draft as in Amina's DA1 draft 1 via instant messaging:

> *Mediator*: are you happy to revise and post it on the wiki?
>
> Amina: yes I will make changes

In this interaction, the mediator was trying to ensure that Amina understood what she had to do next.

2 Accepting a Response

When the learner responded correctly to the mediator mediation, the mediator accepted the response. This move generally occurred when the learner made an appropriate response to the academic writing assessment task or the mediator's abstract hints and clues. Sometimes this move coincided with *showing affect* (mediator move 3). Consider the excerpts below in which the mediator asked Michelle to revise the *hyperTheme* (or topic sentence) in paragraph 3 of her DA1 draft 1 to which she responded correctly:

Excerpt 5.2

> One social factor demonstrated in the case study that has had an impact on Heineken's marketing in European countries is the fact that the population started focusing on a healthier lifestyle and cutting down on alcohol consumption…
>
> *Mediator*: Can you begin this paragraph differently, that is, by telling the reader what this paragraph is about?
>
> [DA1 draft 1]
>
> The case study revealed **many social factors** in Heineken's external environment…
>
> Mediator: It was a good try. **The focus is correct: the words in blue** [in **bold** here].

3 *Showing Affect*

Affect plays a crucial role in our thinking process and motivation which has been recognised in Vygotskian sociocultural theory (Daniels, 2007). The mediator has to consider affect (i.e., learner emotional aspects) in their pedagogical moves. Yet, this aspect of mediator mediation does not appear to be widely recognised in Vygotsky-inspired research (Poehner & Swain, 2016) nor in general literature in assessment in higher education (Dawson et al., 2019). In this study, the mediator frequently took this move to encourage and keep motivating the student to complete the academic writing assessment task successfully. Additionally, it involved the mediator praising the learners for their appropriate responses. Regarding Michelle's DA1 draft 2, this is what the mediator wrote as a wiki comment:

Excerpt 5.3

> Hi Michelle,
>
> Don't worry about the delay - I can understand the pressure from all directions.
>
> Thank you for applying my feedback as closely as it is possible. You have done quite well. Now the analysis is gradually coming together.

This excerpt indicates that the mediator was trying to encourage Michelle. In fact, the student highlighted the value of such affective aspect of mediator mediation during the interview with her.

4 *Asking Learner to Identify the Problem*

Often the mediator asked the learner to identify the problem in the written text as a starting point. This helped the mediator to check how much the learner could control (i.e., self-regulate) their academic writing with very little support from him. This move occurred with all the participants. For example, the mediator asked Michelle to identify the problem in a sentence in her DA1 draft 1 (paragraph 1):

Excerpt 5.4

> … It is important for businesses to be able to identify elements which may have an effect on them and recognize its environments in which it operates…
>
> [Mediator: What is wrong with this sentence? Can you identify this?]

The mediator's intention was to get Michelle to focus on the pronoun 'it' referring to 'businesses' but without indicating what the problem was.

5 *Locating Part of the Text Needing Improvement*

This move which can be indirect (e.g., giving hints) alerted the student to the part of the text that needed improving. But the mediator did not indicate what was wrong. Often the mediator simply highlighted the words or sentences in the text and asked the student to pay attention to those words or sentences. Like the previous move, this one took place at the beginning. The problem areas ranged from spelling to grammar and paragraph themes. For instance, the mediator highlighted the words green in Natasha's DA1 draft 1 (paragraph 5) which had a grammatical inaccuracy (i.e., conjunction) affecting the information flow in the paragraph:

Excerpt 5.5

> **Despite of Heineken** [green highlight in original] has been producing non-alcohol beers mostly for non European market before., there was no good quality non alcohol beer in the market.

Instead of providing the correct solution (e.g., although), the mediator highlighted/located the words to draw Natasha's attention to them.

6 *Asking to Clarify Meaning*

Whilst the previous move simply alerted the student to a potential problem, the mediator used this move when the meaning was not clear in the text or when the content was not appropriate. The mediator did not mention explicitly what the problem was. Instead, he asked the student to think about the problem and resolve it as in the instant messaging interaction between the mediator and Amina below regarding a sentence in her DA1 draft 1 (paragraph 5):

Excerpt 5.6

> Mediator: and "Internet is main factor people use in their laptops."?
> I am not sure what this means?
> paragraph 5.
> Amina: yes
> what is the mistake
> Mediator: I don't understand this sentence: Internet is main factor people use in their laptops.
> Amina: I mean to say that, we use laptop os pc mostly to browse the net
> Mediator: ok. what is the connection with Chrome?

7 *Identifying the Problem in the Text*

Often this move overlapped with move 4 above and sometimes with move 9 below when the student failed to identify the specific problem in the text. To illustrate this move, Michelle wrote the sentence below in her DA2 draft 2 (paragraph 2) and the mediator had to identify the problem because she had an online chat with him that concentrated on the *social factor* prior to completing this draft:

Excerpt 5.7

> ... The advantage that the USA has on most other countries, however, is **their ability to afford 'Safer Syringes'**...
> *Mediator*: This is not linked with the social factor but economic.

8 *Asking to Consider a Possible Solution*

This move was used to direct the student to a suitable solution through questions. The mediator did not offer the actual solution but posed questions regarding the academic writing problem indicated (e.g., appropriate business concept). Here is an example when this move occurred:

Excerpt 5.8

> The analysis will outline how the external factors of the global beer company influenced the **start** of a new non-alcoholic product.
>
> Mediator: Can you use a different word here instead of 'start'?
>
> [Natasha's DA1 draft 1, paragraph 1]

9 *Checking Conceptual Understanding*

The assessment tasks in both DA1 and DA2 required the students to use a business framework (e.g., STEP) and relevant business concepts in their case study analysis. Both the framework and the text organisation needed a good conceptual understanding of what is needed to complete the task. Therefore, the mediator often checked the students' conceptual understanding when needed during the assessment process as shown by the example below:

Excerpt 5.9

> Social factors, covering demographical and cultural aspects of the environment external to the Safer Syringe market are population awareness, **number of workers involved in the industry…**
>
> Mediator: Is the number of workers a social factor? Or something else?
>
> [DA2 draft 1]

In this excerpt, the mediator was checking Michelle's understanding of the *social factor* in the assignment because the words in bold above could actually be related to the *economic factor* as the cost of treating a number of workers injured was high.

10 *Providing Metalinguistic Clues*

The mediator often supported the students by offering metalinguistic clues such as 'pronouns' and 'punctuation marks' to identify problems. In addition, this move also included providing conceptual knowledge in the field (i.e., business studies). This technique was used in order to enhance the students' conceptual knowledge (language and content both) when more implicit moves did not work. This move is illustrated in the two excerpts below where a more implicit move failed with Michelle (the focus is on text development here):

Excerpt 5.10

> … According to Donohue et al. (2008 p. 25) whilst organisations usually have control over the near environment, it is the wider environment which controls **the organisation**…
>
> Mediator: Can you use any other word instead of 'the organisation'?
>
> [DA1 draft 1, paragraph 2]

Excerpt 5.11

> … According to Donohue et al. (2008 p. 25) whilst organisations usually have control over the near environment, it is the wider environment which can greatly influence the business…
>
> Mediator: Can you use **a pronoun** instead of 'the business'?
>
> [DA1 draft 2, paragraph 2]

11 *Providing Content Clues*

It was often necessary to offer support to the students regarding the business content of the case study analysis. For this, the mediator posed questions directed at the relevant business content and concepts in the case study. For instance, the mediator asked questions indicating the pertinent content when Natasha failed to include more social factors in DA1 draft 2:

Excerpt 5.12

> *Mediator:* I also asked you to think about the other sociological factors as indicated in the case study. **What do Italian bars do? Has this affected Buckler?**

12 *Rejecting the Response with Explanation(s)*

There were occasions when the response given by the student in the subsequent draft was rejected by the mediator if the student did not respond correctly to the feedback given previously. This move was geared towards more explicit support which often included the mediator's explanation for his response. The following shows the mediator rejecting the learner response with an explanation (concentrating on conceptual development):

Excerpt 5.13

> The analysis will outline how the external factors of the global beer company influenced **the start** of a new non-alcoholic product…
>
> Mediator: You did not change the word 'start' as I advised. It is alright to use the word 'launch' from the case study. This word is more formal/academic or related to business studies.
>
> [Natasha's DA1 draft 2 introduction]

13 *Explaining the Problem*

There were times when the mediator had to explain the problem in the text explicitly. This move was necessary to make the learner understand the nature of the problem thereby enhancing their conceptual understanding as well. For instance, Amina continued to have problems with using the key concepts from the SWOT framework when she was writing up DA1 drafts 1 and 2 in her Google case study analysis. She tended to combine *opportunities* and *threats* in its external business environment and the mediator had to explain what the problem was via the instant messaging. Excerpt 5.14 illustrates this move:

Excerpt 5.14

Amina: I have mention the threats also

Mediator: in the same paragraph? That is actually true about this paragraph (2).

Amina: yes

Mediator: you compared Chrome with Microsoft.

Amina: I tried to compare the opportunity with a threat

Mediator: I think it is better to separate them out. If they are together, they can be confusing.

Amina: Ok

14   *Exemplifying or Illustrating*

If the student was unable to grasp the concept or understand a problem in the text, the mediator provided support through examples. For example, in DA1 draft 1, Natasha was advised to revise the opening (topic) sentence so as to link it with the analytical framework (STEP) because there was a problem with the text development. However, she did not do this effectively and so the mediator responded with exemplification like this:

Excerpt 5.15

Mediator: As I commented before this sentence needs to be revised because it is not properly connected to the framework of the analysis: STEP/STEEP. You should start with the main idea in the paragraph. **For example, you can say** 'Sociological factors impacted on the development of Buckler beer. One of them is …' Please try yourself once again."

[Natasha's DA1 draft 2, paragraph 2]

15   *Providing a Choice of Possible Solution(s)*

This move was required when the students failed to solve the problem themselves or kept repeating the problem. In this move, the mediator offered choice(s) as to what they could write in the text, thereby providing more explicit assistance to the learner. For example, Natasha kept on using 'despite' where 'although' or 'even though' should have been used in her DA1 drafts. Therefore, the mediator responded as below:

Excerpt 5.16

Despite [highlighted in original] Heineken has been producing non-alcohol beers mostly for non European market before., there was no good quality non alcohol beer in the market.

Mediator: The highlighted words [in bold here] in this sentence need your attention. 'despite' cannot be used here. You can use 'although' instead.

16   *Providing the Correct Solution*

This move provided the highest level of support (i.e., offering an actual 'answer') given to the students when no other techniques worked. For example, Amina continued to have problems with writing the opening sentence (i.e., hyperTheme) in a paragraph that analysed an aspect of SWOT (e.g., strengths) in DA1 drafts 1 and 2. Therefore, the mediator wrote the appropriate hyperTheme for the paragraph that analysed Google's strengths as in Excerpt 5.17 (see **bold** and *italic* words):

Excerpt 5.17

> Mediator: now let's look at *strengths*. The beginning sentence is still a problem.
>
> Amina: yes
>
> Mediator: **actually, I am going to do this first paragraph for you and ask you to do the rest. is that ok with you?**
>
> Amina: ok
>
> Mediator: the main problem is not using the *key concept* (here *strengths*) to frame your paragraph.
>
> **Begin with something at a more general level**: Google has several strengths compared to its competitors.
>
> Amina: heading can not cover that?
>
> Mediator: no, not really. see my example in my previous response. do you see?
>
> Amina: yes

5.6.2 Dynamicity of Mediational Moves

As shown by Table 5.2, each category of mediational moves indicates the type of support given that ranged from implicit hints to explicit corrections, thus, following Aljaafreh and Lantolf's (1994) regulatory scale in principle. The order of these moves was, nevertheless, not linear, but dynamic, unlike in the interventionist DA in which the teacher uses the same move for each learner in the same order (Lantolf & Poehner, 2004). Rather, in line with Vygotsky's discussion of learning and development (1978, pp. 79–91), dialogic mediation designed to address individual learner's needs was offered to each DA learner in each DA session. This resulted in providing different forms of mediation to each learner although their independent performance may have indicated the same level regarding certain aspects of academic writing (e.g., text organisation). This means I did not offer the same type and amount of mediation in the same order in each DA session. Instead, I was free to use any mediational move that I considered appropriate for the learner response. For example, once I (Mediator) identified the problem in the text (mediational move 7), Michelle incorporated the feedback (learner move 12, see Table 5.4 for learner moves) and overcame the problem (learner move 16) in her DA1 drafts 1 and 2 as shown by the teacher/mediator-learner interaction below:

Excerpt 5.18

> Michelle's DA1 draft 1
>
> The STEP framework analyses current and continuing influences on an organisation's external environment and from the case study, it is evident that a number of different **influences impact** on Heineken as an International Organisation.

Mediator: The words in blue [bold here] in this sentence make the sentence difficult to follow. Can you try rephrasing them?

Michelle incorporated the feedback and responded:

The STEP framework analyses current and continuing influences on an organisation's external environment and from the case study, it is evident that a number of external factors have influenced Heineken's marketing approach as an International Organisation. [draft 2, changed text in bold]

Moving from more implicit to increasingly explicit assistance allowed me to identify the learner's maturing academic writing abilities (ZPD), which does not necessarily happen in other forms of formative writing assessment. As an example of an *implicit* mediational move, in Excerpt 6.2 below, I used a highlighter to indicate minor problems without stating the problem (*move 4: Asking learner to identify problem*) in Lou's DA1 first draft and asked her to improve the Theme of the paragraph by locating the text (*move 5*):

Excerpt 5.19

Paragraph 1

Google hopes to **capure** new clients with their ideas for developing a operating system, which they plan to be faster for the future…

Mediator: This beginning sentence does not tell the reader what this paragraph is about. How can you do this?]

A more explicit mediational move was required when the learner was unable to address the academic writing problem identified. For instance, I had commented on Natasha's DA1 drafts 1 and 2 regarding the problem with the Theme (topic) sentence of paragraph 5 in her assessment text. Although she tried to make changes, they were not effective. Therefore, I had to make an explicit move, exemplifying how to write the Theme sentence in her third draft (*move 14: Exemplifying or illustrating*) as shown in Excerpt 6.3 below:

Excerpt 5.20

Paragraph 5

There were obvious benefit of political regulations which helped the company introducing Buckler…

Mediator: You need to introduce the political factors like other factors above. You could begin like this: Finally, political factors also influenced Heineken's marketing of Buckler. The most obvious factor was the government regulations in various countries. For example,
….

Thus, my mediational strategies of moving from implicit to explicit assistance allowed me to identify the students' ZPDs as illustrated by the excerpts above. It is also worth noting in my mediation language that I kept the option open by using the modal verb 'could' instead of making it the only way. Through such strategies, not only could I identify the students' ZPDs in academic writing but also could diagnose problems and provide support accordingly. It should also be mentioned that some moves such as *clarifying the task,* and *showing affect* were included in the list as they contributed to my pedagogical moves and the learner's response.

Now I would like to turn to the frequency and the type of the mediation during the DA procedures in DA1 and DA2 for the four participants to investigate the learners' ZPDs while supporting them with their academic writing.

5.6.3   Academic Writing Support in the ZPD

The analysis of teacher-learner interactions allows educators to identify changing ZPDs over time. Such development is manifested in the type and the amount of mediation required for the learner to complete an assessment task in addition to their improved independent performance (Aljaafreh & Lantolf, 1994; Poehner, 2005). Based on the typologies presented in 5.6.1 (Table 5.2), a summary of the actual mediational moves is given in Table 5.3. The number for each move indicates the instances of each move I made for each learner during DA1 and DA2.

Table 5.3 shows that the teacher employed varied levels of mediational strategies for each learner in each DA session. However, it should be noted that the use of instant messaging with Amina during DA1 increased the number of mediational moves in DA1. These moves indicate different ZPDs of each learner. For example, while I did not apply moves 12, 13 and 16 for Michelle in DA1, I did so for the other three learners, thus applying flexible mediation approach as proposed by Haywood and Lidz (2007). Likewise, some moves such as 5 and 8 were more frequent than others. The large number of these two mediational moves (i.e., 5 and 8) suggests that I employed less explicit mediation strategies where possible (see Table 5.2). For example, *Asking to consider a possible solution* (move 8) involved directing the student to a suitable solution through questions. I did not offer the actual solution but posed questions relating to the problem indicated. The following example (Excerpt 5.21) illustrates how I deployed this move. My comments focus on the introductory paragraph (or macroTheme) in Natasha's DA1 draft 1.

Excerpt 5.21

> P1 The analysis will outline how the external factors of the global beer company influenced the start of a new non-alcoholic product. Although, Heineken was producing non-alcohol beers before, there was a desirable opportunity for launching a new brand. The STEEP analysis lists the circumstances of the Buckler's born.
>
> *Mediator: This [last] sentence is not linked well with the previous sentence. Could you try again?*
>
> *This is your introduction to the analysis, do you need to say what STEEP is?*
>
> [Natasha's DA1 draft 1]

The frequency figures in Table 5.3 additionally indicate that I had made more mediational moves in DA1 than in DA2. One explanation, as mentioned earlier, was the use of instant messaging with Amina during DA1 for the interaction although it was used partially with Michelle too in DA2. The total number of mediational moves

Table 5.3 Type and frequency of mediational moves in dynamic assessment of academic writing

Mediational moves	Amina		Lou		Michelle		Natasha	
	DA1	DA2	DA1	DA2	DA1	DA2	DA1	DA2
1. Clarifying the task	3	2	2	0	1	3	0	5
2. Accepting a response	24	0	7	6	5	4	3	0
3. Showing affect	8	3	11	10	10	7	3	7
4. Asking learner to identify the problem	13	8	8	5	8	0	4	11
5. Locating part of the text needing improvement	9	9	14	8	19	5	10	15
6. Asking to clarify meaning	11	2	6	14	0	1	0	3
7. Identifying the problem in the text	12	1	6	2	2	8	8	3
8. Asking to consider a possible solution	27	12	26	21	18	8	29	11
9. Checking conceptual understanding	14	11	5	4	2	2	2	0
10. Providing metalinguistic clues	24	9	20	13	6	8	17	2
11. Providing content clues	27	7	11	9	2	13	3	2
12. Rejecting the response with explanation(s)	4	2	2	4	0	2	3	2
13. Explaining the problem	14	3	3	2	0	3	3	1
14. Exemplifying or illustrating	6	4	3	3	1	0	6	0
15. Providing a choice of possible solution(s)	11	5	2	6	1	4	5	1
16. Providing the correct solution	20	5	12	12	0	10	9	7
Total	227	83	138	119	75	78	105	70

fell in DA2 for Amina (from 227 to 83) because she opted for email communication instead of instant messaging for the interaction. Particularly influenced by instant messaging was move 2 (*Accepting a response*) which was significantly higher in my interaction with Amina in DA1 than with others. Instant messaging involved an immediate response from participants (i.e., sense of immediacy), almost resembling face-to-face spoken interactions (e.g., see Sweeny, 2010). Such interactions allowed limited reflection and thinking time compared to email interactions. Therefore, there would be more turn-taking and thus an increase in instances of the moves. Again, although not a focus of this study, it would be important to pursue the influence of ICT tools such as instant messaging in future research on dynamic assessment in distance education.

However, from Table 5.3, it can also be seen that the mediational moves for both Lou and Natasha who did not use instant messaging decreased significantly in Natasha's case and slightly in Lou's in DA2. Despite the use of instant messaging with Michelle in DA2, the mediational moves increased only slightly (i.e., from 75 to 78). Therefore, it can be argued that, except for Amina whose final version of DA2 still needed some work (see Chap. 6), the other three learners may have increased their control (i.e., self-regulation) of academic writing skills and conceptual knowledge because they appeared to need less support to accomplish the second assignment task (DA2) which was similar to the first assignment (DA1). Thus, the analysis points to the likely appropriateness of the mediation strategies adopted by the mediator and the enrichment study material on academic writing.

Figure 5.1 demonstrates the distribution of the mediational strategies I used across DA1 and DA2. In total, there were 895 mediational moves. Moves 5 (*Locating part of the text needing improvement*), 8 (*Asking to consider a possible solution*) and 10 (*Providing metalinguistic clues*) featured the most. Among these three, move 10, a more explicit move, had the second highest frequency.

The reason for this was that it not only included teacher comments on metalinguistic clues such as 'pronouns' and 'punctuation marks' to identify problems but also those that related to business conceptual frameworks and text development (i.e., generic stages of a case study analysis). Regarding the latter, as revealed by the learners' performance, I had to concentrate on the application of the STEP/SWOT

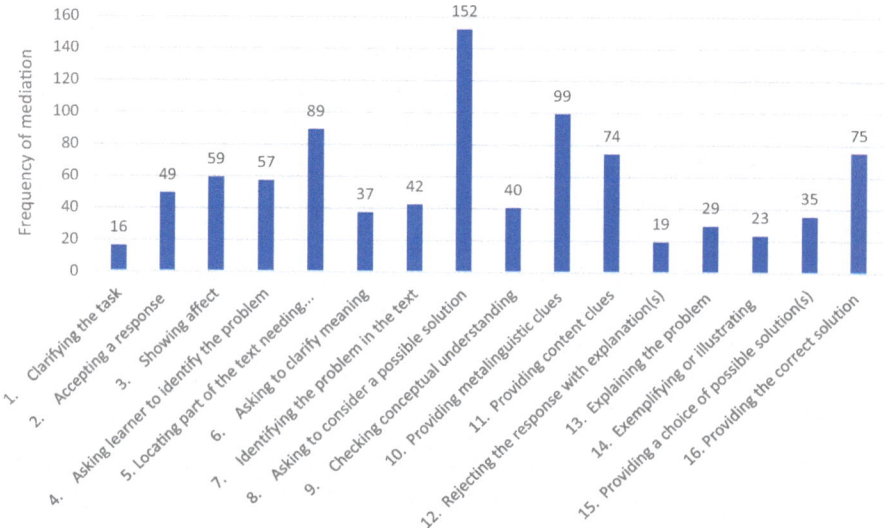

Fig. 5.1 Distribution of mediational moves across DA1 and DA2

frameworks in business studies and text development features such as paragraph hyperThemes and macroTheme (traditionally called topic sentence and Introduction respectively). This technique (i.e., move 10) was used in order to enhance the students' conceptual knowledge (i.e., case study analysis genre awareness, academic language and business content) when more implicit moves did not work. For instance, from Amina's DA1 first draft it was clear that she had not fully grasped the concept of hyperThemes. Almost all her paragraphs had no hyperTheme or had no link with the SWOT framework in the case study analysis. Therefore, I focussed mediation on this aspect (underlined) through instant messaging as illustrated in the example below. Amina (A) and I (M) were discussing her paragraph on Google's Strengths.

Excerpt 5.22

> A: strengths
>
> M: but you have not mentioned it in the text.
>
> in paragraph 1.
>
> A: how can I mention
>
> put a heading
>
> M: yes, one way is to give it a sub-heading but there's one more thing that you need to do - the beginning sentence.
>
> how can the beginning sentence help the reader that this paragraph is about strengths?
>
> [Instant messaging on DA1 draft 1, paragraph 2]

Additionally, Fig. 5.1 demonstrates that the least used strategies were *Clarifying the task* (move 1), *Rejecting the response with explanation(s)* (move 12), *Explaining the problem* (move 13), *Exemplifying or illustrating* (move 14) and *Providing a choice of possible solution(s)* (move 15). Whilst clarifying the task was mainly for managing the interaction (i.e., implicit), the other four strategies were more explicit and concrete. The low number of these moves reflects the flexible mediation principle followed in this study: moving from implicit to explicit mediation. However, the extent of these strategies was not the same for each learner as demonstrated by Table 5.3. These differences suggest varying levels of each learner's ZPD. Additionally, such differences may have been a result of the time and length of interactions between the student and me, or possibly that I was not identifying the ZPDs sufficiently.

In order to observe any microgenetic development of the four learners, it is necessary to compare the mediational moves that I used in DA1 with those in DA2, assuming that I was accurately identifying and working with their changing ZPDs. Figures 5.2 and 5.3 summarise the mediational moves in DA1 and DA2 respectively.

These two figures show that while *Providing metalinguistic clues* (move 10) had the second highest frequency in DA1 (12%), *Locating part of the text needing improvement* (move 5) came second in DA2 (11%). As stated before, the former is a more explicit move than the latter. This indicates the probability that the learners' ZPD level has moved to a higher level.

The difference of all the mediational moves across DA1 and DA2 can clearly be observed in Fig. 5.4. It shows that all the moves had higher frequencies in DA1 than

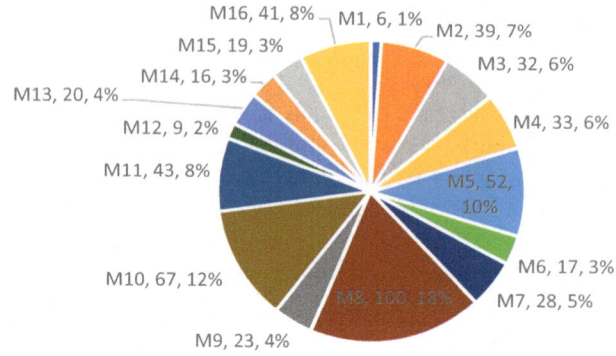

- 1. Clarifying the task
- 3. Showing affect
- 5. Locating part of the text needing improvement
- 7. Identifying the problem in the text
- 9. Checking conceptual understanding
- 11. Providing content clues
- 13. Explaining the problem
- 15. Providing a choice of possible solution(s)

- 2. Accepting a response
- 4. Asking learner to identify the problem
- 6. Asking to clarify meaning
- 8. Asking to consider a possible solution
- 10. Providing metalinguistic clues
- 12. Rejecting the response with explanation(s)
- 14. Exemplifying or illustrating
- 16. Providing the correct solution

Fig. 5.2 Distribution of all mediational moves in DA1

Fig. 5.3 Distribution of all
mediational moves in DA2

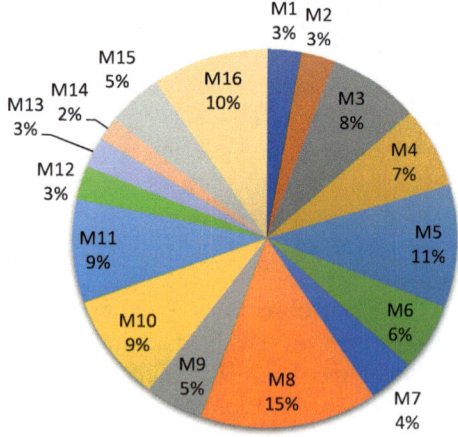

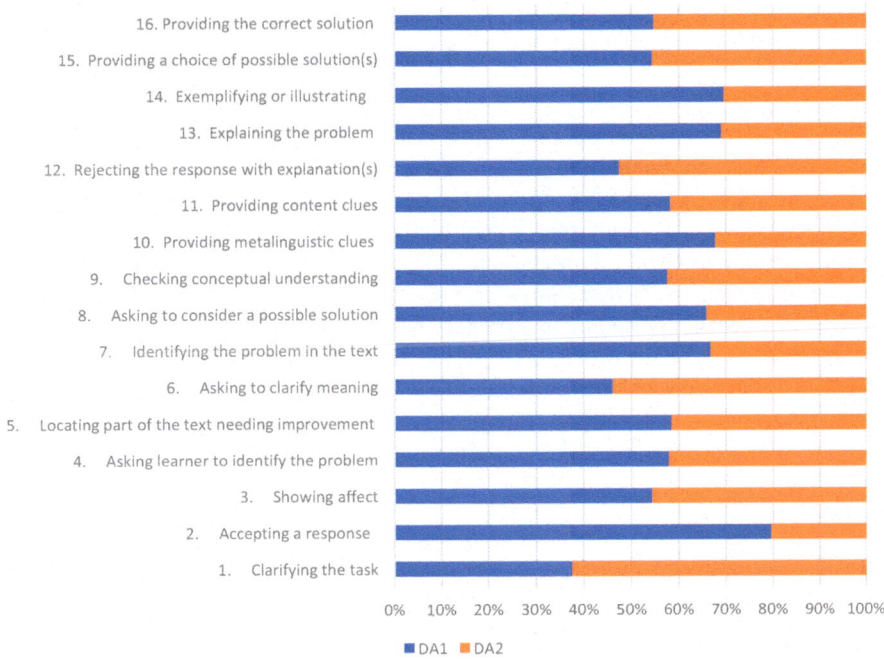

Fig. 5.4   Comparison of mediational moves: DA1 and DA2

those in DA2 except moves 1 (*Clarifying the task*), 6 (*Asking to clarify meaning*) and 12 (*Rejecting the response with explanation(s)*). This difference implies (again based on the assumption that I was correctly identifying and working with learners' ZPDs) that the learners were increasingly taking control of their academic writing (i.e., more student self-regulation). The fewer explicit moves in DA2 also indicate that the dynamic procedures used in DA1 may have been sufficiently sensitive to the learners' ZPDs, with the aim of enhancing their academic writing development.

To sum up, the frequency of mediation with the four DA learners at two different times (i.e., DA1 and DA2) suggests positive changes in their academic writing development although these changes may not be significant in quantity. However, the qualitative changes observed at these two points in time were generally positively different as shown by the type of mediation needed over time.

Next, learners' responsiveness to teacher mediation during the application of dynamic assessment procedures to academic writing in distance education is discussed as revealed by my research.

5.7   Learner Reciprocity: Insights into Academic Writing Development of Distance Learners

Learner reciprocity, as mentioned earlier, is under-researched in DA although learner responsiveness to mediation plays a pivotal role in identifying and developing learners' ZPDs (Ableeva, 2018). In response to this paucity in research, especially in academic writing, my paper which examined two learners' learner reciprocity in the context of dynamic assessment of academic writing in distance education was published as a first step (Shrestha & Coffin, 2012). Since that publication, a few studies have been reported in the literature which, however, do not focus on academic writing. Building on the previous paper, this section expands that paper by examining four learners' reciprocal moves in the context of academic writing assessment. These responses included not only the direct responses to mediation but also those that the learners themselves initiated (e.g., reflection on their progress).

5.7.1   Analysing Learner Reciprocity in Dynamic Assessment of Academic Writing

In order to analyse learner reciprocal moves, Poehner's (2005) *learner reciprocity typology* discussed in Chap. 4 (see 4.6.1, Table 4.9) was used as a starting point. Poehner's list of learner reciprocal moves were adapted and expanded for this study. The list of reciprocal moves which emerged from the data for this study (first introduced in Chap. 4) are re-presented here in Fig. 5.5. These moves are described in detail in 5.7.2.

While the mediational moves were dependent on the degree of their implicitness or explicitness, learner reciprocity moves were analysed by how much the learners took responsibility for handling the assignment tasks (i.e., degree of self-regulation

More dependent	More independent
1. *Asking for task clarification*	9. *Explaining the problem*
2. *Unresponsive*	10. *Evaluating teacher feedback*
3. *Imitating the teacher*	11. *Self-assessing*
4. *Using the teacher as a resource*	12. *Incorporating feedback*
5. *Checking conceptual understanding with teacher*	13. *Suggesting a possible solution*
6. *Responding incorrectly*	14. *Verbalising conceptual understanding*
7. *Asking for content clues*	15. *Rejecting the teacher's feedback*
8. *Identifying the problem*	16. *Overcoming problems*

Fig. 5.5 Learner reciprocity moves

by students). From this perspective, moves 9–16 can be considered more independent than moves 1–8.

The order of these learner moves as shown in Table 5.4 reflects the degree of assistance required by the learner. For instance, *Imitating the teacher* (move 3) comes before *Using the teacher as a resource* (move 4) because the latter requires more learner responsibility than the former.

As explained earlier, one possible reason for the learner variation (i.e., number of responses) is the medium of communication used by Amina in DA1 and Michelle in DA2 although there may be other contextual factors responsible for such variation. While Natasha and Lou communicated by email only, Michelle and Amina used wiki comments, email and instant messaging and their communication with me was more frequent. As with the teacher mediation typologies, the same learner response appeared to function at times as more than one learner move. Therefore, sometimes there were overlaps regarding a particular learner response and so such responses were double-coded.

5.7.2 Descriptions of Learner Reciprocal Moves in Dynamic Assessment of Academic Writing

1 Asking for Task Clarification

This move generally took place at the start of DA when the learners wanted to check their understanding of the academic writing assessment task. Sometimes, it happened later as well although the guidance notes on the task were provided. For example, Michelle wanted to get some clarification regarding the content of her DA1 draft 3:

Excerpt 5.23

> … I have edited the words in blue and **to clarify**, can I go ahead and fill in as much information as needed or stick to the 500 word limit. If I can fill in the political and economical bits, I think it will give it a bit more as an analysis but as I said before I was trying to stick to the word limit. **Please let me know**…
>
> [wiki comment]

2 Unresponsive

The learners did not respond to some of the mediator moves. However, it was not known why they did not respond. For instance, Natasha did not respond to the mediator's comment made in DA1 draft 1 regarding *social factors* when she wrote her draft 2 as shown below:

Excerpt 5.24

> **… The changes in social environment had provided a good base to the success of Buckle**.
> [last sentence in the paragraph]

Mediator: Are there any other social factors?

[DA1 draft 1]

The changes in social environment had provided a good base to the success of Buckler.
[last sentence in the paragraph]

[DA1 draft 2]

3   *Imitating the Mediator*

The learners generally followed this move when they were offered a solution to the problem which they could not resolve themselves. This move indicated the learner's low level of independence (i.e., other-regulation). However, imitating or repeating a more capable peer is considered a step towards learning (e.g., see Chaiklin, 2003). For instance, Michelle repeated the suggestion (in bold) given by the mediator in this sentence:

> Those **who suffer these injuries are mainly** the health care workers who **are** exposed to ... (DA2 final draft).

4   *Using the Mediator as a Resource*

Often this move occurred when the learners were not entirely sure about what they were doing. This move indicated that the learner was taking some responsibility for their academic writing development but needed support. To exemplify this move, in Michelle's DA1 draft 1, the mediator asked her to change the 9th sentence in the text as it was not an effective opening sentence (hyperTheme) in the paragraph. In response, Michelle wrote draft 2 and left a comment in the wiki as shown by Excerpt 5.25:

Excerpt 5.25

> (9) **One social factor** demonstrated in the case study that has had an impact on Heineken's marketing in European countries is the fact that the population started focusing on a healthier lifestyle and cutting down on alcohol consumption.
>
> Mediator: Can you begin this paragraph differently, that is, by telling the reader what this paragraph is about?
>
> [Michelle's DA1 draft 1]
>
> (9) **The case study revealed many social factors in Heineken's external environment**. (10) One factor which greatly influenced Heineken's marketing strategy was their location in Europe and the fact that the culture in these countries started focusing on healthier lifestyles and less alcohol consumption.
>
> Michelle: *Sentence 9 I tried to change the beginning but I am not sure if I was successful so you will let me know. Beginners is something I really have to work on when expressing myself in writing these essays.*
>
> [Michelle's DA1 draft 2]

5   *Checking Conceptual Understanding with Mediator*

An understanding of business concepts and frameworks as well as case study analysis as a genre is important for successfully writing a case study analysis. This move occurred when the participants were unsure about them. Except Natasha, for example, all three DA students checked their conceptual understanding with the mediator regarding the conceptual framework (e.g., STEP framework) to be used in the case study analysis when they needed. Here is an example from Michelle's response:

Excerpt 5.25

> Michelle: in using the first [social] factor
>
> Mediator: yes?
>
> Michelle: changes and attitudes of infected workers, **how do i link this to the effect**
>
> for e.g.
>
> **becasue i dont understand how to link it to the effect**
>
> [Instant messaging, during DA2 draft 2]

6   *Responding Incorrectly*

This type of move occurred when the learner tried to respond incorrectly to the mediator mediation around a problem indicated in the text. Although the response was incorrect, the learner took more responsibility to resolve the problem. Consider the excerpt below in which Natasha changed from 'despite of' in DA1 draft 1 to 'despite' in DA1 draft 2 after the mediator asked her to think about the problem:

Excerpt 5.26

> **Despite** Heineken has been producing non -alcohol beers mostly for non European market before., there was no good quality non alcohol beer in the market. …
>
> [DA1 draft 2, paragraph 5]

7   *Asking for Content Clues*

The learners were sometimes not sure about the information to be retrieved from the case study for their analysis. Therefore, they often asked the teacher-mediator for clues or support. For example, Michelle was not so sure about the social factors in the DA2 task:

Excerpt 5.27

> … **But I am a little stuck and it is only on the social factors** because the others are so clear cut to find but **the social so confuses me …**
>
> [Instant messaging, DA2 draft 2].

8   *Identifying the Problem*

A more independent learner move occurred when the learners were able to identify the problem in the text without the mediator's help. However, this did not mean that they could solve the problem. This kind of move tended to be a form of self-assessment as well:

Excerpt 5.28

> Michelle: … What I also found a bit difficult is the ability to fit the relevant information under the correct headings…
>
> [email with DA2 draft 1]

9 *Explaining the Problem*

In addition to identifying the problem, some students were able to explain the nature of the problem. For instance, when the mediator asked Natasha to add the environmental factors to her DA1 draft 2 which required her to analyse the external macro business environment of a product called Safer Syringe by using the STEEP (Social, Technological, Economic, Environmental and Political) framework, she explained why she had not done this:

> Environmental factors: I have not found relevant information to this category in the case study…

10 *Evaluating Mediator Feedback*

It was notable that two students evaluated the value of the mediator feedback for their writing. Such evaluation indicates what kind of feedback works for them and how the mediator can respond in future. Here is an excerpt from Michelle:

Excerpt 5.29

> … I am ready to finish the step analysis now and **I am confident that the guidelines u sent me will make all the difference. I forgot about cause and effect so that is really good that you reminded me…**
>
> [email during DA2 draft 2]

11 *Self-assessing*

Self-assessment regarding her writing style was quite common in Michelle's response and once in Amina's but never appeared in the other two. Assessing one's progress is a form of reflective learning which contributes to learning and development (Wells, 1999, pp. 159–160). For example, Michelle reflected on her paragraph development thus:

Excerpt 5.30

> … Beginners [topic sentence] is something I really have to work on when expressing myself in writing these essays. I am still adjusting to this style of writing so please bear with me…
>
> [DA1 draft 2]

12 *Incorporating Feedback*

This is naturally the commonest move made by the students in response to the mediator mediation. This move generally led to writing a better text. The learner was able to handle the problem with some mediator support in this reciprocal move.

Natasha, for example, was having difficulty in writing an effective Theme sentence of the paragraph. Once the mediator gave an example, she was able to write such sentences for the rest of her DA1 draft 3 text. Consider the excerpt below which had no theme sentence or hyperTheme (bold) in paragraph 2 of her DA1 drafts 1 and 2:

Excerpt 5.31

> **Social factors**: People awareness of towards a healthier lifestyle has increased in recent years. The demand for less harmful products, for example, non-alcohol beers has grown. In addition, there was already a request for a new enhanced brand in Spain. The changes in social environment had provided a good base to the success of Buckle.
>
> Mediator: *Can you link this factor [in bold above] to your framework by writing a sentence?*
>
> [DA1 draft 1]
>
> Social factors: The public awareness of towards a healthier lifestyle has increased in recent years. The demand for less harmful products, for example, non-alcohol beers has grown. In addition, there was already a request for a new enhanced brand in Spain. The changes in social environment had provided a good base to the success of Buckler.
>
> Mediator: *As I commented before this sentence needs to be revised because it is not properly connected to the framework of the analysis: STEP/STEEP. You should start with the main idea in the paragraph. For example, you can say 'Sociological factors impacted on the development of Buckler beer. One of them is …' Please try yourself once again.*
>
> [DA1 draft 2]
>
> **Social factors have had an effect on the development of Buckler beer**. For example, the public awareness towards a healthier lifestyle has increased in recent years. The demand for less harmful products, for instant, non-alcohol beers has grown. In addition, there was already a request for a new enhanced brand in Spain. Furthermore, the company had to carefully consider the traditional customs of countries when it designed its advertisement. One such a specific element was the fact that bars in Italy offer meals as well.
>
> [DA1 final draft]

13   *Suggesting a Possible Solution*

One learner (Amina) suggested possible solutions to the problems in question during the assessment. This move was considered a more independent one although some assistance was needed. This move is illustrated in the interaction below where Amina suggests a possible theme sentence:

Excerpt 5.32

> Amina: shall we say that, microsoft is a big threat for the chrome because of
>
> *Mediator*: not exactly, your focus is on Google not on Microsoft.
>
> [Instant messaging, DA1 draft 1]

14   *Verbalising Conceptual Understanding*

Asking learners to externalise their thoughts on linguistic concepts has recently been employed in language education research driven by sociocultural theory and this pedagogical technique has been found useful for learners towards solving a problem (e.g., Poehner, 2005; Swain & Lapkin, 2002). This technique was extended in the present study because the learners not only verbalised their thoughts on linguistic forms but also on their conceptual knowledge of a particular discipline (i.e., business studies) and the case study analysis genre. Although only three DA learners made use of this move, this move appeared to help them with their better understanding of the conceptual knowledge they needed to accomplish the given assessment task. The following excerpt from Michelle demonstrates her verbalisation of paragraph development:

Excerpt 5.33

> ... I think after doing the exercises on learning how to develop paragraphs, I have become a little bit more conscious of how I am linking my sentences and this takes a bit of time when producing written assignments to ensure that the sentences within each paragraph are coordinated in the right way to gain the best results...
>
> [email with DA2, draft 1]

15 *Rejecting the Mediator's Feedback*

Although it is not entirely clear why, there were times when the learners rejected the mediator's feedback which sometimes resulted in producing an ineffective case study analysis. However, this move was an independent one. For example, the mediator suggested (i.e., track changed) a Theme sentence for the paragraph on *strengths* in DA1 draft 3 by Lou (DA2 draft 2, paragraph 5) as below but she rejected the suggestion and wrote her own:

Excerpt 5.34

> *Strengths*
>
> **Google has several strengths regarding its new operating system...**
>
> [bold words – mediator's track changes, DA1 draft 3]
>
> *Strengths*
>
> One of the strengths that were facing Google was the ability of designing an operating system that has proven to be easy to work with compared to others...
>
> [DA1 final draft]

16 *Overcoming Problems*

This was the final move made by the learners in relation to a particular problem when they identified and solved it with only a little support from the mediator. For instance, the mediator asked Michelle to change her Theme sentence of paragraph 3 in her DA1 draft 1 as it was too specific. She revised her Theme sentence by making it more effective:

Excerpt 5.35

> **One social factor** demonstrated in the case study that has had an impact on Heineken's marketing in European countries is the fact that the population started focusing on a healthier lifestyle and cutting down on alcohol consumption.

Mediator: *Can you begin this paragraph differently, that is, by telling the reader what this paragraph is about?*

[Michelle's DA1 draft 1]

The case study revealed many social factors in Heineken's external environment. (10) One factor which greatly influenced Heineken's marketing strategy was their location in Europe and the fact that the culture in these countries started focusing on healthier lifestyles and less alcohol consumption.

[Michelle's DA1 draft 2]

5.7.3 *Reciprocal Moves and Academic Writing Development*

As with mediational moves, learner reciprocal moves indicate a learner's developing ZPD in relation to their academic writing development. In other words, these moves show the learner's dynamic control of changing academic writing abilities. These academic writing abilities included writing a case study analysis text, and knowledge and application of business concepts and frameworks such as SWOT in my research. Table 5.4 presents the summary of the actual reciprocal moves made by the four DA learners at two different times (i.e., DA1 and DA2) in the study reported here.

The table shows the frequency of the reciprocal moves and the type of moves made by the learners. As with the teacher mediation moves, the reciprocal moves varied for each learner, indicating their different levels of academic writing abilities (i.e., their ZPDs). Furthermore, in the case of Amina the choice of instant messaging seems to have had an effect on the frequency of moves. It is interesting to note that some of the moves were non-existent in some learners' responses. For example, while move 13 (*Suggesting a possible solution*) was exclusively made by Amina, move 10 (*Evaluating teacher feedback*) was mainly found in Michelle's responses. As illustrated in Excerpt 5.36, when Amina (A) and I (M) were interacting about Amina's missing introductory paragraph, Amina made two suggestions as underlined:

Excerpt 5.36

M: yes, but what about introducing the reader to your analysis?

A: like a report introduction

M: yes, exactly. it is a report.

so where does the SWOT table fit in your text?

A: introduction is missing

M: yes.

A: so it should be

in the first paragraph

[Instant messaging, Amina's DA1 first draft]

However, it is worth noting that this move completely disappeared in DA2.

During the interaction in DA2, Michelle quite frequently evaluated my feedback which was almost non-existent in other students' moves. Excerpt 5.37 elucidates how Michelle made this move. Michelle was working on her DA2 draft 2. She stated

Table 5.4 Quality and frequency of learner reciprocal moves

Reciprocal moves	Amina		Lou		Michelle		Natasha	
	DA1	DA2	DA1	DA2	DA1	DA2	DA1	DA2
1. Asking for task clarification	2	0	0	1	1	0	0	0
2. Unresponsive	4	11	0	2	2	0	10	1
3. Imitating the teacher	13	0	10	12	0	15	15	7
4. Using the teacher as a resource	10	0	0	1	2	7	0	0
5. Checking conceptual understanding with teacher	5	0	0	1	1	4	0	0
6. Responding incorrectly	15	2	14	8	4	6	9	5
7. Asking for content clues	4	0	0	1	1	4	0	0
8. Identifying the problem	7	0	0	0	2	4	0	0
9. Explaining the problem	2	0	0	0	0	6	1	0
10. Evaluating teacher feedback	0	0	0	0	1	6	0	1
11. Self-assessing	1	0	0	0	5	11	0	0
12. Incorporating feedback	9	6	21	39	22	17	24	25
13. Suggesting a possible solution	17	0	0	0	0	0	0	0
14. Verbalising conceptual understanding	19	0	0	1	1	6	0	0
15. Rejecting the teacher's feedback	0	1	3	2	0	3	1	0
16. Overcoming problems	13	4	18	26	20	14	20	23
Total	121	24	66	94	62	103	80	62

via instant messaging that she was 'stuck' regarding the social factors of the STEP analysis and needed some support. Towards the end of the interaction, she wrote:

Excerpt 5.37

Michelle: yes what i needed was the guide and that is what u* did

Mediator: i am glad.

:) [smiley]

Michelle: u clarified the different factors and gave eg's that usually works well with me

[* Any non-standard use of English is retained in IM so as not to lose the context and authenticity]

In this excerpt, not only did Michelle evaluate my support, but she also indicated her learning strategy (underlined). In addition to moves 10 and 13, Table 5.4 also shows that move 14 (*Verbalising conceptual understanding*) featured in Amina's DA1 (n = 19) only and Michelle's DA2 (n = 6) mainly but not in other learners' responses except once in Lou's. Given that conceptual understanding is central to the application of business frameworks and concepts to the case study analysis, verbalising such understanding may have served the purpose of the internalisation of the concepts in question. In fact, verbalisation is a form of externalisation (i.e., interaction with others) that complements internalisation (e.g., see Lantolf & Thorne, 2006, pp. 202–203). Externalisation occurs in social interaction such as the instant messaging context in this study. The teacher presence may have provided a 'sounding board' for both Amina and Michelle.

As I expected, the most frequent move across DA1 and DA2 (shown in Fig. 5.5) was *Incorporating feedback* (move 12), 163 out of 612 reciprocal moves in total. Indeed this move occurred as the most frequent one for all the learners except Amina's DA1. Such heavy use of this move indicates that learners do value formative feedback as long as the feedback is 'usable' (e.g., see Walker, 2009) and meaningful (Hyland, 2013b) as previously discussed in Chap. 1. This finding challenges the previous finding that students are interested in grades rather than formative comments (e.g., Carless, 2006; Mutch, 2003). The reason why students often ignore teacher feedback is due to it not being developmental or usable in future assignments. Therefore, teacher comments that target students' maturing abilities (i.e., ZPDs) are likely to be taken on board by students as shown by this study. However, Fig. 5.6 also indicates

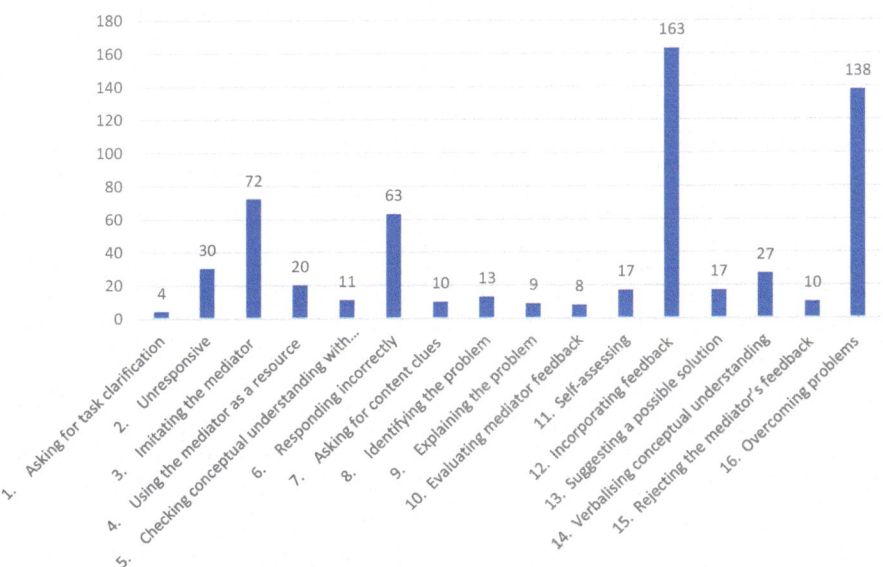

Fig. 5.6 Distribution of reciprocal moves across DA1 and DA2. (1, 2, 3… refer to reciprocal moves. Moves 1–8 are more dependent than moves 9–16.)

that the students made moves 2 (*Unresponsive*) and 15 (*Rejecting the mediator's feedback*), which suggests that some of the teacher feedback was not incorporated. The reason for this is not clear but may be worth investigating in future studies.

The distribution of the other reciprocal moves across DA1 and DA2, as shown in Fig. 5.6, indicates that *Overcoming problems* (move 16) and *Imitating the teacher* (move 3) were the next two most frequent moves employed by the learners over the period of the study. While moves 12 and 16 are more independent moves, move 3 is a less independent one. The third position of move 3 among the reciprocal moves suggests that the students' maturing academic writing abilities and conceptual development needed more explicit support. The students often imitated the teacher for key concepts or paragraph Theme sentences in the case study analysis text they wrote. As explained in Chap. 2, such imitation is an initial step towards internalisation and hence developmental in the context of academic writing development.

Furthermore, as demonstrated by Fig. 5.6, moves 1, 10, 9, 5 and 15 were respectively the five least used responses by the learners. While move 1 is mainly concerned with the clarity of the assessment task, moves 10 (*Evaluating teacher feedback*) and 15 (*Rejecting the teacher's feedback*) may be associated with the power relationship between the teacher (expert and more powerful) and the learner (novice and less powerful) and hence their frequency may have been low. As discussed in Chap. 1 (e.g., Carless, 2006; Hyatt, 2005), teacher-student power relationships often have negative effects on learning and therefore unequal power relationships may hinder identifying learners' ZPDs. The low uptake of move 5 (*Checking conceptual understanding with teacher*) could have resulted from the interpersonal relationship between the teacher and the student and the students' available time for the task. Equally, it is possible that carrying out DA in distance education means a lack of immediacy and face-to-face contact which may have affected the uptake of this move.

When the reciprocal moves in DA1 and DA2 are compared, several things can be observed as demonstrated by Figs. 5.7 and 5.8: (1) the more dependent reciprocal moves (1–8) decreased in DA2 and more independent moves increased; (2) there were fewer instances of incorrect responses in DA2 (7%) than in DA1 (13%); and (3) move 13 (*Suggesting a possible solution*) did not occur at all in DA2.

The increase in more independent moves and the decrease in more dependent moves indicate the learners' maturing academic writing abilities regarding their control of the case study analysis genre and associated conceptual knowledge. In traditional forms of assessment, the assessor considers the present mental functioning of the learner to predict their future, which is already present. Valsiner (2001) calls this model *past-to-present*. On the other hand, semiotic mediation which was employed in my research during the DA sessions allows the researcher to study the *future-in-the-making*. By examining the responses (i.e., what they mention and what they write in the text) made by the learners to mediation (i.e., comments on the student written texts), it is, thus, possible to explore '*the immediate future* of the present psychological processes' (Valsiner, 2001, p.86; emphasis in original).

Most importantly, the significantly low frequency of *Responding incorrectly* (move 6) in DA2 (from 13 to 7%) is an indication that the learners' academic writing abilities may have developed further from DA1. Nevertheless, Michelle made more

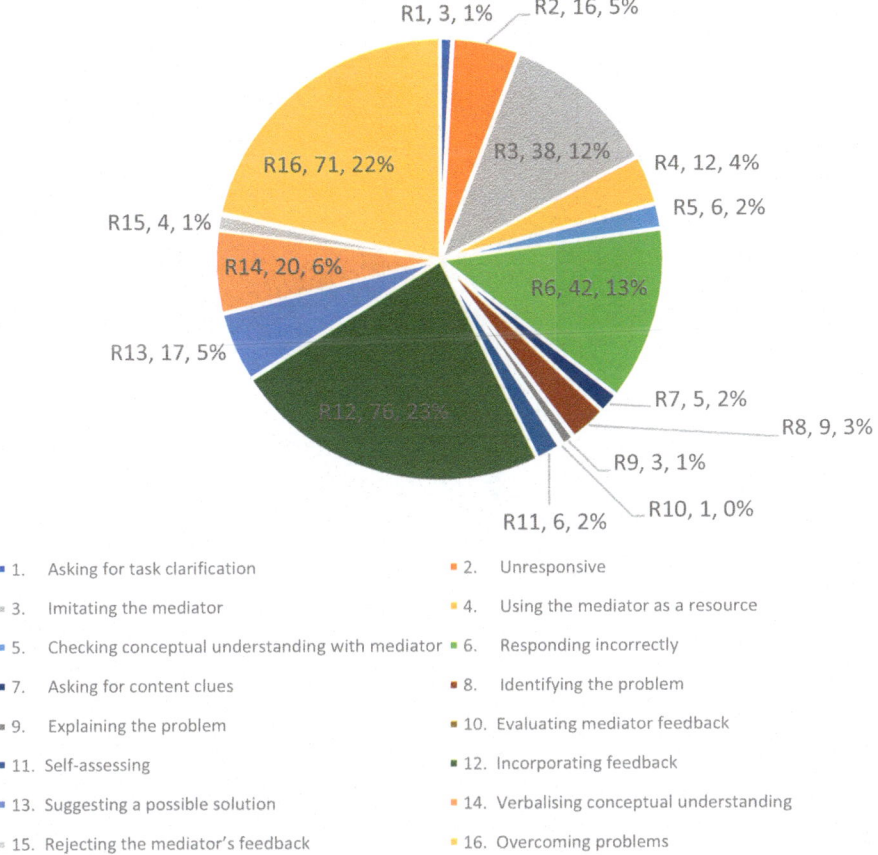

1. Asking for task clarification
2. Unresponsive
3. Imitating the mediator
4. Using the mediator as a resource
5. Checking conceptual understanding with mediator
6. Responding incorrectly
7. Asking for content clues
8. Identifying the problem
9. Explaining the problem
10. Evaluating mediator feedback
11. Self-assessing
12. Incorporating feedback
13. Suggesting a possible solution
14. Verbalising conceptual understanding
15. Rejecting the mediator's feedback
16. Overcoming problems

Fig. 5.7   Distribution of reciprocal moves across learners in DA1

incorrect responses in DA2 than she did in DA1. For example, when she was asked to include the social reason for the growing syringe market in the US, she added an *economic factor* instead to the case study analysis as shown in Excerpts 5.38 and 5.39.

Excerpt 5.38

DA2 draft 1

Paragraph on social factors

Social factors, covering demographical and cultural aspects of the environment external to the Safer Syringe market are population awareness, number of workers involved in the industry and the society's attitude towards safety…

Mediator: Is the number of workers a social factor? Or something else? The three social factors need to be exemplified referring to the case study.

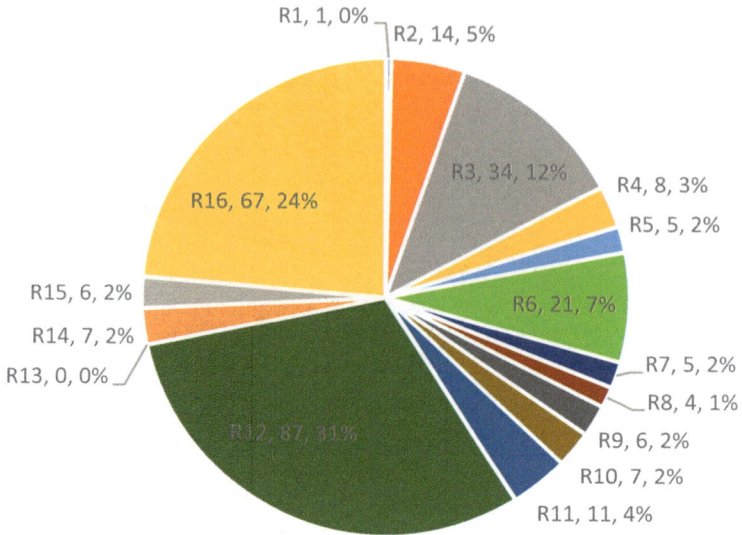

Fig. 5.8 Distribution of reciprocal moves across learners in DA2

Excerpt 5.39

DA2 draft 2

Paragraph on social factors

Social factors, covering demographical and cultural aspects of the environment external to the Safer Syringe market are people's attitude towards safety and their awareness of health and safety… The advantage that the USA has on most other countries, however, is their ability to afford 'Safer Syringes'. According to the 'Case Study, p2' the market will become more open to other countries when people in these countries become more willing to pay for the additional cost of safety. Due to the USA's economic advantage over other countries, they have been able to implement and use 'Safer Syringes' when other countries are not able to afford this.

Mediator: This [first underlined sentence above] is not linked with the social factor but economic. This [second underlined sentence above] is not linked with the social factor either but economic because it's not an impact of a social factor nor is it a social factor.

This may have been due to various reasons including her openness to risk-taking in learning. She may have confused the *social factor* with the *economic factor* in these two drafts as her final draft resolved the issue by putting the above two *economic factor* related sentences in the paragraph on economic factors. Additionally, given that development can be not only evolutionary but also revolutionary in the Vygotskian theory of development and it involves both progression and regression (Vygotsky, 1978, p. 73), Michelle's writing development can possibly be explained from this perspective which is further explored in the next chapter.

5.8 Summary

As highlighted in Chap. 2, all our higher mental functions are mediated by physical and symbolic tools developed within our cultures. Thus, mediation helps us to regulate all our and others' activities. In terms of learning and development, appropriate mediation and targeting learner ZPDs are essential in any domain of learning including academic writing. This chapter illustrated the process of mediation in DA of academic writing in distance education by examining the mediation data in relation to four students' business studies assignments. The main focus was on the students' changing ZPDs (i.e., academic writing abilities) in the context of the teacher support provided. This chapter also provided a list of mediational strategies that may be applicable or adaptable to other formative writing assessment contexts in higher education. In fact, an adapted version of these strategies has been successfully used in English for academic purposes courses at The University of Sheffield English Language Teaching Centre (Chris Smith, personal communication). They call it 'dialogic feedback'.

The illustrative data presented in this chapter showed that an analysis of the teacher-student interaction enables us to observe the students' dynamic academic writing abilities (ZPDs) in the process of writing assessment. It was also noted that identifying such ZPDs requires great skill and attention including sustained motivation, particularly from the teacher. As shown by this study, if the teacher is able to identify the learner's ZPDs accurately and support them accordingly, the learner is likely to benefit from such support and develop their academic writing skills. Therefore, it may be argued that teacher comments on assignments that target students' maturing writing abilities (i.e., ZPDs) are likely to be taken on board by students. However, as noted in this chapter, providing appropriate mediation is challenging and mediation does not automatically lead to writing development (see next chapter).

The analysis of both the mediational and the learner reciprocal moves provided insights into how much control the learners gained over their academic writing in a short span of time. Without such an analysis, it is often difficult to understand the trajectory of learners' writing development by solely considering end products (i.e., a corpus analysis of final student assessment texts).

In order to further complement the examination of the business studies students' academic writing and conceptual development (ZPDs) in distance education, the next chapter considers drafts of their actual written assignments by drawing on the SFL-based genre theory.

References

Ableeva, R. (2010). *Dynamic assessment of listening comprehension in second language learning.* Ph.D., Pennsylvania State University. Retrieved from http://etda.libraries.psu.edu/theses/approved/WorldWideIndex/ETD-5520/index.html.

Ableeva, R. (2018). Understanding learner L2 development through reciprocity. In J. P. Lantolf, M. E. Poehner & M. Swain (Eds.), *The Routledge handbook of sociocultural theory and second language development* (pp. 266–281). New York, NY: Routledge.

Aljaafreh, A., & Lantolf, J. P. (1994). Negative feedback as regulation and second language learning in the Zone of Proximal Development. *Modern Language Journal, 78*(4), 465–483.

Carless, D. (2006). Differing perceptions in the feedback process. *Studies in Higher Education, 31*(2), 219–233.

Chaiklin, S. (2003). The zone of proximal development in Vygotsky's analysis of learning and instruction. In A. Kozulin, B. Gindis, V. S. Ageyev, & S. M. Miller (Eds.), *Vygotsky's educational theory in cultural context* (pp. 39–64). Cambridge: Cambridge University Press.

Coffin, C., & Hewings, A. (2005). Engaging electronically: Using CMC to develop students' argumentation skills in higher education. *Language & Education: An International Journal, 19*(1), 32–49.

Crossouard, B., & Pryor, J. (2009). Using email for formative assessment with professional doctorate students. *Assessment & Evaluation in Higher Education, 34*(4), 377–388.

Daniels, H. (2007). Pedagogy. In H. Daniels, M. Cole, & J. V. Wertsch (Eds.), *The Cambridge companion to Vygotsky* (pp. 307–331). Cambridge: Cambridge University Press.

Davin, K. J., Herazo, J. D., & Sagre, A. (2016). Learning to mediate: Teacher appropriation of dynamic assessment. *Language Teaching Research, 21*(5), 632–651. https://doi.org/10.1177/136 2168816654309.

Dawson, P., Henderson, M., Mahoney, P., Phillips, M., Ryan, T., Boud, D., et al. (2019). What makes for effective feedback: Staff and student perspectives. *Assessment & Evaluation in Higher Education, 44*(1), 25–36. https://doi.org/10.1080/02602938.2018.1467877.

Haywood, H. C., & Lidz, C. S. (2007). *Dynamic assessment in practice: Clinical and educational applications.* Cambridge: Cambridge University Press.

Hyatt, D. F. (2005). 'Yes, a very good point!': A critical genre analysis of a corpus of feedback commentaries on Master of Education assignments. *Teaching in Higher Education, 10*(3), 339–353.

Hyland, K. (2013). Student perceptions of hidden messages in teacher written feedback. *Studies in Educational Evaluation, 39*(3), 180–187. https://doi.org/10.1016/j.stueduc.2013.06.003.

Kozulin, A. (2003). Psychological tools and mediated learning. In A. Kozulin, B. Gindis, V. S. Ageyev, & S. M. Miller (Eds.), *Vygotsky's educational theory in cultural context* (pp. 15–38). Cambridge: Cambridge University Press.

Lantolf, J. P. (2000). Introducing sociocultural theory. In J. P. Lantolf (Ed.), *Sociocultural theory and second language learning* (pp. 1–26). Oxford: Oxford University Press.

Lantolf, J. P., & Poehner, M. E. (2004). Dynamic assessment of L2 development: Bringing the past into the future. *Journal of Applied Linguistics, 1*(1), 49–72.

Lantolf, J. P., & Thorne, S. L. (2006). *Sociocultural theory and the genesis of second language development.* Oxford: Oxford University Press.

Lillis, T. M., & Scott, M. (2007). Defining Academic Literacies Research: Issues of epistemology, ideology and strategy. *Journal of Applied Linguistics, 4*(1), 5–32.

Lund, A. (2008). Assessment made visible: Individual and collective practices. *Mind, Culture, and Activity, 15*(1), 32–51.

Mutch, A. (2003). Exploring the practice of feedback to students. *Active Learning in Higher Education, 4*(1), 24–38. https://doi.org/10.1177/1469787403004001003.

Poehner, M. E. (2005). *Dynamic assessment of oral proficiency among advanced L2 learners of French.* Ph.D., Pennsylvania State University.

Poehner, M. E. (2008). *Dynamic assessment: A Vygotskian approach to understanding and promoting L2 development.* New York: Springer.

Poehner, M. E., & Swain, M. (2016). L2 development as cognitive-emotive process. *Language and Sociocultural Theory, 3*(2), 219–241.

Shrestha, P. N., & Coffin, C. (2012). Dynamic assessment, tutor mediation and academic writing development. *Assessing Writing, 17*(1), 55–70. https://doi.org/10.1016/j.asw.2011.11.003.

Swain, M., & Lapkin, S. (2002). Talking it through: Two French immersion learners' response to reformulation. *International Journal of Educational Research, 37*(3–4), 285–304.

Sweeny, S. M. (2010). Writing for the instant messaging and text messaging generation: Using new literacies to support writing instruction. *Journal of Adolescent & Adult Literacy, 54*(2), 121–130.

Valsiner, J. (2001). Process structure of semiotic mediation in human development. *Human Development, 44*(2), 84–97.

Vygotsky, L. S. (1978). *Mind in society: The development of higher psychological processes.* Cambridge, MA: Harvard University Press.

Walker, M. (2009). An investigation into written comments on assignments: Do students find them usable? *Assessment & Evaluation in Higher Education, 34*(1), 67–78.

Warschauer, M., & Ware, P. D. (2008). Learning, change, and power: Competing discourses of technology and literacy. In J. Coiro, K. M., C. Lankshear, & D. J. Leu (Eds.), *Handbook of research on new literacies* (pp. 215–240). New York: Lawrence Erlbaum.

Wells, G. (1999). *Dialogic inquiry: Towards a sociocultural practice and theory of education.* Cambridge: Cambridge University Press.

Wertsch, J. V. (1985). *Vygotsky and the social formation of mind.* Cambridge, MA: Harvard University Press.

Wertsch, J. V. (2003). Commentary on: Deliberation with computers: exploring the distinctive contribution of new technologies to collaborative thinking and learning. *International Journal of Educational Research, 39*(8), 899–904.

Wertsch, J. V. (2007). Mediation. In H. Daniels, M. Cole, & J. V. Wertsch (Eds.), *The Cambridge companion to Vygotsky* (pp. 178–192). Cambridge: Cambridge University Press.

Williams, C., & Beam, S. (2019). Technology and writing: Review of research. *Computers & Education, 128,* 227–242. https://doi.org/10.1016/j.compedu.2018.09.024.

Chapter 6
Tracking Learners' Academic Writing and Conceptual Development Through Systemic Functional Linguistics

6.1 Introduction

It was argued in Chap. 1 that academic literacy plays a pivotal role in higher education students' ability to build disciplinary knowledge and expertise and communicate that to the discourse community of their discipline. The previous chapter showed that the development of students' academic writing abilities is a dynamic and lengthy social process which is widely accepted in the field of academic writing (e.g., see Manchón, 2017; Prior, 2008; Shrestha & Coffin, 2012). This view is central to the research reported here as dynamic assessment (DA) focuses on the academic writing process and the interaction between the learner and the mediator. It is also important to emphasise that the view about academic writing adopted in this book is the central relationship between texts or genres and their sociocultural environments where they are collaboratively created. In this chapter, I also follow the view that disciplinarity (i.e., 'organisation of knowledge, and of intellectual and educational practices' following Christie and Maton (2011, p. 4)) is a crucial contextual factor in constructing academic writing texts as noted in Chap. 3 (3.4.1).

The research reported in this book aims to shed more insights into business studies students' emerging academic writing abilities through the process of DA in distance education. In Chap. 5, it was argued that the teacher-student interaction assisted the learners in my research increasingly to control their emerging abilities (zones of proximal development (ZPDs)) regarding their academic writing and associated conceptual knowledge. In order to complement this argument, this chapter presents linguistic evidence for the impact of teacher mediation in DA on the learners' *microgenetic* development (i.e., development over a short span of time) by examining their drafts of assessment texts to observe their academic writing and conceptual development (i.e., students' ZPDs in academic writing) during the study period. In particular, this chapter aims to explore what Systemic Functional Linguistic (SFL) based genre analyses of student assessment texts (including drafts) demonstrate regarding students' academic writing and conceptual development within an academic writing course for business studies. It also provides illustrative examples of whether learners following

© Springer Nature Switzerland AG 2020
P. N. Shrestha, *Dynamic Assessment of Students' Academic Writing*,
https://doi.org/10.1007/978-3-030-55845-1_6

non-DA procedures perform differently from those who follow DA procedures as explained in Chap. 4.

As outlined previously, the purpose of DA is to identify learners' ZPDs and support them to develop these ZPDs further during the assessment process. In the context of the research reported in this book, through the first assignment task, DA allowed me to identify the academic writing problem areas of the learners who were studying an academic writing module for business studies (see Chap. 4). Specifically, their problem areas related to the text structure and development of a case study analysis genre and the application within it of two business frameworks (i.e., STEP (Sociological or Social, Technological, Economic & Political) and SWOT (Strengths, Weaknesses, Opportunities & Threats); see Chap. 4). As these were the main problems identified through the DA procedures, they were specifically targeted during my research.

First, I will briefly describe the data sample chosen for this book to explore DA and non-DA business studies students' academic writing development over time in distance education. I will then explain the specific SFL analytical tools which helped me to track these students' emerging academic writing abilities over the duration of my research. A substantial part of this chapter will focus on the results of the SFL-based genre analyses of the participating students' drafts of case study analysis texts across DA1 and DA2, and non-DA1 and non-DA2, particularly by examining text organisation and development and the students' emerging genre and conceptual knowledge.

6.2 Student Written Text Data Used in This Book

This study aimed to investigate the academic writing trajectory of six students over a period of time, as noted in Chap. 4. For this, the assignments from six students (four DA and two non-DA) were selected in order to track their academic writing development (i.e., ZPDs) as evidenced by the linguistic features in their texts. Among these assignments, texts from two students were collected over a period of six months and texts from four further students over 10 months. These different durations were a result of the time they took to complete the assignment tasks and the enrichment study materials designed for the study. For the purpose of this book, only the first and the final assignment drafts from each DA student were selected for text analysis although they produced several drafts. Altogether there were 20 assignment texts, of which 16 were from the four DA students and the other four assignments were from the two non-DA students.

Whilst all other students wrote their assignments in response to the assignment tasks I designed, two students submitted the assignments from the business studies courses they were studying at the time. Amina (DA) submitted the assignment for DA2 from a Level 2 business studies course and Lena (non-DA) for non-DA2 from a Level 3 business studies course. This was done due to their personal circumstances

Table 6.1 Business studies teachers' judgment data

Teachers (Pseudonyms)	Type of data		
	Assessment marks	Summary feedback	In-text Annotation
Annie	6 students × 2 texts	6 students × 2 texts	6 students × 2 texts
Lydia	6 students × 2 texts	6 students × 2 texts	6 students × 2 texts
Mark	4 students × 2 texts (Amina, Lou, Kristie & Lena)	4 students × 2 texts (Amina, Lou, Kristie & Lena)	0

and the assignments required them to produce similar texts (i.e., case study analysis genre).

In addition, other supplementary data was analysed in order to add depth and rigour to the main data set. These included three volunteer business studies teachers' judgments of the student assessment texts and the learner interviews (see 4.5.5 and 4.5.6). The data collected from three business studies teachers is summarised in Table 6.1. Excepting the non-DA student Lena, all other five students (four DA and one non-DA) were interviewed to explore their experiences of the assessment process they went through.

As shown in Table 6.1, three business studies teachers assessed the students' assessment texts (see Chap. 4, 4.5.6). While Annie and Lydia assessed two assessment texts each for six students, Mark was only available for assessing two texts each for four students. Furthermore, unlike Annie and Lydia, Mark did not provide any in-text annotation (i.e., comment within the assignment text). Providing in-text annotations is a common practice in The Open University. While the business studies teachers' judgment provided information regarding the learners' assessment scores and improvement in their conceptual development, the student interview data showed their expressed perception of the DA and the non-DA procedures adopted in my research on academic writing.

6.3   Analysing Academic Writing Assessment Texts Using an SFL-Based Genre Approach

For the analysis of the selected student assessment texts, as explained in Chaps. 3 and 4, the analytical tools were drawn from Hallidayan SFL which considers language as a meaning-making resource to achieve a social purpose (e.g., Halliday & Matthiessen, 2004). As a teacher/mediator, I had identified aspects of Textual (i.e., organisation of text) and Ideational (i.e., representation of experience) meanings as areas for development in the students' first assignment both in DA and non-DA procedures. Therefore, the focus of the textual analysis is on Textual and Ideational meanings as explained in Chap. 4. In relation to Textual meaning, I analysed *macroThemes*, also known as Introductions, and *hyperThemes* defined as 'a clause (or combination of clauses) predicting a pattern of clause Themes constituting a text's method of development' (Martin, 1993a, p. 245) in order to examine if they contributed sufficiently to text development. However, in this book, I have not shown a detailed sentence-level analysis of the text due to space although such an analysis would need to happen in future research. MacroThemes and hyperThemes are considered for their contribution to how students construe Textual meanings.

In terms of Ideational meaning, in this case the use of business concepts and frameworks, the texts were examined using Martin's notion of *Technicality* (Martin, 1993b). As explained in Chap. 4, Technicality also includes technical abstractions (see Woodward-Kron, 2008). For example, the term 'fermentation process' in Excerpt 6.1 is used in the beer industry and thus constitutes a technical abstraction, given its use as a concept rather than an action (i.e., 'fermentation' instead of 'ferment'):

Excerpt 7.1

Paragraph 4

Technological factors affect Heineken's marketing strategy in one main way. Heineken used a specially developed fermentation process where non alcoholic beer had the taste and quality expected of a premium beer without liquor… [Final draft, DA1, Michelle]

In order to identify Technicality in the students' assessment texts, the following criteria were adopted:

1. Terms with a field-specific meaning (processes, things and qualities).
2. Terms defined or in taxonomic relations to other technical terms following Martin and Rose (2007) who define taxonomic relations as 'semantic relations between the particular people, things, processes, places and qualities that build the field of a text' (p. 75).

Technicality was quantified by considering the frequency of the technical terms. If the same term was used more than once, it was counted more than once, given the short length of most student texts (about 500 words) and differing contexts of use.

In addition, the students' conceptual understanding of the case study analysis as a genre was analysed for Ideational meanings as construed in their assignments in response to the assignment tasks. This was mainly considered by examining to what extent the generic features of a case study analysis genre valued in business studies were present in the students' assessment texts.

6.4 What Is Expected of Students in a *Case Study Analysis* Genre?

In Chap. 3, I discussed academic writing genres in higher education drawing on the current research on student writing genre studies (e.g., Nesi & Gardner, 2018). I also argued in view of the current research (e.g., Nathan, 2013) and my own survey of genres found in business studies assignments at The Open University (Chap. 3) that *case study analysis* genre is the most commonly used genre in business studies assignments. There are certain expectations by business studies teachers in terms of how their students write a case study analysis. The case study analysis which students wrote as part of the research reported in this book draws on business concepts or framework(s) to analyse business situations (i.e., various business scenarios of an organisation) as explained in Chap. 3. Business studies students are required to demonstrate their understanding of business concepts and frameworks by applying them to business situations (also see QAA, 2007, 2019). Therefore, the emphasis in such assignments is not on theoretical explanations but on the application of a theory or framework such as SWOT to a new real business world situation. These texts not only describe and classify business phenomena but also simultaneously explain them. Students are also expected to draw some conclusion and make recommendations based on their analysis although there may be some variations because sometimes recommendations are implied rather than explicitly mentioned in the assignment task as highlighted by Table 4.2 in Chap. 4.

As highlighted above, students need to know a set of business concepts/frameworks and their purposes in business studies so that they can produce an effective case study analysis. In order for this to happen, they are provided with various common frameworks or models as tools which they can apply to analysing an organisation's external environment (e.g., see Preston, Fryer, & Watson, 2007). In this study, students were given assessment tasks that required them to apply either the STEP or the SWOT framework which are widely used to analyse the external environment of an organisation (see Chap. 4). An example is given in Fig. 6.1 from the first assignment in my research.

Typically, in a case study analysis, students are asked to use a conceptual framework (such as SWOT) to explain the (hypothetical) effects of phenomena in the external environment on the business. As explained in Chap. 3, a genre such as case study analysis contains a number of stages to achieve a social goal in the context of a culture where it is used. These stages are recurrent in a certain type of text and recognised by the concerned discourse community. By the same token, a case study analysis genre also has a recognisable pattern indicated by the stages it is expected to follow as shown in Table 3.3 in Chap. 3. Since the students in my research were asked to apply two business frameworks to the case study analysis, namely SWOT and STEP, the case study analysis applying each framework has slightly different generic stages. Figures 6.2 and 6.3 below show the genre staging of a STEP and a SWOT analysis which is typically expected from the student.

The figures show how STEP or SWOT serves as the overall superordinate (taxonomising) conceptual framework. In the opening stage of the genre, writers typically provide some kind of Orientation to the conceptual framework and to the organisation in question and then work through the four explanatory components of the framework. In other words, the genre follows certain stages to achieve its purpose. If a stage is left out, the analysis may be incomplete and the text unsuccessful. There are two types of generic stages shown in these figures: obligatory and optional. While Orientation and Components 1–4 are obligatory, Recommendation

---

Assignment

Read the following case study carefully. Then, use the STEP framework to critically analyse the external environment of Heineken in terms of its marketing strategy. Your analysis should not exceed 500 words.

[case study – not included here]

Session 1: Heineken's Buckler beer (case study)

Guidance

This case study explains how Heineken used the marketing strategy to promote its new non-alcoholic brand into the international market. As you are using the STEP framework to analyse Heineken's external environment based on this case study, look for examples that illustrate the factors in the STEP framework in order to produce an effective STEP analysis while you are making notes. If you are not sure about what STEP means, please read the documents attached to the wiki home page for this task. You can also ask me for clarification or more information.

Please note that you can ask me (the researcher) any questions related to the assessment task during any time of the writing process by email or chat or any appropriate method that allows me to record your queries and my response. For this we are very likely to use a wiki to produce the text and msn chat for our interaction according to your convenience. Nearer the time, I will let you know which tool we will be using. Before I make a decision on this, I would like to know your preference.

For writing your text, I would prefer a wiki because it allows me to see all the process you follow and the changes you make to your text which are crucial to my study. You will receive information regarding the wiki shortly.

Fig. 6.1 Assignment task in DA1 for Michelle and Natasha

and/or Conclusion is optional. The Orientation introduces the relevant conceptual framework(s) and the business scenario. The Component introduces one of the four Components in SWOT or STEP and frames the analysis.

The final stage is presented as optional here because business studies teachers seem to have different views regarding the inclusion of this stage in the analysis as indicated by these quotes:

> I think different academics will answer you differently but I would include the recommendations as well. SWOT or STEP frameworks are rather like tools, and if you are looking for evaluations you should consider the recommendations they make out of their analyses and application of these tools in a given context. (Lecturer 1, personal communication, 29 September 2010)

> My view is that a SWOT or STEP would not necessarily include recommendations – unless the question asked for them.

> If you wanted the students to include recommendations for the organisation concerned, you should say to them, clearly and specifically, that you want them to go beyond a list of factors, and ask them to spell out the implications and recommendations for the organisation … (Lecturer 2, personal communication, 29 September 2010).

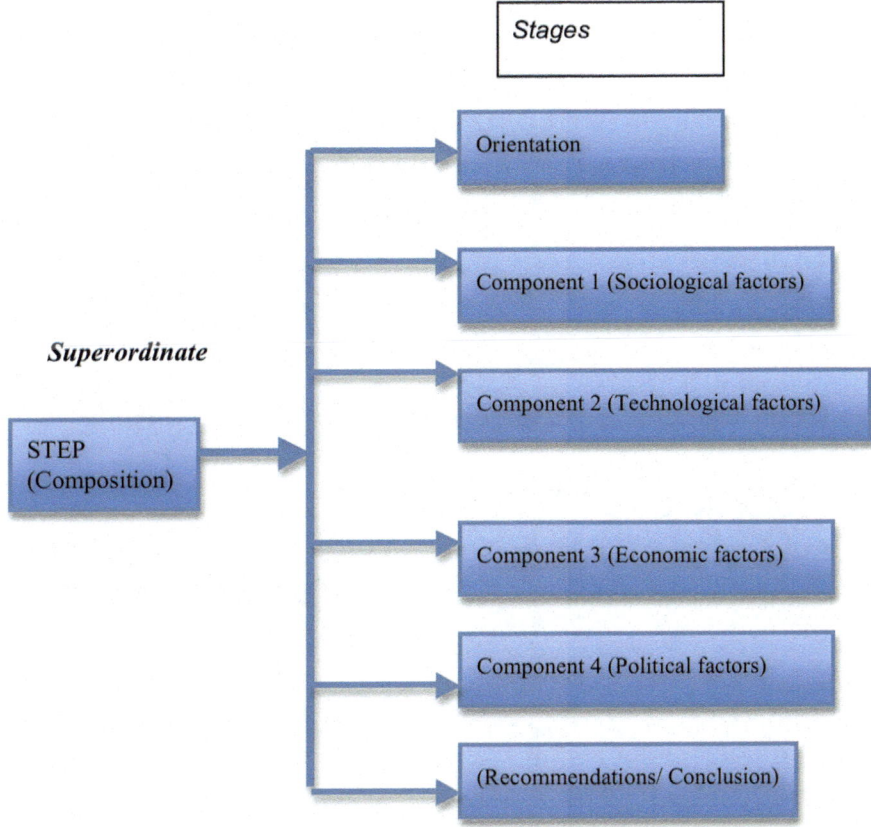

Fig. 6.2 The genre staging of a typical STEP analysis

Given this situation and the fact that students were not specifically asked to make recommendations in the assignment task, the Recommendation stage is presented as optional although it was encouraged during mediation (DA) and in the feedback (non-DA). Recommendation is sometimes implied (i.e., not obvious) in the assignment task as noted in Table 4.2 in Chap. 4. Additionally, each component includes three distinct phases: Description, Explanation and Analysis. Readers may recall from Table 3.1 (Chap. 3) that these three were presented as *elemental genres*. In the case of a case study analysis like a SWOT analysis, elemental genres like these three become parts of the case study analysis macrogenre because they contribute to the meaning of a stage of that genre. For example, once a business phenomenon is identified, described and classified (e.g., as a Strength), its effect on the organisation is explained in the analysis.

For the purpose of this study, the generic stages for a STEP or SWOT case study analysis presented in Figs. 6.2 and 6.3 were followed while analysing the student assessment texts and during the mediation to DA students and in my feedback to

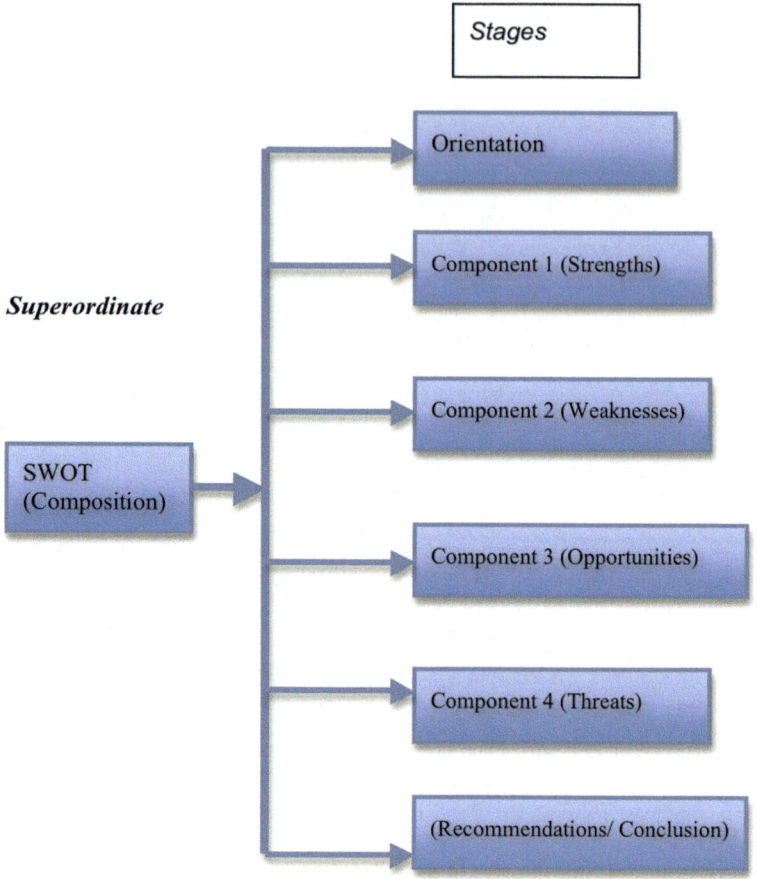

Fig. 6.3 The genre staging of a typical SWOT analysis

the non-DA students. The main reason for this was that texts closely following these generic stages were highly valued by business studies teachers.

6.5   Tracking DA and Non-DA Students' Academic Writing Performance Through SFL

In this section, I will present the ways SFL was used to track both DA and non-DA students' academic writing and conceptual development in the first and the second assignments. While doing so, I demonstrate how SFL offers insights into these students' emerging abilities to write the case study analysis genre in question.

Specifically, I provide SFL-based illustrations of the participating students' production of case study analysis genres, focusing on their control of Textual and Ideational meanings. Where appropriate, I also draw on the supplementary data (i.e., business studies teacher judgements and student interviews) to support my discussion.

6.5.1 Identifying Genres in Students' Assignment Texts

In this section, I will consider the genre and its stages as produced by both the DA and non-DA students in their assignments. Each student's assignment was analysed by examining the generic stages the text followed (see 4.4.3 for a profile of all students). These were analysed because they posed different levels of challenges to the learners as identified through their drafts of the first assignment. In order to help the reader get a sense of the assignment texts, two examples of full assignment texts (first draft), one written by a DA student and another by a non-DA student, are given in Figs. 6.4 and 6.5.

As stated in the previous section, the students' texts written in response to the assignment tasks in this study were expected to be a case study analysis genre that successfully applied one of the business frameworks (i.e., STEP or SWOT) to an organisation's business environment as in the examples given in Figs. 6.4 and 6.5. Tables 6.2 and 6.3 summarise the results of the genres used in the student response texts. As shown in the tables, most students wrote the expected genre: SWOT or STEP case study analysis. However, there was some variation among the learners. For example, it was only Natasha's texts that were in the expected genre across DA1 and DA2. Although her response texts were written as a case study analysis at the higher level, they lacked lower level essential features which I discuss in the next section. Likewise, Lou and Michelle produced case study analyses across DA1 and DA2 but they wrote one incomplete analysis each. In contrast, Amina was not able to produce the expected genre during her independent performance (i.e., DA1 draft 1 and DA2 draft 1) although she did so when assisted (i.e., DA1 and DA2 final drafts).

There was also a distinction between the two non-DA students as shown by Table 6.3. While Lena wrote an effective case study analysis (as represented by the generic stages) for her non-DA1, she did not achieve the same level of success with her second non-DA text. Kristie, however, seemed to have made some improvement in her academic writing in non-DA2 because, unlike her non-DA1 text, the non-DA2 text contains some features of a SWOT case study analysis in addition to Description.

As mentioned before, all six students' texts were also analysed for the generic stages. The SFL genre theory proposes that each genre follows distinct stages to achieve its social purpose as noted earlier. Tables 6.4 and 6.5 provide a summary of the generic stages in each student's texts in the first assignment texts. ˆ is used to mean 'followed by' in SFL genre theory.

A Google SWOT analysis

Strengths

Google hopes to capure (Any errors in the student written texts are maintained throughout this book for their authenticity.) new clients with their ideas for developing a operating system, which they plan to be faster for the future. The company hopes to produce a system that is smart, agile and successful. Google has develped a system called ANDROID which has been tailored for netbooks and able to run programmes that can manage displays, handling keyboard and mouse, which is larger but complex piece of software. Google has a strong postition for online advertising, messaging, photo-editing software. Googles chrome Internet browser with the ability in allowing its operating systems to work at a faster paste with other personal computers.

Weakness

Microsoft has a huge customer service department, on the other hand, google does not and needs to attract a lot more investment in this field.

Opportunites

Google hopes to expand their share of the market by working with Acer by selling netbooks to Google. With the Chome operating system it will help Google to conduct searches on mobiles, allowing the company to break into another market and generating future sale growths and more investment. Google provides a free operating system for consumers. It is not totally available when consumers purchase new PC.

Threats

Competition against Microsoft Office and Windows programmes. Developing new documents , internet explorer to be faster. A growing but deep relationship with other software developers and retailers. Google will find this hard to compete against, from external competition. Internally, google provides free online word processing for customers such as spreadsheet and presentation programes whilst their main competitor trails behind.   google still holds a threatening position over Microsoft by adating a new operating system at a fraction of the cost for manufactures. Consumers are yet to be convinced that google can supply a better or reliable operating system.

Fig. 6.4 First draft of the first assignment written by DA student Lou

As Tables 6.4 and 6.5 show, three of the six students (Michelle, Natasha and Lena) included all the obligatory generic stages in their first assignment:

Orientation^ Component 1^ Component 2^ Component 3^ Component 4^

Michelle, Lena and Amina wrote optional stage(s) too:

[Conclusion/Recommendations]

It appears that these optional stages were valued by the business studies teachers (i.e., subject experts as described in Chap. 4). For example, Annie commented on Lena's Conclusion in the non-DA1 text:

> Here you had opportunity to comment on possible solutions to the immense challenge of going up against a company the size of Microsoft and claiming a larger segment of the market.

Google SWOT analysis

The new technology developed in the form of the PC Operating Systems (OS) by Google has had a strong impact on its major competitor Microsoft and on the users at large. This essay will concentrate on a SWAT analysis of the effects of the Operating Systems is having on Google, Microsoft and the worldwide users.

By announcing that it was in the process of developing an operating system, Google had now firmly put a firm foot in Microsoft market strengthening its own position by developing a new product using technology based on systems used back in the 80's.

This has been welcome news for all users as Google products and technology are free, unlike Microsoft, although its Linux system is sometimes free it also is difficult to use. Google itself being the greatest search engine seems to be hedging itself slightly ahead of the market, but where Google can't deliver Microsoft can such as their marketing and customer support which is a non existent service at Google. Microsoft Windows is still the most popular computer software package purchased by the average PC user, but it comes at a price like all its other products.

The problem with new technology is that it nearly always involves new learning processes. The users will have to train themselves to use a new product and the question remains at to whether a larger proportion of these users would be happy to go through that process. This in turn may affect the popularity and marketing viability of the product, and therefore put Google in a precarious position as its only income comes from advertising, therefore the necessity to be successful at launching this OS is vital. However its flexibility being it greatest asset it is bound to get a great deal of interest from the public.

Google has now the opportunity to provide all services on line, no more complex technology and easy access, the browser becomes the PC where all software is stored and can be used at the push of a button; the question is will Microsoft come up with a new product of their own to try and reclaim a share of that market. This remains unlikely for the time being although Microsoft will probably strengthen its position with its retailers and software developers and review its prices to become more competitive.

The competition is fierce on the market to develop more adaptable and user friendly products and there are concerns as to whether or not Google and Microsoft have the potential and capacity to move forward to more diverse products. Of course Bill Gates of Microsoft as already been in that position once before when Netscape's came up with the same concept as Google to offer everything on line although Bill Gates was successful in getting himself out of the situation once he is now dealing with a much more powerful competitor and it remains to be seen as to who is going to win the battle of the computer giants.

Fig. 6.5 First draft of the first assignment written by non-DA student Kristie

Lydia commented on Michelle's DA1 first draft:

Your conclusion is very general with no mention of Buckler or the points you raised in your analysis.

These comments suggest that the Conclusions that Michelle and Lena wrote were not effective enough although they included these. On the other hand, when there was no Conclusion/Recommendation, Annie wrote the following regarding Lou's DA1 first draft:

Table 6.2 Results for genres written by the DA students

Students	Genres			
	DA1 draft 1	DA1 final	DA2 draft 1	DA2 final
Amina	Description [no link with SWOT]	Case study analysis	Description [no link with STEP]	Case study analysis [less effective than expected]
Lou	Case study analysis [incomplete]	Case study analysis	Case study analysis	Case study analysis
Michelle	Case study analysis	Case study analysis	Case study analysis [incomplete]	Case study analysis
Natasha	Case study analysis	Case study analysis	Case study analysis	Case study analysis

Table 6.3 Results for genres written by non-DA students

Students	Genre	
	Non-DA1	Non-DA2
Kristie	Description	Description [mainly] and Case study analysis [very limited]
Lena	Case study analysis	Case study analysis [partial] and Description/Evaluation [partial]

> It might also be useful to add a concluding paragraph where you comment on the business implications of your analysis above. This is your opportunity to consider elements of your analysis holistically…

From these comments, it is clear that there is an expectation to conclude the case study analysis with some implications of the analysis or recommendations based on the analysis. This may suggest that, after all, students need to include this stage to be successful in writing a case study analysis genre in business studies. As a professional genre (see Nesi & Gardner, 2012), Recommendation seems important and thus, this should be made explicit in the assignment task so that students understand the requirement of the assignment.

The other three students (Amina, Lou and Kristie) had either (1) no Orientation stage or (2) mainly Description or (3) only a few mandatory stages in their first assignment text (see Tables 6.4 and 6.5). The dissimilarities of the stages in the assessment texts indicate different levels of academic writing and conceptual development and thus different level of ZPDs among the six students. Therefore, DA sessions focussed on this.

However, when the DA students' DA1 final (Table 6.4), DA2 draft 1 and DA2 final (Table 6.6) are examined, there is some evidence of progress regarding generic stages. For example, unlike DA1 draft 1, all these texts contain the mandatory Orientation stage. Furthermore, all four DA students (except Michelle's DA2 draft 1) incorporated optional stages into their texts: Conclusion/Recommendations and References (Amina and Lou). These student texts additionally showed that the students' conceptual knowledge increased as indicated by the use of the four Components from the business frameworks (i.e., SWOT or STEP) to frame their case study analysis text.

Table 6.4 Generic stages in DA students' first (DA1) assignment texts

Students	Generic stages	
	DA1 draft 1	DA1 final
Amina	Visual^* Description (Google)^ Description^ Definition? (Chrome)^ Comparison^ Explanation (usefulness of Chrome)^ Comparison (Microsoft and Chrome)^ [Review]	Orientation (SWOT)^ Visual (SWOT table) Component 1 (Strengths) Component 2 (Opportunities) Component 3 (Weaknesses) Component 4 (Threats) [Recommendations]
Lou	Component 1 (Strength)^ Component 2 (Weaknesses)^ Component 3 (Opportunities)^ Component 4 (Threats)	Orientation (SWOT)^ Visual (SWOT table)^ Component 1 (Strengths)^ Component 2 (Weaknesses)^ Component 3 (Opportunities)^ Component 4 (Threats)^ [Conclusion]^ [References]
Michelle	Background information/Orientation^ Classification (STEP)^ Component 1 (Factor 1—Social)^ Component 2 (Factor 2—Technological)^ Component 3 (Factor 3—Economic)^ Component 4 (Factor 4—Political)^ [Conclusion]	Background information/Orientation^ Classification (STEP)^ Component 1 (Factor 1—Social)^ Component 2 (Factor 2—Technological)^ Component 3 (Factor 3—Economic)^ Component 4 (Factor 4—Political)^ [Conclusion]
Natasha	Orientation (STEP)^ Component 1 (Factor 1—Social)^ Component 2 (Factor 2—Technological)^ Component 3 (Factor 3—Economic)^ Component 4 (Factor 4—Political)^	Orientation (STEP)^ Component 1 (Factor 1 Social)^ Component 2 (Factor 2—Technological)^ Component 3 (Factor 3—Economic)^ Component 4 (Factor 4—Political)^ [Conclusion]

Table 6.5 Generic stages in non-DA students' first (non-DA1) assignment texts

Students	Generic stages
Kristie	Orientation (SWOT)^ Background information^ Comparison (Google vs. Microsoft)^ Problem^ Component 3 (Opportunities)^ Description (market competition)
Lena	Classification (SWOT)^ Component 1 (Strengths)^ Component 2 (Weaknesses)^ Component 3 (Opportunities)^ Component 4 (Threats)^ [Conclusion]

Table 6.6 Generic stages in DA students' second (DA2) assignment texts

Students	Generic stages	
	DA2 draft 1	DA2 final
Amina	Orientation (STEP)^ Description (abstract ideas)^ Description^ Recount^ Description^ Classification (type of services)^ Description 1^ Description 2^ Description 3^ Description 4^ [Conclusion]	Orientation (STEP)^ Description (abstract ideas)^ Description^ Recount^ Description^ Classification (type of services)^ Description 1^ Description 2^ Description 3^ Description 4^ [Conclusion]^ [References]
Lou	Orientation (SWOT)^ Component 1 (Strengths)^ Component 2 (Weaknesses)^ Component 3 (Opportunities)^ Component 4 (Threats)^ [Recommendations]^ [References]	Orientation (SWOT)^ Component 1 (Strengths)^ Component 2 (Weaknesses)^ Component 3 (Opportunities)^ Component 4 (Threats)^ [Recommendations]^ [References]
Michelle	Orientation (STEP)^ Component 1 (Factor 1—Social)^ Component 2 (Factor 2—Technological)^ Component 3 (Factor 3—Economic)^ Component 4 (Factor 4—Political) [incomplete]	Orientation (STEP)^ Component 1 (Factor 1—Social)^ Component 2 (Factor 2—Technological)^ Component 3 (Factor 3—Economic)^ Component 4 (Factor 4—Political)^ [Recommendations]
Natasha	Orientation (STEP)^ Component 1 (Factor 1—Social)^ Component 2 (Factor 2—Technological)^ Component 3 (Factor 3—Economic)^ Component 4 (Factor 4—Political)^ [Recommendations]	Orientation (STEP)^ Component 1 (Factor 1—Social)^ Component 2 (Factor 2—Technological)^ Component 3 (Factor 3—Economic)^ Component 4 (Factor 4—Political)^ [Recommendations]

Students	Generic stages
Kristie	Orientation (SWOT)^ Description^ Description^ Description^ Description^ Problem—Solution^ Condition^ Component 4 (Threats)^ [Conclusion/Recommendations]
Lena	Orientation^ Classification (macro and micro environment)^ Classification 1 (macro)^ Classification 2 (micro)^ Evaluation (of marketing strategies)^ Procedure/Process (how the company works with its customers)^ Evaluation (strength of the company)^ Visual (company's market environment)^ Evaluation (of a new product—ConnectWise)^ Visual (product life cycle) Procedure/Process (of marketing the new product)^ [Conclusion]

Table 6.7 Generic stages in non-DA students' second (non-DA2) assignment texts

In contrast, the two non-DA students did not appear to make as much progress as their DA counterparts regarding generic stages as shown in Table 6.7. For instance, Kristie did not really grasp how to make effective use of a SWOT framework in her case study analysis despite my feedback on these aspects on her non-DA1:

'What does 'this' refer to here [first sentence of the paragraph]? You need to be more specific. Also, remember to focus on the one of the four categories of the SWOT framework at the beginning of the paragraph. So far, you haven't done this.' (comment on the paragraph intended to be about SWOT component 1 Strengths, non-DA1).

Lena's case was, however, different. Her non-DA1 contained the generic stages of a typical SWOT case study analysis and hence, it was a relatively successful text (Table 6.5). Therefore, her text achieved its purpose as shown by the marks awarded by business studies teachers (see Table 6.8). Nevertheless, the subject teachers, as noted earlier, pointed out that her Conclusion did not achieve its purpose. This text indicated that she could apply a SWOT framework to analyse a company such as Google. Nonetheless, she did not appear to have the same level of conceptual understanding of the frameworks she used in non-DA2. Lena's non-DA2 assessment task was different from Kristie's as shown below:

Table 6.8 Summary of marks awarded by business studies teachers

Students	Average marks		Annie	Lydia	Mark	Annie	Lydia	Mark
	First assignment	Second assignment	First assignment	First assignment	First assignment	Second assignment	Second assignment	Second assignment
Amina	49	46	60	35	52	38	55	45
Lou	67	65	73	55	72	78	50	68
Michelle	70	67	70	70	–	59	75	–
Natasha	65	63	55	75	–	70	55	–
Kristie	60	68	68	50	62	65	80	60
Lena	77	74	75	80	75	62	75	85

> This part of TMA02 requires you to assess the marketing environment for an organisation of your choice and then to choose ONE element of its marketing activities to illustrate how the organisation is responding to change. For this you will need to use course concepts covered in Block 3 Marketing of this course.

As the assignment brief suggests, Non-DA2 also required the student to produce a case study analysis where she had to apply the concepts of *macro* and *micro marketing environments* and their sub-categories to the analysis of a company. However, in this case, the student is asked to choose a company and no case study reading is provided, unlike in other assignments discussed in this research. This makes Lena's non-DA2 assignment more complex and challenging than non-DA1. In her assignment text, after introducing the marketing concepts (macro and micro marketing environments), she drifts from the framework and describes the processes and procedures the company followed for marketing its products. In this respect, her non-DA2 is not as successful as non-DA1. This raises the question how much Lena internalised the concepts of *macro* and *micro environment* and their application.

The results for the generic stages of student assessment texts were complemented by the business studies teachers' marking as explained earlier in this chapter. The teachers marked two assessment texts from each student as shown in Table 6.8. For comparability of the DA and the non-DA students' performance, DA1 and DA2 first drafts (independent performance) from the DA students and non-DA1 and non-DA2 from non-DA students were marked. The marks for each student from each teacher and the average marks are summarised in Table 6.8.

The table shows individual marks from each teacher for each student. As can be seen in the table, there was a considerable discrepancy between the teachers' marks for the same student. For example, out of 100 marks, Annie awarded 60, Lydia 35 and Mark 52 to Amina's DA1 respectively. It appears that Lydia's marking was less consistent than that of the other two. Interestingly, Lena's non-DA2 was awarded 44% by her own business studies course teacher (i.e., NOT the business studies teachers who participated in my research). In order to resolve this problem, following Weigle (2002), the marks were averaged for both the assignments. The average marks (columns 2 & 3) indicate that Amina's texts were the least successful and Lena's the most effective. Regarding progression between the two assignments, all students' marks are slightly lower for the second assignment than the first one except for Kristie. However, this result is not conclusive given the inter-rater inconsistency on the same assignment mentioned earlier. Furthermore, this inconsistency may have occurred due to two different assessment tasks. Therefore, a more detailed qualitative analysis of these texts was required, which the next section does.

6.5.2   *Tracking* macroThemes *in Students' Academic Writing*

Identifying generic features such as genre type and genre staging is only one aspect of understanding students' academic writing development over time. For a better understanding, it is important to examine their written texts in more detail. For this, all students' assignment texts were analysed for *macroThemes* and *hyperThemes* because they posed challenges to the learners as identified through their first assignments. Although one non-DA student (Lena) performed well in this area in her first assignment, she still had difficulties as will be revealed. This section discusses macroThemes, followed by hyperThemes in the next section.

In this study, following Ravelli (2004), the first paragraph of each assignment text is treated as the macroTheme. Martin and Rose (2007, p. 197) propose that the function of a macroTheme is to predict what the text is about by orientating the reader to its hyperThemes. However, some SFL researchers have argued that this function of macroTheme may not always be necessary for cohesion (e.g., Donohue, 2002). In this study, a macroTheme is considered effective when it (1) introduces the product/service to be examined, (2) states the framework used in the analysis and (3) describes how the analysis will be conducted. For example, a SWOT analysis would introduce the product/service being analysed and state the four Components of SWOT in the macroTheme. An example of a successful macroTheme from my research data is given in Excerpt 6.1 below.

Excerpt 6.1

STEP analysis of safer syringes

The purpose of this STEP analysis is to examine the external macro – environment of the safer syringe market. Although safer syringes are accessible, the number of needlestick injuries is still high. The modern syringes enable the prevention of these injuries and there are signs that the market of safety syringes can grow. This report analyses the safer syringe market from social, technological, economic and political aspects. These factors have a crucial impact on the presence of safety syringes.

[macroTheme (introductory paragraph) in Natasha's DA2 final draft (STEP analysis)]

A summary of the results for macroThemes is presented in Table 6.9 (DA) and 6.10 (non-DA).

Table 6.9 Summary of results for macroThemes and hyperThemes in DA students' texts

Students	Appropriate macroTheme?			
	DA1		DA2	
	Draft 1	Final	Draft 1	Final
Amina	No	Yes	Yes	Yes
Lou	No	Yes	Yes	Yes
Michelle	Yes	Yes	Yes	Yes
Natasha	Yes	Yes	Yes	Yes

These two tables show that while two of the four DA students had a macroTheme in their first assignment (DA1 draft 1), one of the two non-DA students had it in non-DA1. It is also clear from Table 6.9 that all DA students wrote macroThemes in their subsequent assessment texts (see Excerpts 6.2 and 6.3, for examples). The progressive change in the DA students' second assessment texts is an indication of their academic writing development which was targeted during the mediation process. In fact, macroThemes are valued by business studies teachers as demonstrated by Annie's comment on Lou's DA1 first draft: 'You had scope to add a short introduction. This is useful as it places your answer in context.'

Excerpt 6.2

Introduction:

Google is a world famous search engine, introducing the new software called chrome. I am writing the analyses of chrome's market environment using the SWOT model, which describes the four main categories for any organization as follows Strengths, Weaknesses, Opportunities and Threats. Below is the SWOT table, summarizing my analysis.

[macroTheme in Amina's DA1 final]

Excerpt 6.3

Vodafone broadband market SWOT analysis

The following is a SWOT analysis of Vodafone's business environment in relation to the growth of mobile phone usage in the broadband market. The SWOT analysis in this report is taken from different perspectives and three case studies.

[macroTheme in Lou's DA2 first draft]

However, the result for the non-DA students' second assessment texts (non-DA2) was just the opposite to that of non-DA1 as shown in Table 6.10: while Lena left out the macroTheme in her non-DA2, Kristie included it in hers (see Excerpts 6.4 and 6.5). It is interesting that Lena, despite her successful use of the macroTheme in her non-DA1, did not use it in non-DA2. It is likely that her ability to use macroThemes was maturing but not yet internalised or consciously recognised as important which might have been addressed through the dialogic feedback process followed in DA. Therefore, it may be argued that more DA procedures could have helped her to fully internalise this maturing writing ability.

Excerpt 6.4

Google SWOT analysis

The new technology developed in the form of the PC Operating Systems (OS) by Google has had a strong impact on its major competitor Microsoft and on the users at large. This

Table 6.10 Summary of results for macroThemes in non-DA students' texts	Students	Appropriate macroThemes?	
		Non-DA1	Non-DA2
	Kristie	No	Yes
	Lena	Yes	No

essay will concentrate on a SWAT analysis of the effects of the Operating Systems is having on Google, Microsoft and the worldwide users.

[macroTheme in Kristie's non-DA1]

Vodafone announcement of its move into providing fixed-line broadband signals its interest and recognition of an already sizeable and profitable market shared by many competitors. How will Vodafone products compete and how can it succeed in this volatile market? I will use the SWOT analysis model in this paper to analyse this product.

[macroTheme in Kristie's non-DA2]

Excerpt 6.5

SWOT analysis of Google Chrome Operating System

Introduction

Google has recently made an announcement of developing a new operating system for computer users. This will certainly compete with other giants such as Microsoft and Apple who are already dominating the computing world. In this short report I will examine the internal and external business environment of Google Chrome operating system using SWOT model.

[macroTheme in Lena's non-DA1]

Marketing environment of On Line Computing Ltd.

Introduction

In order to answer the question given for this assignment I have chosen an organisation I am the most familiar with. On Line Computing is a company that I have been working for almost two years. The company specialises in IT and communication solutions to small to medium enterprises. Currently the company focuses on proactive and flexible one-stop IT support services within IT, telephony and copier/printer technologies to over 100 clients.

[macroTheme in Lena's non-DA2]

6.5.3 *Tracking* hyperThemes *in Students' Academic Writing*

For hyperThemes, the opening sentence of each subsequent paragraph after the macroTheme is considered as hyperTheme. The functions of a hyperTheme are to predict what the paragraph is about and often to mark a shift in the conceptual development of the text. Martin and Rose (2007, p. 194) suggest that the hyperTheme establishes the reader's expectation as to how the text will unfold. Thus, hyperThemes help the text flow smoothly. As with macroThemes, some researchers have proposed that it is not always necessary to have the hyperTheme in the beginning sentence of a paragraph (e.g., Donohue 2002). In this study, a hyperTheme is considered effective when it (1) predicts the Theme of the paragraph, and (2) uses one of the four Components of SWOT/STEP to frame the paragraph as in Excerpt 6.6 (see the sentence in bold).

Excerpt 6.6

The sociological factors identified in the case study are as follows. The culture of an economy is an important factor. When marketing Buckler, Heineken saw similar cultural developments happening around Europe where focus was placed on having healthier lifestyles and cutting down on alcohol intake. This caused Heineken to adapt the right image for Buckler 'the label', where the cultural focus was foremost in the marketing strategy but also in line with their specific target audience. Another factor that has influenced Heineken's marketing strategy has been the endorsed 'no drinking and driving' campaigns by the Government, to encourage the population to take more responsibility. Because of these social changes, Heineken's marketing strategy has been greatly influenced.

[hyperTheme (first component of STEP framework) in Michelle's DA1 final]

One issue regarding what constitutes a hyperTheme in these case study analyses is the use of sub-headings such as Social/Sociological in a STEP case study analysis. The three business studies teachers in this study did seem to suggest that sub-headings are useful to structure the analysis. However, the bare use of the sub-heading without contextualising it in the paragraph (see Excerpt 6.7) was not considered appropriate by at least one teacher: 'it is always good to indicate what the theory says about this [Social]—then go on and illustrate with application' (Annie commenting on Michelle's DA1 first draft). Her reference to 'theory' of the Social component within STEP was related to a high-level generalisation (hyperTheme) in the paragraph which was lacking.

Excerpt 6.7

SOCIAL

One social factor demonstrated in the case study that has had an impact on Heineken's marketing in European countries is the fact that the population started focusing on a healthier lifestyle and cutting down on alcohol consumption. A second factor that has had an impact on Heineken's marketing strategy is the fact that European governments have endorsed no drinking and driving campaigns to encourage the population to take more responsibility. This has required a social change where people want to have the feel and taste of beer without alcohol present.

[hyperTheme in Michelle's DA1 first draft]

Tables 6.11 and 6.12 show the results for the hyperThemes in both DA and non-DA student assessment texts. The results show that the appropriate hyperThemes either did not exist or only a few did in the DA students' first unassisted performance

Table 6.11 Summary of results for hyperThemes in DA students' texts

Students	Number of appropriate hyperThemes			
	DA1		DA2	
	Draft 1	Final	Draft 1	Final
Amina	0	4	0	4 out of 5 (not always linked with macroTheme)
Lou	4 (indicated by sub-headings)	4	4 (not very effective)	4
Michelle	3 (indicated by sub-headings)	4	4 (one not fully developed)	4
Natasha	2 out of 4	4	4	4

Table 6.12 Summary of results for hyperThemes in non-DA students' texts

Students	Number of appropriate hyperThemes	
	Non-DA1	Non-DA2
Kristie	1 out of 4	1 out of 4
Lena	4	2 out of 9

(DA1 draft 1). For example, Lou's hyperTheme in Excerpt 6.8 (DA1 first draft) is not as effective as it could be. It is indicated by the sub-heading *Strength* which is a Component of SWOT but there is no clear link with it in the paragraph.

Excerpt 6.8

Strengths

Google hopes to capture new clients with their ideas for developing a operating system, which they plan to be faster for the future. The company hopes to produce a system that is smart, agile and successful. Google has developed a system called ANDROID which has been tailored for netbooks and able to run programmes that can manage displays, handling keyboard and mouse, which is larger but complex piece of software. Google has a strong position for online advertising, messaging, photo-editing software. Googles chrome Internet browser with the ability in allowing its operating systems to work at a faster paste with other personal computers.

[hyperTheme indicated by sub-heading 'Strength' in Lou's DA1 first draft]

However, except for Amina's, the hyperThemes are realised better in their second unassisted performance as in Lou's DA2 first draft in Excerpt 6.9. When we compare it with her hyperTheme in Excerpt 6.8, it is markedly different because it specifically uses the key concept 'strengths' and also predicts what the paragraph will be about. This kind of change in hyperThemes in Lou's and other DA students' DA2 first drafts shows their gradual academic writing development.

Excerpt 6.9

The first looks at the strengths that the company has and how the business can improve when entering the broadband market. One of their strengths is delivering a strong cash flow and operational performance. Vodafone has a strong link in developing towards global customer relationships, value compared to their competitors. Vodafone has benefited from obtaining variable cost base within fixed operating costs.

[hyperTheme (Strengths) in Lou's DA2 first draft]

Tables 6.11 and 6.12 also show that all DA students were able to produce effective hyperThemes when assisted (DA1 and DA2 finals). This indicates these students' maturing academic writing abilities and their changing ZPDs which are at various levels of development. For example, while Amina needed continuous assistance with producing effective hyperThemes, Lou, Michelle and Natasha were almost capable of doing so independently.

The result for non-DA students' hyperThemes was remarkably different when compared with their DA counterparts. For instance, despite Lena being able to write effective hyperThemes in the SWOT analysis text in non-DA1, she produced only 2 appropriate ones out of 9 in her non-DA2 (see Case study 3 below). In contrast, Kristie made no progress as she produced only one relatively suitable hyperTheme in each assignment although the formative feedback focussed on hyperThemes in non-DA1. This result suggests that Kristie would have needed more assistance and dialogue in order to fully internalise the ability to produce effective hyperThemes in the case study analysis or she may have required other kinds of pedagogic intervention, extra time and so on. Likewise, Lena would probably have benefited from more interaction which could have sustained the ability that she showed in non-DA1.

6.5.4 Case Studies: A Detailed Look at Three Students' Academic Writing Development

In order to investigate DA and non-DA students' academic writing development in more detail, I would like to present three case studies below as they fairly represent the trend of academic writing development among DA and non-DA participants: two from DA and one from non-DA groups. The DA case studies include one successful participant and one less successful participant as revealed by their case study analysis texts: Natasha (successful) and Amina (less successful). As for non-DA, Lena's texts are selected because her writing trajectory seems to have taken a regressive direction, unlike Kristie's whose text will be discussed in Chap. 7.

Case Study 1: Natasha
The first case to consider is Natasha's assessment texts which were STEP case study analyses. By looking at the use of macroThemes and hyperThemes across her texts it was possible to track her academic writing development. The analysis indicated that she may have gained significantly from both the DA procedures and the enrichment materials. Her DA1 and DA2 first drafts together with the assignment tasks are given in Figs. 6.6 and 6.7. They also contain an analysis of her use of macroThemes and hyperThemes in the case study analysis genre to provide the reader with the text context of my discussion in this section.

Stages of genre	Student text (relevant key concepts underlined)	MacroTheme, hyperThemes and comments

DA1 Assignment task

Read the following case study carefully. Then, use the STEP framework to critically analyse the external environment of Heineken in terms of its marketing strategy. Your analysis should not exceed 500 words.

Stages of genre	Student text (relevant key concepts underlined)	MacroTheme, hyperThemes and comments
	STEEP analysis Of Heineken's Buckler beer	MacroTheme:
Orientation^	P1 The analysis will outline how <u>the external factors</u> of the global beer company influenced the start of a new non-alcoholic product. Although, Heineken was producing non - alcohol beers before, there was a desirable opportunity for launching a new brand. <u>The STEEP analysis</u> lists the circumstances of the Buckler's born.	Indicated by the title but not clear from the introduction; STEP not defined or described.
Factor 1 Social^	P2 <u>Social factors</u>: People awareness of towards <u>a healthier lifestyle</u> has increased in recent years. The demand for less harmful products, for example, non – alcohol beers has grown. In addition, there was already a request for a new enhanced brand in Spain. **The changes in social environment had provided a good base to the success of Buckle.**	HyperTheme: sub-heading (underlined)) used to mark the phase but no linguistic resource used to predict the Theme of the paragraph Last sentence seems to have served as hyperTheme
Factor 2 – Technological^	P3 <u>Technological factors</u>: It was important to create a tasty product for the regular beer consumers. The production process required advanced technologie P4 An other <u>technological advantages</u> of Heineken is its <u>developed distributions system</u>, which provided opportunity to spread the beer in Europe and "To be the first in the market"	HyperTheme: as above A separate paragraph used to expand Factor 2 There is no obvious general to particular movement of information in any paragraph.
Factor 3 – Economic^	P5 <u>Economic factors</u> : Despite of Heineken has been producing non -alcohol beers mostly for non European market before., there was no good quality non alcohol beer in the market. Therefore the company did not have to face <u>big competitors</u>. As Buckler was designed for all nations, the advertising was created centrally and it covered whole Europe, which reduced the cost of expensis.The sponsorship of the Dutch cycling team, was an other positive <u>marketing tactic</u> as the team showed how beer can fit into the active healty lifestyle.	hyperTheme: sub-heading (underlined) used to mark it but no resource used to predict the Theme of the paragraph
Factor 4 – Political^	P6 <u>Political factors</u>. The tendency of reducing the alcohol consumption was desirable by <u>government</u> as well. <u>Government campaigns</u> provided a good opportunity to launch the new line. The company had to deal with different <u>regulations</u> in countries. <u>The legislation in Spain</u> in terms of non – alcohol products was more favourable than in other countries.So it was good chance to introduce Buckler first in Spain.	hyperTheme: as above

Fig. 6.6   Natasha's DA1 first draft STEP case study analysis (P1, P2 … = Paragraph 1, 2 …)

DA2 Assessment task
Read the case study below and write up a STEP analysis of the safer syringe market critically examining its external environment. [Use the STEP table to remind yourself how STEP framework works if necessary.]

Stages of genre	Student text (relevant key concepts underlined)	MacroTheme, hyperThemes and comments
Orientation^	**STEP- Safer syringes** P1 The purpose of <u>this STEP analysis</u> is to examine the <u>external macro – environment</u> of the usage of the safer syringes. This framework analyses <u>the social, technological, economic and political factors</u>, which have an impact on the presence of safety syringes.	MacroTheme: quite clearly defined/ stated – STEP is described and linked with the case study analysis.
Factor 1 – Social^	P2 There is one <u>major social factor</u>, which influences the existence of safer syringes. This factor relates to <u>demographic and cultural features</u> such as safety consciousness in different countries. Take, for example, the article in The Economist, which reveals that America has differing viewpoint from other countries in safety issues. The American opinion is that the world is a dangerous place, therefore everything should be ruled and directed in order to make it safer. This attitude lead to that US have strict regulations on syringes. Although, in Europe and Japan there has been a growing concern by unions and workers there are no statutes on the practice of needlesticks. These <u>social changes</u> have direct effect on the location of the market and explain why USA is the potential market.	HyperTheme: not clearly defined but the information moves from general to particular
Factor 2 – Technological^	P3 **Technology plays a central role in adoption of the safer syringes.** In the past some of the safety syringes were made by <u>manually</u>, which lowered the effectiveness of the production. These days the UK healthcare company invited <u>the cheapest automatically retract syringes</u>, which made by <u>automatic method. The automation of production</u> contributes to increasing the level of production. Consequently, the <u>improvement in technology</u> has an obvious benefit and a central role to go mainstream.	HyperTheme: not clearly stated but opening sentence indicates it; Information moves from general to particular
Factor 3 – Economic^	P4 **Several <u>economic factors</u> have an affect on introduction of safer syringes.** One of the key factors is	HyperTheme: clearly stated; information moves

Fig. 6.7 Natasha's DA2 first draft STEP case study analysis

	applying traditional syringes have <u>high cost</u> from economic aspects and from the aspect of <u>personal health cost</u>. For example, <u>the cost of infection</u> caused by the bloodborne pathogen can cost more than $1 million and the overall economic cost is even higher. These expenses could be reduced by the wider use of safer syringes,. Another important issue is the question of <u>the cost of manufacture</u>. Although, the Medisys company invented the cheapest safety syringes they are still more expensive than traditional needles. This has a negative effect on selling the safety syringes and the company has to focus on USA clients who are able to pay for the more pricy products. Besides, the existing syringe producers are worry about their own market as results of this they hinder the adoption of safer syringes.	from general to particular; Points are made and evidence from case study is used to support them
Factor 4 – Political^	P5 **A number of <u>political factors</u> influence the occurrence of the safety needles.** One such an element is the <u>government regulations</u> on safer needles in 2001. Due to this, <u>The Needlestick Safety Prevention Act</u> decree to use safer needles. It also orders that workers who are involved in direct patient care can decide on which syringe to use. Another USA bill is <u>The Health Care Worker Needlestick Prevention Act</u>, which has been implemented by Pete Stark and his colleague. emphasis the protection of the health workers. These Acts uphold workers to practice <u>their rights</u> and take <u>legal action against employers</u> who do not observe the law. Furthermore, it is fundamental in order to spread the modern syringes.	HyperTheme: quite clearly stated; Examples from case study used to support claims made
Conclusion/ Recommendation	P6 Overall, the analysis represents that <u>the macro environment</u> of the safety syringe business have its opportunities and obstacles. By taking advantage of positive changes in <u>legalization, technology and social attitudes</u> it is possible that safer syringes will attain more <u>market</u> in the future.	Macro-New: summary and recommendation used to conclude text, not previously used in her case study analysis

Fig. 6.7 (continued)

An analysis of Natasha's STEP case study analysis texts showed that the use of macroThemes and hyperThemes is far more effective in her DA2 texts compared to the DA1 ones. The difference is evident between DA1 draft 1 and DA2 draft 1 (both unassisted performance) in particular as shown in Figs. 6.6 and 6.7. For example, she clearly shows what the business framework is (STEP), what it means and then links the framework with the case study of safer syringe market in DA2. DA2 macroTheme is more focussed on the case study analysis and previews the different components of the STEP framework unlike the DA1 one. In the DA2 text, sentences are connected better through the reference pronoun 'this'. It appears that, possibly because of DA-based feedback and intervention, Natasha internalised the concept of macroTheme during this research.

Natasha did not seem to know hyperThemes as shown by her DA1 draft 1 (Fig. 6.6). She did use the sub-heading quite confusingly to indicate the hyperThemes because the factors such as *Social factors* were written within the paragraph rather than being separate as a sub-heading. She, however, used them in her DA1 final version. She seemed to have internalised their use as can be seen in DA2 first draft (see Fig. 6.7). In DA2, she consistently employed hyperThemes to introduce each paragraph that analyses one of the factors in the STEP framework.

As seen in these two figures, whereas DA1 draft 1 uses the sub-heading (e.g., *Economic factors*) to indicate the new stage of the case study analysis genre with no explicit hyperTheme, DA2 draft 1 has no sub-headings but hyperThemes which indicate the method of development of each paragraph. It should also be noted that section headings and sub-headings are often used by students to foreground Ideational and Textual meanings in their assignments (Gardner & Holmes, 2010). In this respect, Natasha's DA1 hyperThemes may fulfil the function of Ideational meaning. However, its Textual meaning (i.e., establishing predictive connections with the conceptual framework used in the text) is not fully achieved. When seen in this light, Natasha's DA2 first draft (Fig. 6.7) shows an effective employment of hyperThemes in her text, demonstrating her better understanding of their application. After introducing each Component (e.g., *Economic factor*), she tells the reader what this paragraph is about effectively except in the paragraph about *Social factors*. Then each of the factors is identified from the case study and exemplified. Thus, the information moves from more general to particular, thereby guiding the reader. This change in Natasha's DA2 suggests the positive impact of teacher mediation on her academic writing development.

An interview with Natasha revealed further how much DA procedures enhanced her academic writing. The main reason for Natasha's participation in the project was to improve her paragraphing skills in her text and practise the application of business frameworks. When asked whether she achieved any of these skills, she responded that she felt more comfortable with writing case study analyses after her participation in the research project. She also stated that she was clearer about the introductory stage (i.e., macroTheme) of the case study analysis which was demonstrated through her performance as discussed earlier.

Furthermore, Natasha mentioned that the new method of assessment was "more relaxed" and helped to build her confidence in academic writing, unlike traditional methods which often caused stress and did not explain why she obtained a particular score on her performance. Concepts related to 'affect' were frequently mentioned by Natasha as an important aspect to her learning, which DA, through mediation, possessed. Some previous studies also found affect as an important but under-researched area of assessment (e.g., Carless, 2006; Evans, 2013) which is supported by this research. 'Patience' and 'encouragement' as attributes of DA were very frequently mentioned throughout the interview by Natasha, also confirmed by the mediational data in Chap. 5. It is crucial to recognise this affective aspect in order to obtain a better picture of any Vygotsky-inspired pedagogic practices (Daniels, 2007; Poehner & Swain, 2016).

Overall, Natasha made good progress during my research by producing effective case study analyses. She also reported that the study materials she received in this study were useful for another business studies course that she started towards the end of this research.

Case Study 2: Amina

Amina, who had major commitments to her family and thus was always busy, was struggling with her academic writing in business studies. Her trajectory of writing in this study turned out to be quite different from Natasha's. Despite my well-intended efforts, her independent performance did not improve during the research. As mentioned previously, Amina wrote a SWOT case study analysis in DA1 and a STEP case study analysis from her business studies course for DA2. Her microgenetic development of academic writing can be tracked through her DA1 and DA2 texts.

When examining Amina's macroThemes and hyperThemes, DA1 draft 1 (Google's SWOT case study analysis) and DA2 draft 1 (Legoland's STEP case study analysis), both unassisted performance, look slightly different from each other (see Figs. 6.8 and 6.9). For example, DA1 draft 1 has no macroTheme as it begins with a SWOT table, followed by a descriptive account of Google's search engine and new operating system (P1). The SWOT table is typically presented after the macroTheme if used. In sharp contrast, DA2 draft 1 (Fig. 6.9) has a clear macroTheme: introduction of the STEP framework and a focus on the effect of the *Social factor* on Legoland's business environment. Thus, this result is drastically different and shows her emerging academic writing ability to write macroThemes. The macroTheme in DA2 is successfully employed although her hyperThemes are less successful. The effectiveness of the macroTheme in DA2 first draft has been acknowledged by Annie: 'Noticeable improvement on assignment one evident in the clear introduction'.

The case of Amina's academic writing development is unique in terms of hyper-Themes. Her case study analysis texts did not demonstrate her control of hyper-Themes as required by the assignment task. However, she was able to write successful hyperThemes when assisted by the teacher. For example, her hyperThemes are effectively written in response to the assignment task in DA1 final version, unlike DA1 draft 1 which contains no hyperThemes that relate to the required conceptual framework (SWOT) as shown in Fig. 6.8 although the hyperTheme exists. A comparison is made between DA1 draft 1 and final versions in Excerpt 6.10

Excerpt 6.10

DA1 draft 1

P2 In July 2009, Google has announced the launch of new operating system, chrome, which will compete against today's most famous and trustable software company's Microsoft…

DA1 final version

Strengths

P2 As a reputable company, Google has certain advantages over its competitors. It is the most visited search engine in the world which can help market this new product effectively…

Stages of Genre	Student Text (relevant key concepts underlined)	MacroTheme, hyperTheme and Comments
Visual^ (SWOT table)	**SWOT Analyses of Google's Chrome** **Strengths** / **Weaknesses** • The world's most visited and well known site. • A very good Reputation. • Successful in Gmail and G talk. • No Customer service. • Nothing special about new product. **Opportunities** / **Threats** • Launch of a full operating system (chrome). • Targeting a billion people in future. • Avery strong competition with microsoft. • Risk of product failure.	SWOT table used with no orientation to the analysis The Opportunities
Description (Google)^	P1 Google is a very well known name for billions of people in the world who use the internet. It is the the most visited search engine in the world. Google has introduced some interesting software's like chrome browser and Gmail and G talk, to 600 million people. Google has made all the information available in seconds on the net. Now a days everyone uses Google for their searches on-line which had made Google the world's no. 1 search engine.	MacroTheme: not clear Description of the company; no mention of the framework (i.e., SWOT) It reads like an introduction to Google

Fig. 6.8 Amina's DA1 first draft SWOT case study analysis

Description^	P2 **In July 2009, Google has announced the launch of new operating system, chrome, which will <u>compete</u> against today's most famous and trustable software company's Microsoft.** The operating system which is <u>in competition</u> with chrome will be window 7. Windows are used by 90% of people using the pc's. Some big companies have already installed windows 7 in new laptops and pc's.	HyperTheme: not clear Narrative style and the hyperTheme does not appear to be working
Definition (Chrome)^	P3 **Chrome is software, which will be free.** This can be very usefull for some hardware comapnies to install and present this software. Google is offering free online office applications which can save a lot space on the hard drive and easy to use.	HyperTheme: focuses on Chrome; last sentence does not extend the meaning in the preceding sentences
Comparison^	P4 **<u>Competition</u> with Microsoft is very tough for Google, as Microsoft's windows are a complete operating system with all the drives and support available all the time.** Free updates and customer support have established very strong customer relationships. Office 7 is also doing very well in the market. Microsoft have such a strong reputation that people go for its products automaticlly without much effort.	HyperTheme: Microsoft's dominance no link with SWOT
Explanation (usefulness of Chrome)^	P5 **The world is changing and technology have a great impact on our lives.** In the modern world lifestyle everyone have a pc or laptop for their personal use. Internet is main factor people use in their laptops. To get the fast and efficient connection to the web, Chrome will be best solution and Google can start marketing by targeting millions of its Gmail and Gtalk users worldwide.	HyperTheme: not clear Focus on technology and changing lives; again no sign of SWOT
Comparison (Microsoft and Chrome)^	P6 **The main market for Microsoft is official use pc's and Google can target the personal use and home pc's with their product Chrome easily.** Although google is not good at customer services which can lead to losing customers and failure of the new product. Google can overcome this problem by establishing a plan for customer services and support centre.	HyperTheme – marketing strategies; no element of SWOT
Conclusion	P7 Chrome is free and easy to use is the main quality of a product, which needs to be marketed right to people. Free instalation can get it on the laptops and personal use pc's by hardware comapnies and it can reduce the prices. Overall we can say that Chrome can be a successful product of IT's world.	Macro-New: no link with SWOT; summarises the description

Fig. 6.8 (continued)

DA2 Assignment task

Because this course relies heavily on you making sense of the academic ideas in light of your own experience, it is helpful to start thinking about your own experience of business organisations and their environments right away. Write a brief account (500 words) of your own experiences to date with business organisations and their environments, using one of the three course themes (theory and practice, ways of thinking, diversity and complexity) to help frame your answer. Remember that your experience need not be solely professional in nature, but you should begin to think about how the ideas you're learning about have some resonance with your own experience.

Stages/ phases of genre	Student text (relevant key concepts underlined)	MacroTheme, hyperTheme and Comments
Orientation (STEP)^	P1 There are various ways of thinking about business environment. Each theory helps to understand how business interacts with each other and with environment. Some theories explain the changes in external environment and others focus on how businesses can become successful. One of the theories is a STEP Model, which describes the business environment by focussing on four factors as follows, • Social • Technological • Economic • Political I am using one of the factors, social, to describe my organisation.	MacroTheme: using the STEP framework to analyse the business environment of Legoland which is not mentioned.
Description (abstract ideas)^ Description of abstract ideas (how experience is shaped up); exemplification - media	P2 **Our experience in everyday life shapes our thinking, built our opinions and we make perspective about how we like doing things and things around us.** People's perspectives can change according to the environment they live in, for example media plays a big role in making people's mind about things. Especially news media can present a story in a positive or negative way which affects people views.	hyperTheme: experience in everyday life? No clear direction and link with the assignment title or the Social factor
Description^ Description/ explanation of how business theories develop	P3 **Theories about business do not have many differences in them.** They are based on collected data and observation of how business work. This data is observed by a human being, so there is great impact of the person who is collecting and presenting that information, which becomes the theory.	hyperTheme: stated but still not linked with the assignment title/ macroTheme
Recount^ Recount of joining the company; background info	P4 **I am working in one of the UK's favourite children park, Lego land.** When I joined the company I was introduced with the training course to help me settle down in the job role and perform my duty accurately. In the training course I learnt about food and hygiene and health and safety at work place.	No clear hyperTheme but concentration on background to the job; no link with macroTheme (Social factor)

Fig. 6.9   Amina's DA2 first draft SWOT case study analysis

Description^ Description of the company – Lego Land	P5 **Lego Land Windsor is one of the four Lego land parks in the world.** First was opened in Denmark, other two are in Germany and USA. This theme park is built with 55million Lego bricks.	HyperTheme: Lego Land; not directly linked with macroTheme (Social factor)
Classification (type of services)^ Description of purpose of the business/ company; looks like classification	P6 **There are four theories or purpose we are working on as follows,** 1. To provide entertainment to children and family. 2. <u>Healthy eating</u> 3. <u>Education</u> 4. Giving <u>value for the money</u> in services.	HyperTheme: purposes of the company; no clear link with the macroTheme (Social factor)
Description 1^ Description of entertainment facilities; exemplification	P7 **At Lego land there are variety of rides and attractions for children and adults including some over 50's attractions.** Activity area in the park includes the beginning, Imagination, Duplo Land, traffic, Land of Vikings, Lego City, adventure land, wild woods and knight kingdom. Average time spent in this area is 5-6 hr. Guest satisfaction 90.8% say they had excellent day.	HyperTheme: entertainment facilities at Lego Land; no clear link with Social factor
Description 2^ Description of eating facilities; exemplification	P8 **We are promoting <u>healthy eating</u> for our customers, especially kids.** There are 7 shops and 11 coffee shops and restaurants in Lego land Windsor. Signature dishes from best-seller children's food expert, Annabel Karmel, feature on the menu. All fizzy drinks have been removed and replaced with milk, fruit juices like caparison and still water. Adults can feature <u>healthy salads,</u> jacket potatoes and low fat, salt and sugar beans etc. There are new fish dishes introduce as well.	HyperTheme: healthy eating at Lego Land; no clear link with Social factor
Description 3^ Description of workshops at Lego Land; exemplification	P9 **All workshops are <u>national curriculum relevant,</u> covering key stage 1- 4 and special needs.** Workshops last for 45 min and they explore different aspects of design, technology and information. The children get help to build design, make robots and complete variety of tasks. School groups receive 15% discount in food and retail, and other extra offers as well. Lego land Windsor nominated charity is Ormond street hospital charity.	HyperTheme: workshops at Lego Land; final sentence un-related to the paragraph; no clear link with Social factor
Description 4^ Description of/ explanation for value for money at Lego Land	P10 **Lego land aims to give <u>value service for the money</u>.** The basic annual pass for child/ senior is £36 and adult £49. 87% of our customers rate the Lego land as good value for money. In 2007 Lego land sold 90000 annual passes.	HyperTheme: value for money; linked with the company's purposes but not Social factors
Conclusion? Explanation of why Lego Land has changed its services	P11 Over the last decade, <u>people livings</u> have been changed. Life have become busier than ever before and <u>stressful,</u> to come out of this <u>stressful life</u> people need breaks and fun out. <u>Eating habits</u> have been changed, people want to eat <u>healthy</u> and been informed of what they are eating. These changes had impacted the Lego land as well. They have changed the way they serve food and salt and <u>sugar</u> been reduced in dishes. Varieties of dishes are introduced to meet the different <u>needs of people.</u> All workshops are representing the national curriculum.	macroNew: people's changing life style. No link with the macroTheme: social factor influencing the company's business environment.

Fig. 6.9 (continued)

Clearly, the latter is directly related to one of the SWOT components (Strength) (abstract and decontextualized) whilst the former simply reports a particular event (contextualised) without connecting it with the SWOT framework. As a result, the purpose of the analysis is not fulfilled. In spite of the mediation focusing on hyperThemes provided to her, Amina was not able to link her analysis with the given conceptual framework. It appears that her DA1 first draft is operating using 'everyday' or 'commonsense' rather than 'scientific' concepts to use Vygotsky's terms (Karpov, 2003).

As in DA1 texts, the hyperThemes are evidently different in paragraphs 7 and 8 in DA2 final version from those in DA2 draft 1 as compared in Excerpt 6.11. However, she did not make any changes to the hyperThemes in paragraphs 9 and 10 despite my comment on her DA2 draft 2:

> The key issue is creating the link between your theoretical concept (STEP) or framework and the information you have about Legoland. As you are applying the sociological aspect of the STEP framework to Legoland's response to its external environment, ensure that each paragraph has a key idea associated with the *social* factor. In other words, your paragraph needs to begin with the high level idea linked with the social factor.

It is also worth noting that those that she changed are not clearly connected with the macroTheme *Social factors* either as can be seen in Excerpt 6.11. This suggests that she needed much more targeted support than Natasha did.

Excerpt 6.11

DA2 draft 1

P7 At Lego land there are variety of rides and attractions for children and adults including some over 50's attractions.

P8 We are promoting healthy eating for our customers, especially kids.

DA2 final version

P7 Lego land is most popular in children and young generation for entertainment and socializing.

P8 To entertain children and their families with different activities Lego land also active in healthy food.

The main challenge for Amina in this assignment (DA2) was using the course concepts to guide her hyperThemes. Although her macroTheme is better in DA2 than in DA1 draft 1, essentially, the rest of her DA2 text is not any different from DA1 draft 1: in both she fails to apply a given framework to conceptualise the business phenomena. This lack of a clear framework guiding DA2 first draft is also evident in Annie's comment:

> Thus far comments have not been related to the 'social' factor. There is no evidence of a logical flow to the line of reasoning here. Proper structure [i.e., hyperThemes] may have assisted this considerably. [Paragraph 4, DA2]

It was not clear why this happened and I could not explore this issue any further due to Amina's lack of availability. However, the interview with her did indicate that she preferred DA to traditional assessment because DA included more 'personal communication and interaction' which made her 'feel comfortable'. From the information that I gathered through email exchanges and telephone conversations with her during the study, the lack of her progress may be explained. It appeared that while she was writing these texts, various personal factors seemed to have affected her work. For example, she had a new-born baby and an ill mother, both of whom needed her continuous attention as Amina had no one else to support her. Given the pressure she had, it is not surprising that she was unable to benefit from the mediational support in DA2.

However, this problem can additionally be linked with the way mediation worked for this assignment. Instead of using instant messaging as for DA1, Amina decided to have annotations and comments on her DA2 texts through emails although her preferred method of communication (i.e., a better mediating tool) was synchronous communication such as instant messaging as mentioned by her during the interview: 'It is better to use chat [than email if] I have time.'

To sum up, Amina benefitted from mediation during DA1 to some extent as discussed above. However, she was unable to sustain her ability to write effective hyperThemes by using a particular business framework in similar contexts and hence, she lacked the self-regulation of writing hyperThemes. Thus, it can be said that her writing development did not progress as expected, unlike Natasha's. From a Vygotskian perspective, however, this may be natural since development does not follow a linear process. Rather it is a dialectical process entailing progression and regression rather than 'gradual accumulation of separate change' (Vygotsky, 1978, p. 73). Amina's regression may still contribute to her academic writing development.

Case study 3: Lena
The third case study relates to Lena's academic writing journey in my research. Since she as a non-DA participant produced only two assessment texts for this study, inevitably, there is limited information regarding how much academic writing development she gained. Her academic writing journey was different from both Natasha and Amina's. Figures 6.10 and 6.11 present Lena's non-DA1 and non-DA2 assignments respectively. Due to the length of non-DA2 text, paragraphs 8–10 (P8–P10) have been removed.

An analysis of Lena's macroThemes and hyperThemes, shown in Figs. 6.10 and 6.11, demonstrates that they are handled better in non-DA1 than in non-DA2 despite both being awarded high marks by the three business studies teachers (see Table 6.8). Whilst the macroTheme in non-DA1 clearly states what the analysis will do (i.e., a SWOT analysis of Google Chrome's internal and external environment), the non-DA2 macroTheme does not state what framework or concepts the analysis uses in the case study analysis of XYZ Computing. It does refer to the assignment question without mentioning specific concept: *marketing environment*. However, the second paragraph introduces the key concepts being used to analyse the organisation's marketing environment. These concepts are *macro* and *micro marketing environments*. Thus, it is evident from Fig. 6.10 that the macroTheme in non-DA1 orientates the reader to the case study analysis effectively by stating how the analysis will be conducted by using SWOT. In contrast, she concentrates on the description

Stages of genre	Student text (relevant key concepts underlined)	MacroTheme, hyperTheme and Comments
Orientation (SWOT)^	*Introduction* P1 Google has recently made an announcement of developing a new operating system for computer users. This will certainly compete with other giants such as Microsoft and Apple who are already dominating the computing world. In this short report I will examine the internal and external business environment of Google Chrome operating system using SWOT model.	MacroTheme states what the text is doing: SWOT analysis of Chrome Does not explain SWOT
Component 1 (Strengths)^	*Strengths* P2 **Google Chrome OS has number of strengths** but one of the important ones is that this software is a browser based OS. It seems to be "a natural extension" of already existing Google Chrome internet browser and is being made for portable netbooks which are currently in a great demand of consumer's usage. Being a browser based operating system it is enabling the software to be faster, smoother and lightweight. A further strength of Google Chrome operating system is that it is free to all its users. This software is an open-source project and therefore outside developers are welcome to work on it. This is a further strength that only creates a demand for such product.	clear hyperTheme: clearly stated - strengths
Component 2 (Weaknesses)^	*Weaknesses* P3 **There are several weaknesses that Google Chrome OS is facing.** Roger Kay, president of Endpoint Technologies Associates says "There're all those drivers and devices that have to be supported." A further weakness is the nonexistent customer service department. If something goes wrong with the software, users seem to be helpless who to turn to for needed support.	Clear hyperTheme: clearly stated - weaknesses
Component 3 (Opportunities)^	*Opportunities* P4 Google now currently have about 60 million users of its Gmail e-mail service. This is a great opportunity to target these users with advertisements of the new operating system. Relating to this, there will be more stuff happening in the internet browser, more web pages will be searched and more relevant the Google search engine becomes.	hyperTheme: though not entirely stated has a focus on opportunities.
Component 4 (Threats)^	*Threats* P5 A typical threat for the Google Chrome OS will be Windows 7 operating system developed by Google's rival Microsoft. Windows 7 will be offered to all consumers when they purchase a new computer or notebook. Even when Google Chrome OS will be out and for free, some consumers may still prefer what they know and therefore stick to Microsoft`s or Apple products.	No clear hyperTheme but concentration on Threats to Google
Conclusion	*Conclusion* P6 Considering the strengths and opportunities and comparing them with weaknesses and threats of Google Chrome operating system it is possible to assume that the software will create a high demand for computer users and therefore a successful product on the market.	MacroNew: Clear conclusion (claim) with no recommendation

Fig. 6.10 Lena's non-DA1 SWOT case study analysis

of what her company does in non-DA2 (Fig. 6.11), thereby making it a less effective macroTheme. Among the three business studies teachers, Annie also pointed out the lack of focus regarding the conceptual framework in the macroTheme: 'Good start at an introduction here—*would however have liked to see mention of the relevant marketing concepts*' (emphasis added, Annie's comment on paragraph 1, non-DA2).

NDA2 assignment task		
Using course concepts/frameworks from Block 3 analyse the marketing environment of an organisation of your choice.		
Stages of genre	**Student text (relevant key concepts underlined)**	**MacroTheme and hyperThemes; comments**
Orientation^	*Marketing environment of XYZ Computing Ltd.* [real company name removed for anonymity] Introduction P1 In order to answer the question given for this assignment I have chosen an organisation I am the most familiar with. XYZ Computing is a company that I have been working for almost two years. The company specialises in IT and communication solutions to small to medium enterprises. Currently the company focuses on proactive and flexible one-stop IT support services within IT, telephony and copier/printer technologies to over 100 clients.	MacroTheme: links with the assignment question but does not state the macroTheme.
Classification (macro and micro environment)^	Marketing Environment P2 Marketing environment is the internal and external influences that can directly or indirectly affect many activities of an organization. Marketing environment divides into macro and micro environment as shown in Table 1.0 below [not shown here].	clear hyperTheme: definition and classification – marketing environment
Classification 1 (macro)^	*Macro Environment* P3 XYZ Computing mainly concentrate on the technology advances in service products means other companies are aggressively marketing to all clients and given the economic situation the company cannot afford to achieve this level of marketing.	hyperTheme: not clearly stated (XYZ's macro environment)
	P4 Economically the company has reduced the spend on the marketing at this point as XYZ is launching a new product. This has been tested and configured for the last five months so there was not any point in marketing the old product. The company has not had any social changes to the marketing in terms of using social media etc as the generation are not yet in a position of power/decision making.	HyperTheme: relatively clear but not linked with the macroTheme which is also not clear!

Fig. 6.11 Lena's non-DA2 marketing case study analysis

Classification 2 (micro)^	*Micro Environment* P5 <u>Micro forces</u> have an <u>organisation-specific impact</u> on the <u>individual business</u>. XYZ Computing strongly consider the reaction of <u>internal environment</u> when <u>implementing</u> <u>marketing</u> <u>strategies.</u> Shareholders are part of <u>the business</u> so they are inconstant <u>marketing mode</u> due to the update from the <u>ops team</u> and <u>general manager</u>. *Internal* – 'men' would include the <u>service team</u> talking directly to <u>clients</u> on <u>site visits</u> and also the company's <u>appointment setter</u> <u>generating</u> <u>new business</u> <u>meetings</u>. *Money*- the company is currently working to a very <u>restrictive marketing budget</u> so no <u>direct marketing</u> is being done. *Machinery* – the company utilise <u>the new system</u> ConnectWise for <u>marketing via email</u> although this at the moment is infrequent. *Materials* used are mainly <u>electronic</u> as of <u>the nature of the company's clients</u> and <u>vertical market</u>. <u>Markets</u> are not as important as the company is well <u>geographically based.</u>	hyperTheme: micro environmental impact on XYZ; link with macroTheme not established
Evaluation (of marketing strategies)^	P6 XYZ Computing <u>positively market</u> to its <u>suppliers</u> to gain <u>leads and favourable discounts</u>. The company has opened <u>accounts</u> with its <u>suppliers</u> with <u>a certain budget</u>. This ensures the <u>speedy orders</u> and <u>deliveries</u> to either to the company's <u>office workshop</u> or to <u>client's sites</u>. <u>Marketing team</u> is also holding a <u>close relationship</u> with the most of its <u>suppliers</u> to ensure that both <u>parties</u> understand the need of <u>quality supplies</u>.	HyperTheme: clearly set out though not linked with the macroTheme
Procedure/ Process (how the company works with its customers)^	P7 <u>Buyers</u> are our <u>customers</u> -<u>other businesses</u>, who are central to the <u>marketing concept</u>. XYZ Computing have four <u>accounts managers</u> who each "look after" its <u>clients</u>. <u>Regular quarterly</u> meetings are being held by <u>accounts managers</u> where any <u>new</u> <u>products</u>, <u>costs</u> and <u>changes to services</u> but also <u>requirements,</u> <u>needs</u> and opinions by the <u>clients</u> are discussed. These meetings bring a vital information to XYZ upon <u>marketers</u> anticipate the future decisions. [paragraphs 8 – 10 removed]	HyperTheme: working with customers
Conclusion	Conclusion P11 XYZ Computing is currently <u>investing</u> in <u>additional</u> <u>programs</u> to ConnectWise such as <u>new antivirus program</u> and <u>online backup</u>. With these <u>features</u> the <u>product</u> is certain to gain a <u>higher value</u> and <u>demand</u> on <u>the market.</u>	MacroNew: no clear link with the macroTheme – marketing environment

Fig. 6.11 (continued)

The same is reflected in the management of the hyperThemes in Lena's non-DA1 and non-DA2. The hyperThemes in non-DA1 are more effective as they directly link with the concepts (i.e., Strengths, Weaknesses, Opportunities and Threats) in the SWOT framework introduced in the macroTheme and operate at a general level. For example, the hyperTheme 'Google Chrome OS has number of *strengths*' in paragraph

2 (emphasis added, see Fig. 6.10) clearly indicates that this paragraph will be about Google's strengths (internal business environment) over its competitors. The key concept *Strengths* is deployed and the paragraph is developed by presenting these strengths. Each strength is also supported by particular examples drawn from the case study reading sources. The same method of paragraph development is followed in the remaining paragraphs that focus on the SWOT components. This academic writing ability in Lena's SWOT case study analysis has been reflected in all three business studies teachers' summary comments:

> Clear points fitted within SWOT framework. (Mark)

> Overall, your structure was excellent. You showed a clear understanding of the case study and you transferred the information correctly giving appropriate evidence to support your claims. (Lydia)

> A well structured and confident piece of writing here. (Annie)

In contrast, most of the hyperThemes in non-DA2 are not directly associated with the concepts (i.e., macro and micro market environment) that Lena intends to apply to the analysis of her company. Compare the hyperThemes in the two paragraphs below (Excerpt 6.12):

Excerpt 6.12

Non-DA1 (SWOT Component 1 – Strengths)

P2 **Google Chrome OS has number of strengths** but one of the important ones is that this software is a browser based OS. It seems to be "a natural extension" of already existing Google Chrome internet browser ….

Non-DA2 (marketing strategies)

P6 **XYZ Computing positively market to its suppliers to gain leads and favourable discounts**. The company has opened accounts with its suppliers with a certain budget….

In contrast to non-DA1, non-DA2 is not linked with the business concept (i.e., *macro marketing environment*) to be applied to the analysis although it predicts what the paragraph will do. The paragraph simply describes the company's marketing strategies. However, the three business studies teachers did not seem to have the same view regarding the use of the course concepts to frame the analysis, which would normally indicate a coherent development of the 'argument' in the analysis. While Lydia and Mark appeared to be satisfied with the application of the concepts, Annie's view of the overall coherence of Lena's text was different as indicated by her summary comment: 'Generally fragmented discussion. Lacks coherence.' In my own view, Lena appeared to be struggling while applying the course concepts to analyse her company's macro and micro environment, which resulted in less effective hyperThemes in non-DA2 than those in non-DA1.

To summarise, Lena showed a good grasp of managing macroThemes and hyperThemes in non-DA1 but she appeared to have failed to do so with her non-DA2. The reasons may be that the latter was conceptually more challenging than the former and potentially she had not fully developed her expertise to write effective macroThemes and hyperThemes as required by this assignment. A more interactive approach to assessment such as DA may have enabled me to explore to what extent Lena grasped the concepts she tried to apply to her case study analysis.

6.5.5 Conceptual Development

Conceptual development is an aspect of Ideational meaning in SFL. In this book, it is concerned with the genre-related aspects (i.e., genre stages, macroThemes and hyperThemes), two business frameworks (i.e., STEP and SWOT) and any directly relevant business concepts in a specific case study analysis text.

Consistent with this view of conceptual development, a learner who produced an assessment text that employed generic stages, macroThemes and hyperThemes drawing on the concepts of STEP or SWOT (or other frameworks, for that matter) better in the second assignment than in the first one was considered to have achieved a degree of conceptual development in the study reported here. Most importantly, social interaction realised through semiotic mediation played an important role in promoting conceptual development, which is central in Vygotskian sociocultural theory of learning. Of particular importance is the view that concept or knowledge is co-constructed rather than being constructed by an individual alone (e.g., see Mercer, 2007).

Conceptual development occurred differently for each learner in my research with some learners developing the targeted conceptual knowledge more than others. For example, most DA learners made progress in this area over time while the non-DA learners showed a limited amount of positive change across two written assignments. It was particularly evident in the application of hyperThemes (see Tables 6.11 and 6.12) and the concepts from the two business frameworks. While three of the four DA students used hyperThemes to operationalise the STEP or SWOT framework in the second assignment, one non-DA student (Kristie) made no progress and another one (Lena) seemed to have regressed in non-DA2 (See three case studies presented in the last section for comparison). On this basis, it can be argued that the non-DA students did not achieve as great a degree of conceptual development as their DA counterparts did.

Conceptual development was also tracked by examining increasing and decreasing *Technicality* in the participants' assignments in my research as it was one of the aspects diagnosed as problematic to them in their first DA/non-DA assignments. Technicality, as defined in Chap. 4 (4.6.2) following SFL traditions, refers to the specialised use of terms in a particular field such as business studies in which commonsense words acquire new meanings (e.g., see Martin, 1993b; Woodward-Kron, 2008). Following this notion of technicality, terms that had taxonomic relationships (e.g., *Technological* in STEP and *Strengths* in SWOT) and business concepts (e.g., *external environment*) in the student assignments were identified and analysed. The analysis was carried out following the two criteria mentioned in 6.3. For comparability across DA and non-DA participants, only unassisted performance (first draft) was analysed. For the coding and analysis of technicality, I used the NVivo qualitative data analysis software. A summary of results for technicality is presented in Table 6.13 and for technical categories and related examples, see Table 6.14. For further examples of technicality in context, please see the underlined words and word groups in the assignments provided in the case studies above (see 6.5.4).

Table 6.13 shows that all students' Technicality increased in their second assignment except for Michelle's. However, the realisation of relevant Technicality in DA students' assignments is remarkably different from that of the non-DA students. For example, although the number of specialised terms increased considerably in both Lena and Kristie's second assignment they were mainly 'other business concepts' rather than those directly related to the frameworks they had used in their case study analysis. Furthermore, Lena's second assignment was considerably longer than the first one. In contrast, almost all the DA students employed more technical terms associated with the framework (e.g., SWOT) used in their second case study analysis assignment than those in their first assignment. These results indicate that the DA students deployed key concepts in a more relevant and meaningful way than their non-DA counterparts did.

These results are supported by the business studies teachers' comments too. For example, Annie commented on Kristie's non-DA2 thus:

> Student in all likelihood has (and relies on) a good common sense understanding of the business world. SWOT not used as a tool for analysis – nor are the concepts explained. No clear evidence of cognitive skill development since previous assignment.

And on Natasha's second assignment: 'STEP factors generally well understood… Clear evidence of writing skills progress since first attempt [assignment]. Student has benefited from guidance [i.e., DA sessions].'

To sum up, the analysis of macroThemes, hyperThemes and Technicality in student assignments suggests that DA students showed more conceptual development than their non-DA counterparts. This may be attributed to the semiotic mediation received by the DA students. Additionally, the results showed that higher frequency of business terms did not necessarily mean writing a successful case study analysis if they did not relate to the associated business framework (cf. Woodward-Kron, 2008).

Table 6.13 Categories and their frequency of Technicality in DA and non-DA texts

Technicality	Amina		Lou		Michelle		Natasha		Kristie		Lena	
	DA1	DA2	DA1	DA2	DA1	DA2	DA1	DA2	Non-DA1	Non-DA2	Non-DA1	Non-DA2
Business environment	1	8	3	12	25	15	4	8	8	9	4	10
STEP—sociological		3			6	12	5	14				
STEP—technological		1			2	5	5	10				
STEP—economic		1			4	9	6	14				
STEP—political		1			3	5	5	16				
SWOT—strengths	1		2	11							5	
SWOT—weaknesses	1		1	2							4	
SWOT—opportunities	1		2	8					1		3	
SWOT—threats	1		4	7							2	
Other business concepts	14	8	15	8	21	2	11	8	22	44	11	31
Macro environment												4
Micro environment												4
Marketing												54
Total	19	22	27	48	61	48	36	70	31	53	29	103

Table 6.14 Technical categories with examples

Technical categories	Examples
Business environment	Market, business environment, reclaim a share of that market
STEP—sociological	Eating habits, a healthier lifestyle
STEP—technological	Technological, specially developed fermentation process
STEP—economic	a number of economic factors, the local economies
STEP—political	the different legislation
SWOT—strengths	A further strength of Google Chrome operating system, a strong position, global customer relationships
SWOT—weaknesses	Several weaknesses,
SWOT—opportunities	A great opportunity, Opportunities
SWOT—threats	A typical threat, price wars
Other business concepts	Organization, Giving value for the money
Macro environment	Macro Environment, recession
Micro environment	micro environment, the reaction of internal environment
Marketing	marketing strategies, marketing mode, direct marketing

6.6   Summary of SFL-Based Examination of Students' Ability to Write a Case Study Analysis Genre

The SFL analyses of the generic stages in the six students' assignments above showed that they were at different stages of development concerning the understanding and internalisation of the generic stages used in a case study analysis genre. It became evident in the first assignment that all the students had difficulty in managing the typical generic stages found in a case study analysis except for Lena (who, however, struggled in her second assignment). Therefore, the mediation (both dynamic and non-dynamic) focussed on these stages. As shown by the subsequent drafts and the second assignment (both DA and non-DA), Lou, Michelle and Natasha handled the generic stages more successfully whilst Amina, despite the significant improvement in her DA1 final version, did not manage these stages effectively in DA2. However, her less effective performance may be linked with the medium of teacher mediation as mentioned earlier, since she was unable to continue using instant messaging for the mediation in DA2. It is also possible that she could have retained her progress regarding writing a SWOT analysis if she had done a similar task as in DA1 instead of a STEP analysis.

On the other hand, Kristie essentially demonstrated no change in her management of the generic stages in the second assignment and Lena handled them less effectively in the second one. In particular, it is intriguing why Lena failed to apply the theoretical concepts chosen by her to guide the generic stages which she applied so successfully to her non-DA1. One reason may be that the chosen theoretical concepts are still not fully internalised or are beyond her ZPD when not mediated by a more capable other.

Like the generic stages, the SFL genre analysis showed that macroThemes and hyperThemes were found more effective in all students' second assignments (DA2 or non-DA2) than in their first assignment (DA1 or non-DA1) except Lena's, presumably because teacher mediation (DA) or normal feedback (non-DA) concentrated on them to help the students improve them. The analysis revealed that Lou, Michelle and Natasha developed their skills in writing effective macroThemes and hyperThemes in the later case study analysis texts, indicating that DA procedures possibly helped them to achieve the effectiveness. Nevertheless, Amina, did not show the same level of her control of the macroTheme and the hyperThemes in DA2 as seen in her DA1 final draft. Again, this could have resulted from the medium of interaction she chose or the nature of the assignment task in DA2 (i.e., STEP instead of a SWOT analysis). While Kristie's handling of the macroThemes and the hyperThemes in her non-DA1 and non-DA2 texts remained the same, Lena did not appear to manage the macroTheme and the hyperThemes in non-DA2 as well as she did in non-DA1. Although it is not clear why Kristie made little progress and Lena performed worse in non-DA2 regarding these two aspects of academic writing, it could be argued that Kristie might have improved her skills and Lena may have retained her skills from non-DA1 through a more dynamic assessment process, a view that Kristie also acknowledged in an interview with her. A similar pattern could be seen in the presence of Technicality in the six participants' case study analysis texts. This presence or absence of Technicality also contributed to the development of both macroThemes and hyperThemes in their texts. The lack of progress by Amina and Kristie and the lack of consistency in Lena's writing could be because, despite the symbolic mediator (i.e., written teacher feedback) having a rich learning potential, it may have remained ineffective due to the lack of an immediate human mediator who could have facilitated its appropriation by these students (Kozulin, 2003, p. 35).

6.7 Summary

Research within DA has rarely reported on academic writing although some studies have attempted to examine aspects of second language writing. The research reported in this book aimed to examine academic writing of distance adult learners from a DA perspective. It also used the powerful tool of SFL-based genre analysis to track the participating students' academic writing development when they wrote a case study analysis genre. This chapter presented how this worked for both DA and non-DA students over their two assignments.

This chapter reported on the SFL-based genre analysis of six students' business studies assignments and the supplementary data by focusing on Ideational and Textual meanings as construed in their case study analysis texts. The findings suggested that DA procedures have the potential to enhance learners' academic writing development, albeit at varying levels. It was also found that while three out of four students that underwent these procedures showed progress regarding their ability to manage generic stages, macroThemes, hyperThemes and Technicality in case study analyses, one of them reverted to her old ways of structuring academic writing in the case study analysis genre. On the other hand, non-DA students showed either no progress or did not maintain consistency in handling these aspects in their academic writing. It was possible to understand these students' academic writing trajectory systematically only by using the well-developed linguistic analysis theory, namely, SFL which has not been deployed in DA research despite the call to use it to provide a rich picture of learners' linguistic development through DA (Gardner, 2010).

Overall, in this study, it appeared that DA procedures in combination with SFL may have helped the DA students improve their academic writing and conceptual development when their potential ability (ZPD) was targeted. To explore the sustainability of the positive changes in these students' academic writing, it is necessary to consider their performance in a new assessment context and this is the goal of Chap. 7.

References

Carless, D. (2006). Differing perceptions in the feedback process. *Studies in Higher Education, 31*(2), 219–233.

Christie, F., & Maton, K. (2011). Why disciplinarity? In F. Christie & K. Maton (Eds.), *Disciplinarity: Functional linguistic and sociological perspectives* (pp. 1–9). London: Bloomsbury.

Daniels, H. (2007). Pedagogy. In H. Daniels, M. Cole, & J. V. Wertsch (Eds.), *The Cambridge companion to Vygotsky* (pp. 307–331). Cambridge: Cambridge University Press.

Donohue, J. P. (2002). *Genre-based literacy pedagogy: The nature and value of genre knowledge in teaching and learning writing on a university first year media studies course.* Ph.D., University of Luton.

Evans, C. (2013). Making sense of assessment feedback in higher education. *Review of Educational Research, 83*(1), 70–120. https://doi.org/10.3102/0034654312474350.

Gardner, S. (2010). SFL: A theory of language for dynamic assessment of EAL. *NALDIC Quarterly, 8*(1), 37–41.

Gardner, S., & Holmes, J. (2010). From section headings to assignment macrostructures in undergraduate student writing. In E. Swain (Ed.), *Thresholds and potentialities of systemic functional linguistics: Multilingual, multimodal and other specialised discourses* (pp. 268–290). Trieste: EUT Edizioni Università di Trieste. Retrieved from https://www.openstarts.units.it/handle/10077/3652.

Halliday, M. A. K., & Matthiessen, C. M. I. M. (2004). *An introduction to functional grammar* (3rd ed.). London: Hodder Education.

Karpov, Y. V. (2003). Vygotsky's doctrine of scientific concepts: Its role for contemporary education. In A. Kozulin, B. Gindis, V. S. Ageyev, & S. M. Miller (Eds.), *Vygotsky's educational theory in cultural context* (pp. 65–82). Cambridge: Cambridge University Press.

Kozulin, A. (2003). Psychological tools and mediated learning. In A. Kozulin, B. Gindis, V. S. Ageyev, & S. M. Miller (Eds.), *Vygotsky's educational theory in cultural context* (pp. 15–38). Cambridge: Cambridge University Press.

Manchón, R. M. (2017). The multifaceted and situated nature of the interaction between language and writing in academic settings: advancing research agendas. In J. Bitchener, N. Storch, & R. Wette (Eds.), *Teaching writing for academic purposes to multilingual students: Instructional approaches* (pp. 183–199). New York: Routledge.

Martin, J. R. (1993b). Technicality and abstraction: Language for the creation of specialised texts. In M. A. K. Halliday & J. R. Martin (Eds.), *Writing science: Literacy and discursive power* (pp. 203–220). London: The Falmer Press.

Martin, J. R. (1993a). Life as a noun: Arresting the universe in science and humanities. In J. R. Martin & M. A. K. Halliday (Eds.), *Writing science: Literacy and discursive power* (pp. 221–267). London: The Falmer Press.

Martin, J. R., & Rose, D. (2007). *Working with discourse: Meaning beyond the clause*. London: Continuum.

Mercer, N. (2007). Commentary on the reconciliation of cognitive and sociocultural accounts of conceptual change. *Educational Psychologist, 42*(1), 75–78.

Nathan, P. (2013). Academic writing in the business school: The genre of the business case report. *Journal of English for Academic Purposes, 12*(1), 57–68. https://doi.org/10.1016/j.jeap.2012.11.003.

Nesi, H., & Gardner, S. (2012). *Genres across the disciplines: Student writing in higher education*. Cambridge: Cambridge University Press.

Nesi, H., & Gardner, S. (2018). The BAWE corpus and genre families classification of assessed student writing. *Assessing Writing, 38,* 51–55. https://doi.org/10.1016/j.asw.2018.06.005.

Poehner, M. E., & Swain, M. (2016). L2 development as cognitive-emotive process. *Language and Sociocultural Theory, 3*(2), 219–241.

Preston, D., Fryer, M., & Watson, G. (2007). *What is a business?*. Milton Keynes: The Open University.

Prior, P. (2008). A sociocultural theory of writing. In C. A. MacArthur, S. Graham, & J. Fitzgerald (Eds.), *Handbook of writing research* (pp. 54–66). London: The Guildford Press.

QAA. (2007). *General business and management*. Gloucester: The Quality Assurance Agency for Higher Education.

QAA. (2019). *Subject benchmark statement for business and management* (4th ed.). Gloucester: The Quality Assurance Agency for Higher Education.

Ravelli, L. J. (2004). Signalling the organisation of written texts: Hyper-Themes in management and history essays. In L. J. Ravelli & R. A. Ellis (Eds.), *Analysing academic writing: Contextualised frameworks* (pp. 104–130). London: Continuum.

Shrestha, P. N., & Coffin, C. (2012). Dynamic assessment, tutor mediation and academic writing development. *Assessing Writing, 17*(1), 55–70. https://doi.org/10.1016/j.asw.2011.11.003.

Vygotsky, L. S. (1978). *Mind in society: The development of higher psychological processes*. Cambridge, MA: Harvard University Press.

Weigle, S. C. (2002). *Assessing writing*. Cambridge: Cambridge University Press.

Woodward-Kron, R. (2008). More than just jargon: The nature and role of specialist language in learning disciplinary knowledge. *Journal of English for Academic Purposes, 7*(4), 234–249.

Chapter 7
Transfer of Aspects of Academic Writing to Similar and New Contexts Through Dynamic Assessment

7.1 Introduction

The value of the transfer of learning in academic and professional contexts is widely recognised (Engle, 2012; Larsen-Freeman, 2013). A large number of studies (e.g., Butler, 2010; Butler, Godbole, & Marsh, 2013; Foley & Kaiser, 2013; MacRae & Skinner, 2011; Thompson, Brooks, & Lizárraga, 2003) have been carried out in education and psychology in order to understand the nature of transfer with regard to learning over the last century, and yet, it is still unclear how and why learning transfer occurs or not (e.g., see Anson & Moore, 2017; Day & Goldstone, 2012; Larsen-Freeman, 2013). Most previous studies have examined students' learning transfer in the context of general academic writing rather than discipline-based academic writing (e.g., James, 2010a, 2010b, 2014; Monbec, 2018) and therefore, there are only a small number of studies on learning transfer in discipline-based academic writing courses (Baik & Greig, 2009) despite the publication of an edited volume on *writing transfer* (Moore & Bass, 2017). Given that a key purpose of such a course in higher education is to enable students to participate in their chosen academic communities as fully as possible (Moore, 2017) as I argued in Chap. 1, the role of learning transfer from such courses to other disciplines is paramount. The notion of writing transfer is helpfully defined by Moore as 'a writer's ability to repurpose or transform prior knowledge about writing for a new audience, purpose, and context' (ibid., p. 2). In this book, this view is broadly taken for the transfer of academic writing to similar and new academic writing contexts.

In the context of higher education, many of the higher order skills and knowledge such as problem-solving are expected to be transferable by educators. For instance, in business and management, skills like structuring a case study analysis, self-reflection

---

A version of this chapter was previously published as: Shrestha, P. N. (2017). Investigating the learning transfer of genre features and conceptual knowledge from an academic literacy course to business studies: Exploring the potential of dynamic assessment. *Journal of English for Academic Purposes, 25*, 1–17. http://dx.doi.org/10.1016/j.jeap.2016.10.002.

© Springer Nature Switzerland AG 2020
P. N. Shrestha, *Dynamic Assessment of Students' Academic Writing*,
https://doi.org/10.1007/978-3-030-55845-1_7

and the application of business frameworks are those higher order skills that are required for all business studies courses (e.g., see QAA, 2019). Business gradu-ates are assumed to transfer the skills and knowledge including cognitive, social and communication skills from their studies to their workplace as well (Jackson, 2013). Therefore, sustaining these skills and knowledge is central to learning and disciplinary writing development. Despite learning transfer being a key purpose in discipline-based academic writing courses, research in the transfer of language and academic skills has only recently started to emerge (Baik & Greig, 2009; Cheng, 2007; Shrestha, 2017).

In this chapter, I focus on the potential of a *dynamic assessment* (DA) approach in the transfer of genre features and conceptual knowledge among undergraduate business studies students in a distance learning context. This chapter builds on Chap. 6 in which I presented the trajectory of six students' academic writing development across two assignments in the context of DA. In this chapter, I begin by explaining the notion of learning transfer as used in this study, and then briefly review the literature with regard to 'learning transfer' in academic writing and DA. Key findings from my research are reported and discussed using the concept of 'transfer' in DA in relation to *generic stages, macro-Themes, hyper-Themes* and *conceptual development* which were also discussed in Chap. 6 from the perspective of academic writing development. I conclude by highlighting the significance of DA in learning transfer.

7.2 Dynamic Assessment and Transfer

As explained in previous chapters, the research reported in this book followed a DA approach known as interactionist DA as described by Lantolf and Poehner (2004, pp. 58–60) and pioneered by Feuerstein and colleagues (2002). In this approach, assistance is expected to emerge from the interaction between the learner and the teacher-examiner, thus responding to the learner's emerging abilities. Both the teacher and the student work together to reach the goal (i.e. in this study, writing academically valued texts in business studies).

To recap as explained in Chap. 3, interactionist DA has certain basic procedures that practitioners need to follow (see Haywood & Lidz, 2007). These include: (1) identifying learners' current abilities through their independent performance; (2) identifying their problems and challenges; (3) designing intervention tasks to address these problems and challenges; (4) working jointly with learners to complete the task by offering feedback targeting their ZPD; (5) ending on a positive note of successful completion of the task; and (6) checking learners' application of newly acquired skills and knowledge to progressively complex tasks and contexts. This final procedure of interactionist DA is the concern of this chapter. In order to understand the learner's application of genre knowledge required by a *case study analysis* genre and conceptual knowledge in business studies, as I argued in Chaps. 4 and 6, Systemic Functional Linguistics (SFL) as an analytical framework enables a researcher to examine *learning transfer* systematically in the participants' academic writing.

Transfer refers to learners' ability to recontextualise their learning in a new context. There are two similar terms used in DA: *transfer* and *transcendence*. While *transfer* was used by Brown and her colleagues (e.g., Brown and Ferrara 1985 cited in Poehner, 2007, p. 338) to describe more complex tasks than those used in DA tasks, *transcendence* is associated with Feuerstein's interactionist DA approach (e.g., Feuerstein et al., 2002). Although DA scholars appear to use these two terms interchangeably, it has been argued (e.g., Poehner, 2007) that the concept of transcendence has been more robustly developed in the DA literature and is more closely in line with Vygotskian theory.

Within academic writing, the terms 'learning transfer' and 'transfer' seem to be used interchangeably to mean learning in one context impacting on performance in another context (e.g., see James, 2014). Recently, scholars like Moore (2017), cited earlier, also use the term 'writing transfer' in a similar sense in the context of First Year Composition courses in universities in the USA. She argues that despite the assumption that students transfer writing and subject knowledge to their subsequent courses or professions, there has been limited evidence to support this claim. Additionally, 'adaptive transfer' was another term proposed by DePalma and Ringer (2011) in second language writing. It refers to 'the conscious or intuitive process of applying or reshaping learned writing knowledge in new and potentially unfamiliar writing situations' (p. 135). Although this concept appeared to be promising, it has been criticised by Grujicic-Alatriste (2013) arguing that it lacks details about its application (e.g., pedagogical tools) and there is little information about language socialisation which plays an important role in academic writing development. Given that 'transfer' has been widely used in DA and is accepted in the academic writing literature, I am using the term 'transfer' in this book to capture both 'transfer' and 'transcendence'.

The notion of transfer in DA is derived from the Feuersteinian concept of *transformability*, defined as the change in an individual's cognitive knowledge that is applicable to other situations (Feuerstein et al., 2002, p. 113). Cognitive knowledge or what Vygotsky calls 'scientific concepts' (e.g., see Karpov, 2003) provide them with cognitive tools for mediating their future problem-solving. As transformability is realised through the application of newly acquired conceptual knowledge or tools to new contexts and tasks, cognitive knowledge becomes one of its essential aspects.

Transfer can be of two types: 'near transfer' and 'far transfer' (Feuerstein et al., 2002, p. 113). These two types are also widely used in a recently edited volume on writing transfer by Anson and Moore (2017) who cite these terms being originated in Perkins and Salomon (1988, 1992) in their introduction to the volume (p. 4). 'Near transfer' refers to the transfer of skills and knowledge to a specific assessment context similar to the ones accomplished in the immediate past. 'Far transfer' is the application of such skills and knowledge to a more complex and challenging context and therefore, entails more sophisticated mental functioning.

While the notion of transfer has been explored in the context of academic writing, as noted earlier, this area is still under-researched and emergent (Cheng, 2007; Moore & Bass, 2017), and results of previous studies have tended to be unclear regarding transfer in general academic writing (e.g., James, 2010a, 2012). In a recent review of studies on transfer in English for academic purposes (EAP), James (2014) reported that there is some evidence of learning transfer in EAP (also see J. H. Green, 2015). However, the reviewed studies tended to focus on accuracy, vocabulary and grammar rather than at the genre level. The review also suggests that there is a need for studies that investigate the nature of EAP instruction and its impact on learning transfer.

Importantly, there seem to be only a few studies conducted in discipline-specific writing contexts which combine an attempt to track transfer of learning with an explicit focus on language. For instance, Shrestha and Coffin (2012) investigated tutor mediation and its impact on academic writing development from one assessment task to another one. This study, however, did not examine transfer as such and did not focus on the actual academic writing performance of the two learners in question. Cheng (2007) examined transferring genre features by an engineering student in his three article introductions. He argued that observing how a learner recontextualises a genre feature in a new academic writing context provides insights into their learning transfer rather than just exploring how much they know about a particular genre. His claim about the lack of research in this area continues to be so as acknowledged in more recent publications (e.g., Anson & Moore, 2017; James, 2014; Moore & Bass, 2017).

The brief review of studies above on transfer in academic writing strongly indicates that there is a gap regarding transfer from general and discipline-specific academic writing courses to other disciplines. Aiming to contribute to address this gap, this chapter specifically explores the extent to which learners undergoing DA and non-DA transfer genre features and conceptual knowledge learned in one academic writing assessment task to another.

7.3   Learning Transfer Data Used

For the purpose of illustrating learning transfer in this chapter, three assignments each from three DA students (Amina, Lou and Natasha) and one non-DA student (Kristie), business studies tutors' feedback on these assignments and interviews with these students were examined. The first two assignment texts from each student were written for two DA sessions discussed in Chaps. 5 and 6. The third assignment text from them was a *transfer assignment* (TA) as explained below.

When the participants completed the second DA (DA2) task, they were studying a business studies module and to which, it was anticipated, they would transfer their learning of academic writing. In order to examine the transfer of genre features and conceptual knowledge observed in the second DA task to another progressively challenging assessment task, the participants were asked to submit their business studies assignments, referred to as transfer assignment (TA) in this book. They submitted the assignments within a month of completing the DA2 task. DA1, DA2 and TA texts written by three students were selected to examine any evidence of genre learning transfer (or otherwise) from DA2 to TA which was much more challenging than the DA ones. Therefore, these TA texts are used to illustrate far transfer in this

---

Lou's TA task from a business studies course

Task

Using tools and concepts from Units 1–4 of Block 3 (including, if you wish, the analysis referred to in Part 1 of this assignment), write a report which identifies the key challenges facing an organisation with which you are familiar (you may use the same organisation you described in Part 1, or in Assignment 01 Part 2 or Assignment 02). (2000 words)

Guidance notes

This question requires you to apply a variety of the tools and concepts you have been introduced to in the 'Analysis' phase of the strategy process (i.e., Units 1–4 of Block 3). We would expect that as part of your analysis you will need to comment upon external challenges (Unit 1), internal challenges (Unit 2), challenges posed by stakeholders (Unit 3), and the challenges posed by the context within which your chosen organisation operates (Unit 4). Your report should emphasise the conclusions you draw from the application of these frameworks, rather than the applied frameworks themselves, though it needs to be clear how you have used them and what, if any, issues they have presented to you in terms of their adequacy or suitability. You are free to include more detailed analyses using the frameworks in appendices attached to your report. These will not feature in your word count for the assignment, but will not attract marks in themselves.

This question is likely to involve some research on your part, locating appropriate data to enable you to perform this analysis. It may be that your final choice of organisation will depend upon the availability of information from a number of sources (for example, the sources you engaged with in Assignment 01 Part 2). Using a number of sources of information means that you will have to weigh up the merits and reliability of each. The section on critical thinking skills towards the end of Block 1 should be helpful in organising your approach to this material.

In marking this section of your assignment, your tutor will take into account the depth and coherence of your analysis, your critical use of a range of tools and data, and your ability to use the report format to argue clearly and convincingly for appropriate recommendations.

Fig. 7.1 Example of TA task completed by Lou (DA participant)

book. Kristie, the non-DA participant, completed the TA that I designed as she was not studying with the OU at that time. It was similar to the two non-DA tasks she completed (i.e., a SWOT[1] case study analysis). Hence, her TA text is presented to illustrate near transfer due to the similarity of the TA task with previous non-DA tasks. Examples of TA completed by both DA and non-DA participants are provided in Figs. 7.1 and 7.2 respectively. Additionally, interviews with the four students about their experience of the assessment procedures they underwent (explained in Chap. 4) and their business studies tutors' feedback on their TA were collected to complement the textual data.

---

[1]SWOT = Strengths, Weaknesses, Opportunities and Threats.

Transfer assignment task for Kristie

Google Nexus One SWOT analysis

Instructions

You are going to read three short case study texts that look at Google's business environment in relation to its brand new smartphone, Nexus One's market:

    i)   'Google challenges iPhone with launch of Nexus One mobile' by Bobbie Johnson (a *Guardian* news report on 5 January 2010)

    ii)   Is Google's Nexus One phone any good?' by Bobbie Johnson (a *Guardian* news report on 13 January 2010)

    iii)   Review: Nexus One good, but no 'super' phone by Rachel Metz (an *Associate Press* news report on 13 January 2010)

These three articles form a case study of Google's Nexus One market. These articles examine the business environment of Google's mobile phone market from different perspectives.

Task

Read the three case study texts about Google's mobile phone market mentioned above and write a SWOT analysis of this product based on the articles. Your SWOT analysis should be of about 500 words. When you have finished writing your SWOT analysis, send it to me (email address) by email as an attachment as soon as you can.

Guidance notes

Using the SWOT framework, analyse the internal and external environment of this new mobile phone by Google by drawing on the three texts. As you are using the SWOT framework to analyse Google's business environment based on this case study, look for examples that illustrate the four categories (Strengths, Weaknesses, Opportunities and Threats) in the SWOT framework in order to produce an effective SWOT analysis while you are making notes. It may also be helpful to use a SWOT table for your notes.

If you are not sure about what SWOT means, please read the documents (about SWOT analysis) that I sent you for the previous assessment tasks. You can also ask me for clarification or more information.

Fig. 7.2 Example of TA task completed by Kristie (non-DA participant)

7.4 Analysing Transfer Data

As noted throughout this book, two theoretical frameworks are deployed as analytical tools in order to examine the potential of DA regarding transfer in this study. One is related to meaning-making through disciplinary writing (e.g., Coffin & Donohue, 2012) and the other is related to learning and development (e.g., Lantolf & Thorne, 2006). The first one draws on Hallidayan SFL, as explained in Chap. 3, which considers language as a meaning-making resource to achieve a social purpose (e.g., Eggins, 2004). The second framework employs the notion of transfer as outlined in Sect. 7.2.

For this chapter, in particular, Ideational (i.e., about topic) and Textual (i.e., about organising message) metafunctions were examined in relation to the four students' assignments following Martin and Rose (2008). *MacroThemes* and *hyperThemes* (Textual meaning) and use of business concepts (Ideational meaning) were identified as areas for development in all three students' first draft of DA1 and were, therefore, targeted in both DA1 and DA2 as explained in Chaps. 4 and 6. These aspects were focused on the feedback for the non-DA participant as well. In addition to macroThemes and hyperThemes, generic stages were examined in each assignment (see Chaps. 3 and 6).

Regarding Ideational meaning, as in Chap. 6, the use of business concepts and frameworks, drawing on the notion of *Technicality* (Martin, 1993b) and students' awareness of case study analysis as a genre were examined to track the effect of DA. To remind the reader (see Chap. 6), the following criteria were adopted in order to identify Technicality in the students' assessment texts:

1. Terms with a field-specific meaning (processes, things and qualities: e.g., external environment)
2. Terms defined or in taxonomic relations to other technical terms (e.g., strengths, weaknesses)

Technicality, coded by using the qualitative data analysis software NVivo 9 (QSR, 2010), was quantified by considering the frequency of the technical terms. If the same term was used more than once, it was counted more than once given differing contexts of use.

The second tool was the notion of transfer developed within Vygotskian socio-cultural theory as explained in Sect. 7.2. In this book, the transfer of skills and knowledge from the first two assessment tasks to a similar assessment task (i.e., a SWOT or STEP[2] analysis) is considered 'near transfer'. As Kristie completed the TA task that was similar to the previous assessment tasks, her TA text is examined for 'near transfer'. The other three DA participants' TA texts were examined for 'far transfer'. There were three main reasons for considering any far transfer from DA students' DA2 to TA: (1) each TA was significantly longer than DA1 and DA2 as compared in Fig. 7.1 (2000 words vs. 500 words); (2) unlike the DA tasks, there were no case study sources provided but the students were asked to choose their own organisation for the analysis and find sources of information to support their analysis as shown in Fig. 7.3; and (3) the TA required the students to apply a range of business concepts and frameworks taught in their modules rather than just one framework as in DA tasks.

---

[2]STEP = Social/ Sociological, Technological, Economic and Political.

DA2 task	Read the three case study texts about Vodafone's broadband market mentioned above and write **a SWOT analysis** of this product based on the articles. Your SWOT analysis should be of about **500 words**.
Business studies assignment (TA)	Question 2 [Question 1 not examined in my research]
	Write **a report of no more than 2,000 words addressed to an interested investor, justifying your proposed marketing and promotion strategy for launching your new creation.** You must also describe the **target markets, the competitive environment, potential risks and rewards, your preferred customer communications and promotion options,** and how you will access or acquire the resources and capabilities to attract and deliver to your target segments.
	Provide an estimate (including a projected cash flow and outline of budgets where appropriate) of the financial implications of your launch and promotion strategy. You should take into account:
	<ul><li>**the concepts covered in Sessions 6 and 7** of Workbook 2. (You may find some of your activities from Session 5 and Activity 8.1 also helpful.)</li><li>your analyses made in response to the questions in the workbook and online activities</li><li>your tutor's feedback on Assignment 02</li><li>online discussions with your tutor group.</li></ul>
	Note: you may refer to or repeat points made in Question 1. You are also encouraged to attach your responses to relevant workbook questions and online activities as appendices in order to support your report. Appendices do not count towards the word limit. [from Natasha's TA]

Fig. 7.3 Comparison between DA task and TA task (key differences highlighted in bold)

7.5   Tracking Learning Transfer in DA Students' Academic Writing Through SFL

Case study genre features and conceptual knowledge as construed in the students' two non-DA and two DA texts are compared with those of their TA to evidence any 'near transfer' and 'far transfer' respectively. Additionally, student interview data and tutor comments are discussed in relation to these features as relevant.

As a reminder to the reader, the students' texts written in response to the DA or non-DA assignment tasks as reported in this book were expected to successfully apply one of the business frameworks, that is STEP (Social, Technological, Economic and Political) or SWOT (Strengths, Weaknesses, Opportunities and Threats), to an organisation's business environment. As mentioned in previous chapters, the SFL genre theory proposes that each genre such as a case study analysis follows a number of stages. As noted previously, a SWOT analysis text for the DA/non-DA assignment included the following generic stages:

Orientation[3] Component 1 (Strengths)^ Component 2 (Weaknesses)^ Component 3 (Opportunities)^ Component 4 (Threats)^

Optional stage(s):
[Conclusion/Recommendations]

A STEP analysis included these stages:

Orientation^ Component 1 (Social)^ Component 2 (Technological)^ Component 3 (Economic)^ Component 4 (Political)

Optional stages:
[Conclusion/Recommendations]

These stages were identified as successful features of a SWOT or a STEP analysis by business school academics in the institution although this might vary in other institutions. However, it should be noted that the optional stages depended on the assignment task because a SWOT or STEP analysis implies drawing conclusions and making recommendations based on the analysis but if the assignment did not make this explicit, students were unlikely to include these stages though highly valued by business studies teachers as noted in Chap. 6.

7.5.1   Near Transfer of Academic Writing

As mentioned above, only one student's (Kristie) assessment texts were analysed for investigating 'near transfer' as she was the only participant who wrote the third SWOT case study analysis in response to the assessment task that I designed. The assessment task required the application of the SWOT framework to the analysis of the market for Google's new smartphone called Nexus One as shown in Fig. 7.2.

As indicated by Fig. 7.2, the nature of the transfer task is identical to the previous two assessment tasks Kristie completed for this study (e.g., see Chap. 6). For example, this task required the student (1) to show an understanding of the SWOT framework by applying it to real business situations; (2) to demonstrate an understanding of the business environment within the communications industry (i.e., the computer operating system [Task 1], broadband market [Task 2] and smartphone market [Transfer task]); and (3) to produce a case study analysis of a similar length (i.e., approximately 500 words). However, there was one difference between Task 1 and this transfer task. While Task 1 had only two case study reading texts for the student to process for the case study analysis, the transfer task had three as in Task 2. This difference is an indication of the increasing complexity of the later tasks.

---

[3] ^ is used to mean 'followed by' in SFL.

Kristie's case study analysis was examined by focusing on her use of generic stages, macroTheme, hyperThemes and conceptual development for 'near transfer' (also see Chap. 6).

Genre and Generic Stages

When Kristie's response to the transfer task was examined regarding its genre and the generic stages, it appeared that she made some progress as shown in Fig. 7.4. Her text contained most of the mandatory stages of a typical SWOT case study analysis genre as shown below:

Orientation^ Component 1^ Component 2^ Component 3^

Although this text still lacks one mandatory stage (i.e., Component 4—Threats) and an optional stage (i.e., Recommendations), it is a more successful case study analysis than her previous two texts (non-DA1 and non-DA2) discussed in Chap. 6. Her previous texts contained only two mandatory stages: Orientation and either Component 3 (non-DA1) or Component 4 (non-DA2). Additionally, except the Orientation stage, the other stages of the (SWOT) case study analysis genre were not obvious in the analysis in the previous two assessment texts whereas her response text to the transfer task included more explicit stages. These changes indicate that Kristie performed better in the transfer task than the previous two tasks. In this respect, she did not actually transfer the genre knowledge demonstrated in the previous assessment tasks to this one. Instead, she appeared to have developed the case study analysis genre knowledge and its application in the transfer task. In other words, her ability to handle the generic stages of a case study analysis employing the SWOT framework was ripening and needed further mediation.

MacroThemes and hyperThemes

Kristie seemed to have internalised the ability to produce a relatively successful macroTheme for the case study analysis. She consistently wrote the macroTheme required for the case study analysis as illustrated in the excerpts below:

Excerpt 7.1

Non-DA1 macroTheme

The new technology developed in the form of the PC Operating Systems (OS) by Google has had a strong impact on its major competitor Microsoft and on the users at large. This essay will concentrate on a SWAT analysis of the effects of the Operating Systems is having on Google, Microsoft and the worldwide users.

Excerpt 7.2

Non-DA2 macroTheme

Vodafone announcement of its move into providing fixed-line broadband signals its interest and recognition of an already sizeable and profitable market shared by many competitors. How will Vodafone products compete and how can it succeed in this volatile market? I will use the SWOT analysis model in this paper to analyse this product.

Stages of genre	Student text (relevant key concepts underlined)	MacroTheme, hyperThemes and comments
Orientation^	**Google Nexus One SWOT analysis** P1 The launch of Google's Nexus One mobile phone was hotly pursued by mobile techno fans after attempts to keep it a secret failed. Would the promise of even more advanced technology at a finger tip ensure its success and overtake its competitors? Using the SWOT analysis framework we will look at the various aspects of this new product in details.	MacroTheme: last sentence indicates the macroTheme but does not define SWOT; Use of journalistic language and style
Component 1 (Strengths)^	P2 <u>The Nexus One strength is not just in its popularity but its high tech touch screen and other updated features, some of them promising to set it apart from the rest.</u> The phone features great access to the web and great new gimmicks such as visual updates, voice recognition and a pretty good camera, but is that enough of a competition to make it profitable?	HyperTheme: not clear but about strengths; particular to particular;
Component 1 (Strengths?)^ Component 3 (Opportunities?)^	P3 <u>Initially, expectations of a new state of the art phone which would surpass even the most advanced phones raised a great deal of interest.</u> After much hype, the new Google Nexus One phone is now firmly established and in direct competition with Apple's iPhone. Its price still could make it an instant success or may hold it back from buyer who may feel it's not worth the extra expense. <u>Either way there is a definite opportunity for Google</u> to break into new markets in the price versus technology world of competition between manufacturers. The price is attractive and reflects the speed and power and the phone can be purchased without a contract or a Sim card or via a contract with T-mobile at much reduced price.	HyperTheme: not related to the macro-Theme; description, not analysis Mixed with another SWOT component (i.e., opportunities)
Component 2 (Weaknesses)^	P4 <u>One of Nexus One weakest point is probably its uninteresting appearance</u>, looks sell in the high-tech world and many will be disappointed by its "nerdy" appearance. In terms of new gadgets it seems to fall down from its original promises of an advanced tool; it has no multi-touch facility, which Apple's clients are familiar with, this is unlikely to sway them to acquire this phone, while others may feel that Apple has the upper end.	Hyper-Theme: some sense but not obvious Particular to particular

Fig. 7.4 Kristie's TA text

Component 2 (Weaknesses)^	P5 <u>Its other weak points are Google's delay in launching the phone to the UK market; (currently under development).</u> If this wasn't bad enough, Nexus One is currently only compatible with GSM wireless technology which restricts it to the US T-Mobile or AT&T network. After all the publicity, it seems as though the Nexus One phone has now become a much less interesting proposition then its counterpart the iPhone.	HyperTheme: not clear; Particular to particular;
Component 3 (Opportunities?)^	P6 <u>The Nexus One phone is Google's opportunity to establish itself as a mobile phone leader, promoting a phone that offers great design improvements on existing phones on the market.</u> Working closely with HTC, Google has been able to develop a technologically advanced product never seen on the market before with enviable features.	Hyper-Theme: not clear but appears to be about Opportunities
Component 3 (Opportunities?)^	P7 <u>A further opportunity to develop services through Google is likely to be based on the fact that it can through the Nexus One know</u> what its client are looking at on the web or what other services they may be using at any time and can tailor it sales according to its clients' needs.	Hyper-Theme: appears to be continued from previous paragraph.
Recommendation		macroNew: none

Fig. 7.4 (continued)

Excerpt 7.3

Transfer task macroTheme

The launch of Google's Nexus One mobile phone was hotly pursued by mobile techno fans after attempts to keep it a secret failed. Would the promise of even more advanced technology at a finger tip ensure its success and overtake its competitors? Using the SWOT analysis framework we will look at the various aspects of this new product in details.

These excerpts indicate her sustained ability to produce a relatively effective macroTheme although she does not explicitly explain what SWOT is. Presumably, she had the assumption that it was a given framework and so did not need any explanation. Nevertheless, one can argue that Kristie's ability to write such a macroTheme is a 'near transfer'.

On the other hand, Kristie demonstrated through her transfer task that she could produce most of the appropriate hyperThemes for a SWOT analysis which were lacking in her previous two assessment texts (see Chap. 6). Whereas the DA students were able to use suitable hyperThemes in their DA2, Kristie (non-DA student) failed to do so in non-DA2. However, her performance as illustrated in Excerpt 7.4 below suggests that her ability to produce successful hyperThemes was maturing but, possibly due to the lack of interactivity with a mediator in her first two assignments, she was unable to fully materialise it unlike her DA counterparts. In fact, she asked me for a telephone 'dialogue' to discuss her problems after non-DA2. During the dialogue, she said: '... But a conversation really helps because sometimes things around a particular part that's the conversation we had earlier that I didn't get because I thought I didn't need to do it because people would understand what I meant...' The reference to 'conversation' indicates the value of a dialogic relationship between the tutor and the student that she missed.

Excerpt 7.4

Non-DA2 hyperThemes

P2 Vodafone already has experience of free broadband and has been able to learn significantly from it...

P6 Problems arise when there is a demand surge, which inevitably slows down customers' connection...

Transfer task

hyperTheme (Component 1)

P2 The Nexus One strength is not just in its popularity but its high tech touch screen and other updated features, some of them promising to set it apart from the rest...

hyperTheme (Component 2)

P4 One of Nexus One's weakest point is probably its uninteresting appearance in the high-tech world and many will be disappointed by its "nerdy" appearance...

As can be seen in the above excerpt, Kristie's non-DA2, despite my comments on her non-DA1 regarding the macroTheme, has no explicit link with the SWOT framework which, however, is obvious in her response to the transfer task. This significant change appears to be further development of her academic writing ability rather than a transfer of such an ability.

Conceptual Development

Conceptual development was analysed in relation to the students' abilities to use appropriate generic schemata and an effective application of the SWOT framework to understand an organisation's business environment as explained in Chap. 6. When examined from this perspective, noticeable conceptual development was found in Kristie's transfer assessment text. For example, she structured her case study analysis by using most of the appropriate generic stages in the text which were absent in her previous assessment texts. Likewise, her use of hyperThemes was more successfully employed in her transfer task as explained above. It should, however, be noted that her conceptual knowledge of the macroTheme from the previous assignments was sustained in the transfer task.

Technicality (i.e., specialised use of terms in business studies) was examined in Kristie's transfer assessment text, following the same method as described in Chap. 6. A summary of the results from the analysis of non-DA1, non-DA2 and TA is presented in Figs. 7.5, 7.6 and 7.7. The figures show the percentage and the frequency count for each category of Technicality. For each category represented in Fig. 7.7 (TA),

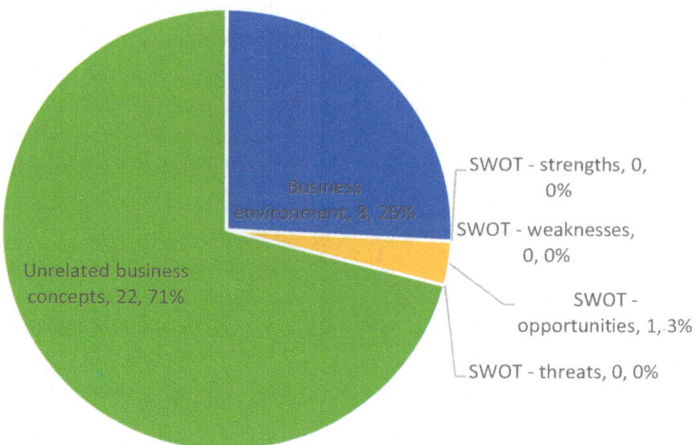

Fig. 7.5 Technicality in Kristie's non-DA1 (% of the total technical terms)

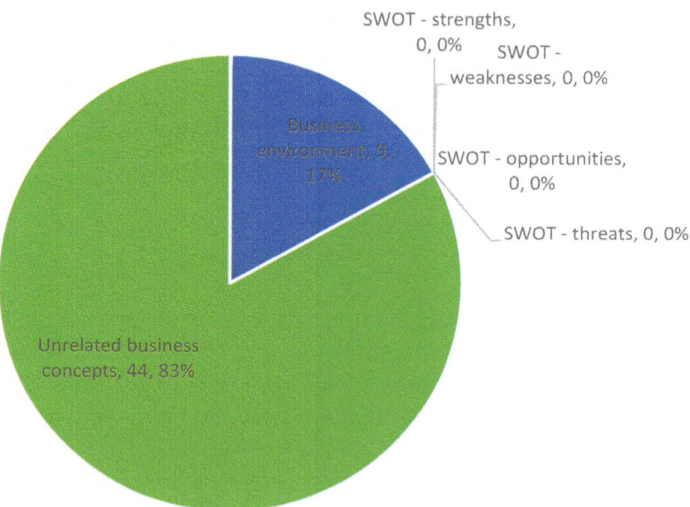

Fig. 7.6 Technicality in Kristie's non-DA2 (% of the total technical terms)

Table 7.1 provides illustrative examples of technicality found in Kristie's transfer text.

As shown by the figures, unlike her previous two assessment texts, the technical terms were more widely distributed although 'other business concepts' still covered 17% of the total technical terms. The most remarkable achievement she made was

Technicality - Kristie's Transfer assignment

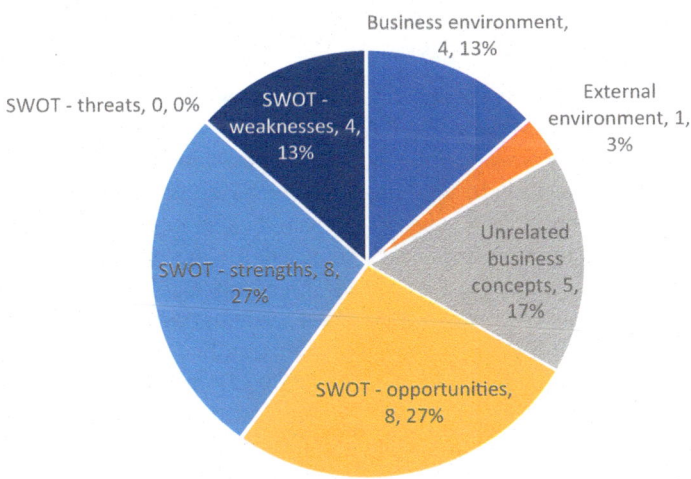

Fig. 7.7 Technicality in Kristie's transfer assignment (% of the total technical terms)

Table 7.1 Examples of technicality under various categories

Categories	Examples from Kristie's transfer text
External environment	Its [Google's] competitors
Business environment	The price versus technology world of competition between manufacturers, the SWOT analysis framework
SWOT strengths	Firmly established, reduced price
SWOT weaknesses	Uninteresting appearance, a much less interesting proposition
SWOT opportunities	A definite opportunity, great design improvements on existing phones on the market
Other business concepts	The extra expense, new product

on the three SWOT categories which were scarcely represented in her previous assignments: Strengths (27%), Opportunities (27%) and Weaknesses (13%). Like her hyper-Themes, Technicality seemed to be an area that further developed in the transfer assessment text. Therefore, I argue that Kristie's ability to write a technically appropriate SWOT analysis was still maturing in her previous two assignments.

7.5.2   Far Transfer of Academic Writing

Genre and Generic Stages

The genre that the students produced for both DA and TA was a *case study analysis*. As stated previously, however, the DA assignment required students to apply only one given business framework while the TA required students to produce a case study analysis of an organisation by applying multiple business concepts and frameworks they studied in the business studies course as indicated in Figs. 7.1 and 7.3.

All three DA students' texts were analysed for the generic stages. Table 7.2 summarises the generic stages found in all three students' DA and TA texts.

All three students were at different levels of academic writing development defined in terms of SWOT or STEP in DA1 as can be seen in Table 7.1. Lou and Natasha seemed to have used almost all stages of a SWOT or STEP case study analysis respectively although Lou used no Orientation and Natasha's text had no Recommendations stage. Amina did not include any mandatory stages of a SWOT case study analysis and produced a description of the organisation. In DA2, after having gone through the DA procedures in DA1, Lou and Natasha successfully followed the generic stages to write a STEP (Natasha) or SWOT (Lou) case study analysis learned in DA1. Their texts begin with Orientation followed by all Components of the analysis in the DA assignment. A similar pattern can be observed in their TA even though they needed to use multiple business course concepts and frameworks. In contrast, except the Orientation, Amina's DA2 indicates generic stages that are not appropriate to the case study analysis she conducted as she fails to apply the concepts from the STEP framework that she introduced. These differences between the three students suggest that while Natasha and Lou seemed to have grasped how to write a case study analysis and thus may have transferred this, Amina seemed to be still developing her writing abilities for a case study analysis. Her emerging writing abilities are exemplified through the first three paragraphs of each assignment in Excerpts 7.5, 7.6 and 7.7. My comments follow each paragraph. The underlined sentences, parts or words are related to hyperThemes.

Excerpt 7.5: Amina's DA1

> [SWOT table]
>
> P1 Google is a very well known name for billions of people in the world who use the internet. It is the[4] most visited search engine in the world. Google has introduced some interesting software's like chrome browser and Gmail and G talk, to 600 million people. Google has made all the information available in seconds on the net. Now a days everyone uses Google for their searches on-line which had made Google the world's no. 1 search engine.
>
> [*Comment: Description^ (of Google). There is no Orientation to the SWOT analysis.*]
>
> In July 2009, Google has announced the launch of new operating system, chrome, which will compete against today's most famous and trustable software company's Microsoft. The operating system which is in competition with chrome will be window 7. Windows are used

---

[4]Student spelling or grammatical errors in all student texts are kept as they were.

Table 7.2 Summary of generic stages in DA student texts

Student	DA1	DA2	TA
Amina	*Genre: SWOT analysis* Description (Google)^ Description^ Definition? (Chrome)^ Comparison^ Explanation (usefulness of Chrome)^ Comparison (Microsoft and Chrome)^ [Review]	*Genre: STEP analysis* Orientation (STEP)^ Description (abstract ideas)^ Description^ Recount^ Description^ Classification (type of services)^ Description 1^ Description 2^ Description 3^ Description 4^ [Conclusion]	*Genre: case study analysis using job characteristics* Orientation^ Criterion 1^ Criterion 2^ Criterion 3^ Criterion 4^ Criterion 5^ Criterion 6^ Conclusion
Lou	*Genre: SWOT analysis* Component 1 (Strength)^ Component 2 (Weaknesses)^ Component 3 (Opportunities)^ Component 4 (Threats)	*Genre: SWOT analysis* Orientation (SWOT)^ Component 1 (Strengths)^ Component 2 (Weaknesses)^ Component 3 (Opportunities)^ Component 4 (Threats)^ [Recommendations]^ [References]	*Genre: case study analysis using various course concepts* Orientation (various business concepts and frameworks)^ Course concept 1 (external business environment)^ Course concept 2 (STEP/PESTL)^ Course concept 3 (internal environment)^ Course concept 4 (Porter's five forces)^ Course concept 5 (identification of internal challenges)^ Recommendations^ Course concept 6 (stakeholder analysis)^ Course concept 7 (strategic context)^ Conclusion^ References
Natasha	*Genre: STEP analysis* Orientation (STEP)^ Component 1 (Factor 1—Social)^ Component 2 (Factor 2—Technological)^ Component 3 (Factor 3—Economic)^ Component 4 (Factor 4—Political)^	*Genre: STEP analysis* Orientation (STEP)^ Component 1 (Social)^ Component 2 (Technological)^ Component 3 (Economic)^ Component 4 (Political)^ [Recommendations]	*Genre: case study analysis using various course concepts* Orientation^ Course concept 1 (market segmentation)^ Course concept 2 (competitive environment—Porter's Five Forces, STEP)^ Course concept 3 (marketing strategies)^ Conclusion

by 90% of people using the pc's. Some big companies have already installed windows 7 in new laptops and pc's.

[Comment: Description^ There is no link with SWOT.]

Chrome is software, which will be free. This can be very useful for some hardware companies to install and present this software. Google is offering free online office applications which can save a lot space on the hard drive and easy to use.

[Comment: Definition?^ There is no link with SWOT.]

Excerpt 7.6: Amina's DA2

There are various ways of thinking about business environment. Each theory helps to understand how business interacts with each other and with environment. Some theories explain the changes in external environment and others focus on how businesses can become successful. One of the theories is a STEP Model, which describes the business environment by focussing on four factors as follows,

Social

Technological

Economic

Political

I am using one of the factors, social, to describe my organisation.

[Comment: Orientation^ She uses the STEP framework to analyse the business environment.]

Our experience in everyday life shapes our thinking, built our opinions and we make perspective about how we like doing things and things around us. People's perspectives can change according to the environment they live in, for example media plays a big role in making people's mind about things. Especially news media can present a story in a positive or negative way which affects people views.

[Comment: Description^ It is a description of everyday experience shaped by media; not focused and has no direct link with macroTheme.]

Excerpt 7.7: Amina's TA extract

Introduction

In this report I am analysing the company in which I am working as customer service assistant named as Alliance Boots UK. Boots is a best place to work, according to the criteria we are agreed in our Forum. This criterion is based on our priorities in a work place. We have agreed to six points, we would like to see in our chosen company, as follows; culture, training, money, flexible work, location and rewards and recognition. The role of work I have chosen is a store manager. All the information about the company is taken by the company website and my personnel experience of work there.

[Comment: Orientation^ analysis of the company using six criteria given; clearer focus on topic.]

Boots is a leading health and beauty retailer with 115000 plus employees. The aim of the company is to become the world's largest health and beauty retailer and key of business is exceptional customer care. The company is providing products and services by expert and friendly people, to help people look and feel better.

[Comment: Description of Boots as a company (background)]

Culture and environment

The first criteria we agreed on, is a culture and environment of the company. Culture is made BY the company's values and behaviour norms shared by company's members. (Edgar Schein). Culture is a key factor in an organization which affects the law implementation, innovation, job satisfaction, organization success and team building.

[Comment: Criterion 1ˆ – sub-heading used]

The other two students, Lou and Natasha, sustained their ability to employ effective generic stages learned in DA1 and DA2 as indicated in their TA. The stages were often marked with sub-headings, particularly in Lou's text (see Extracts 7.8, 7.9 and 7.10 (first two paragraphs) below). Therefore, the particular ability demonstrated by these students can be identified as 'far transfer'.

Excerpt 7.8: Lou's DA 1

Strengths

Google hopes to capture new clients with their ideas for developing a operating system, which they plan to be faster for the future. The company hopes to produce a system that is smart, agile and successful. Google has developed a system called ANDROID which has been tailored for netbooks and able to run programmes that can manage displays, handling keyboard and mouse, which is larger but complex piece of software. Google has a strong position for online advertising, messaging, photo-editing software.
Googles chrome Internet browser with the ability in allowing its operating systems to work at a faster paste with other personal computers.

[Comment: No Orientation; Component 1 (Strengths)ˆ]

Weakness

Microsoft has a huge customer service department, on the other hand, google does not and needs to attract a lot more investment in this field.

[Comment: Component 2 (Weaknesses)ˆ]

Excerpt 7.9: Lou's DA 2

Vodafone broadband market SWOT analysis

The following is a SWOT analysis of Vodafone's business environment in relation to the growth of mobile phone usage in the broadband market. The SWOT analysis in this report is taken from different perspectives and three case studies.

[Comment: Orientationˆ; analysis of Vodafone using SWOT]

The first looks at the strengths that the company has and how the business can improve when entering the broadband market. One of their strengths is delivering a strong cash flow and operational performance. Vodafone has a strong link in developing towards global customer relationships, value compared to their competitors. Vodafone has benefited from obtaining variable cost base within fixed operating costs.

[Comment: Component 1 (Strengths)]

Excerpt 7.10: Lou's TA

Introduction

The following report is based on M&S retail business and using different concepts and tools from units1-4 of block 3and evidence from (M&S Annual report). An introduction of key success factors, listing the knowledge and management techniques has been mentioned with the view that they help the firm. The use of Political, Economic, Social, Technology, Legal and Environment analysis from part 1 focuses on addressing the developments and challenges that faces M&S and meeting its corporate business capabilities or competencies that are required to deal with a very competitive world.

[Comment: Orientation^; analysis of M&S external environment.]

External analysis

In this section it is important to understand the meaning of external analysis and what it means for the organisation. M&S has different external (far) environments that have strong influence on the business. In most cases the business can not control the different levels or changes that operate so therefore the organisation finds itself in the need to adapt to the best changes physically possible. It is necessary to host several observations techniques and develop a strategic response to any problems arising from these environments.

[Comment: Course concept 1 (external environment)^; Sub-heading marks a new phase – external analysis; Defines M&S external environment.]

MacroThemes and hyperThemes

An analysis of macroThemes and hyperThemes in the three students' DA and TA texts was carried out to examine both their frequency and features. The results for the macroTheme showed that all three students wrote a successful macroTheme as learned in DA1 and demonstrated in their DA2. Nevertheless, their macroThemes in the TA task were qualitatively different from one another. For instance, Natasha wrote a macroTheme which did not sufficiently signal the focus of her analysis as shown below in Fig. 7.8.

Natasha's text was an analysis of the market for the new gardening products and services to be provided by her company. This assignment had two parts and only Part 2 was analysed for this study because Part 1 required a different genre even though it provided the background information for Part 2. Despite the macroTheme not sufficiently signalling what the analysis was doing, Natasha's business studies teacher rated her text highly. This may be because Part 1 of her assignment had already

Assignment task	Question 2
	(20 marks)
	Write a report of no more than 2,000 words addressed to an interested investor, justifying your proposed marketing and promotion strategy for launching your new creation. You must also describe the target markets, the competitive environment, potential risks and rewards, your preferred customer communications and promotion options, and how you will access or acquire the resources and capabilities to attract and deliver to your target segments.
Natasha's macro - Theme in her analysis (report)	P1 (P1= Paragraph in the text). Marketing strategy is central question in every business. In this strategy the goal is to launch the company with a minimal marketing budget.

Fig. 7.8 Natasha's macroThemes

Table 7.3 Summary of results for hyperThemes

Students	Number of appropriate hyperThemes		
	DA1	DA2	TA
Amina	0 out of 5	0 out of 5	15 out of 25
Lou	4 indicated by sub-headings	4 out of 4 (not so effective)	13 out of 18
Natasha	2 out of 4	4 out of 4	5 out of 7

set the context and boundary of the analysis. Therefore, the second sentence in Fig. 7.8 specifies the *goal of marketing strategy* but it does not include the aspects regarding her marketing strategies considered later in her analysis. In contrast, both Amina and Lou wrote relatively more successful macroThemes in that they orientated the reader by predicting hyperThemes in the analysis as exemplified below (see Excerpts 7.8–7.9 for a comparison):

Excerpt 7.11: Lou's macro-Theme

P1 The following report is based on M&S retail business and using different concepts and tools from units1-4 of block 3 and evidence from (M&S Annual report). An introduction of key success factors, listing the knowledge and management techniques has been mentioned with the view that they help the firm. The use of Political, Economic, Social, Technology, Legal and Environment analysis from part 1 focuses on addressing the developments and challenges that faces M&S and meeting its corporate business capabilities or competencies that are required to deal with a very competitive world.

A summary of the results for hyperThemes is presented in Table 7.3. As each student wrote their assignment in response to a different TA task, the number of hyperThemes inevitably varied. The table indicates that except Amina the other two students wrote some or all appropriate hyperThemes in DA texts. A hyperTheme, normally the beginning sentence of a paragraph, is considered appropriate when it predicts the Theme of the paragraph (Ravelli, 2004). The table also shows that the majority (over 60%) of the hyperThemes were appropriate in each student's TA.

In relation to the appropriateness of the hyperThemes, when they were connected with the macroTheme in addition to focusing on the Theme of the paragraph, they were classified as appropriate. While some were very effective, some others were less so. For instance, Natasha's DA1 hyperTheme in Fig. 7.9 is indicated by the sub-heading Social factors and the DA2 hyperTheme clearly links back to the STEP framework and is effective although her hyperTheme in TA does not explicitly link back to the macroTheme (i.e., *market strategy*) and, thus, may not be considered as effective as it should have been. Nonetheless, Natasha seemed to have made an assumption that *market segmentation* is an aspect of *market strategy* already made known to the tutor in Part 1 as indicated by her sentence 'I segmented two main group of market segments in Question 1. B' in Fig. 7.9 TA. Therefore, she may not have made the explicit link between the macroTheme and this hyper-Theme.

Lou, as shown in Fig. 7.10, did not write an effective hyperTheme in DA1 except the sub-heading. However, she linked the hyperThemes explicitly with the macroTheme in both DA2 and TA (i.e., SWOT, and challenges faced by Marks &

DA1	P2 Social factors: People awareness of towards a healthier lifestyle has increased in recent years. The demand for less harmful products, for example, non – alcohol beers has grown. In addition, there was already a request for a new enhanced brand in Spain. The changes in social environment had provided a good base to the success of Buckle.
DA2	P2 <u>There is one major social factor,</u> which influences the popularity of safer syringes. This factor relates to <u>demographic and cultural features</u> such as safety consciousness in different countries. Take, for example, the article in The Economist, which reveals that America has differing viewpoint from other countries in safety issues. The American opinion is that the world is a dangerous place, therefore everything should be ruled and directed in order to make it safer. This attitude lead to that US have strict regulations on syringes. Although, in Europe and Japan there has been a growing concern by unions and workers there are no statutes on the practice of needlesticks. These <u>social changes</u> have direct effect on the location of the market and explain why USA is the potential market.
TA	P2 <u>Segmentation is the identification of the customers within a market who demonstrate similar buyer behaviour.</u> I segmented two main group of market segments in Question 1. B. I grouped the customers by using *primary data* such as observation the garden company I used to work for and *secondary data*. The sources of the secondary data based on my *internal sources*, for example, my gardening experience and my experience as a nanny. These sources showed there is a demand on a DIY type gardening and there is a need for a mentor. *Other sources* derived from personal contact networks and from *other external sources*, for instant, from the statistics of the local council […]

Fig. 7.9 Natasha's hyperThemes

Spencer (M&S)) thereby making them effective hyperThemes. In fact, her business studies teacher's feedback comment on TA confirms that her structuring of the analysis was effective: 'You structure your report coherently'. It is her application of the business concepts that the tutor considered needed further development which is discussed in the next section.

In this section, it was shown how the three students construed the Textual meaning in writing a case study analysis genre in DA1 and developed this through to DA2. On the basis of these results, it can be contended that these three students may have transferred their ability to write an appropriate macroTheme to a new and more challenging assessment context (i.e., transfer assignment). Likewise, although these three students did not write all the hyperThemes appropriately, their texts did indicate that they carried over their expertise on writing appropriate hyperThemes from the previous academic writing assessment contexts to the new business studies assessment context. As in Cheng's study (Cheng, 2007), these students may have, at least, developed some genre awareness through the DA process.

DA1	Strengths
	Google hopes to capure new clients with their ideas for developing a operating system, which they plan to be faster for the future. The company hopes to produce a system that is smart, agile and successful. Google has develped a system called ANDROID which has been tailored for netbooks and able to run programmes that can manage displays, handling keyboard and mouse, which is larger but complex piece of software. Google has a strong postition for online advertising, messaging, photo-editing software. Googles chrome Internet browser with the ability in allowing its operating systems to work at a faster paste with other personal computers.
DA2	P4 <u>The second looks at the weaknesses for the business.</u> Vodafone was slow to act and decide to enter the broadband market along with their competitors. They are now forced to think on their feet and find ways of providing a home package with unlimited broadband access, landline calls and now offering 25% off mobile calls.
TA	P3 <u>In this section it is important to understand the meaning of external analysis and what it means for the organisation.</u> Marks & Spencer has different external (far) environments that have strong influence on the business. In most cases the business can not control the different levels or changes that operate so therefore the organisation finds itself in the need to adapt to the best changes physically possible. It is necessary to host several observations techniques and develop a strategic response to any problems arising from these environments.

Fig. 7.10   Lou's hyperThemes

Conceptual Development

The three students' developing genre knowledge and business studies conceptual knowledge in their assessment texts were examined to evidence far learning transfer, drawing on genre studies in SFL and Vygotskian notion of 'scientific concepts'. In particular, the previous section showed that they learned how to write a case study analysis by following suitable generic stages and the macroTheme in DA1 which they applied to DA2 and continued with their TA except for Amina's DA tasks. Despite some less appropriate hyperThemes, these students' knowledge of hyperThemes was also realised in their TA. In this respect, all three students seemed to have transferred their case study genre knowledge to the TA.

All three students showed the transfer of conceptual knowledge albeit at varying levels. For instance, like the DA assignment, the TA required Lou to apply business concepts and frameworks to the analysis (see Fig. 7.1). However, it demanded a wide range of frameworks, including STEP and SWOT. Most importantly, not only did the student have to apply them to the analysis but also evaluate them. Conceptually, such a task was more sophisticated and challenging than those that Lou accomplished for the

DA tasks. However, it may be argued that course materials should have provided her with the required conceptual knowledge for this assignment. Yet, module materials themselves as symbolic mediators may not have been sufficient without a human mediator to fully activate her maturing ability vis-à-vis the application and evaluation of the conceptual knowledge in question (Kozulin, 2003). It is also worth noting that Lou did not explicate SWOT sufficiently in paragraph 5 while applying this framework to the analysis of Marks & Spencer's business environment as shown in Excerpt 7.12 although she accomplished her DA assignments using this framework successfully:

Excerpt 7.12: Use of SWOT framework in Lou's TA

Paragraph 5

P5 When it comes to analysing the near environment, it tends to look a little closer to the organisation and points out the methods in which the business can react to different problems. This is mainly the developments of using the SWOT analysis. This is the strengths that may be hidden within the business, such as through the skills of talents of employees. The weaknesses that could spell trouble for the organisation, asking questions in how they could improve their position in the retail sector, and leading up to the knowledge of improving the business performance compared to the monthly stats in particular areas. Due to the weaknesses of the business which could lead the organisation open to threats from their rivals and therefore taking away competition. What a business regards a threat to some may be an opportunity to others.

[Comment: Lou does not explain why she used the SWOT framework to analyse M&S's external environment. Nor does she show a clear understanding of the concepts such as Strengths and Weaknesses when writing this paragraph.]

In this regard, her ability to apply the SWOT framework might not have fully matured and, consequently, she may not have been able to transfer it to a new and more complex assessment context than DA1 or DA2.

In addition to the conceptual knowledge of writing a case study analysis genre, the Technicality in the writing of the three students was investigated. Categories of Technicality were identified following the process explained in Sect. 7.4. The categories were drawn on the basis of the requirement of the assignment tasks. A summary of results for Technicality (frequency count and %) is shown in Figs. 7.11, 7.12 and 7.13. The technicality in Amina's texts in DA tasks is presented separately for each DA due to the differing business frameworks used.

The figures show that all three students used fewer technical terms in DA1 than in DA2. More importantly, they employed more *unrelated* technical terms than relevant ones in DA1. However, there are a considerable number of relevant technical terms used in all three students' DA2 and TA although their use in the TA looks higher which is due to the length and conceptually complex nature of TA. Most of the terms used in the TA are different from those in the DA given the nature of the specific assignments and field. For example, in DA2, Natasha used *demographic* and *automation of production* under the categories *STEP—sociological* and *STEP—technological* respectively. In her TA, the text included, for instance, *minimal marketing budget* under *Finance* and *market orientation matrix* under *Marketing strategy*. As can be

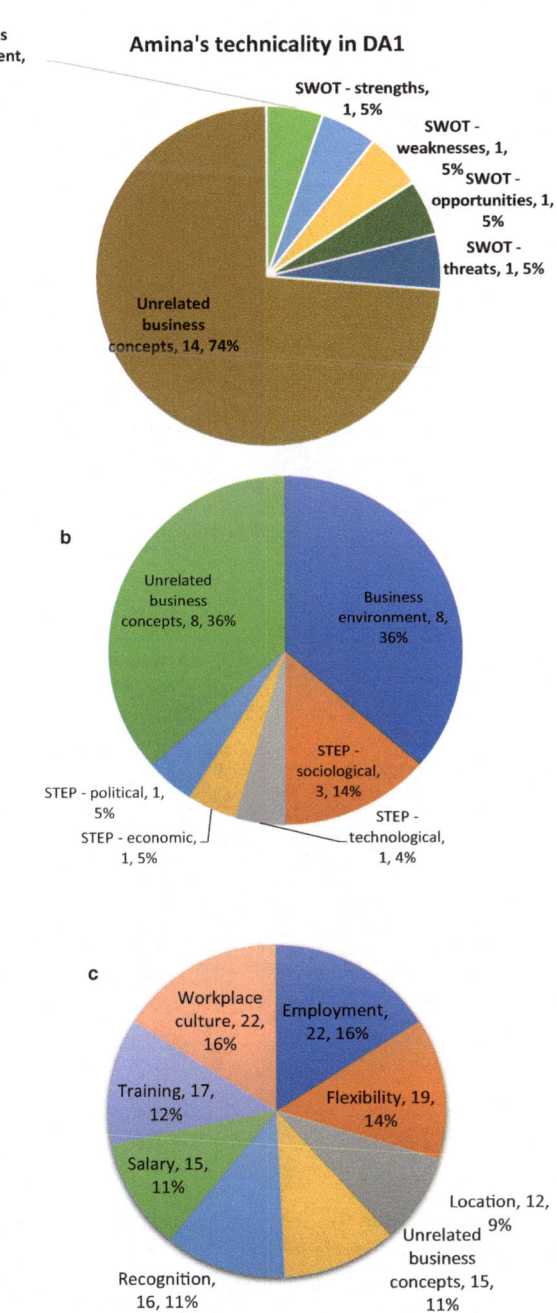

Fig. 7.11 **a** Technicality in Amina's DA1 (count and % of total technical terms). **b** Technicality in Amina's DA2 (count and % of total technical terms). **c** Technicality in Amina's TA (count and % of total technical terms)

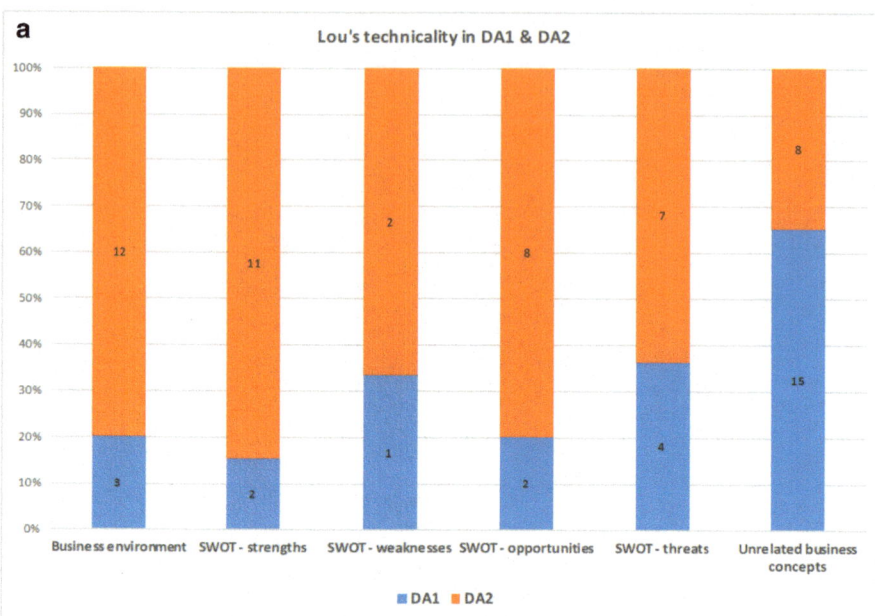

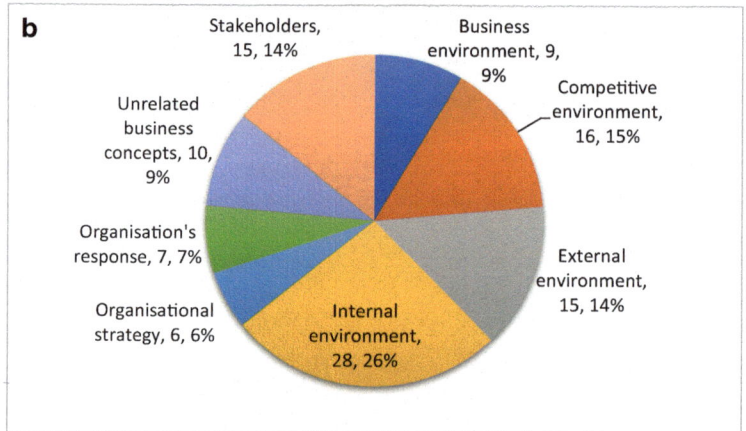

Fig. 7.12 a Technicality in Lou's DA1 and DA2 (count and % of total technical terms). **b** Technicality in Lou's TA (count and % of total technical terms)

seen in these charts, all three students employed a higher percentage of relevant technical terms in their TA.

The three students, nevertheless, demonstrated different levels of transfer of technical terms meaningfully in their TA as evidenced by the proportion of relevant technical terms they used effectively as summarised in Fig. 7.14.

For instance, Natasha appeared to be the most successful by employing almost only relevant terms in her analysis. The majority (89%) of her terms are represented

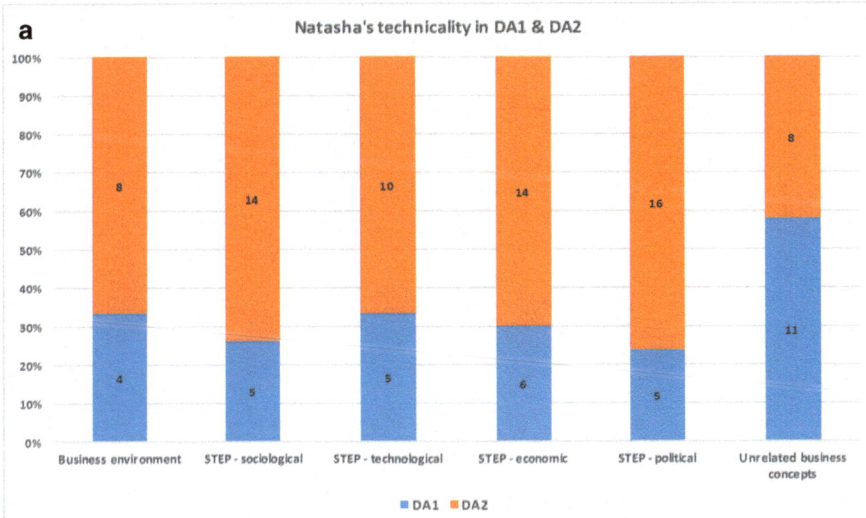

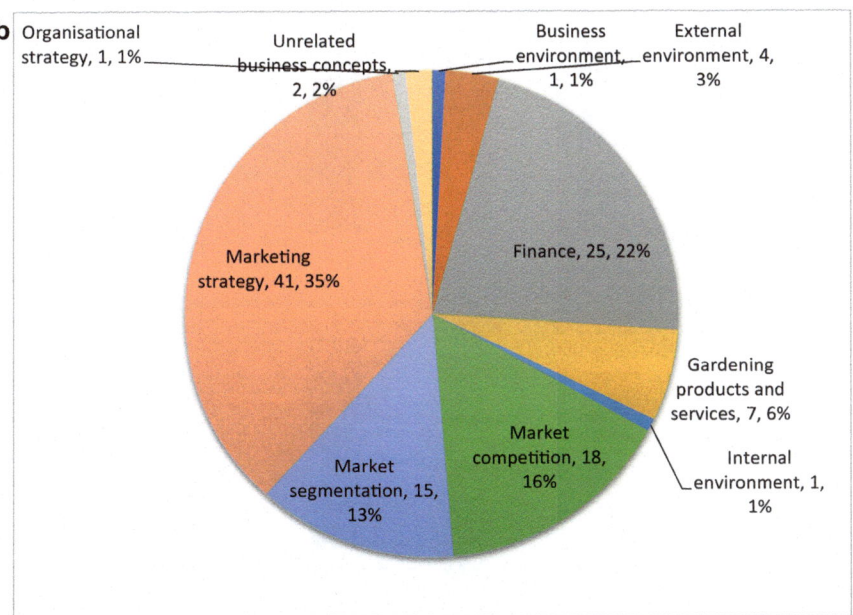

Fig. 7.13 a Technicality in Natasha's DA1 and DA2 (count and % of total technical terms). **b** Technicality in Natasha's TA (count and % of total technical terms)

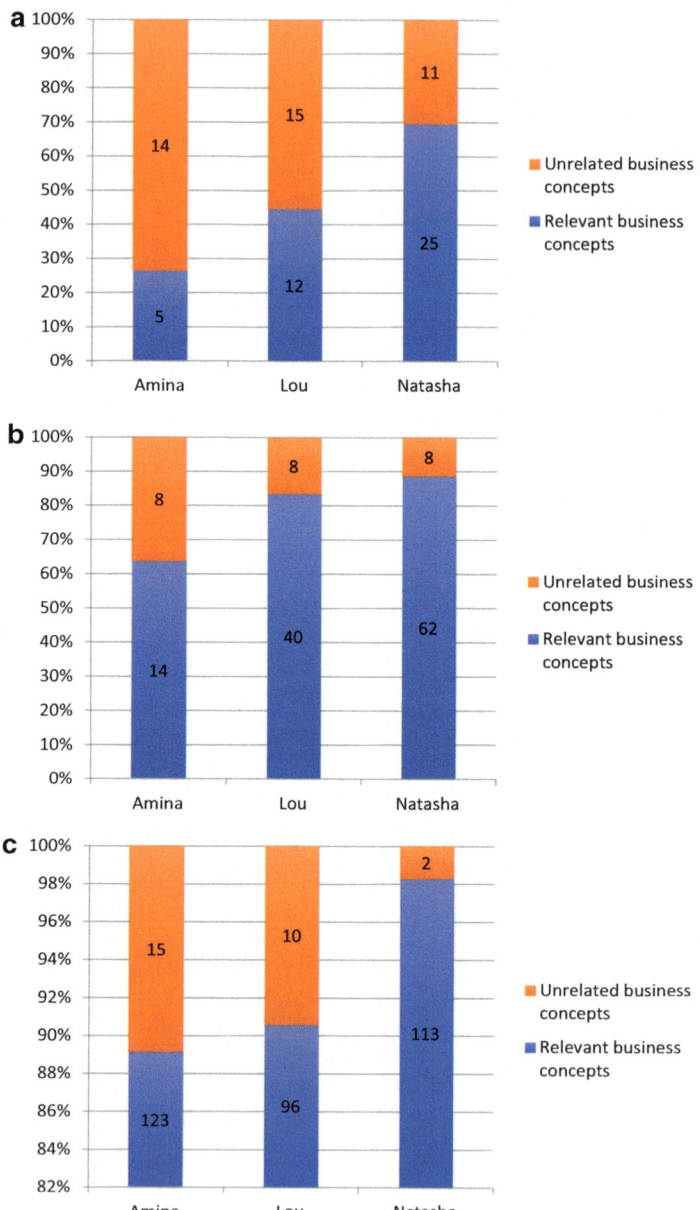

Fig. 7.14 **a** Comparison of technicality in three students' DA1. **b** Comparison of technicality in three students' DA2. **c** Comparison of technicality in three students' TA

by four core aspects of her analysis: *marketing strategy, finance, market competition and market segmentation.*

Business studies teacher comments help shed further light on these students' conceptual development as indicated by their use of technical terms. Natasha appeared to have applied such knowledge effectively to her analysis as confirmed by the business studies tutor's comments when DA2 and TA are compared:

Excerpt 7.13

STEP factors generally well understood. Some e.g. at political could rather be seen as an economic factor. *Has not been able to comment on possible interrelationships between the STEP factors* e.g. political and economic which would be *evidence of higher order thinking.* The interrelationship might be implied in the following though when *student did manage to make some good observations* e.g.: "These social changes have direct effect on the location of the market ...." [my emphasis, business studies teacher (Annie) comments on DA2 assignment]

Lots of evidence that you've based your thinking on course concepts – good. You've made extensive use of the course activities.

[...]

Overall, your style and content are coming on very well – very business-like and well reasoned. [my emphasis, business studies teacher comments on TA]

On the other hand, both Lou and Amina did not apply the business concepts and theories to their analysis in their TAs as expected by their teachers although their texts contained a significant number of technical terms. This may have been the reason why they did not score high marks on their assignments. Lou's business studies teacher's comments below clearly suggest this:

Excerpt 7.14

Has not described the concepts clearly as per course theory – this would have added depth – *has however managed to extract effective examples from the passage to illustrate the theory*: "One of their strengths is delivering a strong cash flow and operational performance" – student does not however reference the source. *Business case is generally well analysed, showing good understanding of the business environment faced by Vodafone.* "different elements effecting Vodafone business, internally and externally" [my emphasis, business studies teacher (Annie) comments on DA2 assignment]

Your use of concepts in units 3 and 4 could have been more expansive, e.g. maybe Grieners theory or the Craig and Douglas reader on globalisation in Unit 4

[...] *Your report did these important conceptual parts of the course to some degree.* (my emphasis, Lou's business studies teacher feedback comments on TA)

Although there may be a variety of reasons for this, a DA approach in assessment in the subsequent course may have revealed further what type of guidance or support these students needed. In this respect, the students' own views on DA can be insightful which the next section explores.

7.5.3 Learner Perspectives on Dynamic Assessment

In order to explore the value of DA from the perspective of the learner-writers, each student was interviewed in a semi-structured style (see Chap. 4). In general all three participants were positive about the DA procedures.

All three DA participants repeatedly stated that they improved greatly through their participation in the DA procedures. They mentioned that the interactive tutor feedback and writing of several drafts enabled them to concentrate on what they needed to develop further. According to Natasha, she was able to develop her skills to write effective paragraphs (hyperThemes) in case studies which she carried over to her TA: 'Particularly beneficial were paragraphing, structure and linking in the text. I am more aware of the linking words and using them to connect sentences. I think about the logical connections more now than I used to.' (Natasha, Interview data).

The participants said that DA was "more relaxed" and comfortable, and helped to build their confidence in academic writing unlike traditional methods of assessment which often cause stress and do not explain why they obtained a particular score on their performance. Concepts related to 'affect' (e.g., 'better relationship through personal communication' as noted by Amina) were frequently mentioned by these learners as an important aspect to their learning, which DA, through tutor mediation, possessed. For example, Amina reported, "… because I think this method is more helpful in a way of life, it means it's in a *better relationship*, it helps to understand better. This [DA] had more *personal communication and interaction*….' (my emphasis). 'Patience' and 'encouragement' as attributes of DA were very frequently alluded to throughout the interview. Natasha, for instance, said 'The tutor had *lots of patience* when I made many mistakes and also *the way the mistakes were pointed out was very helpful* because they were *not shown directly at first but gradually* if I did not notice them' (my emphasis). It is crucial to recognise this affective aspect in order to obtain a complete picture of any pedagogic practices (Daniels, 2007).

When asked how much the tutor mediation enhanced their academic writing development, the participants reported that the DA procedures were very supportive. For example, as quoted above, Natasha thought the tutor had lots of patience when she made many mistakes and also the way the mistakes were pointed out was very helpful because they were not shown directly at first but gradually if she did not notice them. According to her, "… it is a great way of learning because the guidance questions helped me to think about what I did and how I could improve." These students' such expressions suggest that DA offers an innovative pedagogical approach which may not only make learning an enjoyable experience but also enhance academic writing development. It should, however, be noted that their views do not necessarily represent direct evidence of transfer.

7.6 Summary

The goal of this chapter was to explore the value of DA in transferring students' academic writing skills and conceptual knowledge from one academic writing assessment task to a new context of undergraduate business studies. For this purpose, DA was operationalized as a method of instruction and assessment. SFL genre theory was applied to examine the independent learner performance regarding the case study analysis genre schema, macroThemes and hyperThemes (i.e., Textual meanings) which were identified as problematic in the first assignment. Additionally, the students' capacity to make Ideational meaning was tracked through their DA, non-DA and TA texts. Feuerstein's (Feuerstein et al., 2002) notion of 'near transfer' and 'far transfer' was applied to examine the aforementioned aspects in the student assessment texts.

This chapter through four students' academic writing trajectory showed that DA may contribute to the transfer of learning. The transfer of using generic stages, macroThemes and hyperThemes, and conceptual knowledge of these and business studies concepts appeared to take place in the TA texts albeit differently for each of the four participants. The non-DA student (Kristie) demonstrated further development of her academic writing and conceptual knowledge as she received more feedback on her SWOT case study analysis text. It appears that she could have demonstrated stronger evidence of learning transfer if she had had a greater amount of sustained tutor mediation or dialogic feedback. DA participants, on the other hand, seemed to be able to transfer genre features, or show their awareness as in Cheng (2007), and conceptual knowledge to their TA although one student, Natasha, appeared to be the most successful. These students' (except Natasha) reconstrual of their conceptual knowledge was not as successful as their academic writing skills (i.e., genre, macro-Themes and hyper-Themes). This suggests that writing and conceptual development is a lengthy process that may benefit from a greater amount of mediation, learner motivation, engagement and commitment. Additionally, various other factors may have influenced these students' transfer of learning such as time and business course materials.

This chapter contributes to the growing body of academic writing research that uses SFL and sociocultural theory as frameworks. However, in terms of studies on learning transfer in the field of academic writing, these two frameworks do not seem to have been employed together despite them being robust tools. Future studies in learning transfer in academic writing may find them valuable tools.

As the study reported in this chapter is limited to four students only, a larger study may be built on this one in order to evaluate the contribution of DA to students' ability to transfer genre features and conceptual knowledge to their chosen disciplinary areas. The same methodology used in my research may also be deployed for academic writing programme evaluation which seems to be under-researched (Tsou & Chen, 2014).

References

Anson, C. M., & Moore, J. L. (2017). *Critical transitions: Writing and the question of transfer*. Fort Collins, Colorado; Boulder, Colorado: The WAC Clearinghouse; University Press of Colorado.

Baik, C., & Greig, J. (2009). Improving the academic outcomes of undergraduate ESL students: The case for discipline-based academic skills programs. *Higher Education Research & Development, 28*(4), 401–416. https://doi.org/10.1080/07294360903067005.

Butler, A. C. (2010). Repeated testing produces superior transfer of learning relative to repeated studying. *Journal of Experimental Psychology. Learning, Memory & Cognition, 36*(5), 1118–1133. https://doi.org/10.1037/a0019902.

Butler, A. C., Godbole, N., & Marsh, E. J. (2013). Explanation feedback is better than correct answer feedback for promoting transfer of learning. *Journal of Educational Psychology, 105*(2), 290–298. https://doi.org/10.1037/a0031026.

Cheng, A. (2007). Transferring generic features and recontextualizing genre awareness: Understanding writing performance in the ESP genre-based literacy framework. *English for Specific Purposes, 26*(3), 287–307. https://doi.org/10.1016/j.esp.2006.12.002.

Coffin, C., & Donohue, J. P. (2012). Academic literacies and systemic functional linguistics: How do they relate? *Journal of English for Academic Purposes, 11*(1), 64–75. https://doi.org/10.1016/j.jeap.2011.11.004.

Daniels, H. (2007). Pedagogy. In H. Daniels, M. Cole, & J. V. Wertsch (Eds.), *The Cambridge companion to Vygotsky* (pp. 307–331). Cambridge: Cambridge University Press.

Day, S. B., & Goldstone, R. L. (2012). The import of knowledge export: Connecting findings and theories of transfer of learning. *Educational Psychologist, 47*(3), 153–176. https://doi.org/10.1080/00461520.2012.696438.

DePalma, M.-J., & Ringer, J. M. (2011). Toward a theory of adaptive transfer: Expanding disciplinary discussions of "transfer" in second-language writing and composition studies. *Journal of Second Language Writing, 20*(2), 134–147.

Eggins, S. (2004). *An introduction to systemic functional linguistics* (2nd ed.). London: Continuum.

Engle, R. A. (2012). The resurgence of research into transfer: An introduction to the final articles of the transfer strand. *Journal of the Learning Sciences, 21*(3), 347–352. https://doi.org/10.1080/10508406.2012.707994.

Feuerstein, R., Falik, L. H., Rand, Y., & Feuerstein, R. S. (2002). *The dynamic assessment of cognitive modifiability: The learning propensity assessment device: Theory, instruments and techniques* (Revised ed.). Jerusalem: ICELP Press.

Foley, J. M., & Kaiser, L. M. R. (2013). Learning transfer and its intentionality in adult and continuing education. *New Directions for Adult & Continuing Education*, (137), 5–15. https://doi.org/10.1002/ace.20040.

Green, J. H. (2015). Teaching for transfer in EAP: Hugging and bridging revisited. *English for Specific Purposes, 37*, 1–12. https://doi.org/10.1016/j.esp.2014.06.003.

Grujicic-Alatriste, L. (2013). A response to DePalma and Ringer's article "Toward a theory of adaptive transfer: Expanding disciplinary discussions of 'transfer' in second-language writing and composition studies". *Journal of Second Language Writing, 22*(4), 460–464. https://doi.org/10.1016/j.jslw.2013.04.002.

Haywood, H. C., & Lidz, C. S. (2007). *Dynamic assessment in practice: Clinical and educational applications*. Cambridge: Cambridge University Press.

Jackson, D. (2013). Business graduate employability—Where are we going wrong? *Higher Education Research & Development, 32*(5), 776–790. https://doi.org/10.1080/07294360.2012.709832.

James, M. A. (2010a). An investigation of learning transfer in English-for-general-academic-purposes writing instruction. *Journal of Second Language Writing, 19*(4), 183–206.

James, M. A. (2010b). Transfer climate and EAP education: Students' perceptions of challenges to learning transfer. *English for Specific Purposes, 29*(2), 133–147.

James, M. A. (2012). An investigation of motivation to transfer second language learning. *Modern Language Journal, 96*(1), 51–69. https://doi.org/10.1111/j.1540-4781.2012.01281.x.

James, M. A. (2014). Learning transfer in English-for-academic-purposes contexts: A systematic review of research. *Journal of English for Academic Purposes, 14,* 1–13. https://doi.org/10.1016/j.jeap.2013.10.007.

Karpov, Y. V. (2003). Vygotsky's doctrine of scientific concepts: Its role for contemporary education. In A. Kozulin, B. Gindis, V. S. Ageyev, & S. M. Miller (Eds.), *Vygotsky's educational theory in cultural context* (pp. 65–82). Cambridge: Cambridge University Press.

Kozulin, A. (2003). Psychological tools and mediated learning. In A. Kozulin, B. Gindis, V. S. Ageyev, & S. M. Miller (Eds.), *Vygotsky's educational theory in cultural context* (pp. 15–38). Cambridge: Cambridge University Press.

Lantolf, J. P., & Poehner, M. E. (2004). Dynamic assessment of L2 development: Bringing the past into the future. *Journal of Applied Linguistics, 1*(1), 49–72.

Lantolf, J. P., & Thorne, S. L. (2006). *Sociocultural theory and the genesis of second language development.* Oxford: Oxford University Press.

Larsen-Freeman, D. (2013). Transfer of learning transformed. *Language Learning, 63,* 107–129. https://doi.org/10.1111/j.1467-9922.2012.00740.x.

MacRae, R., & Skinner, K. (2011). Learning for the twenty-first century: Maximising learning transfer from learning and development activity. *Social Work Education, 30*(8), 981–994. https://doi.org/10.1080/02615479.2010.520118.

Martin, J. R. (1993). Technicality and abstraction: Language for the creation of specialised texts. In M. A. K. Halliday & J. R. Martin (Eds.), *Writing science: Literacy and discursive Power* (pp. 203–220). London: The Falmer Press.

Martin, J. R., & Rose, D. (2008). *Genre relations: Mapping culture.* London: Equinox.

Monbec, L. (2018). Designing an EAP curriculum for transfer: A focus on knowledge. *Journal of Academic Language and Learning, 12*(2), A88–A101.

Moore, J. L. (2017). Five essential principles about writing transfer. In J. L. Moore & R. Bass (Eds.), *Understanding writing transfer: Implications for transformative student learning in higher education* (1st ed., pp. 1–12). Sterling, Virginia: Stylus.

Moore, J. L., & Bass, R. (2017). *Understanding writing transfer: Implications for transformative student learning in higher education* (1st ed.). Sterling, Virginia: Stylus.

Poehner, M. E. (2007). Beyond the test: L2 dynamic assessment and the transcendence of mediated learning. *Modern Language Journal, 91*(3), 323–340.

QAA. (2019). *Subject benchmark statement for business and management* (4th ed.). Gloucester: The quality assurance agency for higher education.

QSR. (2010). *NVivo qualitative data analysis software (Version 9).* Victoria: QSR International.

Ravelli, L. J. (2004). Signalling the organisation of written texts: Hyper-themes in management and history essays. In L. J. Ravelli & R. A. Ellis (Eds.), *Analysing academic writing: Contextualised frameworks* (pp. 104–130). London: Continuum.

Shrestha, P. N. (2017). Investigating the learning transfer of genre features and conceptual knowledge from an academic literacy course to business studies: Exploring the potential of dynamic assessment. *Journal of English for Academic Purposes, 25,* 1–17. https://doi.org/10.1016/j.jeap.2016.10.002.

Shrestha, P. N., & Coffin, C. (2012). Dynamic assessment, tutor mediation and academic writing development. *Assessing Writing, 17*(1), 55–70. https://doi.org/10.1016/j.asw.2011.11.003.

Thompson, D. E., Brooks, K. I. T., & Lizárraga, E. S. (2003). Perceived transfer of learning: From the distance education classroom to the workplace. *Assessment & Evaluation in Higher Education, 28*(5), 539–547.

Tsou, W., & Chen, F. (2014). ESP program evaluation framework: Description and application to a Taiwanese university ESP program. *English for Specific Purposes, 33,* 39–53. https://doi.org/10.1016/j.esp.2013.07.008.

Chapter 8
Dynamic Assessment of Academic Writing and Its Future in Higher Education

8.1 Introduction

Research on academic writing assessment has constantly revealed that students in higher education have not been satisfied with the assessment feedback and support they receive for a number of reasons. Equally, student engagement with assessment and formative feedback has been limited (Dawson et al., 2019; Lea & Street, 1998; Yang & Carless, 2013) and thus designing engaging academic writing assessment and formative feedback has gained more attention recently. As an academic literacy practitioner and researcher, the issue of student engagement with assessment and formative feedback has been central to my work, particularly because of the nature of the student population in The Open University (i.e., distance education, employed, non-traditional educational backgrounds and open entry). The research I discussed in this book addresses the issue in distance education context. This research was underpinned by the Vygotskian sociocultural theory of learning and Systemic Functional Linguistics (SFL). Following multiple methods including action research, the study explored the process of dynamic assessment (DA) by examining the students' trajectory of academic writing and conceptual development.

In this concluding chapter, first, I present a summary of the key findings. Then, I describe the implications of my research on DA of academic writing for practitioners, especially those teaching academic writing and researchers in the field of academic writing assessment. I conclude this book by considering the most recent and potential developments in DA and their implications for the future of academic writing assessment research and pedagogy.

© Springer Nature Switzerland AG 2020
P. N. Shrestha, *Dynamic Assessment of Students' Academic Writing*,
https://doi.org/10.1007/978-3-030-55845-1_8

8.2 Why Dynamic Assessment for Academic Writing Assessment?

In this section, I highlight the importance of DA in academic writing assessment in higher education in a distance education context as revealed by my research. This study focussed on six undergraduate business studies students at The Open University UK over a period of six to ten months, exploring the application of interactionist DA to academic writing assessment. The focus of the study was the Vygotskian notion of microgenesis (i.e., development over a short span of time) in relation to the students' academic writing. To examine their development, I considered their changing zones of proximal development (ZPDs) in both their independent and mediated perfor- mance. The students' academic writing was examined in relation to their Textual (i.e., organisation of message) and Ideational (i.e., disciplinary and genre knowl- edge development) meanings as evidenced through their written assessment texts. The overarching research question that guided this study was the extent to which DA procedures enhance learners' academic writing development and conceptual development in business studies.

Four of the six students participated in DA and the other two students took part in non-DA. This study had three main stages: DA1 or non-DA1, intervention (enrich- ment study materials) and DA2 or non-DA2 (see Chap. 4). Additionally, four of the six students (3 DA and 1 non-DA) completed a transfer assessment task (i.e., a third assessment task that was similar to but more challenging than the first two). While the DA students received semiotic mediation via emails and instant messaging during the assessment, the non-DA students were provided with one-off traditional teacher feedback on each of their assignments without much interaction.

First and foremost, the analysis of student-tutor interactions around assessment texts provides insights into the DA students' ZPDs (i.e., their potential writing abil- ities) as reported in Chap. 5, thus demonstrating DA's potential to provide academic writing teachers with an in-depth understanding of their students' maturing writing abilities. The qualitative analysis of the mediational strategies suggests that the students benefited from support ranging from implicit mediation such as *Showing affect* and *Asking learner to identify the problem* to explicit mediation such as *Providing a choice of possible solution(s)* and *Providing the correct solution*, hence, supporting the findings of other DA studies such as Ebadi and Rahimi (2019), Poehner (2005) and Ableeva (2010). The qualitative results for the learner reciprocal moves indicate that the learners became more independent in their second assessment (DA2) than the first one (DA1). This may have been a result of the semiotic mediation they received in DA1. The quantitative analysis shows that there was a lower frequency of the more explicit mediational moves in DA2 than in DA1, thereby suggesting the learners' increasing control (i.e., self-regulation) of academic writing. Likewise, the results for the learner reciprocal moves show that the learners made more indepen- dent moves such as *Verbalising conceptual understanding* and *Overcoming problems* in the second assessment than in the first one, an indication of the learner taking more responsibility for their learning.

The analysis also shows, however, that there is not only progression but also regression or no progress during learners' academic writing development. From the Vygotskian perspective (Vygotsky, 1978) on development, such 'twists and turns' in academic writing development are not surprising as development can be both evolutionary and revolutionary. In sum, the results show that through semiotic mediation following DA principles, it is possible to gain insights into learners' maturing academic writing abilities and nurture them further to help the learners internalise them. It also indicates that this process takes a long time and requires sustained motivation from both the teacher and the learner to take advantage of semiotic mediation offered during the DA procedures.

Secondly and more importantly, my research shows that a systematic textual/linguistic analysis of the students' assessment texts serves as a powerful tool for tracking their academic writing and conceptual development. This is necessary to provide further evidence of the students' changing academic writing abilities (ZPDs) and the impact of tutor mediation on their academic writing because the teacher mediation data provides only a partial picture of academic writing development. This was achieved in my research by deploying a well-established theory of language use, namely SFL, as an analytical tool for analysing the students' assessment texts and by so doing provided linguistic evidence for the students' changing ZPDs and the impact of teacher mediation on academic writing development. This aspect of my research is in line with previous SFL-based research on academic writing. SFL has been used extensively and usefully in teaching academic writing in higher education and researching its various aspects including genre types (e.g., Nesi & Gardner, 2012) and subject knowledge (e.g., Woodward-Kron, 2008) but not in DA research.

The findings of the SFL-based textual analysis suggest that the DA students made gains both in their control of a *case study analysis* genre and in their control of business studies concepts. These gains were related to those features of the case study analysis genre which were not successfully realised in the first student assessment text as identified in their unassisted performance (first draft). The students' academic writing development was tracked by examining the development of Textual and Ideational meanings in their assessment texts. The foci of the Textual meaning were on *generic structure, macroThemes* (traditionally called introduction) and *hyper-Themes* (also commonly known as topic sentence) in the assessment texts. The analysis of Ideational meaning was mainly concerned with the application of business concepts and frameworks (e.g., STEP and SWOT) as required by the assessment tasks. Additionally, a conceptual understanding of the *case study analysis* genre as revealed in the assignments was also considered as evidence of conceptual development. Three of the four DA students made steady progress regarding generic stages, macroThemes, hyperThemes and the application of the relevant business concepts and frameworks to their case study analysis texts. The non-DA students' progress over the two assignments, however, was either inconsistent or minimal. Therefore, it can possibly be argued that the DA procedures enhanced the DA students' maturing academic writing abilities as such procedures may have been sensitive enough to help the learners internalise them. In contrast, the non-DA students' academic writing abilities remained either the same or regressed which may be due to the lack of semiotic mediation that could target their ZPDs. It is, of course, difficult to draw any firm conclusions given the scale of the study.

Finally, this study investigated the extent of transfer of academic writing skills and conceptual knowledge from one writing assessment task to another. The twin transfer of academic writing skills and conceptual knowledge gained in the first and the second assignments were examined by using the notions of 'near transfer' and 'far transfer' (Feuerstein et al., 2002). The analysis focussed on the same features of a case study analysis genre and aspects of conceptual development as noted in the previous paragraph to consider their transfer to the transfer assessment text. The findings indicate that the transfer of learning (i.e., the use of generic stages, macroThemes, hyperThemes and the application of business concepts and frameworks) from the previous assessment tasks to the new ones occurred, though differently for each of the four learners. However, there was a contrast between the DA and the non-DA learners. For example, the non-DA student not only transferred her ability to write an effective macroTheme but also developed her ability further to produce successful hyperThemes and application of business frameworks in her transfer assessment text. The DA students sustained their ability to write effective macroThemes and hyperThemes in their transfer assessment texts although, except for one student, they did not show the same level of transfer regarding their conceptual/disciplinary knowledge. The reason for not being able to transfer conceptual knowledge might have been due to the more complicated application of multiple business concepts and frameworks within one case study analysis in the transfer assessment task when compared with the previous two assessments (i.e., DA1 and DA2).

8.3   Implications for Academic Writing Practitioners

This research on DA has a number of implications for academic writing practitioners in higher education. As mentioned throughout the book, the current study employed an innovative approach to assessing students' academic writing in business studies in distance education. Therefore, the findings from the study may provide academic writing practitioners with insights into how such an approach could be used to support their own learners' academic writing and conceptual development.

8.3.1   Implicit to Explicit Mediation

A key aspect of this research was the use of *implicit to explicit mediation* to understand and assess business studies students' academic writing abilities. The study identified a set of teacher mediational moves which appeared to have worked effectively in enhancing participants' academic writing (see Table 8.1 reproduced from Chap. 5). Although these moves were identified in the context of this particular study, they can be applied to other learning contexts. For example, there were three mediational

Table 8.1 Mediational moves in dynamic assessment of academic writing	Implicit (i.e., hints, prompts, etc.)	Explicit (e.g., examples, corrections, etc.)
	1. *Clarifying the task* 2. *Accepting a response* 3. *Showing affect* 4. *Asking learner to identify the problem* 5. *Locating part of the text needing improvement* 6. *Asking to clarify meaning* 7. *Identifying the problem in the text* 8. *Asking to consider a possible solution*	9. *Checking conceptual understanding* 10. *Providing metalinguistic clues* 11. *Providing content clues* 12. *Rejecting the response with explanation(s)* 13. *Explaining the problem* 14. *Exemplifying or illustrating* 15. *Providing a choice of possible solution(s)* 16. *Providing the correct solution*

moves that were frequently used in this study: *Locating part of the text needing improvement, Asking to consider a possible solution* and *Providing metalinguistic clues.* Alongside other effective teaching techniques, an academic writing teacher could employ these moves in their academic writing instruction and assessment. In fact, the mediational moves have been adapted to teaching academic writing and its assessment in a summer English for Academic Purposes programme at The University of Sheffield (Chris Smith, personal communication). The colleagues at The University of Sheffield use a mixture of online synchronous and asynchronous communication (Google docs) and a follow-up face-to-face interaction to discuss challenges faced by students in their written assignments. As I understand, this type of mediation (implicit to explicit mediation) seemed to be popular with students and help with student progression into higher level studies.

Additionally, these mediational moves found in this study also suggest that rather than focusing only on students' sentence grammar (e.g., explicit corrections), the teacher could concentrate on higher level features of a text including the use of conceptual frameworks to frame text and so support students in developing their disciplinary writing (such as business studies as exemplified in this book). In fact, these mediational moves could be applied by any teacher in other disciplines outside academic writing such as a social care lecturer when they mark their written assignments across a course.

8.3.2 Dialogic Feedback

Related to implicit-to-explicit mediation is dialogic feedback which is a central feature of DA and this study. Vygotsky and Vygotskian researchers have long argued that dialogue plays the fundamental role in mediation to enable learning and development (e.g., Wells, 1999). It has also emerged as a key aspect of assessment feedback in higher education (Ajjawi & Boud, 2018; Carless & Boud, 2018). My research on DA of academic writing further supports this and has implications for academic writing and other subject teachers. The DA procedure has the power to diagnose difficulties faced by students by identifying their zone of proximal development and help them overcome such difficulties through a dialogic process. Due to the nature of flexible semiotic mediation followed in this study, it was possible to diagnose different levels of the same problem. For example, Amina and Lou had similar problems regarding the use of hyperThemes in their DA1 draft 1. However, through semiotic mediation it became clear that Amina needed more support in her ability to handle hyperThemes than Lou did as shown by their second unassisted performance.

As an application of the dialogic feedback as revealed by my research, a first year course on business communication for business and management students has adapted it at The Open University. This course has four assignments in the course of eight months (one academic year). The first and the second assignments require students to read the same case study. They are asked to produce notes of key points based on their reading of the case study in the first assignment. Their teachers provide formative feedback and a score on this assignment. In the second assignment, students are required to write a SWOT case study analysis based on the same case study and use their notes for this assignment. They are also asked to apply their teacher's feedback on the .first assignment to their writing in the second assignment. The teachers then provide feedback on the second assignment, commenting on the uptake of the feedback and awarding a score. The third assignment encourages students during a 'formative assessment week' to write a draft of their assignment and email it to their teacher for formative feedback before they submit the final version for summative assessment. The teacher provides high level formative feedback (not too specific and detailed so as not to jeopardise summative assessment) on the draft. The same approach is taken for the fourth assignment. Although this approach is not DA, it follows a dialogic process to support students with academic writing development. The anecdotal evidence from teachers and the end of course evaluation survey results suggest that students have found this approach beneficial for their academic writing although there is a need for further research on the success of this approach. Due to the significantly high number of students on this course (over 1,400 per year), the more flexible version of DA is practically unimaginable but an adapted version like the one described here was possible. Academic writing teachers in other universities could adapt this approach to their academic writing assessment design.

8.3.3   Interpersonal Relationship with Learners

Another finding that has a pedagogical implication for academic writing teachers and other discipline teachers is the importance of the interpersonal relationship (i.e., affect) between the learner and the teacher which is also identified in the litera-ture, and thus corroborating previous studies (e.g., Dawson et al., 2019; Hyland & Hyland, 2006c; Pitt & Norton, 2017). All DA participants stated that the interaction with the teacher was comfortable and relaxing. For example, during the interview, Michelle said, '… It was a lot more comforting for me to do the assignment [i.e., DA]. Before [i.e., traditional assessment] it was a bit stressful…' Likewise, the mediation data included *Showing affect* as one of the teacher moves. These may have a positive effect on learning and learner motivation (cf. Carless, 2006). In fact, affect has long been recognised in Vygotskian sociocultural theory of learning (e.g., Daniels, 2007) and in Feuerstein's Mediated Learning Experience as noted in Chap. 2 (Feuerstein et al., 2002). The current study suggests that the academic writing teacher and other subject teachers need to carefully use their language and any semiotic tools used (and body language in face-to-face interaction for that matter) when they interact with their learners around their academic writing performance. Such an approach is likely to help students feel emotionally supported, thus enhancing the possibility of the uptake of the formative feedback as noted by Pitt and Norton (2017).

8.4 Implications for Academic Writing Researchers

The research I have discussed in this book has importance for educational researchers as well, especially those following Vygotskian sociocultural theory. In particular, it has implications for academic writing assessment research, sociocultural theory based writing research, and DA-based writing research.

This study contributes to the growing body of sociocultural theory oriented writing research and, by the same token, genre studies in relation to student learning. In sociocultural theory, writing is seen as a social activity. This means writing is always situated in a cultural context and often collaboratively constructed through direct or indirect semiotic mediation (see, for example, Bazerman, 2013; Hasan, 1992; Prior, 2008, p. 58). This study explored academic writing situated in a discipline (i.e., business studies) 'housed' in an institutional context (i.e., The OU). As sociocultural theory oriented writing research, the study supports previous studies that academic writing development benefits from semiotic mediation (e.g., Coffin & Donohue, 2014; Mahboob, Dreyfus, Humphrey, & Martin, 2010; Wegner, 2004).

The most significant contribution of this study is the use of SFL as a theory of language use to analyse data which provided evidence of students' ZPDs and the impact of teacher mediation on academic writing development over time. This is new to ZPD research and DA-based research, a response to Gardner's (2010) call for combining DA with SFL to track students' writing development. Despite quite a large number of DA studies within second language learning, to my knowledge, no studies have deployed SFL to analyse students' linguistic development. My research shows the value of this powerful tool without which it might have been challenging to gain insights into the participating students' emerging academic writing repertoire in business studies. Given that SFL is a well-established theory of language use which is widely used in educational research, DA or sociocultural theory oriented writing researchers should keep an open mind towards the use of SFL for data analysis in their research. It is particularly so in the field of English for academic purposes including academic writing due to the influence that SFL has on it as shown by the recent special issue of *Journal of English for Academic Purposes* edited by Gardner and Donohue (2020).

DA-based research on (academic) writing has not, to date, been reported in the literature extensively apart from a few such as Antón (2009) which, however, lacks details of the DA procedures for writing assessment and my own research (Shrestha & Coffin, 2012) which reports only on the mediation process. Two later studies (i.e., Alavi & Taghizadeh, 2014; Ebadi & Rahimi, 2019) have some similarities with the current study but they were conducted in a face-to-face foreign language teaching and test preparation context. My research has shown that it is possible to apply DA principles to academic writing assessment in a discipline (i.e., business studies). Additionally, it has demonstrated that DA procedures can be implemented in a distance education context. In particular, this study has extended previous DA studies such as Poehner (2005) by identifying mediational strategies for academic writing which did not seem to exist in the DA literature prior to my own publication (Shrestha & Coffin, 2012) based on some of the data used in this book, and using independent subject tutors' comments as complementary data. DA researchers can draw on both the mediation moves and reciprocal moves when they examine their mediation data.

The research methodology used in this study can be of direct relevance to those who are involved in academic writing assessment research. Of particular importance is the combination of the two theoretical frameworks, namely, DA and SFL which allowed the researcher to examine not only the product but also the process. Given the predominance of product-oriented research on academic writing assessment, this study provides an alternative way of investigating the process of academic writing assessment.

8.5 Challenges in Conducting Dynamic Assessment

In this section, before discussing the future of DA of academic writing, I would like to discuss some of the potential issues future DA practitioners and researchers in the field of academic writing may need to be aware of. In the last three chapters of this book, I have argued that the findings indicate the potential power of DA. There are, nevertheless, a number of considerations to bear in mind when implementing DA in academic writing assessment.

8.5.1 Expertise of the DA Practitioner

DA has its origin in Vygotsky's sociocultural theory of mind. Likewise, the success of conducting DA depends on the quality of mediation which in turn relies on the DA practitioner in addition to the learner reciprocity. For example, an inexperienced DA practitioner may find it challenging to diagnose, identify and work with students' ZPDs regarding their academic writing (e.g., see Davin, Herazo, & Sagre, 2016; Haywood & Lidz, 2007).

Working in the learner's ZPD is a challenging task. In particular, DA following a flexible approach heavily relies on the mediation skill of the teacher/mediator (Haywood & Lidz, 2007). This means that a wrong judgment made by the teacher can have a negative impact on the learner's development. Some previous DA studies have noted instances of improper mediation, leading to undermining learners' opportunities to develop (e.g., Ableeva, 2010; Poehner, 2005). In the current study, the analysis of the tutor mediation data shows that I may have focussed on aspects of academic writing that were potentially not significant for the learner's academic writing development. Therefore, it is essential for the DA practitioner to constantly reflect on the mediation process and its sensitivity towards the learner ZPDs.

8.5.2 Time Constraints

Time commitment is essential for the success of DA. It is even more crucial in the distance education context because most students have only a limited amount of time for study due to their full-time jobs and other personal commitments as explained in Chap. 1 (Chetwynd & Dobbyn, 2011). This means carefully planning how frequently it is necessary to interact with the learner between written drafts or assignments. In a face-to-face context, it may be possible to hold an oral (synchronous) discussion with the learner around their written text because there is a physical campus (though the pandemic such as COVID-19 can change this drastically) and the student-teacher interaction is normally spoken as several previous studies have shown. In distance education, however, synchronous communication whether written text-based or spoken (e.g., online conferencing) may not be practically possible because the time availability of both the teacher and the student may be different. In that case, finding a suitable time in sufficient amount becomes extremely challenging as shown by my research. This challenge may be encountered even in a face-to-face context as reported by some recent studies in non-DA contexts in higher education (e.g., Henderson, Ryan, & Phillips, 2019). One way to address this issue is by using asynchronous text-based communication methods such as emails and online forums which can, nevertheless, be a lengthy process, depending on how soon both the teacher and the student respond.

8.5.3   Difficulty on Large-Scale

Despite being valuable, implementing a DA approach on a large scale has practical constraints due to the time needed and the intensive nature of the one-on-one dialogue. As previous studies and my own research show, most of these studies were on a small scale. To follow a flexible mediation approach of DA with hundreds of students in a study programme may be almost impossible unless a less flexible approach (i.e., interventionist DA) such as that adopted in Poehner, Zhang, and Lu (2014) is employed. In the context of distance education which tends to have a large number of students within a study programme (e.g., over 500), using a flexible DA approach like the one discussed in this book may be immensely challenging. The same may apply to traditional classrooms where there are many students. It is, however, possible to adapt this approach by making it less burdensome for both the teacher and their students. The teacher could make their feedback interactive and dialogic by making links between the current assignment and the feedback on the previous assignment(s) and asking students to respond how they want the feedback in each future assignment. Alternatively, an online forum discussion could be run inviting groups of students to discuss how the formative feedback has helped or hindered their academic writing development. This helps to make the feedback dialogue continuous and sustainable.

8.5.4   Choice of Semiotic Mediation Tools

In this study, a range of semiotic mediation tools were deployed during the mediation process. They were all text-based (i.e., written). However, each tool had its own benefits and challenges. For example, the email communication tended to be quite limited to the teacher providing formative feedback and the students responding to the feedback via their revised written drafts. For some students this tool worked well. For others, a synchronous communication mode for mediation (e.g., instant messaging) served them better as they felt the need of immediacy for the interaction. For an academic writing teacher with a large number of students, it may not be possible to use many semiotic mediation tools and may need to limit to, for example, online forum discussion or simply a face-to-face one-on-one dialogue if the time allows. My own research suggested that, if possible, it is helpful to have a range of options for the mediation purpose, depending on student preferences and the practical constraints of the learning context.

8.5.5   Labour-Intensiveness

The great amount of time needed for applying DA to academic writing assessment has already been mentioned. Additionally, the DA process involves carefully identifying the student's emerging academic writing abilities (ZPDs) and providing 'implicit to explicit' mediation. This means the teacher has to spend a good amount of time going through what the student has been able to do and what they are yet to develop in their academic writing. Then, they need to craft their response which is sensitive enough to the student's ZPD. This process is lengthy and thus labour-intensive. Given that resources are always limited in higher education (Henderson et al., 2019; Tuck, 2018), finding time for such a lengthy and labour-intensive DA process may face institutional constraints despite the power of DA to support learners with what they need.

8.6 Future Directions for Dynamic Assessment of Academic Writing

Future studies in this area can take a number of directions. First and foremost, more DA studies need to be conducted in academic writing and distance education. Despite the introduction of DA to applied linguistics in 2004 by Lantolf and Poehner (2004), only a handful of studies in writing assessment and too few in distance education exist. There are some specific directions that future studies within academic writing could pursue, which are briefly outlined below to conclude the book.

8.6.1 Group DA

The majority of DA studies have focussed on individual learners (Lantolf & Poehner, 2011; Poehner, 2009). Only recently has there been some interest in group DA (GDA) in which the focus of mediation is not limited to an individual learner but to a group of learners or even the whole class (Poehner, 2009). The lack of research in GDA may not be surprising given the individualised nature of mediation offered in DA approaches by targeting a particular learner's ZPD. Conducting GDA requires much more carefully planned procedures for making semiotic mediation sensitive to group ZPDs which may be much more complicated and challenging than working in one individual learner's ZPD. Therefore, there have been only a few studies on GDA reported in the literature. The earliest example appears to be one by Haywood and Lidz (2007, pp. 224–225) who mention an example from their work with the US Army. They also propose a number of GDA principles to be followed while conducting GDA. These principles include things like homogenous groups (i.e., people with the same level of ability), and standardised mediation. However, these principles have not yet been applied to educational contexts and every learner tends to have different needs although they may have similar 'actual' ability to others'. A recent study by Bakhoda and Shabani (2019) shows that it is possible to conduct GDA for reading comprehension in a foreign language learning context by using computerised implicit to explicit mediation which is standardised as in Poehner et al. (2014). However, research examining group ZPD in academic writing following a GDA approach has not been conducted yet and thus merits further research although this will be more complex and requires more careful planning than in the reading comprehension context.

8.6.2 Computer-Based DA

The current study was conducted in a computer-mediated environment whereby almost all interactions (e.g., emails) took place through computers (see Chap. 4 and Shrestha & Coffin, 2012). However, the potential of using computers as an *automated* mediating tool was not a focus of the investigation. This area of DA research, known as computer-based DA (C-BDA), is quite new (e.g., Guthke & Beckmann, 2000; Tzuriel & Shamir, 2002). Tzuriel and his colleagues have, for instance, explored the potential application of computers for assisting mediation in DA (e.g., Shamir, Tzuriel, & Guy, 2007; Tzuriel & Shamir, 2002). Mostly they have worked with primary school children, investigating changes in their cognitive ability. In their C-BDA approach, both computers (programmed with DA procedures) and a human mediator work together so as to maximally attune mediation to individual needs.

Guthke and Beckmann (2000) report that they adapted their *Leipzig Lerntest* for a computerised version (i.e., automated). It provides standardised five-level assistance (i.e., mediation) to the learner. Questions are sequenced in the order of difficulty and they are provided according to the learner response. Unlike Tzuriel and Shamir's, this C-BDA does not include a human mediator. The programme generates both the score and the learner profile for each learner regarding the number of attempts a learner makes at responding to a task and the amount of assistance they need to complete it.

More recently, a few studies have been reported in this area. These studies were, however, in a foreign language learning context rather than in academic writing in a discipline. Two of these studies are worth mentioning. First, Poehner et al. (2014) carried out a study examining the mediation effect of computerised (automated) Chinese as a foreign language reading and listening tests on a group of students (82 and 68 respectively) to diagnose their language development. Implicit to explicit prompts were provided for each multiple-choice test item which the automated computer programme used according to the accuracy of the student response to the test item. The authors argue that this type of DA helps to diagnose leaners' language abilities on a large scale and also offers information required to design subsequent curriculum. Following the same approach, a second study (Bakhoda & Shabani, 2019) reports that C-BDA of reading comprehension helped the teacher to identify group ZPDs and expand them by using implicit to explicit electronic mediation via computers in a classroom context.

Given the potential contribution of DA to academic writing development, C-BDA may be a useful direction for future research. In particular, it can be used to diagnose potential areas for students to develop in academic writing at the beginning of a study programme. However, assessing disciplinary writing and learning is much more complex and different than other contexts such as foreign language learning because the former is conceptually very challenging, and therefore, C-BDA, without a human mediator, may not be able to respond to learners' ZPDs effectively. For this reason, a considerable amount of planning and piloting may be needed initially which Poehner et al. (2014) have also acknowledged.

8.6.3 Online Synchronous Communication for Mediation

As explained above, computers have the potential for DA. More importantly, technological tools mediated by computers seem to play an important role in different ways for different learners as observed in my research although the focus was not on the investigation of the affordances of technological tools. For example, one of the participants (Amina) was offered mediation through synchronous communication (i.e., instant messaging) which she really liked. However, due to her personal circumstances, she could not participate in the same way in DA2 as she did in DA1. This was possibly the reason why she did not do as well on DA2 as she did on DA1. As only one participant interacted through a synchronous communication tool which was in DA1 only, this study had very limited data as to how mediation could be provided via synchronous communication such as instant messaging.

A useful future direction for this research could be investigating how DA principles work via synchronous online communication tools compared to the asynchronous medium such as emails and forums. There is only one study in this area reported in the literature (i.e., Oskoz, 2005). Oskoz's study was on adult Spanish learners' language development in a synchronous computer-mediated environment. To date, there has been no study of academic writing in such a context and thus investigation is needed to add to our understanding regarding the application of semiotic mediation via synchronous computer-mediated communication. This has become even more important because increasingly learners use smartphones and tablets for communication and study whether in distance education or face-to-face universities which are also forced to use online platforms to teach in a pandemic such as COVID-19. Although a significant amount of research has been conducted in other areas of language learning by using tools such as WhatsApp (e.g., Andujar, 2016 investigating grammatical, lexical and mechanical accuracy of second language learners), and Skype (e.g., Terhune, 2016 examining oral communication), there is little research on the use of online synchronous communication tools like WhastApp in academic writing assessment and mediation within DA. Future research could explore not only affordances of online synchronous communication tools for mediation but also what effects they would have on students' academic writing development.

8.6.4   Interpersonal Aspects of Mediation and Dialogic Feedback

The interpersonal relationship between the mediator/teacher and the learner was an aspect of the findings in my research. However, it has not received a detailed treatment in this book because it is an area that deserves an extended discussion and further evidencing due to its high pedagogical importance. Indeed, in most recent studies on assessment feedback in higher education, aspects of interpersonal relationships including affect and students' emotional experiences caused by assessment feedback have been suggested as areas for further research because there is extremely limited research in these areas which has only recently emerged (e.g., see Ajjawi & Boud, 2018; Carless & Boud, 2018; Dawson et al., 2019; Evans, 2013; Henderson et al., 2019). Within the DA literature, despite its importance in mediation and the dialectical nature of thinking/cognition and emotion as accepted in Vygotskian sociocultural theory of learning (Poehner & Swain, 2016), there is almost no research conducted on learner emotions and their impact on mediation and the ZPD activity and thus research in this area is in dire need (Poehner, 2018, pp. 262–263).

The research on various aspects of interpersonal relationships between the mediator/teacher and the learner during the mediation and feedback dialogue can also benefit from examining the use of language and other semiotic tools in them from a Systemic Functional Linguistic perspective by focusing on the Interpersonal dimension. For example, the Appraisal framework developed by Martin and White (2005) could be deployed to examine the evaluative language used by the mediator during the interaction. This framework allows us to examine mediator-learner attitudes, feelings involved (affect) and values attached to different things/sources during the mediation and the ZPD activity. This SFL perspective will certainly enable us to understand the Interpersonal dimension of mediation and dialogic feedback better in DA research.

References

Ableeva, R. (2010). Dynamic assessment of listening comprehension in second language learning. *Ph.D. Pennsylvania State University*. Retrieved from http://etda.libraries.psu.edu/theses/approved/WorldWideIndex/ETD-5520/index.html.

Ajjawi, R., & Boud, D. (2018). Examining the nature and effects of feedback dialogue. *Assessment and Evaluation in Higher Education, 43*(7), 1106–1119. https://doi.org/10.1080/02602938.2018.1434128.

Alavi, S. M., & Taghizadeh, M. (2014). Dynamic assessment of writing: The impact of implicit/explicit mediations on L2 learners' internalization of writing skills and strategies. *Educational Assessment, 19*(1), 1–16. https://doi.org/10.1080/10627197.2014.869446.

Andujar, A. (2016). Benefits of mobile instant messaging to develop ESL writing. *System, 62*, 63–76. https://doi.org/10.1016/j.system.2016.07.004.

Antón, M. (2009). Dynamic assessment of advanced second language learners. *Foreign Language Annals, 42*(3), 576–598.

Bakhoda, I., & Shabani, K. (2019). Enhancing L2 learners' ZPD modification through computerized-group dynamic assessment of reading comprehension. *Innovation in Language Learning and Teaching, 13*(1), 31–44. https://doi.org/10.1080/17501229.2017.1286350.

Bazerman, C. (2013). *A theory of literate action: literate action* (Vol. 2). Fort Collins, Colorado: The WAC Clearinghouse and Parlor Press.

Carless, D. (2006). Differing perceptions in the feedback process. *Studies in Higher Education, 31*(2), 219–233.

Carless, D., & Boud, D. (2018). The development of student feedback literacy: Enabling uptake of feedback. *Assessment and Evaluation in Higher Education*, 1315–1325. https://doi.org/10.1080/02602938.2018.1463354.

Chetwynd, F., & Dobbyn, C. (2011). Assessment, feedback and marking guides in distance education. *Open Learning: The Journal of Open, Distance and e-Learning, 26*(1), 67–78.

Coffin, C., & Donohue, J. (2014). *A language as social semiotic based approach to teaching and learning in higher education*. Malden, MA: Wiley.

Daniels, H. (2007). Pedagogy. In H. Daniels, M. Cole, & J. V. Wertsch (Eds.), *The Cambridge companion to Vygotsky* (pp. 307–331). Cambridge: Cambridge University Press.

Davin, K. J., Herazo, J. D., & Sagre, A. (2016). Learning to mediate: Teacher appropriation of dynamic assessment. *Language Teaching Research, 21*(5), 632–651. https://doi.org/10.1177/1362168816654309.

Dawson, P., Henderson, M., Mahoney, P., Phillips, M., Ryan, T., Boud, D., et al. (2019). What makes for effective feedback: staff and student perspectives. *Assessment and Evaluation in Higher Education, 44*(1), 25–36. https://doi.org/10.1080/02602938.2018.1467877.

Ebadi, S., & Rahimi, M. (2019). Mediating EFL learners' academic writing skills in online dynamic assessment using google docs. *Computer Assisted Language Learning, 32*(5–6), 527–555. https://doi.org/10.1080/09588221.2018.1527362.

Evans, C. (2013). Making sense of assessment feedback in higher education. *Review of Educational Research, 83*(1), 70–120. https://doi.org/10.3102/0034654312474350.

Feuerstein, R., Falik, L. H., Rand, Y., & Feuerstein, R. S. (2002). *The dynamic assessment of cognitive modifiability: The learning propensity assessment device: theory, instruments and techniques* (Revised ed.). Jerusalem: ICELP Press.

Gardner, S. (2010). SFL: A theory of language for dynamic assessment of EAL. *NALDIC Quarterly, 8*(1), 37–41.

Gardner, S., & Donohue, J. (2020). Introduction to the special collection: Halliday's influence on EAP practice. *Journal of English for Academic Purposes, 44*, 100831. https://doi.org/10.1016/j.jeap.2019.100831.

Guthke, J., & Beckmann, J. F. (2000). The learning Test concept and its application in practice. In C. Lidz & J. G. Elliot (Eds.), *Dynamic assessment: Prevailing models and applications* (pp. 17–70). New York: Elsevier.

Hasan, R. (1992). Speech genre, semiotic mediation and the development of higher mental functions. *Language Sciences, 14*(4), 489–528.

Haywood, H. C., & Lidz, C. S. (2007). *Dynamic assessment in practice: Clinical and educational applications*. Cambridge: Cambridge University Press.

Henderson, M., Ryan, T., & Phillips, M. (2019). The challenges of feedback in higher education. *Assessment and Evaluation in Higher Education, 44*(8), 1237–1252. https://doi.org/10.1080/02602938.2019.1599815.

Hyland, K., & Hyland, F. (2006). Interpersonal aspects of response: constructing and interpreting teacher written feedback. In K. Hyland & F. Hyland (Eds.), *Feedback in second language writing: Contexts and issues* (pp. 206–224). Cambridge: Cambridge University Press.

Lantolf, J. P., & Poehner, M. E. (2004). Dynamic assessment of L2 development: Bringing the past into the future. *Journal of Applied Linguistics, 1*(1), 49–72.

Lantolf, J. P., & Poehner, M. E. (2011). Dynamic assessment in the classroom: Vygotskian praxis for second language development. *Language Teaching Research, 15*(1), 11–33. https://doi.org/10.1177/1362168810383328.

Lea, M., & Street, B. V. (1998). Student writing in higher education: An academic literacies approach. *Studies in Higher Education, 23*(2), 157–172.

Mahboob, A., Dreyfus, S., Humphrey, S. L., & Martin, J. R. (2010). Appliable linguistics and english language teaching: The scaffolding literacy in adult and tertiary environments (SLATE) project. In A. Mahboob & N. Knight (Eds.), *Appliable linguistics: Texts, contexts and meanings* (pp. 25–34). London: Continuum.

Martin, J. R., & White, P. R. R. (2005). *The language of evaluation: appraisal in English.* Basingstoke, New York: Palgrave Macmillan.

Nesi, H., & Gardner, S. (2012). *Genres across the disciplines: Student writing in higher education.* Cambridge: Cambridge University Press.

Oskoz, A. (2005). Students' dynamic assessment via online chat. *CALICO Journal, 22*(3), 513–536.

Pitt, E., & Norton, L. (2017). 'Now that's the feedback I want!' students' reactions to feedback on graded work and what they do with it. *Assessment and Evaluation in Higher Education, 42*(4), 499–516. https://doi.org/10.1080/02602938.2016.1142500.

Poehner, M. E. (2005). *Dynamic assessment of oral proficiency among advanced L2 learners of French.* Ph.D., Pennsylvania State University.

Poehner, M. E. (2009). Group dynamic assessment: Mediation for the L2 classroom. *TESOL Quarterly, 43,* 471–491.

Poehner, M. E. (2018). Probing and provoking L2 development: The object of mediation in dynamic assessment and mediated development. In J. P. Lantolf, M. E. Poehner, & M. Swain (Eds.), *The Routledge handbook of sociocultural theory and second language development* (pp. 249–265). New York, NY: Routledge.

Poehner, M. E., & Swain, M. (2016). L2 development as cognitive-emotive process. *Language and Sociocultural Theory, 3*(2), 219–241.

Poehner, M. E., Zhang, J., & Lu, X. (2014). Computerized dynamic assessment (C-DA): Diagnosing L2 development according to learner responsiveness to mediation. *Language Testing.* https://doi.org/10.1177/0265532214560390.

Prior, P. (2008). A sociocultural theory of writing. In C. A. MacArthur, S. Graham, & J. Fitzgerald (Eds.), *Handbook of writing research* (pp. 54–66). London: The Guildford Press.

Shamir, A., Tzuriel, D., & Guy, R. (2007). Computer-supported collaborative Learning: Cognitive effects of a peer mediation intervention. *Journal of Cognitive Education and Psychology, 6,* 373–394.

Shrestha, P. N., & Coffin, C. (2012). Dynamic assessment, tutor mediation and academic writing development. *Assessing Writing, 17*(1), 55–70. https://doi.org/10.1016/j.asw.2011.11.003.

Terhune, N. M. (2016). Language learning going global: Linking teachers and learners via commercial skype-based CMC. *Computer Assisted Language Learning, 29*(6), 1071–1089. https://doi.org/10.1080/09588221.2015.1061020.

Tuck, J. (2018). *Academics engaging with student writing: Working at the higher education textface.* Milton: Taylor and Francis.

Tzuriel, D., & Shamir, A. (2002). The effects of mediation in computer assisted dynamic assessment. *Journal of Computer Assisted learning, 18*(1), 21–32.

Vygotsky, L. S. (1978). *Mind in society: The development of higher psychological processes.* Cambridge, MA: Harvard University Press.

Wegner, D. (2004). The collaborative construction of a management report in a municipal Community of practice. *Journal of Business and Technical Communication, 18*(4), 411–451. https://doi.org/10.1177/1050651904266926.

Wells, G. (1999). *Dialogic inquiry: Towards a sociocultural practice and theory of education.* Cambridge: Cambridge University Press.

Woodward-Kron, R. (2008). More than just jargon—the nature and role of specialist language in learning disciplinary knowledge. *Journal of English for Academic Purposes, 7*(4), 234–249.

Yang, M., & Carless, D. (2013). The feedback triangle and the enhancement of dialogic feedback processes. *Teaching in Higher Education, 18*(3), 285–297. https://doi.org/10.1080/13562517.2012.719154.

Printed by Printforce, the Netherlands